Reality in Movement

Reality in Movement

Octavio Paz as Essayist and Public Intellectual

MAARTEN VAN DELDEN

VANDERBILT UNIVERSITY PRESS
Nashville, Tennessee

Copyright 2021 Vanderbilt University Press
All rights reserved
First printing 2021
This study was funded in part by the Latin American Institute and the Office of the Dean of Humanities at UCLA.

Cover photo of Octavio Paz ©Archivo Manuel Álvarez Bravo, S.C.

Library of Congress Cataloging-in-Publication Data

Names: Van Delden, Maarten, 1958- author.
Title: Reality in movement : Octavio Paz as essayist and public intellectual / Maarten van Delden.
Description: Nashville : Vanderbilt University Press, [2021] | Includes bibliographical references and index. | Summary: "Comprehensive study of Octavio Paz's essayistic work and his role as a public intellectual"— Provided by publisher.
Identifiers: LCCN 2020045512 (print) | LCCN 2020045513 (ebook) | ISBN 9780826501493 (hardcover) | ISBN 9780826501486 (paperback) | ISBN 9780826501509 (epub) | ISBN 9780826501516 (pdf)
Subjects: LCSH: Paz, Octavio, 1914-1998--Criticism and interpretation. | Mexico—Intellectual life—20th century.
Classification: LCC PQ7297.P285 Z96535 2021 (print) | LCC PQ7297.P285 (ebook) | DDC 861/.62—dc23

LC record available at https://lccn.loc.gov/2020045512
LC ebook record available at https://lccn.loc.gov/2020045513

In memory of my mother

Contents

Acknowledgments   ix

INTRODUCTION	1
1. The Rebel	11
2. Revolution	31
3. Mexico and the United States	58
4. India	79
5. Psychoanalysis	101
6. Feminism	127
7. The Left	152
8. Conservatism	179
9. Poetics	199
10. Octavio Paz as a Literary Character	222

Notes   263
Bibliography   323
Index   345

Acknowledgments

Portions of Chapter 7 appeared previously in "The War on the Left in Octavio Paz's *Plural* (1971–76)," *Annals of Scholarship* 11.1/2 (1996): 133–55. An earlier, shorter version of Chapter 2 was included in Roberto Cantú, ed., *The Willow and the Spiral: Essays on Octavio Paz and the Poetic Imagination* (Newcastle upon Tyne: Cambridge Scholars Publishing, 2014), 156–69. Permission to reprint is gratefully acknowledged. Other sections of this book appeared previously in Spanish. Chapter 1 of this book has its origin in an essay titled "El rebelde en Paz," in José Antonio Aguilar Rivera, ed., *Aire en libertad: Octavio Paz y la crítica* (Mexico City: Fondo de Cultura Económica/Centro de Investigación y Docencia Económicas, 2015), 171–93. An earlier version of Chapter 3 was published under the title "¿Dentro o fuera de la historia? El pensamiento de Octavio Paz en torno a México y los Estados Unidos," translated by Álvaro Uribe, *Anuario de la Fundación Octavio Paz* 2 (2000), 88–99. A section of Chapter 7 and portions of Chapter 10 appeared in Spanish in *Zona Octavio Paz*, zonaOctaviopaz.com. I am grateful to Guillermo Sheridan for having opened the (virtual) pages of this website to my work.

Many friends, colleagues, and students shared ideas, offered comments, and suggested readings as I worked on this book. Others gave me the opportunity to publish earlier versions of my work on Octavio Paz or present it in a public setting. I extend my heartfelt gratitude to José Antonio Aguilar Rivera, Maricela Becerra, Roberto Cantú, Adolfo Castañón, Isaura Contreras, Daniel Cooper, Esteban

Córdoba, Willivaldo Delgadillo, Roberto Ignacio Díaz, Liesbeth François, Armando González Torres, Manuel Gutiérrez, Robert Lane Kauffmann, Efraín Kristal, Carlos Lechner, Nadia Lie, Miguel Enrique Morales, José Antonio Moreno, Ignacio Sánchez Prado, Julio Puente García, and Kristine Vandenberghe. Deserving of special mention are my fellow *pacianos* Yvon Grenier and Malva Flores, who have been rigorous and perspicacious interlocutors for many years, and Verónica Cortínez, my incomparably generous colleague in the Department of Spanish and Portuguese at UCLA. Support provided by the Office of the Dean of Humanities at Rice University and the Latin American Institute and Academic Senate at UCLA was essential in allowing me to advance my research on Paz. I am grateful to these entities for their confidence in me. I would also like to salute Zack Gresham at Vanderbilt University Press for the expert way in which he guided my manuscript through the review process, as well as the two anonymous readers for the press, who provided invaluable comments and suggestions. My beloved wife, Illa Cha, and our three sons, Reinier, Derek, and Edward, gave me many reasons to persevere with my work. My mother, sadly, passed away as I was working on this book. I dedicate it to her.

Introduction

Octavio Paz (1914–1998) was a towering presence in twentieth-century Mexican literature. Working largely in the symbolist and modernist traditions, he produced a vast poetic oeuvre of uncommon power and innovativeness. His essays, in turn, cover an astonishing range of subjects, including pre-Columbian art, Mexican national identity, international politics, economic reform, Asian religious traditions, avant-garde poetry, structuralist anthropology, utopian socialism, sexuality and eroticism, psychoanalysis, Marxism, the Mexican muralist movement, the nature of poetry, and a host of other topics. He was just as comfortable writing in sweeping terms about issues such as the nature of modernity or the development of Mexican history as he was drawing intimate character sketches of the many well-known people—primarily from the world of literature and the arts—he came to know in the course of his long and extremely active career. He was deeply immersed in Mexican culture, having produced in *El laberinto de la soledad* (1950; *The Labyrinth of Solitude*) what is perhaps the most enduring interpretation of the Mexican character, while also possessing an extraordinarily cosmopolitan vision, one that encompassed not only a large part of the Western tradition, as one can see from a work such as *Los hijos del limo* (1974; *Children of the Mire*), a history of modern poetry from German Romanticism to the 1960s avant-garde that remains unparalleled in its reach, but also other world civilizations, most notably those of Asia.

Paz participated in crucial political debates, both at home and abroad, from the 1930s to the 1990s. As a young poet, he caught the eye of Pablo Neruda, who in 1937 invited him to participate in a congress of anti-fascist writers in Spain, where a brutal Civil War was raging.¹ From his sojourn in Spain, Paz learned the value of solidarity in the face of the onslaught of fascism, but he also received an early lesson in the dangers of leftist dogmatism. The writers who gathered in the Spanish city of Valencia expressed their opposition to the Francoist rebels who had risen up to overthrow the country's democratically elected government, but also demonstrated their animosity toward writers such as André Gide, who had dared to criticize the Soviet Union. For Paz, the attack on Gide was the beginning of a long process of disenchantment with a sizeable sector of the international Left. A key episode took place when he was living in Paris in the late 1940s and became embroiled in a dispute surrounding the existence of concentration camps in the Soviet Union. In an article published in Paris in November 1949, a French writer and political activist named David Rousset called attention to the existence of a vast network of forced labor camps in the Soviet Union. Even though Rousset, as a survivor of a Nazi concentration camp, appeared to possess a unique authority to speak up on this topic, leading leftist intellectuals, including Jean-Paul Sartre, responded by denouncing not the Soviet Union, but Rousset.² Paz sided with Rousset, publishing an article on him in the Argentine journal *Sur*, with extensive documentation on the affair.³ His support for Rousset left him isolated within the Mexican intellectual world. Yet even while courting controversy with his principled stand against Soviet abuses, Paz was serving quietly in the Mexican diplomatic service in various world capitals, including Paris, New Delhi, and Tokyo, penning thoughtful and generally supportive expositions of the policies—primarily in the economic realm—of Mexico's post-revolutionary regimes.⁴ His career as a diplomat came to an end in 1968 when the Mexican government, led by President Gustavo Díaz Ordaz, decided to use the army, as well as paramilitary units, to crush the student movement that had emerged that year in Mexico, culminating in a massacre on October 2, 1968, in Mexico City's Tlatelolco square. Paz submitted his resignation as ambassador to India, where he had been posted since 1962, and after a few years spent mostly at British and American universities, he eventually returned to Mexico City, where he remained, although with frequent sojourns abroad, until his death in 1998. During this period, Paz became a vocal supporter of liberal democracy and free-market economics, as well as a strong critic of Communist regimes around the world. In spite of the fact that he never abandoned the anti-capitalist strain in his thinking, his positions provoked much hostility in Mexican intellectual circles, leading to frequent polemics between Paz and his antagonists, something the Mexican poet often seemed to relish. In sum, for much of his life Paz found himself at the center of key political debates of his era.

Paz was extraordinarily alert to the cultural and philosophical currents flowing through the world around him, and throughout his career he eagerly absorbed and commented on the latest ideas, forms of cultural expression, and systems of thought that caught his attention. In the 1930s, as a beginning poet still seeking an identity as a writer, he responded both to the call for a politically committed poetry that was particularly salient in those turbulent years and to the equally insistent need to carve out a separate realm for poetry, untouched by non-poetic concerns. In the 1940s, after moving to Paris, he gravitated toward the surrealist movement, especially its leader, André Breton. Even though he spurned surrealist ideas about poetic technique, most notably the practice of automatic writing, he became a strong advocate of surrealism as a spiritual attitude, celebrating its utopian vision of the transformation of the world through poetry. At the same time, Paz had delved into existentialist philosophy, and his readings of Heidegger left a clear imprint on the idea of existence and the nature of the self he developed in works such as *El arco y la lira* (1956; *The Bow and the Lyre*). The Mexican poet's essays of the 1960s also stand at the confluence of multiple cultural movements of the period. For instance, living in India gave him an exceptional vantage point from which to contribute to the critique of the West that surged through the intellectual world in these years. Paz was especially focused on questioning the Western ideology of progress, and one can recognize in some of his writings from this period the expression of an early environmental consciousness. At the same time, he continued his dialogue with key figures from the Western philosophical tradition, primarily Marx, Nietzsche, and Freud, while also showing a keen interest in the latest intellectual trend coming from Paris—that of structuralism, in particular structuralist anthropology. Paz had long been an advocate of the artistic avant-garde, what he called the "tradition of rupture" in Western literature, but in the 1970s he began to question whether the avant-garde was not in fact undermining itself, becoming routine instead of revolutionary. In the same years, he became increasingly skeptical of other ostensibly "critical" currents in Western thought, primarily Marxism, and began to show more interest in liberal and anti-statist standpoints. The resurgence of various forms of nationalism and religious fundamentalism in this period also attracted a great deal of commentary from Paz, who had been concerned with questions of cultural identity as well as religion since the beginning of his career. In short, if there was ever a writer who matched the definition of being someone who is "interested in everything," Paz would surely come as close as anyone to meeting the criteria. To read Paz is to immerse oneself in an entire era in Mexican and international cultural and intellectual history.

For Paz, writing was not something done in isolation; rather, it was part of an intense and ongoing literary and cultural conversation. The dialogue with the intellectual currents of his time that I have just sketched was at the same time a dialogue with specific individuals in the literary world. Paz was close to the poets of the *Contemporáneos* group in Mexico City in the 1930s, especially Xavier Villaurrutia and Jorge Cuesta; he befriended André Breton, Albert Camus, and many others in Paris in the late 1940s and early 1950s; he carried out an extensive correspondence over a period of many years with numerous notable figures in the Mexican literary world, including Alfonso Reyes, Carlos Fuentes, José Luis Martínez, and Tomás Segovia; and in the final quarter century of his life, after returning to Mexico City, he was the founder and editor of two cultural journals, *Plural* (1971–1976) and *Vuelta* (1976–1998), where he gathered around him a group of younger writers who would themselves go on to play central roles in Mexican cultural life.[5] In the 1970s, Paz held a regular visiting appointment at Harvard University, which facilitated a dialogue with East Coast liberal intellectuals, including John Kenneth Galbraith, Irving Howe, Susan Sontag, and Daniel Bell, whose work he published in his journals. He also opened the pages of *Plural* and *Vuelta* to numerous writers and intellectuals from different parts of Latin America, including Cuban exile authors such as Severo Sarduy and Guillermo Cabrera Infante, writers affiliated with the Argentine journal *Sur*, such as Jorge Luis Borges and José Bianco, and prominent liberal thinkers such as Mario Vargas Llosa. And, of course, Paz kept up his dialogue with France, which, like many Latin American writers of the nineteenth and twentieth centuries, he regarded as a kind of second homeland.[6] All in all, it is clear that he stood at the center of a vast network of cultural activity, encompassing authors from many different countries.

Paz influenced many writers, especially in Mexico. The work of Carlos Fuentes, Mexico's preeminent twentieth-century novelist, cannot be fully understood without taking the impact of Paz's work into account. Fuentes wrote powerfully and movingly about his relationship with his older colleague, portraying him in several works of fiction and integrating Paz's ideas, especially his ideas about Mexican history and culture, into his essays and novels. There is no doubt that his literary career would have had a different shape in the absence of Paz's example. The end of their friendship in the late 1980s was perhaps inevitable, as their political ideas began to diverge, but it was surely painful for both of them. Also striking for a student of Paz's career is the devotion he inspired among the circle of intellectuals who worked with him on his various cultural initiatives. Consider the fact that several of his collaborators, including Fabienne Bradu, Adolfo Castañón, Christopher Domínguez Michael, Enrique Krauze, and Guillermo Sheridan, have written book-length studies of Paz.[7] The launch in fall 2018 of a website devoted exclusively to Paz's life and work, a website that has been releasing a constant stream of articles about his work, selections from his correspondence, and reflections and impressions of Paz authored by people who knew him, testifies to the vast and ongoing reach of his influence.[8] The Mexican poet and essayist Gabriel Zaid, one of the most eminent figures in the Mexican literary world, who collaborated with Paz over a period of several decades, put it very simply in an essay on the occasion of the centenary of the poet's birth. Paz's appearance in Mexican literature was, Zaid claimed, nothing short of a "miracle."[9] Whether one agrees with Zaid's generous assessment or not, it is surely a testimony to the intense admiration Paz inspired in those who knew him. And few would doubt that he was a deserving winner of the Nobel Prize in literature, which he was awarded in 1990, still the only Mexican recipient of the prize.

Alongside admiration, Paz was also the object of much criticism, and even scorn and animosity. Entire books were written attacking his ideas about literature, about Mexican history, and, above all, about politics. After his return to Mexico in the early 1970s, and as he became increasingly critical of leftist regimes and leftist ideas, Paz found himself embroiled again and again in fierce intellectual debates with his colleagues in the Mexican intellectual world. Most of these polemics played out in Mexico City newspapers and magazines, and occasionally on television, a medium in which Paz had become increasingly interested and whose possibilities he eagerly explored in the 1980s and 1990s. Why was Paz's work so controversial? Surely Paz's own polemical temperament had much to do with it.[10] However, one can also point to a number of cultural and political trends that helped place Paz in the midst of the battles that swirled through the Mexican intellectual world in the final decades of the twentieth century. To begin with, Paz was hugely influential, yet he was also out of step with the predominantly leftist orientation of the country's intellectuals, especially those who worked in Mexico's rapidly growing academic sector. Add to this the fact that Mexican intellectuals work in an unusually close proximity to the state and one can understand why the debates often turned exceptionally vehement. In Mexico, there was much at stake, since what intellectuals said actually mattered. Paz himself exemplified this phenomenon, as his support for Carlos Salinas de Gortari in the wake of the presidential elections of 1988, elections whose legitimacy was called into question given the high likelihood that the governing party had engaged in fraud to ensure its victory, surely helped the official candidate secure his hold on power. A final factor contributing to the antipathy Paz generated among a relatively large portion of his potential audience was the increasing influence of anti-canonical and anti-elitist viewpoints, especially (and paradoxically) in academia. More than twenty years after the poet's death, the controversies surrounding his writings still have not died down, as evidenced by the recent publication of new attacks on his legacy.[11] Still, it is also worth noting that Paz succeeded in drawing into his orbit a number of prominent Mexican intellectuals who had long opposed him, most notably Roger Bartra and Carlos Monsiváis, and that many of his critics also generously acknowledge the importance of his oeuvre, or, at a minimum, the power and seductiveness of his literary style.[12]

Reality in Movement: Octavio Paz as Essayist and Public Intellectual offers detailed discussions of key themes in Paz's essayistic oeuvre. I approach Paz from a perspective that is admiring and generous, as an author of his stature deserves, but that does not sidestep criticism when warranted. It is not my purpose to write a hagiography of Paz, but I am even less inclined to take up the aggressively debunking style, closer to denunciation than criticism, that has become so widespread in the literary and cultural criticism of our era. Paz's writings merit careful analysis, and where necessary it is surely helpful to point out contradictions or blind spots. But the harsh ideological attacks frequently aimed at Paz are not only unfair and overstated; they generally misconstrue the purpose of literature and indeed of literary and cultural criticism. The underlying assumption in much of the criticism levelled at Paz is that his writings are at bottom a bid for power, and that this struggle for dominance within the literary and cultural field must be unmasked.[13] The first question that such an approach raises is whether it cannot also be applied to the critics articulating their reservations about Paz. If everything in the cultural realm is part of a struggle for dominance, would it not make sense to regard the arguments of Paz's critics in the same light? More importantly, however, attacks of this nature are rooted in a reductive and unconvincing view of literature. If works of literature were merely moves in a game of self-legitimation, what would make them deserving of our attention? As I have argued elsewhere, readers and critics would have no reason to spend time on literary works if such works had nothing to offer beyond their own desire to gain recognition.[14] The assumption underlying the readings of different aspects of Paz's work that follow is that his work deserves to be understood on its own terms, that it needs to be placed in as broad and complex a historical and cultural context as possible, and that to approach his work in this way can be a rich and rewarding experience. Needless to say, such an approach does not translate into automatic agreement with everything Paz says.

I open with two chapters that seek to understand a fundamental feature of Paz's literary career: his lifelong engagement with the subversive, critical, and adversary culture of his era. I begin, in a chapter titled "The Rebel," with Paz's portrait of the figure of the *pachuco* in *El laberinto*, one of his earliest works. I show how Paz's depiction of the *pachuco* is much more sympathetic than has generally been recognized, and that this portrait is in consonance with a fascination with the figure of the rebel that was part of the culture of the post-war era and that persisted throughout Paz's career. The next chapter, titled "Revolution," deals not with the individual who rises up against an unjust social order, but with the broader political upheavals that played such a crucial role in twentieth-century history, and that Paz assiduously followed and commented upon. We will see that there is a bifurcation in his approach to this phenomenon: whereas he became disenchanted with the Russian Revolution and other revolutions in the Marxist-Leninist mold early on, he saw the Mexican Revolution in a different light and continued to regard it as a kind of polestar until the end of his life.

I then move on to two chapters that address questions of cultural identity, a topic of great interest to Paz. I analyze first his writings about the differences between Mexico and the United States, and subsequently his thought on India. In the chapter "Mexico and the United States," I uncover a revealing paradox in Paz's approach, centered on how each country relates to history. Relying on notions of "organic" versus "inorganic" historical processes, Paz suggests that the development of US history has been, in a sense, natural, whereas Mexican history is characterized by deep fractures. And yet, when Paz describes the type of society that has emerged in each country, he comes to the conclusion that American society is abstract and machine-like, whereas in Mexico people entertain a far more natural (and humane) relationship to the world they live in. In the chapter titled "India," I zero in on Paz's views on India's relationship to the West, and on how the Mexican poet uses his writings on the subcontinent to reflect more broadly on the question of cultural contact.

Following the two chapters on cultural identity, I offer two chapters that place Paz in conversation with central cultural and philosophical currents of his era. In the chapter titled "Psychoanalysis," I show how Paz's writings on national identity rely on psychoanalytical models of interpretation, and I pay attention to how he gravitated in the 1960s toward the "utopian Freudians," in particular Norman O. Brown. I also show how Paz eventually moved away from the psychoanalytical perspective on desire, a shift that is especially visible in his late book on the topic of love, *La llama doble: Amor y erotismo* (1995; *The Double Flame: Love and Eroticism*). In "Feminism," I propose that Paz's views on gender have been widely misconstrued. Through close readings of passages from *El laberinto* and other works, I argue that contrary to the view put forward by feminist critics of his work, Paz was by no stretch of the imagination a sexist; indeed, his views on the social construction of gender were in tune with the arguments advanced by the eminent feminist thinker Simone de Beauvoir, who Paz cites in *El laberinto*.

In the next two chapters, I take up the question I had already begun to address in the opening chapters of this book: that of Paz's complex political profile. In the chapter titled "The Left," I examine three key episodes from Paz's long and often conflictive dialogue with leftist thought: first, I look at his response to the publication of Alexander Solzhenitsyn's *The Gulag Archipelago*; next, I explore his reflections on the Sandinista Revolution in Nicaragua; and last, I review Paz's role in the large international gathering of writers and intellectuals he organized in Mexico City in August 1990 to discuss the consequences of the fall of the Berlin Wall. My conclusion is that Paz remained much closer to leftist ideas and ideals than most of his enemies, and some of his friends, have acknowledged. In the chapter titled "Conservatism," I examine Paz's relationship with conservative thought, specifically in the Mexican context. I look at two aspects of the topic: first, I examine his surprisingly favorable assessment of the colonial period in Mexican history; next, I discuss his rapprochement in the 1990s with the PAN (*Partido Acción Nacional*), Mexico's main conservative party during Paz's lifetime. I show that the Mexican poet's gravitation toward conservative historiography and politics responded to considerations that were not conservative in the orthodox sense.

The next chapter addresses the question of aesthetics in Paz's work. In "Poetics," I uncover a fundamental tension in Paz's theory of poetry between an emphasis on the autonomy of the art work, deriving from the tradition of symbolist aesthetics, and a very different view in which poetry fuses with life, a dream Paz shared with the surrealists. The closing chapter of *Reality in Movement* offers a shift in perspective. Paz was an extraordinarily compelling person with an exceptionally visible public profile; this is reflected in the surprisingly large number of writers who included him as a character in their fictional works. In "Octavio Paz as a Literary Character," I study what is surely a significant aspect of the poet's reception in the literary world: his image as it appears in other literary works. In sum, by studying Paz from multiple angles, it is my hope that a portrait will emerge of a writer of unusual richness and complexity, a writer who throughout his career sought to capture what he himself once called the movement of reality.[15]

CHAPTER 1
The Rebel

Octavio Paz has often been portrayed as a conservative thinker, and one cannot deny that significant elements of cultural and political conservatism influenced his thought. However, to claim that Paz was a conservative *tout court* amounts to a grave distortion of his work, for if there is one thing that stands out in the Mexican poet's career it is his lifelong fascination with the themes of rebellion and revolution. Consider the fact that one of his most widely read essays is "Rebelión, revuelta, revolución" from *Corriente alterna* (1967; *Alternating Current*).[1] It is surely also significant that when Paz decided in the early 1990s to tell the story of his itinerary as an intellectual, he organized his recollections around the theme of revolution and his changing views of the topic.[2] And what to say of the circumstance that the author's account of modern poetry centers on the idea of "the tradition of rupture," that is, on the idea of poetic modernity as a long series of breaks or rebellions within the poetic tradition?[3] Any reading of Paz's intellectual profile that overlooks his insistent concern with different modes of dissidence in the modern world will fail to do justice to the poet's thinking. Paz had a complex and often conflictive relationship with the political and cultural Left, but for most of his career he was a participant (albeit an often critical one) in the rebellious, adversary culture of his era.[4]

In the exploration that follows of Paz's engagement with the idea of rebellion, I begin with a discussion of the *pachuco*, as Paz describes him in the opening chapter of *El laberinto*. The *pachuco* is surely the most noteworthy representative in Paz's oeuvre of the figure of the rebel.[5] I will argue that the portrait of the *pachuco* in *El laberinto* is not degrading and disparaging, as many critics believe. A detailed reading of Paz's portrayal of this character will reveal that the author of *El laberinto* felt a great deal of sympathy for the *pachuco*, and even identified with him, a sense of empathy rooted to a great extent in the link the author sees between the *pachuco* and the figure of the rebel. After my discussion of *El laberinto*, I will explore Paz's approach to the theme of rebellion in his later work, principally from the 1960s and 1970s, the era of the counterculture, with which Paz also identified.

Paz's portrait of the *pachuco* has generated a great deal of negative commentary. Critics complain that Paz's depiction of the *pachuco* is hostile and disdainful. They accuse the author of *El laberinto* of adopting a snobbish and superior attitude toward the young Mexican Americans he describes in the opening pages of his famous meditation on the Mexican character. Instead of trying to understand the *pachuco*, Paz allegedly repudiates him. Rather than sympathizing with him, he looks down on him. Some commentators argue that by depicting the *pachuco* as someone who behaves in an instinctive fashion, without self-awareness, Paz deprives his actions of the political dimension they might otherwise possess. Critics also accuse the author of *El laberinto* of removing the *pachuco* from his immediate social and historical context, and of transforming him into a mythical—and not very plausible—character. Finally, the disparagement of the *pachuco* is taken to constitute a disparagement of the Mexican American community as a whole.[6]

A close reading of the four or five pages Paz devotes to the *pachuco* reveals a much more complicated picture than his critics have recognized. Clearly, there are negative elements to the description of the *pachuco*. When Paz speaks of him as "un *clown* impasible y siniestro" (18; an impassive and sinister clown),[7] or when he describes the *pachuco*'s behavior as "enfermiza" (21; unhealthy), it is impossible not to recognize the disapproval in the author's tone. But in Paz things are rarely black and white. The pejorative elements in the portrait of the *pachuco* are combined with a tone of understanding, sympathy, and even admiration. We will see that deep down Paz is on the *pachuco*'s side. This is clear not only from the portrait of the *pachuco* itself, but also from the larger context in which we must place this portrait. When we examine the overall thematic structure of *El laberinto*, the cultural milieu in which the book was written, and Paz's enduring interest in the figure of the rebel, we realize how wrong critics have been to accuse Paz of disparaging the *pachucos*.[8]

"El pachuco y otros extremos" ("The *Pachuco* and Other Extremes"), the opening chapter of *El laberinto*, outlines a series of analogies linking the *pachuco* to other figures in the text. One cannot properly understand Paz's vision of the *pachuco* without recognizing these links. Consider the fact that Paz begins the chapter not with the *pachuco*, but with the image of an adolescent discovering the uniqueness of his own existence: "A todos, en algún momento, se nos ha revelado nuestra existencia como algo particular, intransferible y precioso. Casi siempre esta revelación se sitúa en la adolescencia" (11; All of us, at some point, have had a vision of our existence as something unique, untransferable, and precious. Almost always, this revelation takes place during our adolescence). What is the significance of this beginning? Why start a work on the Mexican character with these reflections on the figure of the adolescent? And how do we get from the adolescent of the essay's opening lines to the *pachuco* of a few pages further on? In short, who is this adolescent and what does he represent?

The reader soon learns that the adolescent shares with the *pachuco* an anguished questioning of his own identity. But Paz links the adolescent of his opening paragraph not only with the *pachuco*, but also with Paz himself, with the Mexican nation and, in the end, to all human beings who struggle to understand who they are. The parallel between the adolescent and Mexico is stated explicitly in the chapter's second paragraph. Having concluded his description of the adolescent's discovery of his own identity, Paz remarks that "A los pueblos en trance de crecimiento les ocurre algo parecido" (11; Something similar happens to nations going through a growth process). In other words, nations are like individuals. They are born, they grow up, they reach maturity, and eventually they age and go into decline. Mexico, Paz proposes, is like the adolescent of the opening lines of his essay. Using a biological metaphor, the author suggests that Mexico is a young country seeking to define its identity. "¿Qué somos y cómo realizaremos eso que somos?" (11; What are we and how will we fulfill what we are?), Mexico asks itself, hoping to grasp its own unique character, like a young person standing on the brink of adulthood.

Paz also suggests that there is a resemblance between the adolescent of the opening paragraph of his essay and himself. Note, to begin with, the image he uses to depict the adolescent's interrogation of his own identity: "inclinado sobre el río de su conciencia se pregunta si ese rostro que aflora lentamente del fondo, deformado por el agua, es el suyo" (11; as he leans over the river of his consciousness, he wonders whether the face that rises up slowly from the bottom, deformed by the water, is his own). And now observe how, a few pages later, Paz uses a similar image to describe his experiences as a Mexican living in the United States: "Recuerdo que cada vez que me inclinaba sobre la vida norteamericana, deseoso de encontrarle sentido, me encontraba con mi imagen interrogante" (14; I remember that whenever I leaned forward and gazed into North American life, hoping to discover its meaning, I would encounter my own questioning image). The image of Paz looking into North American life only to encounter his own reflection explicitly recalls—through the repetition of the verb *inclinar* (to lean)—the image of the adolescent looking into the stream of his own consciousness in search of his own features. Both Paz and the adolescent are Narcissus figures, absorbed in the contemplation of their own reflections. The adolescent becomes aware of his difference from other people and as a result begins to wonder who he is. Paz discovers his difference from the Americans and so becomes conscious of his identity as a Mexican. For both Paz and the adolescent, their identity is a problem, a question mark, something unresolved and uncertain.

At the end of the opening paragraph of "El pachuco y otros extremos," Paz states that in the adolescent "La singularidad de ser—pura sensación en el niño—se transforma en problema y pregunta, en conciencia interrogante" (11; the singularity of existence—pure sensation in the child—becomes a problem and a question, an interrogating consciousness). The ideas that Paz introduces here foreshadow the themes he develops a few pages later in his portrait of the *pachuco*. Let us begin with the notion of identity as a problem. Paz's adolescent discovers that he has an identity, but at the same time he is unsure as to the nature of that identity. When Paz shifts his focus from the adolescent to the Mexican, he depicts a similar psychological configuration. Like the adolescent, some Mexicans (not all) have entered a phase in their existence of being conscious of their own Mexicanness (13). But the Mexican, too, experiences this identity not as something he securely possesses, but as a conundrum.[9] Paz's desire to highlight the idea of identity as a problem explains the subsequent transition in his essay to the figure of the *pachuco*. For Paz, the *pachuco* represents first and foremost that person for whom his Mexican identity is "un problema de verdad vital, un problema de vida o muerte" (15; a truly vital problem, a problem of life and death). Insofar as for Paz being a Mexican means being unsure of who one is, the *pachuco*, who experiences this uncertainty more sharply than anyone else, is the most Mexican of all Mexicans.[10]

Why is their Mexicanness a problem for the *pachucos*? Paz describes the situation of people of Mexican descent in the United States as that of being trapped between two worlds, neither of which will accept them, and to neither of which they wish to belong. Mainstream American society rejects the *pachuco*, but at the same time the *pachuco* rejects that society. Yet even as he spurns the United States, the *pachuco* refuses to return to his Mexican roots: "El 'pachuco' no quiere volver a su origen mexicano; tampoco—al menos en apariencia—desea fundirse a la vida norteamericana" (16; the *pachuco* does not wish to return to his Mexican roots, nor—apparently—does he wish to become a part of North American life). Here, in a nutshell, we have the "problem" of *pachuco* identity. Like the adolescent, the *pachuco* has acquired an awareness of his own self, but he has not succeeded in defining that self. He knows that he has an identity, but he does not know what that identity is. He floats in an in-between state, unable to find a home for himself in the world he inhabits.

How does the *pachuco* respond to this situation? In answering this question, Paz returns repeatedly to the notion of a kind of stubborn self-affirmation on the part of these young Mexican Americans. Consider some of the phrases he uses to capture the *pachuco*'s spirit: "obstinada y casi fanática voluntad de ser" (16; obstinate and almost fanatical will-to-be); "exasperada afirmación de su personalidad" (16; exasperated affirmation of his own personality); "obstinado querer ser distinto" (17; obstinate wish to be different); "no afirma nada, no defiende nada, excepto su exasperada voluntad de no-ser" (20; he does not affirm or defend anything, except for his exasperated desire not-to-be). A persistent paradox runs through Paz's description: even though the *pachuco* has a powerful will-to-be, he has no being. Again and again he affirms his identity, in spite of the fact that he has no identity to affirm. The one thing he possesses is a sense of his singularity. Paz tells us that the *pachucos* "se singularizan tanto por su vestimenta como por su conducta y su lenguaje" (16; stand out through their clothing as well as their behavior and speech). He also notes that "su peligrosidad brota de su singularidad" (19; their menace arises from their singularity). The notion of the *pachuco* as someone unmistakably different from the rest of society takes us back to the solitary adolescent of the opening page of *El laberinto*. We begin to understand, then, that the *pachuco* is the concrete expression of a universal human condition. After all, Paz emphasizes in his essay's opening sentence that *everyone* experiences their identity as "particular, intransferible y precioso" (11; unique, untransferable, and precious). The *pachuco* is different from everyone else, but for that same reason he is like everyone else. For this sharp sense of difference is part of the experience of every single human being. In short, Paz's message is that, in some way, *we are all pachucos*.[11]

There is another manner in which Paz connects the concrete experiences of the *pachuco* to an all-encompassing narrative about the human condition. Toward the end of his discussion of the *pachuco*, Paz introduces the concepts of sin and redemption, thereby linking the *pachuco* to a Christian world-view. But how does Paz arrive at a Christian reading of the *pachuco*'s trajectory? What is the *pachuco*'s sin and how does he hope to achieve redemption? In order to answer these questions we need to recognize that the key to *pachuco* psychology is the way in which he relates to mainstream American society. As we saw earlier, Paz claims that the *pachuco* does not want to become a part of that society. Now, it is clear that the *pachucos* refuse to assimilate into American society not only because they are "rebeldes instintivos" (16; instinctive rebels), but also because they are the victims of racial discrimination. Paz notes that Mexican Americans live surrounded by "hostilidad" (16; hostility) and "intolerancia" (17; intolerance). The interesting thing about the *pachucos* is that they respond to this lack of acceptance on the part of the dominant society by underlining their "voluntad personal de seguir siendo distintos" (17; personal desire to persist in being different). This lack of interest in adapting to American society is expressed above all through their extravagant outfits, which serve to set them apart and draw attention to themselves. Paz describes the *pachucos*' style of dress as "deliberadamente estético" (deliberately aesthetic) and adds that such a style is strikingly at odds with American preferences in matters of clothing, which stress comfort above all (17–18). For Paz, this desire to stand out rather than blend in is a sign of the *pachuco*'s blatant rejection of American society.

At this point, however, Paz's argument takes a different turn. Underneath the *pachuco*'s defiant stance, Paz uncovers an additional layer of meaning: the *pachuco* seeks not only to negate American society, but also to pay homage to it. The author of *El laberinto* draws attention to the ambiguity of the style of dress of the *pachucos*: "por una parte, su ropa los aísla y distingue; por otra parte, esa misma ropa constituye un homenaje a la sociedad que pretenden negar" (18; on the one hand, their clothing sets them apart and makes them appear different; on the other hand, that same clothing amounts to an homage to the society they presume to reject). For Paz, every aspect of the *pachuco*'s behavior turns out to have a double meaning. The *pachuco* challenges American society in order to attract its attention. He attacks it in order to join it. To oppose mainstream society turns out to be a way of establishing a relationship with it. In the end, the *pachuco*'s rebellion is only the first step on the path to a symbolical reintegration with American society. It is at this point that Paz inserts the *pachuco*'s trajectory within a Christian framework. The two stages in the narrative that Paz has sketched—the rejection of American society, on the one hand, and the longing for integration with that society, on the other—correspond to the two key stages in the Christian narrative about salvation. The *pachuco*'s association with the realm of the forbidden makes him a sinner in society's eyes, but the persecution that is subsequently unleashed upon him paves the way for his ultimate redemption. Paz speaks of a cycle that begins with the *pachuco* representing "el pecado y el escándalo" (sinfulness and scandal) and ends with him being ripe "para la redención, para el ingreso a la sociedad que lo rechazaba" (19; for redemption, for rejoining the society that rejected him). The *pachuco* is saved because he is persecuted: "La persecución lo redime y rompe su soledad: su salvación depende del acceso a esa misma sociedad que aparenta negar" (20; Persecution redeems him and allows him to break out of his solitude: his salvation depends on his access to the very society he appears to be negating). But what is the effect of resorting to Christian concepts in the account of the *pachuco*'s behavior? Ultimately, it is to link him to a narrative with universalizing pretensions, to a story that is, in a sense, everyone's story. From a Christian perspective, we are all sinners and we all have the opportunity of finding salvation. Once we see how Paz relates the *pachuco* to one of the most deeply ingrained narratives of Western culture, it becomes impossible to claim that the *pachuco* is simply an object of disdain.[12]

Paz devotes only a few pages of the opening chapter of *El laberinto* to the *pachuco*. Having completed his account of the *pachuco*'s character, the author shifts his focus to a broad comparison of Mexican and US society. If we recall Paz's claim that he became aware of his identity as a Mexican during the time he lived in the United States, we can understand the logic of this section of "El pachuco y otros extremos." The Mexican discovers who he is by comparing himself with his northern neighbors. But the examination of the differences between Mexico and the United States—even as it appears to amount to a shift in focus—is also closely linked to the earlier discussion of the *pachuco*. Many of the themes Paz introduces in his exploration of the *pachuco*'s psychology reappear in the pages devoted to comparing and contrasting Mexicans with Americans. For example, when Paz describes the condition of the Mexican as "una orfandad" (23; an orphanhood), we hear an echo of his earlier description of the *pachuco* as "huérfano de valedores y de valores" (17; an orphan shorn of values and lacking anyone to defend him). In sum, the portrait of the *pachuco* prefigures that of the Mexican. In fact, Paz explicitly states that the *pachuco* is an extreme version of the Mexican: "estos seres son mexicanos, uno de los extremos a que puede llegar el mexicano" (16; these individuals are Mexicans, one of the extremes the Mexican can reach). The *pachuco* helps us better understand the Mexican. By the same token, Paz's portrait of the Mexican—and how he differs from the Americans—helps us better understand his evaluation of the *pachuco*. An examination of how Paz develops the comparison between Mexico and the United States in *El laberinto* can cast helpful light on his views of the *pachuco*.

In "El pachuco y otros extremos," Paz looks at how strikingly different the fundamental dispositions are that Mexicans and Americans adopt in relation to the world. He begins by recalling an aspect of the American mind-set that made a deep impression on him when he first arrived in the United States: "Cuando llegué a los Estados Unidos me asombró por encima de todo la seguridad y la confianza de la gente, su aparente alegría y su aparente conformidad con el mundo que los rodeaba" (24; When I arrived in the United States, I was astonished above all by the assurance and self-confidence of the people, their seeming cheerfulness and conformity with the world that surrounded them). He notes that this satisfaction with the way things are and confidence in the future does not mean that Americans never criticize anything. But the criticisms one hears in the United States are of the kind that does not call society's basic structure into question: "Casi todas las críticas que escuché en labios de norteamericanos eran de carácter reformista: dejaban intacta la estructura social o cultural y sólo tendían a limitar o a perfeccionar estos o aquellos procedimientos" (24; Almost every criticism I heard from the North Americans was of a reformist nature: the basic social or cultural structures were left intact and the goal was simply to restrict or improve upon certain procedures). Americans, according to Paz, are a profoundly optimistic people. They are content with the ideals they have formulated for themselves, and they feel confident in their ability to fulfill their ideals. But this optimism also has its unattractive side, for it is tied to the American tendency to negate "todos aquellos aspectos de la realidad que nos parecen desagradables, irracionales o repugnantes" (26; all those aspects of reality that strike us as disagreeable, irrational, or repugnant). In Paz's view, Americans have a very positive view of the world in which they live, but their cheerfulness is purchased at the price of a troubling lack of depth.

Mexicans, by contrast, do not shy away from the dark side of reality; on the contrary, they are powerfully drawn to it: "La contemplación del horror, y aun la familiaridad y la complacencia en su trato, constituyen contrariamente uno de los rasgos más notables del carácter mexicano" (26; The contemplation of horror, and even a certain familiarity and pleasure in dealing with it, constitute, by contrast, one of the most noteworthy features of the Mexican character). Paz goes on to enumerate various other traits, all of which serve to demonstrate how far Mexicans are from sharing the basic contentedness of their neighbors to the North: Mexicans, according to Paz, are suspicious, sad, nihilistic, sarcastic, and passive. In trying to identify the roots of such strikingly different attitudes toward the world, the author of *El laberinto* concludes that "para los norteamericanos el mundo es algo que se puede perfeccionar; para nosotros, algo que se puede redimir" (27; for the North Americans, the world is something to be perfected; for us, it is something to be redeemed). The belief in progress and in the human ability to shape the world makes the United States a fundamentally modern country. And insofar as Mexico is the polar opposite of the United States, we cannot help but conclude that it is an anti-modern country. With their view of "el pecado y la muerte" (sinfulness and death) as "el fondo último de la naturaleza humana" (27; what ultimately defines human existence), Mexicans have remained much closer to an older religious worldview in which the purpose of life is not progress or improvement, but redemption. The Mexican world-view also entails a different relation to the body: whereas in the United States, with its emphasis on work and hygiene, the body is kept at a safe distance, in Mexico, with its celebration of contact and communion, the body is an ever-present element in social life.

In concluding his discussion of the differences between Mexico and the United States in "El pachuco y otros extremos," Paz notes that the attitudes he has analyzed are diametrically opposed to each other. But he adds that neither attitude is preferable to the other: "Ambas actitudes me parecen irreconciliables y, en su estado actual, insuficientes" (27; Both attitudes strike me as irreconcilable and, in their present state, insufficient). What Americans and Mexicans share, according to Paz, is a "común incapacidad para reconciliarnos con el fluir de la vida" (29; a common inability to become reconciled with the flow of life). Neither Mexicans nor Americans have found a way to overcome the solitude that afflicts them. On both sides of the border, the author of *El laberinto* sees attitudes toward life that are incomplete and ultimately damaging to the people that hold them. It appears, then, that Paz adopts an even-handed position, criticizing both countries equally. He does not celebrate Mexico, but he does not idealize the United States either. Still, Paz's air of impartiality is not entirely persuasive. It is true that at one point in the text he describes the religious sentiment of the Mexicans as fruitless: "su fervor no hace sino darle vueltas a una noria exhausta desde hace siglos" (28; for centuries, our religious fervor has done nothing but go in circles around an exhausted waterwheel). It is also true that Paz's account of the Mexican character highlights some of its negative and self-destructive aspects. Critics have focused on these passages in *El laberinto* and have jumped to the conclusion that Paz wrote a kind of insult to the Mexican people.

But in reality, Paz sides with the Mexicans. When compared to the Americans, the Mexicans come across as infinitely more authentic. Whereas American life is cold and antiseptic, the Mexican world is intense and colorful. Americans may be more advanced as a society, but Mexicans are more profound. Even the occasionally unpleasant features of Mexican life are seen as a reflection of the country's deep spirituality. In speaking of the Mexican cult of death, Paz notes that this obsession with mortality expresses not just a masochistic mindset, but a religious one, as well (26). When he states that Mexicans lie "por fantasía, por desesperación, o para superar su vida sórdida" (26; from imaginativeness, from despair, or in order to overcome the sordidness of their existence), Paz is endowing this otherwise negative habit with a certain grandeur. Lying, in this description, is not a cowardly evasion of the truth; instead, Paz turns it into a courageous and creative act. However, it is in his description of the Mexican tradition of the *fiesta* that Paz most clearly expresses his preference for Mexican over American culture.[13]

According to Paz, Americans believe in happiness, but they are unacquainted with true joy (27). Conversely, Mexicans may be obsessed with death, but they know how to celebrate life. While Paz hints at this theme in "El pachuco y otros extremos," he develops it at greater length in the opening pages of "Todos santos, día de muertos" ("The Day of the Dead"), chapter three of *El laberinto*. So what is it that makes the Mexican *fiesta* special? How does it illustrate the idea that Mexicans live closer to the wellsprings of life? And how does Paz's description of the *fiesta* reveal where his deepest sympathies lie? In answering these questions, I will focus on two aspects of the *fiesta*: first, its status as a communal event; and second, the way in which it overturns the structures and hierarchies of everyday life. I will then look at how Paz explicitly contrasts the Mexican tradition of the *fiesta* with the way in which the inhabitants of modern, industrialized nations spend their free time. Finally, I will show how certain themes that appear in Paz's examination of the *fiesta* refer back to the portrait of the *pachuco* at the beginning of *El laberinto*, and in doing so help us to better understand that portrait.

Mexicans use the *fiesta* as a form of release from the repression they suffer in their everyday lives. In the second chapter of his book, Paz describes the Mexican as someone who closes himself off from the world around him. The Mexican wears a mask in order to protect his inner self from the aggression he fears will be directed at him by others. Unable or unwilling to establish contact with his fellow human beings, he remains a profoundly solitary creature. But since it is impossible to repress one's instincts permanently, the Mexican resorts to the *fiesta* as an escape valve for all that remains concealed in his everyday existence. The *fiesta* is a kind of explosion—an explosion provoked by the Mexican's bottling up of his true self. Or, as Paz puts it, the *fiesta* is "el revés brillante de nuestro silencio y apatía, de nuestra reserva y hosquedad" (54; the brilliant reverse of our silence and apathy, our reserve and gloom). The *fiesta* is, more than anything else, a profoundly social event. The Mexican abandons his usual reserve and opens himself up to others. He embraces the surrounding world and even the universe itself: "Todas (esas ceremonias) le dan ocasión de revelarse y dialogar con la divinidad, la patria, los amigos o los parientes" (53; All these ceremonies give him a chance to reveal himself and to converse with God, country, friends, or family). In the night of the *fiesta*, the Mexican sheds the usual suspicion he feels toward his fellow human beings and becomes filled with brotherly love: "Esa noche los amigos, que durante meses no pronunciaron más palabras que las prescritas por la indispensable cortesía, se emborrachan juntos, se hacen confidencias, lloran las mismas penas, se descubren hermanos y a veces, para probarse, se matan entre sí" (53; On that night, friends who have not spoken to each other for months, except to exchange certain indispensable courtesies, get drunk together, confide in each other, weep over the same sorrows, discover their brotherly feelings for each other, and occasionally, in order to prove themselves, kill each other). Does the violence in which the *fiesta* sometimes culminates mar the sense of joy and celebration? Surely it does. And yet, at the same time, Paz presents the killing that explodes amidst the partying as a form of fraternizing with the other. Ultimately, the key feature of the *fiesta* is its profoundly communal nature: "La Fiesta es un hecho social basado en la activa participación de los asistentes" (57; The *Fiesta* is a social event rooted in the active participation of the people).

The *fiesta* binds the members of a community together, but it also dissolves the community's rules and structures. It is as if the community has to be destroyed in order to be restored. The idea of the *fiesta* as a subversive event that overturns the conventions of everyday life is a crucial element in Paz's interpretation. He explains that in the *fiesta* "la noción misma de Orden" (55; the very notion of Order) is annihilated. In the *fiesta* everything is permitted. All of the common hierarchies that structure a society—having to do with gender, class, profession, and so on—are swept aside. The world is turned upside down: "Los hombres se disfrazan de mujeres, los señores de esclavos, los pobres de ricos" (55; Men dress up as women, owners as slaves, poor men as rich men). Taboos are destroyed: "Se ridiculiza al ejército, al clero, a la magistratura" (55; The army, the clergy, and the judiciary become the object of ridicule). Nothing is sacred: "Se burlan de sus dioses, de sus principios y de sus leyes" (56; They mock their gods, their principles, and their laws). The *fiesta* allows the group to free itself from its own normative expectations. Is there something slightly terrifying about this vision of confusion and disorder? Perhaps there is. But there is surely also something deeply compelling about the possibility of liberating oneself from the suffocating strictures of society. And as a poet with a strong connection to the artistic avant-gardes of the first half of the twentieth century, Paz undoubtedly wants us to see the rupture that the *fiesta* introduces into everyday life as something fundamentally creative and inspiring.

That Paz was promoting a favorable view of the Mexican tradition of the *fiesta* becomes even clearer when we see what he has to say about the recreational activities of the inhabitants of the developed parts of the world. Paz notes that the way in which people in the world's rich countries spend their free time shows their lack of a sense of community: "En las grandes ocasiones, en París o en Nueva York, cuando el público se congrega en plazas o estadios, es notable la ausencia de pueblo: se ven parejas y grupos, nunca una comunidad viva en donde la persona humana se disuelve y rescata simultáneamente" (52; On large occasions, in Paris or New York, when people congregate in squares or stadiums, one is struck by the absence of community: one sees couples and groups of people, but never a living community in which the individual is simultaneously dissolved and redeemed). Public spaces in the industrialized world are pervaded with feelings of alienation and anonymity. The modern masses are the opposite of a genuine community; they constitute, in Paz's words, "aglomeraciones de solitarios" (52; agglomerations of solitary individuals). The note of disparagement rings even louder when the author of *El laberinto* declares that modern-day vacations are "individuales y estériles como el mundo que las ha inventado" (56; as individualistic and sterile as the world that has invented them). What they lack, in other words, is the creative and communal dimension of the Mexican *fiesta*. It is clear, then, that Paz is not a neutral observer of the differences between Mexico and the United States; on the contrary, his sympathies are firmly on the side of the customs and cultural traditions of his native country.

How does all this relate to the portrait of the *pachuco*? To begin with, one might note that the *fiesta* and the *pachuco* share certain traits. Consider the fact that for Paz the *pachuco* incarnates "la libertad, el desorden, lo prohibido" (19; freedom, disorder, the realm of the forbidden)—exactly the same qualities that the *fiesta* embodies. If Paz celebrates the *fiesta* for its subversiveness, it makes sense to assume that he sees the *pachuco*'s subversiveness as attractive, too. More broadly speaking, both the theme of the *fiesta* and the theme of the *pachuco* fit into Paz's meditation on the differences between Mexico and the United States. The *fiesta*, as we have seen, is the prototypical Mexican cultural practice. The deep appreciation Paz shows for this practice reveals his overall preference for Mexican over American culture. The *pachuco*, in turn, plays the role of a representative Mexican in the opening chapter of *El laberinto*. If Paz sympathizes with Mexico, it makes sense to assume that he sympathizes with the *pachuco* as well.[14] Once again, I am not claiming that there are no negative elements in the portrait of the *pachuco* in the opening chapter of *El laberinto*. But one cannot assess Paz's evaluation of the *pachuco* without taking into account the *pachuco*'s place in the book's larger thematic structure. For Paz, one of the defining features of the *pachuco* is that he is not an American. The fact that he is not American is, in itself, a reason for liking the *pachuco*.[15]

Paz wrote *El laberinto* at a moment in time when fascination with the figure of the rebel was reaching a high point in Western culture. Influential books of the postwar years such as Albert Camus' *L'homme révolté* (1951; *The Rebel*) in France and Colin Wilson's *The Outsider* (1956) in England reveal the widespread preoccupation of the period with the solitary individual who is at odds with society.[16] With the rise of the countercultural movements of the 1960s, the celebration of protest and dissent became an even more pervasive feature of Western culture. In a sense, of course, the spirit of rebellion has been an integral part of Western modernity from its beginnings. Modernity—in the form of scientific progress, technological advances, industrialization, secularization, individualism, and democratization—brought about immense changes to society, but it also spawned powerful movements of resistance to these changes. In fact, if we follow Paz's idea that modernity is rooted in the spirit of criticism, then it makes sense to see the rebellion against modernity as a key component of modernity itself. Paz's work on what he calls the "tradition of rupture" in Western art and literature—that is, the tradition of constant innovation and unremitting iconoclasm—perfectly illustrates the idea that modernity has always been at war with itself. For Paz, this tradition begins with the Romantic revolt against the Enlightenment and continues well into the second half of the twentieth century, when it begins to fall victim to its own contradictions. As I pointed out at the beginning of this chapter, Paz was for much of his career a kind of fellow traveler in the huge movement of revolt that traversed the Western world. This movement of revolt—with its keen concern with the figure of the rebel—was especially potent in the aftermath of World War II, perhaps because no other event had left so ugly a stain on modernity's reputation. It was in this cultural milieu that Paz wrote *El laberinto* and it is this milieu that helps account for the sympathy he expresses for his own rebel figure—the *pachuco*. In short, Paz was not immune to his era's fascination with the theme of rebellion—on the contrary, he offered some of the most eloquent examples of this fascination in Latin America.

Over the course of his long career, Paz returned many times to the theme of rebellion, especially in the 1960s and early 1970s. Paz's 1967 collection of essays, *Corriente alterna*, is well known for its proclamation that the era of revolutions was over. But the book is just as noteworthy for its defense of the profound social and cultural upheavals of the period: "La rebelión juvenil y la emancipación de la mujer" (The youth rebellion and women's liberation), Paz declares, "son quizás las dos grandes transformaciones de nuestra época" (175; are perhaps the two most significant transformations of our era). Even though Paz regularly draws attention in *Corriente alterna* to the self-refuting nature of the ethos of rebellion—if everyone is a rebel, then no one is a rebel—his writing remains imbued with the profoundly critical and questioning spirit of the political and aesthetic avant-gardes that had from very early on shaped his thinking. Striking in this regard is the fact that Paz closes his book with an essay on what he calls "la sublevación de los pueblos del 'tercer mundo'" (213; the uprising of the nations of the "Third World"), suggesting that it is in the Third World that the desire for a drastic transformation in the order of things now finds its most significant expression. In a sense, Paz is proposing that the Western tradition of dissent has migrated in the post-war period to the Third World. According to Paz, the insurrection of the Third World is the central fact of the contemporary era. Here the spirit of uprising is flowering, without, however, becoming entrapped in the modern ideology of revolution, with its one-dimensional concept of progress. Instead, what Paz sees in the Third World is a spontaneous, non-ideological search for an identity—and it is precisely this that he finds appealing. Or, to use Paz's own words, "El 'tercer mundo' no sabe lo que es, excepto que es voluntad de ser" (214; The "Third World" does not know what it is, except that it is a will-to-be). But isn't this exactly what Paz had said about the *pachuco* almost twenty years earlier?

Paz again meditated on the rebellions of the 1960s in *Posdata* (1970; "The Other Mexico"), his response to the October 1968 Tlatelolco massacre in Mexico City. *Posdata* is both a defense and a critique of modernity. Insofar as modernity is linked to the ideology of progress, Paz questions its worth. The blind pursuit of progress has produced disastrous results; therefore, the very tendency of modern societies to measure themselves solely in terms of their ability to increase material well-being must be thoroughly criticized. Yet insofar as modernity is linked to freedom, criticism, and democracy, Paz defends it. In *Posdata* he calls for an end to authoritarianism—of the PRI regime in Mexico, but also of the leftist revolutions of the twentieth century—and instead advocates for the development of new forms of "control democrático y popular lo mismo del poder político y económico que de los medios de información y de la educación" (democratic and popular control over political and economic power, as well as over the media and educational institutions).[17] But what exactly does this have to do with rebels and rebellion? Throughout *Posdata* we see Paz drawing parallels between his own support for democracy and the sensibility of the rebels of the 1960s. In observing the upheavals taking place in the United States, Paz approvingly notes the tremendous "capacidad de crítica y autocrítica" (17; capacity for criticism and self-criticism) that characterizes the countercultural movements of the period. It is this ability to think critically and question authority that is perhaps the most promising feature of the cultural landscape of the time. But there is something else that appeals to Paz about the youthful rebels of the 1960s. In effect, he places them in the very same Romantic tradition to which he himself as a poet belongs.[18] Like William Blake and the French surrealist poets, and like Paz himself, the young rebels have understood that "La definición del hombre como un ser que trabaja debe cambiarse por la del hombre como un ser que desea" (27; The definition of man as a creature who labors needs to be exchanged for that of man as a creature who desires). They have also understood that the modern world urgently needs to put in place a new system of values, one in which the present is no longer sacrificed for the sake of the future, and in which "pleasure" ceases to be a forbidden word (27). It is clear that Paz profoundly identifies with the Romantic aspects of the countercultural movements of the 1960s.

Paz's attitude toward the 1960s rebels was not, however, one of uniform approval. Even though he applauded the new concern with "pleasure" and "desire," he regularly expressed his reservations about certain aspects of the contemporary movement for sexual liberation. In the closing section of *Conjunciones y disyunciones* (1969; *Conjunctions and Disjunctions*), for example, he complains that modern eroticism has become too politicized—that is, it has ceased to be erotic. Paz makes it clear that he fully supports "la pelea por el amor libre, la educación sexual, la abolición de las leyes que castigan las desviaciones eróticas" (117; the fight for free love, sex education, and the abolition of laws that punish erotic deviations),[19] but he feels uncomfortable with the manner in which these causes are being promoted. By using a vocabulary associated with the world of politics, the fighters for sexual liberation end up destroying the realm of the erotic. Paz exults in what he calls "la rebelión de los sentidos" (120; the rebellion of the senses), that is, the rediscovery of the human body. But by adopting the form of a political cause, this rebellion ends up undermining itself, for political causes are essentially intellectual—and non-erotic—in nature. As a political cause, the fight for sexual liberation must be rooted in a theory. And theory, Paz suggests, does not cohabit well with eroticism. This is why the rebels of the period come across as so fanatical, and, in the end, not so different from the people they attack: "El fanatismo de nuestros rebeldes es la contrapartida de la severidad puritana; hay una moral de la disolución como hay una moral de la represión y las dos agobian a sus creyentes con pretensiones igualmente exorbitantes" (118; The fanaticism of our rebels is the counterpart of Puritan severity; there is a morality of dissolution just as there is a morality of repression and both leave their followers exhausted with their equally exorbitant demands). In acting according to ideological imperatives, one has ceased to listen to the dictates of desire. But Paz's critique of the movement for sexual liberation does not mean that he is against rebellion per se. On the contrary, his critique is rooted in his sense that some features of this movement—specifically, its political nature—remained too closely tied to a culture of repression. In sum, the problem is that the movement for sexual liberation does not offer a sufficiently far-reaching alternative to Western modernity.

I have been suggesting that Paz's favorable assessment of the rebels of the 1960s can help us better understand the view he had of the *pachuco* in the late 1940s.[20] Indeed, it is worth noting that the bifurcation in his evaluation of the rebellions of the 1960s—he likes the Romantic dimensions of these rebellions, but disapproves of their ideological side—has implications for our reading of the *pachuco* as well. Consider the fact that the *pachuco*'s rebellion against American society is entirely nonpolitical. The whole point about the *pachuco* is that he rebels in an instinctive, spontaneous manner and that he has no political program to back him up. For some, this might be a problem. Not so for Paz. Insofar as politics and ideology were sources of alienation, it was probably better to strip oneself of the illusions they created. When asked in a 1977 interview on Spanish television how the *pachucos* were related to the Chicanos who had burst onto the American scene in the 1960s, Paz answered that the Chicano was "un pachuco con conciencia política" (a *pachuco* with a political consciousness).[21] Given Paz's views on the negative consequences of having a political consciousness, one surmises that by this he meant not that the Chicanos had gained something in comparison with the *pachucos*, but rather that they lost something. In short, Paz was indirectly reiterating his sympathy for the *pachuco*.

CHAPTER 2

Revolution

When the *Zapatista* rebellion erupted in the state of Chiapas in January 1994, Paz responded with surprise, even horror. In a series of articles that appeared in *Vuelta* and other Mexico City publications in the aftermath of the uprising, the Mexican poet expressed his strong opposition to the *Zapatista* insurrection. The idea he came back to again and again in discussing the events of early 1994 was that the Chiapas rebellion was out of step with the movement of history. "Es un regreso al pasado" (It is a return to the past), he declared in one of his articles on the subject.[1] Paz described the ideology of the rebels as "restos del gran naufragio de las ideologías revolucionarias del siglo XX" (the remains of the great shipwreck of twentieth-century revolutionary ideologies),[2] and referred to the reactions of the Mexico City intellectuals who applauded the rebellion as examples of "una recaída en ideas y actitudes que creíamos enterradas bajo los escombros—cemento, hierro y sangre—del muro de Berlín" (a relapse into ideas and attitudes we thought had been buried under the rubble—cement, iron, and blood—of the Berlin Wall).[3] The Mexican poet believed that the collapse of the Berlin Wall had signaled the end of left-wing revolutionary ideology. In light of the grand historical turning point of 1989, the *Zapatista* insurrection appeared archaic and anachronistic.

Paz's response to the events in Chiapas in early 1994 was both predictable and surprising. It was predictable because for several decades Paz had devoted much effort to analyzing the failures of twentieth-century revolutions. At the same time, it was surprising because at different stages of his career Paz had celebrated the

Mexican Revolution in terms that might well remind the reader of those he used to condemn the *Zapatista* rebellion. In what follows, I will examine the two itineraries Paz traced in his thinking about the great revolutions of the twentieth century. In the first part of my discussion, I will explore Paz's views of the world's leftist revolutions, first and foremost the Russian Revolution. As a young man in the 1930s, Paz was sympathetic to the ideals that had inspired the Russian Revolution. As he put it in a 1984 interview with Enrique Krauze, "como tanta gente de mi generación, fui marxista . . . o estuve cerca del marxismo" (like so many others of my generation, I was a Marxist . . . or perhaps I should say that I felt close to Marxism).[4] In *Itinerario* (1993; Itinerary), he explains that "entre 1930 y 1940, lo mismo en Europa que en América, la mayoría de los escritores que entonces éramos jóvenes sentimos una inmensa simpatía por la Revolución rusa y el comunismo" (between 1930 and 1940, both in Europe and in America, the majority of writers who were young at that time felt a great sympathy for the Russian Revolution and for Communism).[5] But Paz's career can be understood as the story of his gradual distancing from the passions of his youth. There was no sudden break in his outlook; instead, when we examine Paz's writings over the decades, we observe a steadily increasing disillusionment with both the theory and practice of twentieth-century leftist revolutions, a disillusionment that explains the position he adopted in response to the *Zapatista* rebellion of 1994. However, there is another narrative to be uncovered when one studies the development of Paz's political thought: it is the story of someone who was born as a revolution was raging across his nation; of the son of a *Zapatista* militant; of a poet and essayist who meditated again and again on the meaning of the Mexican Revolution; of a man, finally, who in the 1990s was still calling himself "hijo de la Revolución Mexicana" (a son of the Mexican Revolution).[6] As his disenchantment with Communist revolutions grew, Paz's view of the Mexican Revolution remained favorable, even celebratory. Although he was sometimes a supporter and sometimes a critic of Mexico's post-revolutionary regimes, he never questioned the legitimacy of the Revolution itself. In short, in his thinking about the Mexican Revolution, Paz was not against the revolution, but for it. This will be the focus of the second part of my discussion in this chapter. In approaching one of the key dimensions of Paz's political thought, my purpose is to give a sense of the complex configuration of his ideas.[7]

Paz believed that the idea of revolution was one of the defining features of the modern era. In "Poesía, mito, revolución" (Poetry, myth, revolution), an essay based on the speech he gave in June 1989 upon receiving the Alexis de Tocqueville Prize from President François Mitterand of France, he described the idea of revolution as "el signo distintivo, la señal de nacimiento de la edad moderna" (the distinguishing feature, the birth signal of the modern era).[8] But Paz also believed that revolution as an ideal had become exhausted in the second half of the twentieth century. Over the years, he referred repeatedly to what he called "el ocaso del espíritu revolucionario" (the waning of the revolutionary spirit),[9] or "el fin de la revolución en la acepción moderna de la palabra" (the end of the idea of revolution in the modern sense of the word).[10] There were different reasons, in Paz's view, for this exhaustion. Some were rooted in concrete observations regarding the actual outcomes of the twentieth century's leftist revolutions. Paz regularly noted that the trajectories of these revolutions had not matched Karl Marx's predictions. According to Marx, Communist revolutions would take place in the most economically advanced nations. Furthermore, Marx expected the proletariat to lead the revolution. Neither of these predictions came true. The major Communist revolutions of the twentieth century, such as the ones in Russia, China, and Cuba, took place in underdeveloped rather than developed countries, and nowhere did the proletariat play a significant role. Still, the most significant way in which actual revolutions contradicted Marxist prophecy was in their betrayal of the Left's grand emancipatory hopes. Instead of bringing about Communist utopias, the revolutions of the twentieth century had everywhere resulted in brutally authoritarian regimes. For Paz, the failure of revolutionary practice to live up to revolutionary ideals undermined the idea of revolution itself.

Paz was deeply concerned with the actual record of the revolutionary regimes that had taken power in the twentieth century. Nevertheless, in discussing the exhaustion of the idea of revolution in the second half of the twentieth century, his focus was often theoretical rather than empirical. He was as interested in demonstrating the philosophical bankruptcy of the idea of revolution as in detailing the poor record of actual revolutions. In a trenchant series of essays from *Corriente alterna*, Paz argues that the idea of revolution itself is based on false premises. The problem with revolution is related in the first place to the idea of linear time that is inscribed in the concept of revolution—a notion of time Paz associates with modernity and believes has become exhausted: "La acepción de la palabra *revolución* como cambio violento y definitivo de la sociedad pertenece a una época que concibió la historia como un proceso sin fin. Rectilínea, evolutiva o dialéctica, la historia estaba dotada de una orientación más o menos previsible" (196; The use of the word *revolution* to refer to a violent and definitive change in society belongs to a period that viewed history as an endless process. Whether rectilinear, evolutionary, or dialectical, history was endowed with a more or less predictable direction). According to Paz, the idea that there is a march of history—that history follows a single and predictable path—is no longer plausible. In fact, he argues that in the contemporary era the very idea of the future has fallen into disrepute. "El futuro," he says, "ha perdido su seducción" (176; The future has lost its seductiveness). And once the idea of the future loses its central position in contemporary society's understanding of the world, the idea of revolution too loses its appeal. In short, Paz was trying to show that the very concepts that undergirded the idea of revolution had lost their credibility.

Another problem with revolution was that it involved a misguided introjection of a utopian outlook into the realm of politics and history. Why, Paz wonders in *Corriente alterna*, have so many twentieth-century revolutions spawned regimes of terror? Paz suggests that revolutions become derailed when the utopian vision of the future that inspired the desire for change during the prerevolutionary period serves to justify the resort to violence during the post-revolutionary phase. Prior to the revolution, violence is vindicated in the name of the utopian goal being pursued. After the revolution, this justification vanishes, since, as Paz argues, "al asumir la autoridad, el revolucionario asume la injusticia del poder, no la violencia del esclavo" (206; once he assumes a position of authority, the revolutionary is no longer an instrument of the violence of the slave but of the injustice of power). Twentieth-century Communist revolutionaries had failed to make this distinction. They believed that violence was justified both prior to the revolution and after the revolution. Prior to the revolution, violence served to overthrow an unjust order, and after the revolution, violence was justified in the defense against the revolution's enemies. But with the revolutionaries in power, their acts of violence were no longer blows against oppression; they were now in themselves acts of oppression. And since the sought-after utopia could in reality never be achieved, violence, oppression, and persecution became permanent features of the new revolutionary order. The key mistake was the belief in utopia. To think that one could arrive at a utopia was to assume that history followed a single, predictable path. For Paz, on the contrary, history is the realm of indeterminacy. In *Corriente alterna*, he writes that "La historia ya no es una pieza escrita por un filósofo, un partido o un Estado poderoso; no hay 'destino manifiesto': ninguna clase o nación tiene el monopolio del futuro. La historia es diaria invención, permanente creación: una hipótesis, un juego arriesgado" (212; History is no longer a play written by a philosopher, a party, or a powerful state; there is no such a thing as a "manifest destiny": no class or nation has a monopoly on the future. History is a daily invention, a permanent creation: a hypothesis, a risk-filled game). The attempt to impose an ideal blueprint on society in ignorance of these facts grants revolutionaries carte blanche to practice terror in the name of the perfect state to be achieved in the future.

In *Corriente alterna*, Paz maintains a certain allegiance to utopianism, in spite of his devastating analysis of what he regards as its philosophical flaws. This is clear from his comments on Marxism, which he continues to regard as a grand and inspiring philosophy.

"Renegar de su herencia moral" (To reject its moral heritage), he claims, "sería renegar al mismo tiempo de la porción más lúcida y generosa del pensamiento moderno" (199; would be at the same time to reject the most lucid and generous part of modern thought). However, by the time of *Tiempo nublado* (1983; Cloudy weather, published in English as *One Earth, Four or Five Worlds*), Paz had sharpened his critique of utopian politics and established a greater distance from Marxism. Paz now argues that utopianism has religious origins; in short, it does not belong in the realm of politics. It is a fundamental error to seek from revolution "lo que los antiguos pedían a las religiones: salvación, paraíso" (what people in the past sought from religion: salvation, paradise). The failure to distinguish between politics, which for Paz belongs to the realm of "la realidad inmediata y contingente" (immediate and contingent reality), and religion, which deals not with contingencies but with the domain of the absolute, sets the stage for the conversion of politics itself into a religion.[11] This in turn leads to the horrors of political persecution that had disfigured all twentieth-century revolutions. Once politics is yoked to the realm of absolute truth, everything is permitted in the name of politics. The ends justify the means. Note that the historical backdrop to Paz's analysis of utopianism in *Tiempo nublado* is the link between Marxist philosophy, with its conspicuously utopian vision of politics, and twentieth-century totalitarianism, which had converted the dream into a nightmare.

In *Itinerario*, Paz claims that the distinguishing feature of the modern era is "la preeminencia, desde fines del siglo XVIII de la palabra revolución" (43–44; the preeminence, starting in the late eighteenth century, of the word revolution). It makes sense, therefore, for him to organize the story of his life around the question of his conflictive relationship to the theory and practice of twentieth-century revolutions. As Paz explains, "Estas páginas son el testimonio de un escritor mexicano que, como muchos otros de su generación, en su patria y en todo el mundo, vivió esas esperanzas y esas desilusiones, ese frenesí y ese desengaño" (46; These pages are the testimony of a Mexican writer who, like many others of his generation, at home and around the world, experienced those hopes and disillusions, that frenzy and that disappointment). If we accept Paz's view of the interconnectedness of modernity and revolution, then the preeminence of the word *revolution* in his account of his ideological itinerary stamps Paz as a thoroughly modern thinker. At the same time, the critical distance he adopts with regard to twentieth-century revolutions marks his detachment from his own era.

In the account Paz provides in *Itinerario*, the problem with revolution is that it promises something that it cannot deliver. Again and again, Paz returns to the idea that twentieth-century revolutionary ideology acted as a substitute religion. But whereas the absolutes of religion can never be refuted—since they will be fulfilled in another world, and therefore are not subject to any rational or this-worldly test—the absolutes of revolution inevitably collide with the reality of human nature, which is such that it can never accomplish the perfect state invoked by revolutionary ideology. Paz argues that "las revoluciones de la Edad Moderna [han] pretendido substituir a las religiones en su doble función: cambiar a los hombres y dotar de un sentido a su presencia en la tierra. Ahora podemos ver que fueron falsas religiones" (45; the revolutions of the Modern Age have aspired to take the place of religion and fulfill its dual function: to change man and to grant meaning to his presence on earth. We can now see that these revolutions were a false religion). Elsewhere in the same essay, he tries to explain why so many eminent twentieth-century intellectuals became vocal supporters of Communist regimes all over the world, even after it had become clear that these regimes were betraying their own utopian goals. In essence, Paz sees a hankering after the kinds of answers traditionally provided by religion: "Hay una falla, una secreta hendedura en la conciencia del intelectual moderno. Arrancados de la totalidad y de los antiguos absolutos religiosos, sentimos nostalgia de totalidad y absoluto. Esto explica, quizá, el impulso que los llevó al comunismo y a defenderlo. Fue una perversa parodia de la comunión religiosa" (78; There is a flaw, a secret fissure in the modern intellectual's consciousness. Severed from totality and from ancient religious absolutes, we feel a nostalgia for wholeness and for the absolute. This perhaps explains the impulse that led so many intellectuals to convert to Communism and to defend it. It was a perverse parody of religious communion). In spite of the harsh judgment, this is a story told from the inside. At certain points in his career, as we have seen, Paz identified with the dreams he here condemns.

Paz's critique of utopianism is reminiscent of the ideas of twentieth-century liberal thinkers, such as Isaiah Berlin and Leszek Kolakowski. Both Berlin and Kolakowski argue that given what we know about human nature a perfect world can never be attained. People who are foolish or naive enough to believe the contrary are likely to resort to or condone unacceptable methods to try to bring about the elusive utopian goal. As Kolakowski puts it in "The Death of Utopia Reconsidered," "any attempt to implement [utopia] is bound to produce a highly despotic society which, to simulate the impossible perfection, will stifle the expression of conflict and thus destroy the life of culture by a totalitarian coercion."[12] Berlin, in turn, argues in "The Decline of Utopian Ideas in the West" that since "no perfect solution is, not merely in practice, but in principle, possible in human affairs," therefore "any determined attempt to produce it is likely to lead to suffering, disillusionment and failure."[13] In short, the search for utopia is not merely futile, it is in fact dangerous.

There is a clear affinity between Paz and the anti-utopian and anti-revolutionary ideas of Berlin and Kolakowski. What is curious about Paz—perhaps perplexing—is that in other parts of his oeuvre, he expresses the very same utopian outlook he criticizes in the passages I have examined from *Corriente alterna*, *Tiempo nublado*, and *Itinerario*. This is clear from the exalted, poetic account he gives of the Mexican Revolution in *El laberinto*. It is also clear from the fact that even as—over the decades—he distanced himself from his favorable view of Marxist ideology and the revolutions this ideology had spurred, he remained largely faithful to his early idealization of the Mexican Revolution.

In *El laberinto*, Paz identifies certain rhythms that characterize Mexican culture and history. In Mexican everyday life, he detects an oscillation between two behavioral poles. On the one hand, Paz describes the Mexican as a person who wears a mask and adopts a closed and defensive posture in relation to the outside world. This is the well-known analysis he develops in "Máscaras mexicanas" ("Mexican Masks"), the second chapter of *El laberinto*. On the other hand, Paz presents the Mexican as someone who loves festivals and delights in communal activities. He develops this idea in "Todos santos, día de muertos," the third chapter of *El laberinto*. The two stages in Paz's argument are closely intertwined. In masking himself, the Mexican represses his inner being; this repression, in turn, provokes a reaction. A behavioral trait sustained with too much force ends up generating an opposite behavioral trait. This is why, as Paz puts it in a characteristically paradoxical manner, "el solitario mexicano ama las fiestas y las reuniones públicas" (51; the solitary Mexican is enamored of *fiestas* and public gatherings). Unable to remain in the state of solitude and isolation that characterizes his everyday life, the Mexican resorts to the ritual of the *fiesta* in order to release his repressed emotional energies.

If the alternation between the mask and the *fiesta* is the key to understanding Mexican culture, it turns out that it is also the key to interpreting Mexican history. In the second half of *El laberinto*, Paz shows how the rhythms of everyday life are replicated at the level of the Mexican historical process. Most striking in this regard is Paz's reading of the relationship between Mexico's nineteenth century and the Mexican Revolution. Paz describes the former as a period of "mentira e inautenticidad" (145; lies and inauthenticity)—a period, in other words, of self-masking—and the latter as a kind of socio-political and military *fiesta*—a "fiesta de las balas" (162; *fiesta* of the bullets), as he describes it, quoting the title of a vignette from Martín Luis Guzmán's *El águila y la serpiente* (1928; *The Eagle and the Serpent*).

For Paz, the fundamental problem facing nineteenth-century Mexico is the mismatch between the ideological projects of the nation's elites and the actual elements of the country's social reality. The leaders in the struggle for Independence adopted the ideas of the European Enlightenment, but, according to Paz, these ideas did not correspond to the true social forces at play during this phase of Mexican history. As Paz puts it, the continent's independence was achieved under the aegis of progressive political ideas imported from abroad; in reality, however, "Los grupos y clases que realizan la Independencia en Sudamérica pertenecen a la aristocracia feudal nativa" (131; the groups and classes that brought about Independence in South America belonged to the local feudal aristocracy). As a result, "las ideas enmascaran la realidad en lugar de desnudarla o expresarla" (131; ideas mask reality instead of disclosing or expressing it). In sum, the masking of the self that Paz observes at the level of everyday behavior in Mexico also occurs at the level of the nation's socio-political process.

The same conflict characterizes the period of rule by the dictator Porfirio Díaz, known as the *Porfiriato*. Once again, the country's elite imports its guiding ideology from abroad. "Sus ideales" (Their ideals), Paz argues, "son los de la burguesía europea" (are those of the European bourgeoisie). And once again there is a mismatch between ideology and reality: "Esos grandes señores amantes del progreso y la ciencia no son industriales ni hombres de empresa: son terratenientes enriquecidos por la compra de los bienes de la Iglesia o en los negocios públicos del régimen" (141; These great gentlemen who loved progress and science were neither industrialists nor businessmen; they were landholders who had grown rich from the purchase of Church properties or in the public affairs of the regime). Bourgeois ideology becomes a patina covering feudal socio-economic arrangements. The country's guiding ideas are nothing more than a fraud.

In the historical narrative Paz develops in *El laberinto*, the Mexican Revolution acts as the revenge of reality on the country's attempt to adopt a fraudulent appearance. According to Paz, the Mexican Revolution does not respond to an ideological program nor is it propelled by the force of ideas. Instead, it constitutes a spontaneous eruption of the nation's hidden reality. In Paz's words, the Revolution is "una verdadera revelación de nuestro ser" (148; a true revelation of our nature), "una explosión de la realidad" (153; an explosion of reality), "un volver a nuestra raíz, único fundamento de nuestras instituciones" (157; a return to our roots, the only proper foundation for our institutions), "una insurgencia de la realidad mexicana" (157; a rising up of Mexican reality), and "un movimiento tendiente a reconquistar nuestro pasado" (160; a movement tending toward the reconquest of our past). As Anthony Stanton comments, "Rarely has the Mexican Revolution received such a total and passionate defence as a popular movement of deep authenticity."[14] For Paz, the Revolution's power and grandeur derive from its raw and spontaneous quality. Ironically, this quality also turns out to be a fatal weakness. Paz consistently links the Revolution to the realms of instinct and feeling—but it is precisely because the Revolution is devoid of ideas that it cannot, in the end, produce a coherent plan for the reorganization of society. In the final account, the Revolution is for Paz no more than "un punto de partida, un signo oscuro y balbuceante de la voluntad revolucionaria" (158; a point of departure, an obscure and stammering reflection of the revolutionary will). The leaders of the revolution failed to develop a "plan orgánico" (organic plan) for the nation (148). The revolution's spontaneity was both its glory—for this is what guaranteed its authenticity—and its downfall—for no lasting social order can emerge out of mere unstructured spontaneity.

When Paz spoke of the Mexican Revolution as a revelation or liberation of the real Mexico, he was thinking of one strand within the Revolution in particular, what is sometimes known as the Revolution of the South, led by Emiliano Zapata. In a handful of pages in *El laberinto*, Paz offered an unforgettable portrait of the man he describes as having died as he had lived, "abrazado a la tierra" (155; embracing the land). For Paz, Zapata was the antidote to the deception and falsehood characterizing the *Porfiriato* period. The revolutionary leader from the state of Morelos understood that Mexico's political and economic system was a kind of straitjacket that needed to be ripped off. His program, Paz explains, "contenía pocas ideas, estrictamente las necesarias para hacer saltar las formas económicas y políticas que nos oprimían" (155; contained few ideas, strictly the ones necessary to blow up the political and economic structures that were oppressing us). Zapata sought to overcome the longstanding breach between the real nation and the legal nation through the promulgation of "una legislación que se ajustara a la realidad mexicana" (155; laws that were adapted to Mexican reality).[15] What did this mean in practice? It meant a return to pre-Hispanic forms of land ownership, which were of a profoundly communal kind. It meant, in other words, that the new political and economic structures that were to emerge from the revolution had to take as their point of departure "la porción más antigua, estable y duradera de nuestra nación: el pasado indígena" (157; the oldest, most stable, and most enduring part of our nation: the indigenous past). Paz spoke of the Mexican Revolution as an explosion, but it was an explosion that set the stage for a return to the past. What he was describing was, in a way, a profoundly conservative, backward-looking revolution.[16]

Paz returned to a discussion of Zapata many years later in *Posdata*. In the context of a series of reflections on whether the Mexico of the late 1960s was ripe for a new revolution, Paz offers a far less exalted portrait of the revolutionary leader from Morelos. He now describes Zapata not as someone who understood the truth about his country, but as a sadly ineffective politician. In *Posdata* Paz puts forward a different perspective on the role of the peasantry in politics. He acknowledges that the harsh conditions that prevail in the Mexican countryside—he speaks of "medio México semidesnudo, analfabeto y mal comido" (the illiterate, barely clothed, and poorly fed half of Mexico)—would appear to be conducive to a new revolutionary insurrection (86). He notes, furthermore, that there have been outbreaks of violence in Mexico's rural areas in recent times. Nevertheless, Paz states firmly that it would be absurd to claim that the situation in the countryside was revolutionary. Why does Paz think this? In the first place, he notes that the conflicts in the country's rural areas were fundamentally of a local nature (87). More importantly, Paz believes that there is an inherent contradiction or incompatibility between the peasantry and the role of the state in society. "Los campesinos" (The peasantry), he points out, "nunca han querido ni quieren tomar el poder" (88; has never wanted to and still does not want to take power). And to back up this claim

Paz reminds the reader of what happened when Zapata's army of peasants occupied Mexico City during the Revolution. When Zapata paid a visit to the National Palace, he was horrified by the sight of the presidential chair and refused to sit in it. He eventually withdrew his troops from the country's capital city, returning to Morelos. In the end, as we know, he was assassinated at the orders of Venustiano Carranza, a rival revolutionary leader. For Paz, the lesson is clear: "a aquél que rehúsa el poder . . . el poder lo destruye" (89; he who refuses to take power . . . will be destroyed by power). Through his own actions, Zapata had made himself marginal to Mexico's future. In Paz's new reading, Zapata no longer represented what was most promising and inspiring about the Mexican Revolution; instead, he stood for "el aislamiento, la segregación" (90; isolation, segregation). Rather than pointing the way forward for the nation, Zapata had made himself irrelevant.

Paz was by no means the only thinker of his time to interpret the Mexican Revolution as a spontaneous explosion of the nation's submerged reality—and as a movement lacking a systematic ideology. Max Parra has shown that the pages devoted to the Mexican Revolution in *El laberinto* repeat key motifs (though surely in a more poetic fashion than any of his precursors) in the historiography of the Mexican Revolution of the preceding decades.[17] Consider, for example, Frank Tannenbaum's *Peace by Revolution* (1933), one of the foundational works of the historiography of the Mexican Revolution. The author underlines the very same opposition Paz depicts in his reading of the Revolution. Tannenbaum claims that the uprising "was essentially the work of the common people. No organized party presided at its birth. No great intellectuals prescribed its program, formulated its doctrine, outlined its objectives."[18] He goes on to note how different the Mexican Revolution was from the French and Russian Revolutions: "There was not a Rousseau, a Voltaire, a Montesquieu, a Diderot in Mexico. . . . There is no Lenin in Mexico."[19] Tannenbaum compares the Mexican Revolution to a force of nature: it was "unheralded and unguided . . . like a cyclone."[20] Consider, too, how closely Alfonso Reyes follows in the footsteps of Tannenbaum in a reading he put forward of the Mexican Revolution in 1939. Reyes claims that "la Revolución Mexicana brotó de un impulso mucho más que de una idea. No fue planeada. . . . No fue preparada por enciclopedistas o filósofos, más o menos conscientes de las consecuencias de su doctrina, como la Revolución francesa. No fue organizada por los dialécticos de la guerra social, como la Revolución Rusa" (The Mexican Revolution sprang from an impulse rather than from an idea. It was not planned. . . . It was not prepared for by encyclopedists or philosophers, more or less conscious of the consequences of their doctrines, as was the case with the French Revolution. It was not organized by dialecticians of social warfare, as was the Russian Revolution).[21] In sum, Paz hews closely to a well-known interpretation of the Mexican Revolution.

In order to understand Paz's thinking about the Mexican Revolution, it is imperative to examine his ideas not just about the Revolution, but about the post-revolutionary period as well. The relationship between the two periods is a crucial (and complicated) issue, in part because there is considerable disagreement among historians as to exactly when the Revolution ended, and in part because the regime that evolved out of the Revolution, and remained in power until the year 2000, explicitly based its legitimacy on its connection to the Revolution. Paz reflected as extensively on the post-revolutionary period as he did on the Revolution itself, developing a nuanced (some might say contradictory) point of view as both critic and defender of the *Partido Revolucionario Institucional* (PRI; Institutional Revolutionary Party), which ruled the country for over seventy years. He regularly accused the post-revolutionary regimes of betraying the ideals of the Mexican Revolution, but he also spoke frequently of the achievements of these regimes, and of how these achievements could be linked to the original goals of the revolutionaries.

Let us note, to begin with, that Paz's tone changes drastically when he shifts in *El laberinto* from a discussion of the Revolution to a discussion of the post-revolutionary period. He abandons his poetic style of writing, and becomes far more practical and prosaic in his approach. According to Paz, the primary goal of the post-revolutionary governments was not the search for national identity nor the reconciliation with the past (although these aspects were not cast aside entirely), but rather economic development. In *El laberinto*, Paz speaks at length of how the post-revolutionary regimes mobilized the state's resources in order to "hacer de México una nación moderna" (189; transform Mexico into a modern nation). But he explains that these regimes opted for a capitalist economic model to achieve this goal. A state-led capitalist model, to be sure, but capitalist nevertheless. In short, by the middle of the twentieth century, Mexico had developed into a capitalist country, with the proviso, that is, that the nation's capitalist class operated under the wings of the state. As Paz puts it in *Posdata*, "la nueva clase [capitalista] es una criatura del régimen revolucionario" (66; the new capitalist class is a creation of the revolutionary regime). Was this what Mexico's revolutionaries had envisioned? Certainly not Zapata, Paz's favorite revolutionary. But in his writings from the 1950s and 1960s, Paz does not hesitate to describe this model for Mexico's development as at least a partial success. In *El laberinto*, he states that it is owing to the policies of Mexico's post-revolutionary governments that "nuestra evolución es una de las más rápidas y constantes en América" (195; our development is among the fastest and most consistent in the Americas). In *Corriente alterna*, he claims that Mexico's one-party system paved the way for "un avance considerable de nuestra economía" (180; a considerable improvement in our economy), although he hastens to add that the system's democratization is an urgent necessity. A few years later, in *Posdata*, he speaks of how Mexico's "desarrollo económico ha sido excepcional" (32; economic development has been exceptional), and celebrates the fact that "al fín México es un país moderno" (70; at last Mexico has become a modern nation).

Paz suggested that what he called the "logros" (achievements) of the Mexican Revolution had not been sufficiently acknowledged.[22] In addition to crediting the post-revolutionary regimes with achieving strong economic growth (especially from the 1940s to the 1960s), Paz praised them for creating stability in the country,[23] and for avoiding one of the banes of revolutionary states throughout the twentieth century: the imposition of state-sponsored regimes of terror.[24] And yet, at key moments of his career, Paz was among the most vocal critics of the PRI regime. In October 1968, he resigned his position as Mexico's ambassador to India to protest the massacre by government forces of a large number of students who had gathered in Mexico City's Plaza Tlatelolco to demand social and political reform. Paz subsequently authored a lengthy analysis of the events of 1968 in which he linked the current PRI regime not to any of the political, cultural, or ideological strands within the Mexican Revolution, but rather to the violent, hierarchical, and repressive political-theological system of the Aztecs. In *El laberinto*, Paz had already suggested in passing that the Mexican Revolution was dead. "La Revolución Mexicana" (The Mexican Revolution), he argued, "ha muerto sin resolver nuestras contradicciones" (has died without resolving our contradictions).[25] Over the years, the skeptical note in Paz's reflections began to ring louder and louder. In *Posdata*, he argued that the PRI regimes had usurped the revolutionary heritage.[26] In the same work, he suggested that Mexico's regime suffered from sclerosis.[27] A few years later, he claimed that the Mexican Revolution had been "confiscado" (confiscated)[28] or "congelado y desfigurado" (frozen and disfigured).[29] Writing in the early 1990s, he argued that there was a dividing line, rather than continuity, between the revolutionary and post-revolutionary periods in Mexican history. These two stages were not as connected as some might think: "el segundo período, el llamado institucional, no sólo presenta radicales diferencias con el primero sino que no puede llamarse con propiedad revolucionario" (the second period, known as the institutional period, is not only radically different from the first one, it cannot properly be called revolutionary).[30] Although this perspective did not preclude Paz from identifying the achievements of the post-revolutionary regimes, he did not view these achievements as fulfilments of the revolutionary struggles of the early twentieth century.

Taken together, the reflections on the post-revolutionary period that Paz produced over the course of approximately half a century leave us with an ambiguous picture. Paz returned occasionally to the idea that the Revolution had allowed Mexico to deepen and solidify a sense of nationhood. In *El ogro filantrópico* (1979; The philanthropic ogre), for example, he wrote that "la Revolución ha dado una conciencia de nación a la mayoría de los mexicanos" (the Revolution has endowed a majority of the Mexican people with a sense of their national identity),[31] while in *Itinerario* he made a similar claim, stating that the Mexican Revolution "consiguió crear una conciencia de identidad nacional que antes apenas existía" (succeeded in forging a national consciousness that until then barely existed).[32] For Paz, this was an enduring accomplishment on the part of the Revolution, one that the post-revolutionary regimes had sustained. Yet many of the other achievements he mentioned seemed singularly *negative* in nature and came into focus only when one compared Mexico with other countries. Unlike the Soviet Union, Mexico had not experienced a reign of terror, or the imposition of a rigid ideological orthodoxy.[33] Unlike other Latin American countries, Mexico had not suffered constant military coups.[34] Such qualified praise made it difficult to view the PRI regime as having fulfilled the goals for which the revolutionaries had fought. Indeed, as we have seen, Paz was much more likely to depict the post-revolutionary order as amounting to a betrayal of the original revolutionary impetus.[35]

One of the ways in which Paz addressed the ambiguity in his own picture of twentieth-century Mexican history was by speaking of the system that emerged from the country's upheavals as a "compromise." He introduced this concept in *El laberinto*: "La Revolución mexicana" (The Mexican Revolution), he claimed, "ha sido un compromiso entre fuerzas opuestas: nacionalismo e imperialismo, economía dirigida y régimen de 'libre empresa', democracia y paternalismo estatal" (has amounted to a compromise between opposing forces: nationalism and imperialism, a planned economy and a 'free-enterprise' system, democracy and state paternalism).[36] He used it again in *Posdata* where he describes the Mexican political system as "un compromiso entre la dictadura personal de los caudillos y el programa democrático de la Revolución mexicana" (a compromise between the personal dictatorship of the strongmen and the democratic program of the Mexican Revolution).[37] In *Itinerario*, Paz relied once more on this concept in an attempt to capture the complex and mixed nature of the post-revolutionary order, which he now described as "un compromiso entre la herencia liberal de 1857, las aspiraciones comunitarias populares y fragmentos de otras ideologías" (a compromise between the liberal heritage of 1857, the communitarian aspirations of the people, and fragments of other ideologies).[38] In all of these comments, one gets the sense that for Paz this "compromise" failed to match the ideals for which Mexico's revolutionaries had fought; nevertheless, it was a compromise that worked, at least for a time.

One of Paz's main complaints about pre-revolutionary Mexican society was that it suffered from the malady of inauthenticity. As we have seen, Paz believed that a severe mismatch had developed during the *Porfiriato* between the regime's official ideology and Mexico's actual social and economic conditions. In Paz's account, the falsehood that enveloped Mexican society of the late nineteenth and early twentieth century helped precipitate the revolutionary explosion of 1910 and the years that followed. From this perspective, the Mexican Revolution offered a kind of psychological cleansing, an overcoming of the state of inauthenticity in which the country had lived until then, or, to use Paz's own metaphor, the possibility of removing the mask that had concealed the nation's true being. Clearly, Paz has not been alone in developing this theme of the incongruous, fractured nature of Latin American reality.[39] One wonders, however, whether the diagnosis Paz applied to the *Porfiriato* could not apply equally well to Mexico's period of PRI rule. Did the PRI governments not offer the consummate example of a gap between rhetoric and reality? Could the very idea of a regime that presumed to be "institutional" and "revolutionary" at the same time not be seen as an example of the masking of reality that Paz denounced in the *Porfiriato*? Paz did indeed denounce the PRI regime in precisely such terms, above all in *Posdata*, the work in which he developed his harshest criticism of the post-revolutionary order. He speaks, for example, of how in the 1940s a new phase took hold in Mexican history, characterized by a kind of disfiguring of the original revolutionary impetus: "las ideas se transforman en fórmulas y las fórmulas en antifaces" (ideas turn into formulas and formulas become masks).[40] This is, of course, highly reminiscent of Paz's description of the *Porfiriato*. It was not, however, the dominant theme in his approach to the post-revolutionary era, as it was in his description of Mexico's nineteenth century.

Even though Paz ends up suggesting in *El laberinto* and other works that the Revolution had not been a success, he continued throughout his career to use the Mexican Revolution as a guidepost and legitimating device. In *Corriente alterna*, for example, Paz offers a highly sympathetic account of the rise of the Third World in the decades following the end of World War II and ends up wondering which model the countries of the Third World will choose to follow: that of the Mexican Revolution or the Cuban Revolution.[41] Clearly, the implication is that the Mexican Revolution constitutes a viable model for other countries. Even more striking is the answer Paz gives to a question posed to him in a 1984 interview by Enrique Krauze. When Krauze inquires whether Paz's vision of the revolution might not be described as "demasiado Zapatista" (too *Zapatista*), Paz responds as follows:

> ¿Es demasiado Zapatista mi visión de la revolución? No lo creo. La Revolución es el momento en que nuestro pueblo busca la forma política e histórica que lo exprese. No es el momento en que los mexicanos encuentran esa forma, sino en el que se deciden a buscarla o a inventarla. . . . La crisis revolucionaria mostró que el pueblo mexicano estaba huérfano de esas ideas madre que simultáneamente fundan, alimentan y forman a una sociedad. Ante la petrificación o la invalidez de las ideas que le habían dado una raison d'être, el pueblo mexicano busca, instintivamente y casi sin ideas, nuevas ideas. No afuera, como antes, sino dentro de si. Este es el sentido profundo, para mí, de la Revolución mexicana. No las encontró, pero se conoció a si mismo.
>
> *Is my vision of the Revolution too Zapatista? I do not believe so. The Revolution is the moment when the Mexican people begin to search for*

> *a political and historical form that expresses the nation's identity. It is not the moment when we discover that form; rather, it is the moment when we decide to look for it or invent it. . . . The revolutionary crisis revealed that the Mexican people were lacking in those life-giving ideas that simultaneously create, nourish, and give shape to a society. In the face of the petrification or lack of validity of the ideas that had served as its raison d'être, the Mexican people, instinctively and almost without ideas, begin to search for new ideas. Not outside of Mexico, as they had done in the past, but within itself. This, for me, is the profound significance of the Mexican Revolution. Our country didn't find the ideas it was searching for, but it discovered itself.*[42]

We see here how thirty-five years after *El laberinto* Paz continues to depict the Mexican Revolution from the same psycho-cultural perspective he had settled on at the beginning of his career.

Striking, too, is Paz's use of the Mexican Revolution in his 1990 essay "México: modernidad y patrimonialismo," a response to a speech by President Carlos Salinas. Salinas was promoting the idea of the "estado justo" (just state) as a replacement for the "estado propietario" (owner state), and the goal of Paz's essay was to demonstrate that the "estado justo," contrary to critics who viewed it as a betrayal of the Mexican Revolution, in fact fit into the tradition of the Mexican Revolution. Paz begins by noting that there were several Mexican Revolutions. He is no longer interested in arguing—as he did in *El laberinto*—that one dimension of the Revolution (*Zapatismo*) was more authentic than the others. Instead, he claims that the very multiplicity of strands within the Revolution is what gives it its "vigencia" (relevance) in the present.[43] The Revolution, says Paz, had many faces: "la de Madero, política y democrática; otra la de Zapata, agraria y milenarista; otra la de Carranza, nacionalista; otra la de Obregón y Calles, más dedicada a construir que a derribar" (the political and democratic revolution of Madero; the agrarian and millenarian revolution of Zapata; the nationalist revolution of Carranza; and the revolution of Obregón and Calles, more focused on construction than on destruction).[44] Still, the recognition of the Revolution's many faces does not mean that Paz declines to express his preference for one or the other of its dimensions. Whereas in 1950 Paz had celebrated *Zapatismo* as the most stirring and authentic current within the Revolution, he now argues that "Las aspiraciones democráticas de Madero tienen hoy una actualidad que no tenían hace cincuenta años; el afán de Calles por modernizar nuestra economía parece ser de hoy" (Madero's democratic goals seem relevant today in a way that they did not fifty years ago; Calles's efforts to modernize our economy are similar to what we are currently witnessing).[45] And he goes on to claim that in the debate between the "estado propietario" and the "estado justo," the latter has precedence, for it is the "concepción más . . . antigua y . . . permanente" (the idea that is . . . older . . . and more enduring).[46] What is most revealing about this exercise is the need to use the Mexican Revolution as a point of reference and a legitimating device for political projects in the present. It is as if a political agenda cannot work in Mexico unless it can be linked to some ideological strand within the Revolution.

Paz's continued fidelity to the inheritance of the Mexican Revolution went hand in hand with a clear position *against* the idea that Mexico might have been ready, at any point during the poet's lifetime, for another revolution. This was especially noteworthy in 1968, the year in which a revolution appeared to be just over the horizon in countries across the globe. Indeed, in his earliest responses to the May 1968 uprising in Paris, Paz seemed completely caught up in the revolutionary fervor of the times. "Los acontecimientos de Francia me tienen exaltado" (The events in France have put me in a state of exaltation), he reported in a May 27, 1968, letter to Vicente Rojo.[47] The next day, in a letter to Arnaldo Orfila Reynal, he reiterated his enthusiasm and expressed confidence that the student-worker uprising in France would take a revolutionary turn: "Sigo con pasión los sucesos de Francia. . . . Si los obreros continúan con su firme actitud . . . asistiremos a la primera revolución socialista en un país desarrollado. Esto es, seremos testigos de la verdadera revolución socialista" (I'm following what is happening in France with great excitement. . . . If the workers maintain their firm stance . . . we will be in the presence of the first socialist revolution in a developed nation. In other words, we will be witnessing the first truly socialist revolution.)[48] Within a few weeks, however, as the French insurrection began to lose steam and the French government reasserted its authority, Paz was already revising his point of view. In a June 11, 1968, letter to Emir Rodríguez Monegal, he acknowledged that his prediction of a revolution in France had been wrong: "Al principio creí que estábamos realmente ante una verdadera revolución—la primera en un país desarrollado y el comienzo de la revolución europea. O sea: la revolución que todos hemos esperado, la verdadera. No ha sido así" (At first, I thought we were witnessing a true revolution—the first revolution in a developed nation and the beginning of the European revolution. That is: the revolution we have all been waiting for, the true one. It has not been so).[49] Although Paz still saw much that was inspiring in the May 1968 movement—especially its libertarian spirit—there was no doubt that he was writing with a feeling of frustrated hopes.

When a student movement emerged a few months later in Mexico, Paz's responses were much more moderate in tone. He never once interpreted the events in Mexico as an incipient revolution. On the contrary, he repeatedly insisted that the students wanted to reform the system, not overturn it. The letters Paz wrote to different people in the months after the beginning of the unrest in Mexico offer ample evidence of his reading of the movement as reformist, not revolutionary. It is important to note in this context that reform was both what the students wanted (according to Paz) and what Paz thought was best for the country. In an August 19, 1968, letter to Jean-Clarence Lambert, he explained the differences between France and Mexico: "El movimiento tiene un sentido diferente al de París: no es una 'contestación' total sino algo menos ambicioso pero, dentro de México, más factible" (The movement has a different meaning from the one in Paris: it is not a total "contestation," but something less ambitious, although, in the Mexican context, more feasible).[50] In a subsequent letter to the same Parisian correspondent, Paz offered more detail on what he regarded as the feasible changes the country needed: "se trata de lograr lo que rechazan los jóvenes europeos y norteamericanos—la democracia burguesa" (it is a matter of achieving what young people in Europe and North America reject—bourgeois democracy).[51] In late October, a few weeks after the Tlateloco massacre, Paz repeated the same point in a letter to Carlos Fuentes. "México," he wrote, "necesita . . . una reforma, no una revolución" (needs . . . reform, not a revolution).[52] In later writings, Paz would make it clear that this reformist orientation was not simply his personal preference. It also matched the political sentiments of the Mexican people as a whole. In *Posdata* he noted that "ni el temple del pueblo mexicano es revolucionario ni lo son las condiciones históricas del país" (the Mexican people are not in a revolutionary mood, and the historical conditions of the country are not revolutionary either).[53] Completely gone, by this time, was the desire for a *real* revolution he had so strongly expressed in his initial responses to the events in Paris in May 1968.

Was the 1968 student movement in Mexico reformist or revolutionary in its goals? The leaders of the movement itself have weighed in on this complicated and controversial question, often from divergent perspectives. One student leader, Raúl Álvarez Garín, insists that the student movement was democratic both in its aims and in its organization, and he emphasizes that the movement did not seek to overthrow the government.[54] But he also notes that one of the outcomes of the peaceful 1968 uprising—and its defeat— was the emergence in Mexico of guerrilla movements that sought to overthrow the PRI regime through violent means. And he sees these armed movements as "una continuación . . . un segundo momento del propio Movimiento del 68" (a continuation . . . a second stage of the 1968 Movement).[55] Another student leader, Luis González de Alba, rejected the idea of revolution, and depicted the movement as unabashedly reformist in its aims. In *Los días y los años* (1971; The days and the years), an account of the student movement that he wrote in Lecumberri prison, González de Alba records a conversation with student radicals from Germany, who express their surprise at the fact that the Mexican students are demanding *respect* for the Constitution, whereas in Western Europe, by contrast, the student movements sought to *abolish* the constitutions in their countries. González de Alba explains that in Mexico the Constitution has never been respected; to demand that its ideals be upheld—including the ideal of "libertades democráticas" (democratic freedoms)—could potentially bring about a profound change in the system. González de Alba realized that in other countries it might make sense to make more radical demands; he insisted, however, that in Mexico "seguimos manteniendo exigencias puramente reformistas" (our demands continue to be purely reformist).[56] Jorge Volpi, in his overview of debates in the Mexican intellectual world surrounding the events of 1968, draws a complex portrait of the sensibility and ideological tendencies of the time. On the one hand, he notes that a variety of developments around the world—among others, the Cuban Revolution and the Vietnam War—led to a vigorous rebirth of "la idea revolucionaria" (the revolutionary idea).[57] On the other hand, he notes that what he calls "la principal bandera de los estudiantes" (the students' principal banner) was democracy, not revolution.[58]

We have already seen that Paz sided with the reading of the student movement as reformist. However, as time passed he put forward a new reading of the student movement. He still believed that it was essentially a reformist movement, but he now began to argue that the students themselves had misinterpreted the meaning of the movement in which they were participants. He explained his views in some detail in the preface to the English translation of Elena Poniatowska's book on the 1968 massacre, *La noche de Tlatelolco* (1971; The night of Tlatelolco, published in English as *Massacre in Mexico*). Paz begins by praising the students for their political skill, and above all for "la moderación de sus demandas, englobadas en la palabra *democratización*, aspiración nacional de los mexicanos desde 1910" (the moderate nature of their demands, summed up in the word *democratization*, which has been a goal of the Mexican nation since 1910).[59] But he then goes on to argue that the commonsensical dimension of the movement vanishes when one hears the students discuss their goals: "En lugar del realismo táctico y estratégico: las fórmulas huecas, los esquemas rígidos, el simplismo doctrinario, las frases gaseosas" (Instead of tactical and strategic realism: hollow formulas, rigid schemes, simplistic doctrines, misty phrases).[60] The students thought they were participating in a completely different movement from the one that was in actual fact developing around them: "Era como si el México de 1968 fuese una metáfora de la Comuna de París o de la toma del Palacio de Invierno: México era México y simultáneamente era otro tiempo y otro lugar, otra realidad" (It was as if the Mexico of 1968 were a metaphor of the Paris Commune or of the storming of the Winter Palace: Mexico was Mexico and at the same time it was another time and another place, another reality).[61] The students were experiencing one thing, but they thought that they were experiencing something completely different: "Sus actos eran reales, sus interpretaciones imaginarias" (Their actions were real, their interpretations imaginary).[62] Paz would reiterate and elaborate on this reading of the events of 1968 on many occasions in the course of the years to come.[63] It was a reading of the 1968 student movement and its (distorted) theorization that clearly expressed Paz's evolving opposition to revolutionary politics.

In short, there is a tension between Paz's anti-revolutionary position in many of his writings and his celebration—throughout his career—of the Mexican Revolution. To be clear: it is not inherently contradictory to support one revolution while opposing another one. Revolutions take place at different times and in different places, and such variations can provoke a range of judgments, leading to either favorable or unfavorable assessments. Only a very simplistic thinker will support every single revolution, regardless of the circumstances, and Paz was obviously not such a thinker. But in Paz's case there is a genuinely puzzling quality to his thought. He was a utopian thinker who developed a subtle and insightful critique of utopian thought. He was a man who valued prudence in politics, but who was thrilled by the idea of poetry turning into action. He poeticized the Mexican Revolution, but also offered very practical analyses of its achievements and failings. One could go on listing the multifarious tensions in his work. But these tensions were also a source of richness, and a reflection of the broad reach of Paz's mind. One important explanation for the bifurcation in Paz's thinking about twentieth-century revolutions is that the Russian Revolution resulted in a highly repressive state that murdered tens of millions of its citizens, whereas the Mexican Revolution did not. Furthermore, Paz was attracted to the Mexican Revolution's cultural and nationalist dimension, which he did not observe in the Russian Revolution. But the complex configuration of Paz's ideas about twentieth-century revolutions can also be connected to a certain underlying structure one detects in his thought, and the way his thought draws on different—sometimes competing—cultural and intellectual traditions within the modern world.

Throughout Paz's work one encounters an ur-opposition between ideas and reality, reason and instinct, thought and feeling. When Paz lamented the fact that Spanish America lacked an eighteenth century (by which he meant an Enlightenment), he was proposing that ideas have the power to transform reality. If only we had had the right intellectual tradition, Paz was suggesting, Spanish American history would have taken a different course from the one it did. Yet the realm of ideas and reason also seemed to have a pernicious dimension to it. When in *Corriente alterna* Paz discusses the decline of what he calls "las antiguas utopías geométricas" (the old geometrical utopias),[64] the use of the term "geometrical" suggests that what is declining is in fact the power of reason to mold reality. And the implication, as we saw before, is that the belief in reason's power to mold reality is in itself foolish or even dangerous. It is worth recalling Paz's allusion in the final paragraph of *El laberinto* to Goya's famous etching "El sueño de la razón produce monstruos" (The dream/sleep of reason produces monsters), which the Mexican poet appears to be reading as a statement on the dangers of an excessive reliance on reason. Note that the reference to Goya is part of an attack on a modern world in which "los espejos de la razón multiplican las cámaras de tortura" (the mirrors of reason cause the torture chambers to multiply).[65] Reason, instead of freeing human beings from their bondage, as the thinkers of the Enlightenment had predicted, in fact made their enslavement worse. Consider, also, the fact that one of Paz's main reservations about the 1994 Chiapas rebellion was that the *Zapatistas* did not represent a "spontaneous" uprising of the indigenous people of the region, but rather that the rebellion was the result of a premeditated and lengthily prepared effort led by urban intellectuals. "No estamos ante una revuelta espontánea" (We are not witnessing a spontaneous uprising), he wrote in his first response to the events in Chiapas, "sino ante una acción militar premeditada" (but rather a premeditated military action).[66] This fact in itself made the rebellion, for Paz, questionable. He regarded it as the product of an ideological—and therefore distorted—view of the world. But doesn't Paz argue elsewhere that without ideas we cannot change the world? Clearly, there is an ambiguity in Paz's views on the relationship between the power of the human intellect on the one hand and the force of raw, unstructured reality on the other. The ambiguity can be attributed to the fact that Paz draws simultaneously on two interrelated, but also competing, intellectual traditions in Western culture: the Enlightenment and Romanticism. Helpful, in this regard, is Yvon Grenier's description of Paz as a "liberal romantic."[67] Paz's attachment to the ideals of the Enlightenment and of the liberal tradition leads him to press for the importance of rational, critical debate in bringing about social change; his Romantic side leads him to celebrate spontaneity and to dismiss thinkers who think that ideas can be used to mold reality.[68] In his criticisms of the Russian Revolution and other Communist revolutions that followed in its wake, Paz speaks as a believer in the Enlightenment ideal of the free, rational individual (although the great revolutions of the twentieth century could also be seen as a product of the Enlightenment run amok); in his celebration of the Mexican Revolution, he speaks (at least some of the time) as an adherent of the Romantic ideals of "expressive individuation" and communal integration.[69]

CHAPTER 3

Mexico and the United States

It is well known that discussions of identity generally involve the postulation of an Other. It is also well known that in the long Latin American tradition of writings on national or continental identity, the role of the Other has most commonly been assigned to the United States of America. Octavio Paz is no exception in this regard. Following in the footsteps of nineteenth-century authors such as Domingo Sarmiento, José Martí, and José Enrique Rodó, and writers of the first half of the twentieth century such as José Carlos Mariátegui and José Vasconcelos, Paz's reflections on the question of his nation's identity are often paired with investigations into the history, culture, and politics of the United States. Indeed, over the course of his career, Paz authored a series of powerful meditations on what he regarded as the profound differences between the two countries. Again and again, he sought to define Mexico by contrasting it with the United States.

In spite of having written some of his era's most important works on the topic, Paz was ambivalent about the question of national identity. Consider, for example, an observation Paz makes in a 1949 letter to Alfonso Reyes. Having recently completed *El laberinto*, the Mexican poet goes on a tirade *against* the topic of the very book he had just written. "Le confieso" (I have to admit), he writes, "que el tema de México . . . empieza a cargarme" (that the topic of Mexico . . . is starting to irritate me). Paz then proceeds to explain why—in spite of his exasperation—he had decided to devote an entire book to the theme of national identity: "si yo mismo incurrí en un libro fue para liberarme de esa enfermedad—que sería grotesca si no fuera peligrosa y escondiera un deseo de nivelarlo todo" (if I myself incurred in a book, I did so in order to free myself of that disease—a disease that would be grotesque if it weren't dangerous and if it did not conceal a desire to cut everything down to size).[1] In short, he writes the book in order to put the theme of the book behind him. Indeed, the desire to overcome or go beyond the question of national identity is reflected within the work itself. Take, for example, *El laberinto*'s much-quoted (and frequently criticized) concluding lines. After describing the years following the end of World War II as an era in which all belief-systems have collapsed—Paz speaks of "el derrumbe general de la Razón y la Fe, de Dios y la Utopía" (the general collapse of Reason and Faith, of God and Utopia)—he goes on to declare that the resulting state of solitude is a universal human condition: "Estamos al fin solos. Como todos los hombres" (Finally, we are alone. Like all men). This, in turn, leads into his eloquent (though controversial) conclusion: "Somos, por primera vez en nuestra historia, contemporáneos de todos los hombres" (For the first time in our history, we are contemporaries of all mankind).[2] In sum, it is irrelevant whether one is Mexican or from some other country. Paz's lengthy probe into the nature of Mexican identity ends with the claim that national identities have ceased to matter.

In spite of his attack in his letter to Reyes on what he describes as "el nacionalismo torcido" (the twisted nationalism) of many of his contemporaries,[3] Paz frequently defended the idea that collective identities exist, and often used the concepts of "nation" and "civilization" as the building blocks of his thinking about the world. In a lengthy digression inserted into his 1964 essay on Rubén Darío, Paz takes a strong stance against the Marxist idea that history should be regarded as a battle between rival socio-economic systems. Such a viewpoint implies that civilizations are mere ideological masks covering up "la verdadera realidad social" (the true social reality).[4] Countering this idea, Paz defends the concept of "el genio de los pueblos" (the genius of a people), defining it as "la realidad concreta de unos hombres en un paisaje determinado, con una herencia semejante y cierto número de posibilidades que sólo se realizan por y gracias a la acción del grupo" (the concrete reality of a group of men in a specific environment, with a similar heritage and a certain number of possibilities that can only be realized by the group and thanks to the actions of the group).[5] In *Corriente alterna*, Paz notes that Marx overlooked "la morfología de las sociedades y las civilizaciones, aquello que las separa y distingue por encima de los sistemas de producción económica" (the morphology of a society or a civilization, that which more than its economic system distinguishes it and sets it apart from other civilizations),[6] creating a blind spot in Marxist theory that severely limited its usefulness as a tool for understanding the world. For Paz, the Sino-Soviet conflict of the 1960s was evidence of the enduring influence of civilizational differences.[7] From a Marxist perspective, it was impossible to explain why two Communist countries had gone to war with each other, since the proletariat was assumed to hold power in both China and the Soviet Union. If social class was the real driver of history, then national differences would not matter. But the fact was that such differences did seem to matter. Paz finds a further refutation of the Marxist notion that the worker "no tiene patria ni color local" (has no nationality and no local identity) in the idea—also emerging in the 1960s, specifically as a result of developments in Yugoslavia—that each nation "debe llegar al socialismo por su propio camino y por sus propios medios" (should find its own path to socialism).[8] In short, Paz repeatedly zeroed in on the importance of national or civilizational identity and did so in order to downplay the significance of socio-economic class.

Paz used the idea of civilizational differences to explain the contrast between Mexico and the United States. In one of his best-known essays on the topic, "México y Estados Unidos: Posiciones y contraposiciones," first published in 1978, he argues that even if the economic gap between the two countries were to disappear, that is, even if Mexico were to become as prosperous as the United States, the two countries would still not become alike. The reason for this is clear, Paz claims. The differences between Mexico and the United States belong to "el orden de las civilizaciones" (the order of civilizations), a domain in which change occurs only at a very slow pace.[9] A mere shift in economic circumstances cannot alter differences that are a product of history and as a result are deeply embedded in culture and society. This is not to dismiss altogether the relevance of economic factors. But these factors are less important than the civilizational elements, which Paz refers to as being of a more permanent nature and describes as "esa zona fluida, de contornos indecisos, en la que se funden y confunden las ideas y las creencias, las instituciones y las técnicas, los estilos y la moral, las modas y las iglesias" (that fluid domain, of uncertain contours, in which are mixed together ideas and beliefs, institutions and techniques, style and morality, fashions and churches).[10] It is important to note, however, that for Paz Mexico and the United States do not belong to different civilizations; rather, they constitute separate branches within a single civilization, that is, Western civilization. Even so, the gulf separating them is deep and wide.[11]

Paz wrote about the relationship between Mexico and the United States repeatedly over the course of his long career. He produced his most important writings on the topic during two periods, the 1940s and the 1970s, both of which coincided with his longest sojourns in the United States. He first came to the United States in 1943, having received a Guggenheim fellowship to work on a study of the poetry of the Americas. After a brief stay in Los Angeles, he settled in the Bay Area, living first in Berkeley and later in San Francisco. He remained there until 1945, writing poetry, working at the Mexican Consulate in San Francisco, attending classes at the University of California at Berkeley, and writing articles for journals and newspapers back home, including a series of reports on the 1945 San Francisco Conference at which the United Nations charter was drafted.[12] In 1945, Paz moved to the East Coast and later that year he was appointed Third Secretary in the Mexican Embassy in France. In Paris he wrote *El laberinto*, a work on the Mexican character into which Paz wove his impressions of the United States. Indeed, Paz himself stated in the opening chapter of the work that the encounter with Mexico's northern neighbor—a country utterly different from his own—precipitated his thoughts about his Mexican identity. Although there were occasional visits to the United States in the interim, Paz's next period of prolonged contact with the country did not occur until the late 1960s and 1970s. Following his resignation as Mexico's ambassador to India in October 1968, Paz became a frequent guest on American university campuses, and for several years in the 1970s he held a visiting appointment at Harvard University. Paz penned some of his most important essays on the relationship between Mexico and the United States, including "El espejo indiscreto," "La mesa y el lecho," and "México y Estados Unidos: Posiciones y contraposiciones," during these years.

Although it is clear that his writings on the topic were informed at least in part by his personal impressions, Paz tended to eschew anecdotes drawn from his own experience, preferring to adopt a broad historical perspective on the cultural differences between Mexico and the United States. In his discussions of this topic, he did not fail to acknowledge the changes taking place over the years in Mexico's northern neighbor. There was a significant difference between the repressive nature of US society in the 1940s and the permissiveness of the 1960s and 1970s. Paz was deeply interested in the counterculture of the 1960s,[13] as well as in the rise of multiculturalism in the 1980s and 1990s.[14] Toward the end of his life he even began to argue in favor of an "association" of the United States and Latin America.[15] But his principal focus was on the enduring substratum of US society—the *longue durée*, we might say—and its persistent contrast with Mexico. Indeed, one of the recurring themes of his writings on the topic was that the gap between the two nations had such profound historical roots that it might well be unsurpassable. On one occasion, he even went so far as to compare the breach between Mexico and the United States to the vast gulf separating Hindus from Muslims in India.[16]

Paz often described history as a realm of chance and accident. "La historia siempre está encinta de accidentes, infortunios y catástrofes" (History is always filled with accidents, misfortunes, and catastrophes), he states. "La historia no es un absoluto que se realiza sino un proceso que sin cesar se afirma y se niega. La historia es tiempo; nada en ella es durable y permanente" (History is not an absolute seeking its fulfilment; it is a process that ceaselessly affirms and negates itself. History is time: nothing in it is durable or permanent).[17] Such a stance was probably a reaction against the grand narratives of Marxist historiography that dominated the intellectual debates of his era. Yet in his writings on Mexico and the United States, Paz adopts a very different perspective. The overriding concern of his reflections on this topic is the question of each nation's relationship to history, but history not as a domain where randomness and unpredictability reign, but as the medium through which nations or civilizations establish an authentic identity and define a meaningful trajectory for themselves. In a 1988 interview with conservative thinker Carlos Castillo Peraza, Paz explicitly states that "La historia no carece de sentido o, mejor dicho, de sentidos" (History is not lacking in meaning or, better said, in meanings), but then goes on to note that history's meaning is multiple: "Hay tantas historias como civilizaciones y, dentro de cada proceso histórico, aparecen diversos sentidos y caminos, unos convergentes y otros divergentes" (There are as many histories as there are civilizations and, within each historical process, different meanings and paths arise, some that converge, while others diverge).[18] However, it is not simply by virtue of existing that a civilization achieves historical meaning. There are certain modes of civilizational being that, according to Paz, are anti-historical. Paz approaches the comparison between Mexico and the United States with precisely this conceptual tool in hand: the opposition between what is historical and what is not historical. Not surprisingly, he argues that Mexico and the United States are polar opposites: whereas one country is authentically historical, the other is not. What is surprising, however, is that the nation chosen to represent historical being changes depending on the context.

In contemplating the history of the United States, Paz is repeatedly struck by how natural and organic the country's evolution seems to be. In "México y Estados Unidos" he puts forward his core thesis about the origins of US society and culture: "Los Estados Unidos son hijos de la Reforma y de la Ilustración. Nacieron bajo el signo de la crítica y la autocrítica" (The United States is a child of the Reformation and the Enlightenment. It was born under the sign of criticism and self-criticism).[19] Note the use of biological metaphors to describe the moment at which the United States comes into existence. Such metaphors suggest that we are dealing with a natural process resembling the way in which human beings come into the world. In a subsequent passage from the same essay, he uses a botanical image to restate his thesis that the origins of the United States are to be found in the seventeenth-century Puritan settlements: "en las pequeñas comunidades religiosas de Nueva Inglaterra estaba ya en germen el futuro: la democracia política, el capitalismo y el desarrollo social y económico" (in the small religious communities of New England, the seeds of the future had already been planted: political democracy, capitalism, and social and economic development).[20] In "El espejo indiscreto," Paz repeats the botanical motif when he describes Puritanism as the "raíz enterrada" (buried root) of North American democracy.[21] The use of these images suggests that the evolution that led from colonial North America to twentieth-century democracy and capitalism resembles a natural process. The history of the United States reminds Paz of the growth of a living organism.[22]

The emphasis on organic interconnectedness emerges not only from Paz's account of how the past gave birth to the present in the United States, but also from the way he portrays the relations between the different components of society in Puritan New England. In an essay on Latin American poetry commissioned in 1967 by the *Times Literary Supplement*, Paz speaks of how "entre el protestantismo, las instituciones democráticas anglosajonas, la idea del progreso y el capitalismo hay una relación orgánica" (there is an organic relationship between Protestantism, Anglo-Saxon democratic institutions, the idea of progress, and capitalism).[23] Note, in this passage, the emphasis on the interconnectedness of religion, politics, ideology, and economics, all of which are fused into an integrated whole.[24] Speaking of the early Puritan settlements in "México y Estados Unidos," Paz returns to the same theme, this time stressing the interrelations between religious beliefs, national sentiment, and political institutions: "en aquellas comunidades se había operado la fusión entre las convicciones religiosas, la embrionaria conciencia nacional y las instituciones políticas" (in these communities, religious convictions, an embryonic national consciousness, and political institutions had become fused together).²⁵ As he continues to develop his argument, Paz again underlines the idea that the different dimensions of this society existed in a profoundly harmonious relationship with each other: "entre las convicciones religiosas de los norteamericanos y sus instituciones democráticas no hubo contradicción sino armonía" (between the religious convictions of the North Americans and their democratic institutions, there was no contradiction, only harmony).²⁶ As we will see, the constant resort to notions of coherence and continuity sets the stage for the discussion of Mexican history as characterized by the lack of precisely these qualities.

Paz describes US history as having the appearance of a natural evolution, yet his account of twentieth-century American society suggests that this organic process produced an inorganic society. Again and again, when portraying modern-day America, Paz evokes an abstract, machine-like world filled with individuals who have been robbed of essential elements of their humanity. In *El laberinto*, Paz depicts the average American as a person lost "en un mundo abstracto de máquinas, conciudadanos y preceptos morales" (in an abstract world of machines, fellow citizens, and moral precepts).²⁷ In the same text, drawing on the Marxist concept of alienation, Paz argues that capitalism—and the United States is, of course, the capitalist nation par excellence—deprives the worker of his humanity, "puesto que reduce todo su ser a fuerza de trabajo, transformándolo por este solo hecho en objeto. Y como a todos los objetos, en mercancía, en cosa susceptible de compra y venta" (given that it reduces his being to his labor, thus transforming him into an object. And as with all objects, into merchandise, into a thing that is susceptible to being bought and sold).²⁸ Furthermore, in the United States—as in other modern nations—there is little sense of community. In "México y Estados Unidos," Paz notes that "los Estados Unidos no han conocido realmente el arte de la fiesta" (the United States has never truly known the art of the *fiesta*). "Es natural" (It's natural), he adds, "una sociedad que afirmaba con tal energía el valor redentor del trabajo, tenía que reprobar como una depravación el culto a la fiesta" (a society that so vigorously promoted the redeeming value of work, can be expected to condemn the cult of the *fiesta* as something depraved). And he makes it clear that he regards this rejection of the *fiesta* as a failure to understand its communal nature: "la conciencia puritana no podía ver que el valor de la fiesta era precisamente un valor religioso: la comunión" (the Puritan mind was incapable of understanding that the value of the *fiesta* was of a religious nature: it offered a form of communion).[29] Paz links the atomized and individualistic nature of social life in the United States to the Puritan identification of health with purity, an identification that produces a view of human contact as a form of contamination, and results in the eerie absence of the human body—"la inexistencia del cuerpo en tanto posibilidad de perderse—o encontrarse—en otro cuerpo" (the absence of the body as the possibility of losing—or finding—oneself in another body)—from social and cultural life in the United States.[30] At the same time, Paz joins a long line of observers who have argued that the American stress on individual liberty has resulted in a strangely homogeneous society. In *El laberinto*, Paz explains how American society blocks the natural growth of a person's character and shapes a profoundly conformist mind-set: "Desde la infancia se somete a hombres y mujeres a un inexorable proceso de adaptación; ciertos principios, contenidos en breves fórmulas, son repetidos sin cesar por la prensa, por la radio, las iglesias, las escuelas. . . . Presos de esos esquemas, como la planta en una maceta que la ahoga, el hombre y la mujer nunca crecen o maduran" (From childhood on, men and women are subjected to an inexorable process of adaptation; certain principles, summed up in brief formulas, are ceaselessly repeated in the newspapers, on the radio, in churches, and schools. . . . Trapped inside these structures, like a plant in a pot that suffocates it, men and women never grow up or become mature).[31] The natural and harmonious evolution of American society, from the Puritan era to the present, produces an arid society that represses the instincts, banishes the body, and dissolves the sense of community, in sum, that stunts the full growth of our human faculties. The history of the United States may have unfolded in an organic fashion, but the outcome of this history is a society that strikes Paz as profoundly inorganic.[32]

There is another paradox at the heart of Paz's description of the United States. It is not just that the natural evolution of history produces an unnatural way of life; it is that American history has culminated in a nation that exists *outside of history*. In *El laberinto*, Paz alludes on various occasions to the American belief that a society can be invented or re-invented through an act of the will. He notes, for example, that the notion that "la historia es el resultado de la sola voluntad humana" (history is the outcome of the human will alone) is one of the key assumptions undergirding American life.[33] Earlier, Paz had contrasted the Mexican view of reality, according to which "el mundo que nos rodea, existe por sí misma, tiene vida propia" (the world that surrounds us exists in itself and has a life of its own) with the American view, which holds that the world "ha sido inventada... por el hombre" (has been invented... by man).[34] In "La democracia imperial," he expands on the consequences of this view. For one thing, if society is the product of acts of human volition, then it must be possible to break with the past in order to create a wholly new society. This is precisely what happened in the United States: "La sociedad norteamericana se fundó por un acto de abolición del pasado. Sus ciudadanos, a la inversa de ingleses o japoneses, alemanes o chinos, mexicanos o portugueses, no son los hijos sino el comienzo de una tradición. No continúan un pasado: inauguran un tiempo nuevo" (North American society was founded through the abolition of the past. Its citizens, unlike the English or the Japanese, Germans or Chinese, Mexicans or Portuguese, are not the descendants of a tradition, but its beginning. They do not carry forward the past: they inaugurate a new era).[35] In short, the United States is a nation founded upon the rejection of the past. After explaining that each civilization is characterized by a peculiar stance with regard to time, Paz claims that the distinguishing feature of the United States is that it is "una sociedad orientada hacia el futuro" (a society that is oriented toward the future).[36]

The break with the past initiated by the United States was a break with Europe. In "La democracia imperial," Paz states that it was also a break with the burden of church and state: "los Estados Unidos fueron fundados para que sus ciudadanos viviesen entre ellos y consigo mismos, libres al fin del peso de la historia y de los fines metahistóricos que el Estado ha asignado a las sociedades del pasado" (the United States was created so that its citizens could live with each other and with themselves, free at last from the weight of history and the metahistorical goals that the state had assigned to societies of the past).[37] The turn away from the past is also a turn from the public to the private sphere. Paz views the United States as a society that is organized around the needs of the individual; he deplores the consequent weakening of the political sphere. He believes that the deepest questions about human life—"confiscados tradicionalmente por las Iglesias y los Estados" (traditionally confiscated by the church and the state) —have devolved in the United States upon each person's private life.[38] But he regards this process as both anti-political, since politics is what human beings in society do together, and anti-historical, since history is the realm of collective action. In the United States, "el bien común no consiste en una finalidad colectiva o metahistórica sino en la coexistencia armoniosa de los fines individuales" (the common good does not consist in a collective or metahistorical goal, but in the harmonious coexistence of individual goals).[39] For Paz, however, where there is no meta-history, there is no history.[40]

In Paz's account, Mexico is virtually the exact opposite of the United States. Whereas the foundational break of the United States with the past makes it an exception among the world's nations, Mexico's rootedness in history makes it a normal country. In "La mesa y el lecho," another essay from the 1970s, Paz claims that like most countries "México es el resultado de las circunstancias históricas más que de la voluntad de los ciudadanos" (Mexico is the product of historical circumstances rather than of the will of its citizens).[41] Whereas in the United States the past is constantly being erased, in Mexico each individual bears the nation's history within him or herself. In "México y Estados Unidos," Paz evokes the succession of cities that have arisen on Mexico's central plateau—Teotihuacán, Tula, Mexico-Tenochtitlan, Ciudad de México—and claims that each of these stages in the nation's past is part of a continuum that lives on in each individual Mexican: "Esta continuidad de dos milenios está presente en cada mexicano. No importa que esa presencia sea casi siempre inconsciente y que asuma las formas ingenuas de la leyenda y aun de la superstición. No es un conocimiento sino una *vivencia*" (This continuity of two millennia is present in every Mexican. It does not matter that this presence is almost always unconscious or that it takes on the naïve shapes of legend or even of superstition. It is not something known, but something *lived*).[42] In the same essay, he notes that the most radical—and therefore most authentic—faction in the Mexican Revolution, the *Zapatistas*, proposed not so much the construction of a new future as a return to the past, to the nation's origins. Emiliano Zapata and his followers fought for the reinstatement of forms of collective ownership of the land that can be traced back to the pre-Columbian era: "La imagen instintiva que los revolucionarios se hacían de la edad de oro se situaba en el pasado más remoto" (The revolutionaries instinctively created an image of the golden age as situated in the most remote past).[43] In short, Paz believes that in Mexico the past is still a living presence.

In his critical ethnography of contemporary Mexico—the focus of the opening chapters of *El laberinto*—Paz draws out qualities of harmony, wholeness, and integration that echo his description of the country's deep and palpable relation to its past. In almost every aspect of the Mexican's behavior, Paz detects a desire for contact and communion. The masses of modern society are mere agglomerations of isolated individuals. Mexicans, by contrast, retain an authentic sense of community, a sense expressed above all in the tradition of the *fiesta*. Paz describes the *fiesta* as a vehicle for social integration: "gracias a la Fiesta el mexicano se abre, participa, comulga con sus semejantes" (thanks to the *Fiesta*, the Mexican opens himself up, participates, and communes with his fellow human beings).[44] Whereas in modern society work has turned into an abstract and impersonal activity, in Mexico it still involves a personal, even amorous relationship with the products of one's labor. In *El laberinto*, Paz evokes "la lentitud y cuidado en la tarea, el amor por la obra y por cada uno de los detalles que la componen" (the deliberate and careful attention to the task at hand, the love of the object being made and of every detail of its composition), all qualities he observes in his fellow Mexicans.[45] Whereas the Puritan heritage of the United States has resulted in the disappearance of the human body from the nation's social and cultural life, in Mexico the body is still a vivid and tangible reality. Paz notes that for Mexican women, "el cuerpo, el suyo y el del hombre, es una realidad concreta y palpable. No una abstracción ni una función sino una potencia ambigua y magnética en la que se entrelazan inextricablemente placer y pena, fecundidad y muerte" (the body, her own and that of the man, is a concrete and palpable reality. Neither an abstraction nor a function, but rather an ambiguous and magnetic force in which pleasure and pain, fecundity and death, are inextricably linked).[46] This view of the body as something supremely real is also reflected in the mind-set of Mexican murderers. According to Paz, in Mexico a killer always kills "una persona . . . un semejante" (a person . . . a fellow human being), which is to say that he maintains a personal relationship with his victim. "La antigua relación entre víctima y victimario, que es lo único que humaniza al crimen" (The ancient relationship between victim and victimizer, which is the only thing that humanizes crime) has not yet been abolished in Mexico, Paz claims, contrary to what has happened in modern societies.[47] The nature of Mexican murder is reflected in Mexican society's broader outlook on death: "la muerte mexicana es corporal, exactamente lo contrario de la muerte norteamericana, que es abstracta y desencarnada" (Mexican death is corporeal, exactly the opposite of North American death, which is abstract and disembodied).[48]

Paz's depiction of Mexico as a country of contact and communion, presence and palpability, suggests that Mexican society must be viewed not as a machine—as is the case of the United States—but as a living organism.[49] And yet, when we examine Paz's reading of Mexican history, a reading that remained largely consistent over the course of his long career, it is remarkable to observe how much he emphasizes the ideas of disjunction and fragmentation. What predominates is not the notion of natural growth, as in his account of the history of the United States, but the sense that things are out of joint. Paz's meditations on Mexico's past are haunted by the feeling that "Desde el siglo XVIII hemos bailado fuera de compás" (Ever since the eighteenth century we have been dancing out of step).[50] Again and again, Paz argues that far from unfolding in a coherent and harmonious fashion, Mexican history is marked by a series of deep and traumatic ruptures. Perhaps the best example of this reading of Mexico's past in Paz's oeuvre is found in the opening pages of his monumental 1982 book on Sor Juana Inés de la Cruz, in which he introduces and then rejects the organicist metaphor for understanding Mexican history.

Paz notes that there are two principal interpretations of Mexican history. In one version, "México nace con el estado azteca o aun antes; pierde su independencia en el siglo XVI y la recobra en 1821. . . . Nueva España es un interregno, un paréntesis histórico, una zona vacía" (23; Mexico is born at the time of the Aztec state or even earlier; it loses its independence in the sixteenth century and recovers it in 1821. . . . New Spain is an interregnum, a historical parenthesis, an empty zone).[51] The second reading builds upon "una metáfora a un tiempo agrícola y biológica: las raíces de México están en el mundo prehispánico; los tres siglos de Nueva España, especialmente el XVII y el XVIII, son el período de gestación; la Independencia es la madurez de la nación, algo así como su mayoría de edad" (23; a metaphor that is both agricultural and biological: Mexico's roots are in the pre-Hispanic world; the three centuries of New Spain, especially the seventeenth and eighteenth centuries, are a period of gestation; Independence is when the nation reaches maturity, something like adulthood). In relation to these two interpretations of Mexican history, Paz's aim is twofold. First, he wishes to return the colonial period to its central place in Mexican history, a place it has been denied in the standard readings of the country's past. Second, his purpose is to refute the view that Mexican history is characterized by "una continuidad lineal" (25; a linear continuity).

The latter point is of particular interest to my argument. Opposing the interpretation of Mexican history as "una ininterrumpida evolución progresiva" (an uninterrupted progressive evolution), as suggested by the agricultural and biological imagery used by certain historians, Paz argues that "la historia de México es una historia a imagen y semejanza de su geografía: abrupta, anfractuosa. Cada período histórico es como una meseta encerrada entre altas montañas y separada de las otras por precipicios y despeñaderos" (24; the history of Mexico is abrupt and uneven, like its geography. Each historical period resembles a plateau surrounded by tall mountains and separated from the other periods by cliffs and chasms). Paz identifies two principal breaks in the flow of Mexican history: the Conquest and Independence. So profound were these ruptures that when we contemplate Mexico's past we see "no tanto una continuidad lineal como la existencia de tres sociedades distintas" (25; not so much a lineal continuity as the existence of three distinct societies). In order to evoke the relationship between these different societies, Paz resorts to the image not of a plant and its natural growth, but to that of Mexico's fractured topography.

If Mexican history seems broken and discontinuous in Paz's eyes, so does the country's intellectual culture. Paz repeatedly draws attention to the mismatch between ideas and reality in Mexico, and indeed throughout Latin America. In his account, the continent's elites have tended to behave ever since Independence as if they were Europeans or North Americans. They have assumed that their countries could be remade with the help of social, economic, and political blueprints borrowed from the world's advanced nations. But in Mexico the weight of tradition, habit, and culture has repeatedly frustrated these dreams. Building upon this insight, Paz reads Mexican history as the manifestation of an ongoing conflict between the modernizing projects of the nation's elites on the one hand, and the pre-existing structures of Mexican society on the other. The basic shape of this conflict emerges in an especially forceful way in Paz's account of Mexico's nineteenth century in the sixth chapter of *El laberinto*, "De la independencia a la revolución"

("From Independence to the Revolution"). Paz distinguishes three stages in this period: Independence, the Reform movement, and the *Porfiriato*. Each of these stages is characterized by a dual agenda: Mexico seeks to join the circle of modern nations, while at the same time wishing to shape for itself a cohesive, authentic sense of nationhood. The problem is that to some extent these two aims are at cross-purposes with each other. The ideas that inspire Mexico's elites do not correspond to the reality of the nation as it actually exists. The result is that the entire period leading from Independence to the Revolution of 1910 is marked by a sense of falsehood and inauthenticity. The official ideologies promulgated by the nation's leaders mask reality rather than revealing or disclosing it.

Paz has been criticized for viewing ideas as the engines of history.[52] And yet, in *El laberinto*, Paz portrays ideas as failed motors. In his reading of the first century of Mexico's existence as an independent nation, Paz repeatedly emphasizes the inability of ideas in Mexico, and more broadly throughout Spanish America, to change the world. The principal feature of Spanish American Independence for Paz is the disjunction between the rhetoric deployed by the movement's leaders and the interests they represented. "Aquel lenguaje era 'moderno,' eco de los revolucionarios franceses y, sobre todo, de las ideas de la independencia norteamericana" (Their language was "modern," echoing the French revolutionaries and, above all, the ideas of North American Independence), Paz claims. And yet, "los grupos que encabezaron el movimiento de independencia no constituían nuevas fuerzas sociales, sino la prolongación del sistema feudal" (132; the groups that headed the movement for Independence did not represent new social forces, but rather the prolongation of the feudal system). After Independence, Mexico's liberals, whose efforts culminated in the 1857 Reform Laws, made the mistake of thinking that it was enough to "decretar nuevas leyes para que la realidad se transforme" (136; pass new laws in order to transform reality). The problem, however, was that the nation's elites never obtained "la adhesión de todo el país a las nuevas formas políticas" (140; the entire nation's support for the new political structures). According to Paz, there was a glaring lack of correspondence between the nation-building projects initiated from above and the actually prevailing conditions in Mexico. During the *Porfiriato*, finally, the regime adopted positivism as its official ideology and promoted the progressive and enlightened ideals of science and progress, while in practice its key economic policies had the effect of reinforcing the nation's feudal character. In late nineteenth-century Europe, Paz sees a firm link between ideas and reality. The positivist philosophy of Auguste Comte in France and Herbert Spencer in England "expresa a la burguesía europea en un momento de su historia. Mas la expresa de una manera natural, orgánica" (143; expresses the European bourgeoisie at a specific moment of its history. But it expresses it in a natural and organic fashion). But this is not the case in Porfirio Díaz's Mexico. The regime's adoption of positivist ideas is profoundly incongruous: "Basada en la gran propiedad agrícola, el caciquismo y la ausencia de libertades democráticas, la dictadura de Díaz no podía hacer suyas esas ideas sin negarse a sí misma o sin desfigurarlas" (144; Based on large agricultural properties, the power of the local strongmen, and the absence of democratic freedoms, the Díaz dictatorship could not make those ideas its own without disfiguring them or negating itself).

The result of this persistent rift in the social body, a rift that contrasts, as we have seen, with the organic interconnectedness of class and ideology in Europe and the United States, is a profound and enduring state of discord: "Una discordia más profunda que la discordia política o la guerra civil, pues consistía en la superposición de formas jurídicas y culturales que no solamente no expresaban a nuestra realidad, sino que la asfixiaban e inmovilizaban" (145; A discord that was deeper than political discord or civil war, for it consisted in the imposition of juridical and cultural forms that not only failed to express our reality, but in fact asphyxiated and immobilized it). It is this history of discord that helps account for the other noteworthy aspect of the Mexican character: not the Mexican who entertains an authentic relationship with his or her body, who participates fully in communal rituals, who loves the products of his or her labor, but the Mexican as someone locked within artificial cultural forms, estranged from the surrounding world, indifferent to both life and death—in sum, the Mexican as a wearer of masks.

Paz attributes the differences between Mexico and the United States to the different transatlantic legacies that have shaped the two societies. England and Spain are both part of Western civilization, but they represent opposite poles within that civilization. For Paz, the fundamental difference between the two nations is of a religious nature: "en Inglaterra triunfó la Reforma mientras que España fue la campeona de la Contrarreforma" (in England the Reformation triumphed whereas Spain was the champion of the Counter-Reformation).[53] The opposition between Spain and England results in a corresponding contrast between their New World colonial offshoots.

In order to understand the complex and paradoxical account Paz gives of the historical trajectories of Mexico and the United States, and of the main features of culture and society in the two countries, it will be helpful to introduce the concept of modernity into our argument. It is this concept that explains certain assumptions Paz makes when discussing the historical development of Western civilization, as well as the sometimes contradictory stances he adopts when evaluating Mexican and US society. In what way, then, might the concept of modernity be relevant to the discussion? Recall, to begin with, that Paz sees the Anglo-Saxon branch of Western civilization as rooted in the Reformation. Consider, furthermore, that Paz believes that the Reformation paved the way for the modern world. In discussing what he calls "la radical diferencia entre las dos Américas" (the radical difference between the two Americas), Paz notes that the English-speaking part of the continent "es hija de la tradición que ha fundado al mundo moderno: la Reforma con sus consecuencias sociales y políticas, la democracia y el capitalismo" (is a child of the tradition that has created the modern world: the Reformation and its social and political offshoots, democracy and capitalism), whereas the Spanish- and Portuguese-speaking nations are products of "la monarquía universal católica y la Contrarreforma" (the universal Catholic monarchy and the Counter-Reformation), that is, historical currents that represent the resistance against modernity.

Richard Morse has spoken of Latin America's "shunning" of the "great modern 'revolutions'—commercial, scientific, political, and religious," and of its "recalcitrance" with regard to "industrial capitalism and political rationality."[54] Morse, whose work parallels that of Paz in its examination of the differences between the United States and Latin America, does not place this resistance to modernity in a negative light. Instead of interpreting Latin America's reluctance to modernize as a sign of "ineptitude," Morse suggests that it may "betoken an intransigent historical identity" with "durable ... psychic resources,"[55] as well as containing important "messages for the world."[56] Interestingly, given that he is a Latin American, whereas Morse is not, Paz's position on this issue is much more ambivalent. This ambivalence helps account for the peculiar configuration of his writings on Mexico and the United States.

Paz has consistently invested the rise of modernity with an aura of inevitability. This is the implication of the use of terms such as "natural" and "organic" to describe the historical development of certain countries. Such terms serve to establish the notion of a historical norm.[57] To interpret modernity as the inevitable outcome of the unfolding of history has obvious implications for the assessment of Mexico's place in the world. It is clear that Mexico cannot remain disconnected from the historical norm. And this is precisely what Paz repeatedly stated over the course of his career. Two examples will suffice to illustrate the point. In *El laberinto*, in the passage contrasting Mexican with American attitudes toward work, Paz states that it is only a matter of time before Mexicans become modern, too: "nada, excepto un cambio histórico cada vez más remoto e impensable, impedirá que el mexicano deje de ser un problema, un ser enigmático, y se convierta en una abstracción más" (nothing, except for a historical shift that appears increasingly remote and unthinkable, will prevent the Mexican from ceasing to be a problem, an enigmatic being, and becoming one more abstraction).[58] Approximately forty years later, in *Pequeña crónica de grandes días*, Paz spoke even more confidently, as well as less mournfully, of Mexico's inevitable modernization: "si México quiere ser, tendrá que ser moderno" (if Mexico wants to be, it will have to be modern).[59] On the question of becoming modern, Paz sees no choice for Mexico.

And yet, at the same time, throughout his career, Paz adopted the role of critic of modernity.[60] Consider, for example, his profoundly unappealing, almost dystopian portrait of the United States in the opening chapters of *El laberinto*. Paz's repudiation of the social, economic, and cultural consequences of modernity is also evident from a passage in *Posdata* describing conditions in Western Europe and the United States. In fervent tones, Paz denounces "la destrucción del equilibrio ecológico, la contaminación de los espíritus y los pulmones, las aglomeraciones y los miasmas en los suburbios infernales, los estragos psíquicos en la adolescencia, el abandono de los viejos, la erosión de la sensibilidad, la corrupción de la imaginación, el envilecimiento de Eros, la acumulación de los desperdicios, la explosión del odio" (the destruction of ecological balance, the contamination of both our souls and lungs, the agglomerations and miasmas in the infernal suburbs, the psychological ravages suffered by our adolescents, the abandonment of the elderly, the erosion of our sensibilities, the corruption of the imagination, the debasement of Eros, the accumulation of waste products, the explosion of hate).[61] By the late 1980s, Paz appeared to have made his peace with the economic system responsible for the economic devastation he had so eloquently described in *Posdata*, for he emerged at that time as a strong supporter of the free-market policies of President Carlos Salinas de Gortari. Yet Paz remained a reluctant convert to the capitalist creed, a skeptical proponent of his country's modernization. In *La otra voz* (1990; *The Other Voice*), he claimed that the workings of the free market resemble a "pesadilla circular" (a circular nightmare),[62] and asserted, moreover, that the economic system he himself was defending as Mexico's best hope for the future was a process "sin rostro, sin alma, sin dirección" (without a face, without a soul, and without a sense of direction).[63]

Insofar as Paz identifies the advance of modernity with the march of history, he makes this development appear natural. Yet insofar as Paz regards this same process as responsible for a stunning series of social, cultural, economic, and environmental disasters, he presents it as unnatural. The oscillation between these two positions ultimately accounts for his seemingly contradictory approach to the question of how Mexico and the United States relate to history.

CHAPTER 4

India

In 1951, Octavio Paz held a modest post as a diplomat in the Mexican embassy in Paris. Somewhat unexpectedly, he was notified of his transfer to India, where Mexico had recently opened a diplomatic mission. Paz arrived by boat in Bombay in November 1951, from where he traveled to New Delhi to take up his position in the Mexican legation.[1] His stay in India turned out to be short. In May 1952, Paz was notified of a new transfer, this time to Japan, a country with which Mexico had reestablished diplomatic relations—severed as a result of World War II—the previous month. Paz arrived in Tokyo in June of that year, but was to remain there for fewer than five months. Struggling financially, and confronted with persistent illness on the part of his wife, Elena Garro, Paz requested to be transferred again so that Garro could receive the medical treatment she needed, a request that was soon approved.[2] In October 1952, Paz, Garro, and their daughter left Japan for Switzerland, where Paz joined Mexico's delegation to the United Nations in Geneva.[3] Paz's brief sojourns as a diplomat in India and Japan in the early 1950s had a truncated feel to them. Nevertheless, they were the beginning of an intense dialogue with the cultures of Asia that would last until the end of his life.

As Roberto Cantú has pointed out, India was the "unequivocal cornerstone" of Paz's relationship to Asia.[4] Paz returned to India as Mexico's ambassador in New Delhi in 1962, and would remain there until late 1968, when the Mexican government's massacre of students in Tlatelolco square led Paz to resign his post and move first to Europe and later to the United States. Paz kept up an engagement with India over a period of several decades, culminating late in his life in the publication of *Vislumbres de la India* (1995; *In Light of India*), a book that begins as a narrative about the author's personal encounters with India but then switches to a characteristically Pazian discussion of the core features of Indian civilization, focusing, among other things, on the religious history of the subcontinent, on India's social structure, on its nation-building efforts in the twentieth century, and on the world-views of its people. Paz approaches these topics with an astonishing sweep and breadth of vision. He also tackles the question of India from the profoundly comparative perspective he commonly brings to bear on issues of culture and identity. Running through *Vislumbres* is an ongoing preoccupation with the impact of the West on India, and with the differences separating East from West. The latter question leads into a lengthy comparison between India and Mexico. A recurring theme in the book is that of otherness itself, that is, of how a civilization relates to other civilizations. Indeed, the stance a civilization adopts toward otherness becomes for Paz a key measure for assessing that civilization. In the discussion that follows of *Vislumbres*, I will focus on the topics just mentioned. First, I will look at the theme of how the West transformed India (and did not transform it at the same time). Next, I examine the comparison between East and West, and how this discussion evolves into a three-way comparison between India, the United States, as a paradigmatically Western nation, and Mexico, as a peripherally Western one. Finally, I discuss Paz's reflections in *Vislumbres* on identity and otherness. Paz had, of course, written a great deal about India before *Vislumbres*. An examination of Paz's approach to India in *Corriente alterna* will bring to light important continuities in Paz's views of India, but also a significant shift.

In *Vislumbres*, Paz shows a deep interest in tracing the impact of the West—especially Great Britain—on India. He shows how Western influences helped shape the careers of key figures in the story of India's emergence as an independent nation, such as Nehru and Gandhi, and how Western political and intellectual currents changed the course of Indian history. His assessment of the role of the West in India's development is often favorable. As one reviewer of the English translation of *Vislumbres* put it, "Mr. Paz is quite flattering about the British raj."[5] This does not mean that Paz sides with the British in India; on the contrary, a large part of his narrative is organized around the Indian struggle for independence, a struggle with which the Mexican poet whole-heartedly identifies. It also does not mean that he fails to pinpoint the lack of success of certain Western efforts to change India. Finally, the perhaps surprisingly sympathetic account of British imperialism does not imply that Paz hews to a simplistically pro-Western stance. On the contrary, he makes clear his distaste for certain Western values and regularly adopts the Indian perspective on the cultural conflicts he brings to light. Still, there is no doubt that one of the main arguments Paz puts forward in *Vislumbres* is the idea that India owes central aspects of its modern identity—such as the adherence to democratic values and the nation-building effort itself—to Western influences.[6]

Paz expresses great admiration for both Nehru and Gandhi. He also places the two men firmly within a Western cultural orbit. For Paz, Gandhi was not only "un hindú tradicional" (a traditional Hindu) but also "un occidental" (131; a Westerner). He notes the influence of Tolstoy on Gandhi's pacifism, of Kropotkin on his concept of social reform, and of Thoreau on his idea of passive resistance (131–32). He also draws attention—with a hint of ironic amusement—to Gandhi's repudiation of the technological advances of the West. "Veía en el ferrocarril y en el telégrafo inventos funestos" (He viewed trains and telegraphs as calamitous inventions), Paz observes, "pero los usaba" (133; but he used them all the same). Still, he adds, one should not judge a saint, only venerate him.[7] In Nehru's case, Western influences were, if anything, even more salient. "Nehru era un hombre de cultura occidental" (38; Nehru was a man of Western culture), Paz states, adding that the Indian statesman felt especially drawn to the rationalist and socialist currents within Western culture. For the Mexican poet, in a twist that he restates when he turns to a broader discussion of India's appropriation of Western ideas, Nehru's anti-imperialism was in fact a consequence of his Western education. "Su misma política anti-occidental" (His anti-Western political stance), Paz explains, "fue el producto de sus años de estudiante en Harrow y en Cambridge: allí aprendió a odiar no a los ingleses sino al imperialismo" (147; was a product of his years as a student at Harrow and Cambridge: that is where he learned to despise not the English, but imperialism). In short, there were ingredients in Western culture that taught Nehru how to fight against Western domination.[8]

Paz's account of how Gandhi and Nehru responded to Western influences expresses on the level of individual biography how the West and India interacted on a broader historical scale. Again and again, we read in *Vislumbres* that Western ideas paved the way for Indian nationhood. "El imperialismo" (Imperialism), claims the Mexican poet, "trajo consigo su propia negación" (88; brought with it its own negation). In other words, British imperialism contained the seeds of its own destruction. And what were these seeds? Paz identifies the ideas of democracy and nationalism as Western exports that helped set the stage for the fight for Indian independence. The idea of the nation, he insists, was "un concepto moderno importado por los ingleses" (63; a modern concept imported by the English). He repeats the same idea when he states later in *Vislumbres* that "la idea de fundar una nación llegó a la India por la vía inglesa" (91; the idea of founding a nation arrived in India via England). British ideas of democracy introduced notions of intellectual criticism and self-determination that helped inspire and energize the movement for Indian independence. All of the Western influences identified by Paz are part of a larger story about the arrival of modernity in India, for democracy and nationalism are essentially modern ideologies. The British brought modernity to India; modernity, in turn, created the conditions for the critique of British domination. As Paz puts it, "el imperialismo introdujo en la India a la modernidad y, con ella, la crítica de su dominación" (121; imperialism implanted modernity in India, and with it the criticism of its own domination). In sum, British imperialism was a self-undermining enterprise.[9]

One of the principal tools used by the British to spread their influence was the educational system. Paz devotes several pages of *Vislumbres* to the adoption in 1835 of the British system of education in

India. Paz mentions that the man who spearheaded this initiative—Lord Macaulay— based his decision on his disdain for the cultural traditions of the East—a disdain that was, Paz points out, rooted in Macaulay's ignorance of these traditions (122). But the author of *Vislumbres* also notes that important figures in the Indian community, including Rāmmohun Roy, widely known as the "father of modern India," had themselves supported the idea of implanting the British educational system in India's schools. The Mexican poet further argues that even though Macaulay's project of educational reform was the expression of an ethnocentric point of view, it brought immense benefits to the Indian population. One important consequence was the creation of what Paz calls "esa clase intelectual de indios anglicistas, primero en Bengala y después en los principales centros del subcontinente, como Bombay, Delhi y Madrás" (124; an intellectual class of anglicized Indians, first in Bengal and later in the principal cultural centers of the subcontinent, such as Bombay, Delhi, and Madras). This educated elite eventually played a key role in the fight for independence. Another important consequence of the introduction of the British educational system was to provide the subcontinent with a common language. Paz explains that the British Empire "unió bajo su dominio, por primera vez en la historia de la India, a todos los pueblos" (86; created unity, for the first time in the country's history, amongst all the peoples of India). The English language played a crucial role in the process of unification.[10]

The West helped transform India, but only partially, obviously enough. In his description of the voyage by ship that took him to India in late 1951, Paz mentions a group of mostly Polish nuns, en route to a convent in Madras. He reports that he felt moved listening to the mass sung by the nuns as they arrived in Bombay. But Paz also wonders whether the nuns realized "que su llegada a la India era un episodio tardío del gran fracaso del cristianismo en esas tierras" (10; that their arrival in India was a late episode in the story of the failure of Christianity in that part of the world). In brief, if there was one domain in which the West failed to change India, it was in that of religion. Paz mentions, of course, that the British colonial enterprise started as a commercial undertaking and that it never aimed at the conversion of the colonial subjects to Christianity. He also acknowledges that even though the British Empire did not have evangelization as one of its goals, it did introduce Christian beliefs into the subcontinent. Paz notes how certain nineteenth-century Hindu reformers tried to ward off the attacks on their religion on the part of Western missionaries by, in effect, making Hinduism more Christian. Swam Vivekananda's call in 1899 for all Hindus to embrace each other as brothers had, according to Paz, an unmistakable Christian flavor to it. "Su religión secreta fue el cristianismo" (His secret religion was Christianity), Paz claims in his discussion of the Hindu reformers, "sin saberlo ni quererlo habían hecho suyos sus valores" (126; without knowing it and without wanting it they had made its values their own). But even though a small Christian community emerged in India, and Christian values may have filtered into Indian culture, the country did not enter the orbit of Christianity. Indeed, Paz emphasizes repeatedly that India's complex non-Western religious identity—specifically the coexistence of Islam and Hinduism—is among the country's most distinctive features (44).

Another striking feature of Indian society—one that may well leave the observer perplexed, according to Paz—is the caste system. The discussion of this system in *Vislumbres* stands at the core of the book's exploration of the differences between India and the West. Paz explains that castes, like social classes, are "elementos de un todo jerárquico" (69; parts of a hierarchical totality). But whereas in the West social hierarchies are rooted in domination, either political or economic, in India the hierarchy created by the caste system is not based upon power or money, but upon religious notions of purity and impurity (69). One can be rich, yet belong to a lower caste. Conversely, a person of a higher caste can have very limited worldly resources. Alongside the religious function, castes play a crucial social role in providing their members with a sense of belonging. People are part of a specific caste because of their trade or profession, or because of the place where they were born. Clearly, in the West people identify with larger communities, too. But the social order instituted by the caste system is far more powerful, and more rigid, than Western forms of communal organization.

Paz's discussion of the caste system leads him to posit two broad contrasts between India and the West. First, he observes that in modern Western culture "el individuo es el elemento primordial" (68; the individual is the primordial element). In the West, even communities are fundamentally collections of individuals. In India, by contrast, "la realidad primordial es la colectiva" (the primordial reality is the collective). A caste is not "un conglomerado de individuos sino un círculo de familias" (71; a conglomerate of individuals but a circle of families). There is no escape from one's caste, except through renunciation of the world itself (71). The second broad contrast Paz sketches in this section of his book is between a static society and a society that embraces change. "En Occidente" (In the West), Paz states, "desde fines del siglo XVIII se ha sobrevalorado al cambio" (from the end of the eighteenth century on, change has been overvalued). In India, on the other hand, "se ha valorado a la inmutabilidad" (75; immutability has been valued). The value of a caste is precisely its unchanging nature. It provides comfort and shelter and to abandon one's caste is comparable, in Paz's striking comparison, to leaving the mother's womb (72). The two oppositions, between change and immutability, and between the individual and the collective, are of course interlinked, for individualism thrives in an environment where change is possible, whereas the collective tends toward immobility.

It is not conceivable that Paz would wish to defend the caste system, yet his discussion of this feature of Indian society leads into a critique not of India, but of the West. The poet's suggestion that Western societies *overrate* change, whereas India is said merely to *value* immutability, reveals the direction in which the argument will be taken. In the pages that follow, Paz launches into a vehement denunciation of Western modernity. He does not limit himself to expressing disagreement with certain features of Western society; instead, he describes himself as feeling "repelled" by these features, which, as we have seen, consist in the first place of individualism and the orientation toward change (77). Following Tocqueville, Paz establishes a distinction between egoism, which is an age-old element of human nature, and individualism, which is a modern phenomenon. Individualism, paradoxically, does not lead to a more fulfilled life for the individual. In a world in a constant process of change, the individual ends up divided both from his forebears, and from his fellow citizens. The isolated condition of the modern individual explains two of the signal defects of modern democratic societies: indifference and envy (76–77). What repels Paz, then, is both the solitude that characterizes life in the modern world, and the fact that a true sense of individuality is lost. "Las sociedades modernas" (Modern societies), he argues, "han convertido a los hombres ... en una masa homogénea; los modernos parecen todos salidos de una fábrica y no de una matriz" (77; have transformed people ... into a homogeneous mass; modern populations give the impression of having come out a factory, not a womb). But why attack modern individualism in a discussion of the caste system? Paz explains that he has no intention whatsoever of justifying the existence of castes in India; his goal is merely to attenuate "el hipócrita escándalo" (78; the hypocritical shock) that this institution causes among Western observers. In sum, an understanding of the caste system helps the poet cast light on the defects of modern Western societies.

Paz's position vis-à-vis India is shaped by the fact that as a Mexican author he is positioned on the West's periphery. Mexicanness is a constant topic of reflection in *Vislumbres*, allowing Paz to claim a certain privileged access to India. After all, if India is extraneous to the West, and Mexico is, too, then it makes sense to posit that there is a link between the two countries. In an essay from the mid-1960s, Paz had speculated about possible connections between the populations of Asia and the Americas.[11] In *Vislumbres* he does not bring up these ideas; instead, he discusses affinities between Mexico and India rooted in a shared historical condition, that is, the relationship to the West. Early in the book, as he recalls the November 1951 journey by train that took him from Bombay to Delhi, Paz speaks of how the encounter with India caused images of Mexico to burst forth in his mind. "Desde el principio" (From the start), he explains, "todo lo que veía provocaba en mí, sin que yo me lo propusiese, la aparición de imágenes olvidadas de México"

(20; and without wanting it, everything I saw brought forth forgotten images of Mexico). And what is the resemblance that sparks the connection between the two countries in Paz's mind? Interestingly, it is a common *lack* of resemblance that brings India and Mexico together. Paz puts it as follows: "La extrañeza de la India suscitaba en mi mente la otra extrañeza, la de mi propio país" (20; The strangeness of India reminded me of that other strangeness, the strangeness of my own country). The key word here is, of course, *strangeness*, which suggests a departure from a certain norm. Paz does not say so explicitly, but the reader understands that what Mexico and India have in common is their distance from a Western standard. Paz will come back to this idea later in *Vislumbres*, speaking now not of "strangeness," but of "difference." "El hecho de ser mexicano" (The fact of being a Mexican), he claims, "me ayudó a ver las diferencias de la India . . . desde mi diferencia de mexicano" (95; helped me see India's differences . . . from the perspective of my difference as a Mexican). Both Mexicans and Indians are in some sense outsiders; the condition of being on the outside brings the two countries together.

What exactly is the relationship of these two countries to the West? Let us note, to begin with, that Paz's discussion of India's and Mexico's links with the West is at the same time a discussion of the two nations' relationship to modernity. And since the United States is, for Paz, the paradigm of modernity, it is not surprising to see his commentary on India and Mexico evolve into a three-way comparison between these two countries and the US. In *Vislumbres*, the Mexican poet reiterates key ideas about the United States that he had already explored at length in his extensive writings about Mexico's northern neighbor. He argues once again that the United States is a nation that is oriented toward the future and that its founding in the eighteenth century represented a new beginning and a break with the past. According to Paz, "la piedra de fundación de los Estados Unidos no es el pasado sino, gran paradoja histórica, el futuro" (91; the foundation stone of the United States was not the past, but, paradoxically, the future). Unlike Europeans, who are "hijos de sus respectivas tradiciones" (the offspring of their respective traditions), Americans do not lean on the past. When the United States declares its independence, it is not so much a nation as "el proyecto de hacer una nación" (91; the project of making a nation). This project of building a nation free from the burden of the past, as a kind of emanation of the human will, is in essence the project of modernity.

Paz notes that the example of the United States had a significant influence on the struggle for independence and subsequent nation-building efforts in Latin America. The idea of political nationhood was introduced in India by the British, but its origins, according to Paz, must be sought in the experience of the United States (91). Mexico and India, however, faced challenges on the path to modernity that were utterly different from those confronted by the United States. Whereas the United States, as a nation without a past, started its existence as a kind of blank slate, India cannot avoid looking backward, where it encounters "un pasado milenario, rico en tradiciones y creaciones" (91; a millenarian past, rich in traditions and creations). In addition, India's past is immensely heterogeneous: "religiones, lenguas, tradiciones diversas y, a veces, enemigas entre ellas" (91; diverse religions, languages, and traditions that are at times each other's enemies). In seeking a path forward as an independent nation, India adopts a contradictory approach: it must both overcome its past, for the past is an obstacle on the road to modernity, and rescue the past, for it is in its history that the new nation finds its identity. According to Paz, Mexico finds itself in the same situation as India. The new nation's perspective on its past is critical and polemical. But in Mexico, as in India, the nation-building effort also entails a recovery of the past. Paz points out that "lo mismo en México que en la India siempre ha habido elocuentes e inteligentes defensores de la cultura tradicional no europea" (both in Mexico and India there have always been eloquent and intelligent defenders of traditional non-European culture), and he goes on to note that there is nothing surprising about this. In both countries, the past is immensely rich, and, more importantly, it has the quality of being "vivo todavía" (93; still alive). Paz does not offer a solution to the dilemma he outlines; in *Vislumbres*, his interest is primarily in drawing attention to the resemblances between Mexico and India in their struggles to become modern nations.

There are, of course, significant differences between Mexico and India as well as resemblances. What most separates the two countries is the fate of their native populations in the wake of Western colonization. Nothing could be more divergent than the histories of India and Mexico in this regard. As Paz puts it, "En México la civilización prehispánica fue destruida y lo que queda son supervivencias; en la India la antigua civilización es una realidad que abarca y permea toda la vida social" (93; Mexico's pre-Hispanic civilization was destroyed and what survives are the remnants of that civilization; in India, the ancient civilization is a reality that encompasses and permeates the entirety of the nation's social world). One consequence of this difference is that Mexico is part of the West, whereas India is not. The author of *Vislumbres* notes that "La Conquista y la Evangelización unieron a los distintos pueblos prehispánicos; hoy la inmensa mayoría de los mexicanos es católica y habla en español" (94; the Conquest and the evangelization of the New World unified the diverse pre-Hispanic peoples; nowadays, the vast majority of Mexicans are Catholic and speak Spanish). And yet, Mexico's integration into the West does not mean that its path toward modernity will necessarily be smoother than that of India. Indeed, for both nations, as we have already seen, the past is, at least in part, an obstacle to be overcome. The reason for this is that Spanish colonization in the Americas did not introduce the cultural and political elements that would have helped Mexico evolve more rapidly in the direction of modernity. According to Paz, "La cuestión a la que se enfrenta México es cómo dar el salto a la modernidad sin haber pasado por las experiencias culturales y políticas de los siglos XVIII y XIX, que cambiaron radicalmente a los europeos y a los norteamericanos" (94; The question Mexico faces is how to make the leap to modernity without having undergone the cultural and political experiences of the eighteenth and nineteenth centuries, which had a profoundly transformative impact on Europe and the United States). Several pages later he notes that the Spanish legacy in the New World did not include "los principios modernos" (the modern principles) which the British introduced in India (110). As a nation shaped by the Counter-Reformation, Mexico's inheritance is Western, but fundamentally anti-modern. Paz observes that the challenge for India in reconciling its immensely diverse and ancient traditions with the demands of the modern world is of a greater magnitude than the challenge faced by Mexico. However, the nature of the dilemma is essentially the same for both nations.

Why did the intrusion of the West have such drastically different consequences in the New World compared to India? In posing this question, Paz is led into some reflections on the nature of inter-civilizational contact, and on the question of otherness. The fundamental difference, according to the Mexican poet, between ancient Mexico and India is that the former had existed in a state of complete isolation until the arrival of the Spaniards in the early sixteenth century, whereas the history of India is marked by constant interaction with other civilizations. Here is how Paz puts it: "Las culturas mesoamericanas nacieron y crecieron en un aislamiento total hasta el siglo XVI; la India, en cambio, estuvo siempre en relación con los otros pueblos y culturas del Viejo Mundo, primero con Mesopotamía y, más tarde, con persas, griegos, kuchanes, romanos, chinos, afganos, mongoles" (106; Mesoamerican civilizations existed in complete isolation from the rest of the world until the sixteenth century; India, by contrast, always maintained contact with other Old World peoples and cultures, first with Mesopotamia and later with Persians, Greeks, the people of Quchan, Romans, Chinese, Afghans, Mongols). The lack of contact between the Mesoamerican world and other civilizations explains why that world suddenly collapsed in the face of an onslaught from the outside. "Las culturas mexicanas" (Mexican civilizations), he explains, "vivieron en una inmensa soledad histórica; jamás conocieron la experiencia cardinal y repetida de las sociedades del Viejo Mundo: la presencia del *otro*, la intrusión de civilizaciones extrañas" (107; lived in an immense historical solitude; they never underwent the cardinal and repeated experience of the societies of the Old World: the presence of the *other*, the intrusion of foreign civilizations).

He restates the problem further on in the same section of *Vislumbres*: "A Mesoamérica le faltó el contacto con gentes, ideas e instituciones extrañas" (107; Mesoamerica lacked contact with foreign peoples, ideas, and institutions). Not having the experience of interacting with different cultures left the Mesoamerican world "desarmado ante toda influencia de fuera" (115; defenseless in the face of external influences). This defenselessness was, in Paz's view, a psychological condition: "Los antiguos mexicanos vieron a los españoles como seres sobrenaturales llegados de otro mundo porque no tenían categorías mentales para identificarlos" (107; The ancient Mexicans viewed the Spanish as supernatural beings who had arrived from a different world, for they did not possess the mental categories that would have allowed them to identify them as who they really were). In short, the defeat of the indigenous civilizations of the Americas at the hands of the Spanish had to do with the lack of a certain type of cultural experience: the encounter with the other.

A reader familiar with Paz's writings would not have been surprised at the interpretation of the Conquest of America that he advances in his book on India, as he had explored similar ideas over the course of several decades. In a 1965 essay from his collection *Puertas al campo* (Doors to an open field), Paz notes that he had always marveled at "el carácter cerrado de la civilización mesoamericana, la ausencia de cambios de orientación, el movimiento circular de su evolución histórica" ("Dos apostillas," 147; the closed nature of Mesoamerican civilization, the absence of change in its orientation, the circular nature of its historical development). He does not deny that one can identify ruptures in the course of Mesoamerican history; however, he insists that these changes occurred within a narrow range and never altered the essential outlines of Mesoamerican civilization. He contrasts the isolation of the pre-Columbian world with the constant intercultural exchanges that took place in other parts of the globe: "Los pueblos americanos no conocieron nada que se pareciese a esa inyección de ideas, religiones y técnicas extrañas que fertilizan y cambian una civilización, tales como el budismo en China, la astrología babilonia en el

Mediterráneo, la filosofía y las letras chinas en Japón, el arte griego en la India" (147–48; The peoples of the Americas never experienced anything resembling the injection of foreign ideas, religions, and technological advances that fertilize and transform a civilization, as we see with Buddhism in China, Babylonian astrology in the Mediterranean, Chinese philosophy and literature in Japan, Greek art in India). Paz goes on to explain that "el Viejo Mundo fue una pluralidad de civilizaciones" (the Old World was made up of a plurality of civilizations), whereas in the Americas "crecieron plantas distintas pero semejantes de una raíz única" (148; different but similar plants grew up from a single root). He concludes, in words strikingly similar to the words he would use several decades later in his book on India, that this distinctive feature of Mesoamerican civilization was the explanation for its defeat at the hands of the Spanish: "Sucumbieron ante los europeos no sólo por su inferioridad técnica, resultado de su aislamiento, sino por su soledad histórica: no tuvieron nunca, hasta la llegada de los españoles, la experiencia del *otro*" (149; They succumbed to the Europeans not only as a result of their technological inferiority, which was a result of their isolated condition, but because of their historical solitude: they had never had, until the arrival of the Spanish, the experience of the *other*).

More than ten years later, in a text that served as prologue to the catalogue of a 1977 exhibition of Mexican art in Madrid, Paz repeated the same ideas about the isolation of the pre-Columbian world. Once again, Paz sketches a contrast between an Old World in which different cultures continuously interacted with each other and a New World that existed in a kind of civilizational solitude. "Por más aislados que hayan estado los centros de civilización en el Viejo Mundo" (However isolated the centers of civilization in the Old World may have been), says Paz, "siempre hubo relaciones y contactos entre los pueblos del Mediterráneo y los del Cercano Oriente y entre éstos y los de la India y el Extremo Oriente" (there always existed relations and contacts between the peoples of the Mediterranean and the Middle East, and of those of the Middle East with India and the Far East). He goes on to provide some examples of the contacts he is referring to: "Los persas y los griegos estuvieron en la India y el budismo indio penetró en China, Corea y Japón" (The Persians and the Greeks visited India and Indian Buddhism reached China, Korea, and Japan). Among pre-Columbian civilizations, there was nothing of the kind: "es claro ... que no conocieron nada equivalente a la transfusión de ideas, estilos, técnicas y religiones que vivificaron a las sociedades del Viejo Mundo" (it is clear that they never experienced anything resembling the transfusion of ideas, styles, technologies, and religions that vivified the societies of the Old World). Paz notes that there was some contact between Mesoamerican and Andean civilizations, but neither civilization owes anything significant to outside influences. In short, "Las dos civilizaciones americanas jamás conocieron algo que fue una experiencia repetida y constante de las sociedades del Viejo Mundo: la presencia del *otro*, la intrusión de civilizaciones y pueblos extraños" (The two American civilizations never lived through what was a repeated and constant experience of the societies of the Old World: the presence of the *other*, the intrusion of foreign peoples and civilizations).[12] Paz concludes his discussion by attributing the defeat of the Aztecs, Incas, and other pre-Columbian nations to this isolation: "La razón de su derrota no hay que buscarla tanto en su inferioridad técnica como en su soledad histórica" (We must seek the reason for their defeat not so much in their technological inferiority as in their historical solitude).[13] A world that had never been in contact with the other turned out to be deeply vulnerable once the other arrived on its shores.[14]

In *Vislumbres*, Paz repeatedly returns to the idea that cultural contact and cultural diversity are key features of Indian civilization. He begins by noting that "la peculiaridad más notable y la que marca a la India no es de índole económica o política sino religiosa: la coexistencia del islam y el hinduismo" (44; India's most striking trait is not economic or political, but religious in nature: the coexistence of Islam and Hinduism). In brief, the nation itself is defined by a profound internal difference. Later on, Paz will insist that "Uno de los temas recurrentes de la historia de la India es el choque de civilizaciones" (106; One of the recurring themes of the history of India is the clash of civilizations). He notes that

India absorbed influences from the outside and exported elements of its culture to other countries: "El pensamiento, las religiones y el arte de la India fueron adoptados por muchos pueblos asiáticos; a su vez, los indios absorbieron y transformaron ideas y creaciones de otras culturas" (106–7; The thought, religions, and art of India were adopted by many other Asian peoples; at the same time, India absorbed and transformed the ideas and creations of other cultures). Paz does not have a naïve view of the subject of cultural contact, for he acknowledges that what he calls the "incompatibilidad" (incompatibility) of Islam and Hinduism has left India with a profound wound (44). Overall, however, the interaction between different civilizations is assessed positively, as the comparison with pre-Columbian civilizations illustrates. Indeed, Paz maintained throughout his career that civilizations thrive when they enter into contact with foreign influences. In a 1973 essay titled "El uso y la contemplación," Paz links the problem of civilizational persistence with the rise of modern technology. Technology homogenizes the world and threatens history itself. Why does Paz think technology spells the end of history? Because history, he explains, cannot exist in the absence of cultural diversity. "La asombrosa variedad de las sociedades" (The astonishing diversity of societies), he argues, "produce la historia: encuentros y conjunciones de grupos y culturas diferentes y de técnicas e ideas extrañas" (18; generates history: encounters and conjunctions of different groups and cultures and of foreign technologies and ideas).[15] Once civilizations become uniform, and there is no longer an outside to contend with, they lose the capacity to change. "La experiencia del *otro*" (The experience of the *other*), says Paz, "es el secreto del cambio" (is the secret of change). And, he adds, "También el de la vida" (19; Also that of life). In light of these ideas, we are in a better position to understand the meaning of India for Paz. *Vislumbres* is a book about India, but it is also about the encounter with otherness. India stands for many things in Paz's mind; most centrally, it stands as a vibrant example of a civilization shaped by its contacts with other civilizations.

Paz had already written extensively about India in the 1960s, in works such as *Corriente alterna* and *Conjunciones y disyunciones*.

Since I will be discussing the latter work in the next chapter, I will focus here on the former, an examination of which will allow me to identify important continuities in Paz's vision of India, but also a significant shift in perspective that emerges in *Vislumbres*. As is often the case with Paz's collections of essays, *Corriente alterna* ranges across a variety of topics, including avant-garde art and literature, experiments with drugs, the rise of the Third World, and philosophical debates surrounding the death of God, to name only a few. If we were to identify one theme that binds the essays together, it would be the crisis of Western values. Paz describes this crisis in terms of what he calls "el fin del tiempo rectilíneo" (the end of rectilinear time), a phrase that appears repeatedly in the course of the book and points to what the Mexican poet regards as the bankruptcy of the Western ideology of progress, and its related ideals, such as the belief in the individual. *Corriente alterna* also includes sections addressing Eastern philosophy and religion. What is the function of these sections within the overall conception of the book? It is quite clear: Paz uses the East as a lens through which to bring his critique of the West into focus.

Let me briefly show how Paz introduces aspects of Eastern philosophy and religion in *Corriente alterna* to draw attention to the limitations of Western culture. To begin with, we may note how in an essay on Henri Michaux's account of his experiences with mescaline Paz observes a resemblance between the drug-induced alteration of consciousness undergone by Michaux and the overwhelming impact of India on Paz during his first sojourn there. What did consuming mescaline disclose to Michaux? Paz speaks of how the Belgian-French poet's eyes were opened to "la confusión cósmica . . . la revelación del caos" (88; cosmic confusion . . . the revelation of chaos). And how does Paz describe his initial reaction to India? Like Michaux under the influence of mescaline, Paz felt that he had come into contact with a primordial dimension of reality. "Caído en la gran boca jadeante" (Having fallen into the heaving mouth of Indian reality), he writes, "el universo me pareció una inmensa, múltiple fornicación" (88; the universe struck me as an immense and multiple fornication). He then explains the broader significance of the sensation he underwent in India when he first lived there in 1951 and 1952: "La visión del caos es una suerte de baño ritual, una regeneración por la inmersión en la fuente original, verdadero regreso a la 'vida anterior'" (88–89; The vision of chaos is a kind of ritual bath, a regeneration through immersion in the original source, a true return to "prior life"). And Paz makes it clear that the description of his experience in India possesses a normative dimension; it is not merely a neutral description of a different view of life. He begins by noting that "Primitivos, chinos taoístas, griegos arcaicos y otros pueblos no temen al contacto tremendo" (89; Primitives, Chinese Taoists, ancient Greeks, and other peoples do not fear contact with what is terrifying). The implication is clear: Westerners do fear that contact and this fear must be identified as the crippling weakness that it is. "La actitud occidental es enfermiza. Es moral" (The Western attitude is unhealthy. It is moralizing), says Paz. "Gran aisladora" (Great insulator), he continues, "gran separadora, la moral parte en dos al hombre" (89; great separator, morality splits human beings in two). Instead of the cleaving of humans into two, what is needed is an approach to life that restores unity and allows us to "reconciliar cuerpo, alma y mundo" (89; reconcile the body, the soul, and the world). In conclusion, the discussion of the alteration of consciousness brought about by mescaline in Michaux's account and the description of Paz's powerful response to the utterly different reality of India serve parallel purposes: to unmask the Western worldview, revealing its aridity and repressiveness.

In a later section of *Corriente alterna*, Paz develops a more extended comparison between India and the West. He draws attention to a fundamental difference in the very structure of thought in these two cultural zones. "El pensamiento de Occidente" (Western thought), he claims, "arranca de la idea de sustancia, cosa, elemento, ser; el de la India de la relación, la interpenetración, la interacción, el flujo" (139; is rooted in the idea of essence, object, element, being; India's thought evolves out of the idea of relationships, interpenetration, interaction, flux). This leads into a consideration of the status of change in each cultural context. Whereas in India change is negated, in the West it is affirmed. In the case of India, the argument runs as follows: if the real has no substance, then change is an illusion: "Si lo real es la negación, el cambio es irreal" (139; If the real is negation, then change is unreal). In the West, by contrast, "lo real es positivo y de ahí que el cambio no sea sinónimo de irrealidad" (139; the real has a positive existence and as a result change is not synonymous with unreality). The confidence that the real is real leads the West to affirm change: "es el ser al desplegarse o manifestarse" (139; it is being as it unfolds or manifests itself). The key is to understand that in India the real is understood as negation. In the West, Paz claims, it is unthinkable to think of nothingness, whereas in India it is impossible to think of being. The Mexican poet's complex meditation segues into a consideration of how this difference in conceiving reality shapes the way in which the two civilizations approach the question of liberation. He creates a counterpoint between the figure of the *sanyasi*, the Hindu religious ascetic who has renounced the world, on the one hand, and the artist and the revolutionary, on the other. The *sanyasi* does not oppose the world, but negates it. The artist defies the world, whereas the revolutionary seeks to destroy the world in order to create a better one. "La primera relación" (The former relationship), says Paz, referring to the *sanyasi*, "es religiosa y de indiferencia; la segunda es secular, activa y de oposición" (147; is religious and characterized by indifference; the latter is secular, active, and one of opposition). The different forms of seeking freedom from the world in India and the West are related to the different conceptions of reality existing in each civilization. Paz concludes his discussion by citing the mantra "cambiar el mundo y cambiar la vida" (to change the world and to change life), a formula which he claims sums up the wisdom of the modern West. If a *sanyasi* were to hear this phrase, says Paz, he would probably respond first with stupefaction and then with laughter. In pointing to such a response, the Mexican poet wishes to distance the reader from the Western point of view, to see it not as natural or universal, but as relative and partial, as the potential object, that is, of ridicule.

The counterculture of the 1960s offered a sweeping critique of the Western tradition, or at least the elements of that tradition that appeared dominant in the postwar era. It developed this critique by seeking out adversary elements within the Western tradition itself, for example in Romantic poetry. Paz himself often noted the affinity of the rebels of the 1960s with the poetry of Blake or Arthur Rimbaud. The counterculture also sought alternatives outside the West. The religious and cultural traditions of India offered a particularly rich terrain for exploration for people disenchanted with the modern West. The vagaries of ambassadorial appointments in the Mexican foreign service had brought Paz to India in 1962, where he remained until 1968, experiencing a formative period in his life. Paz's approach to India in these years was very much attuned to that of the counterculture. For Paz, too, India's multifaceted civilization offered a point of view from which to observe the deficiencies of the dominant Western models. In *Vislumbres*, similarly, India served as a lesson, modeling an alternative to what was already known, and providing a way of broadening one's mind. It offered, in Paz's terminology, the experience of the other. But in *Vislumbres*, as we have seen, there was an element that was absent in Paz's writings about India from the 1960s. He was now as interested in how the West—Great Britain in particular—had molded India, as he was in the teachings that India might offer the West. In this regard, *Vislumbres* brings to light a significant shift in Paz's outlook: he was far more pro-Western in the 1990s than he had been three decades earlier.

In the wake of the publication of Edward Said's path-breaking study on orientalism, a discussion emerged (although with some delay) of orientalism in the Hispanic world.[16] Given Paz's extensive writings on Asian cultures, it is not surprising that the Mexican poet's work often figured in this discussion. Since Said's study had focused on orientalist practices in two countries—Great Britain and France—the question was posed whether Hispanic orientalism suffered from the same biases and was part of the same imperialist enterprise as its counterparts in other parts of Europe, or whether it constituted, by contrast, a case apart. In one of the first responses to Said's work from the field of Hispanism, Julia A. Kushigian argues that Hispanic orientalism was indeed different from other European expressions of the phenomenon. Spain's proximity to and interaction with the Arab world had laid the foundation, in Kushigian's view, for "a spirit of respect for the Orient unparalleled by other Western European nations."[17] Hispanic orientalism, Kushigian insists, "comprises a generosity toward, and respect for, diversity."[18] She offers studies of the orientalist vein in works by Jorge Luis Borges, Severo Sarduy, and Paz to illustrate her point. Silvia Nagy-Zekmi puts forward a less sympathetic point of view, dismissing the argument that because Latin America was not a colonizing continent there could be no orientalism in Latin American culture. She draws attention to an internal colonialism in Latin America, involving criollo oppression of indigenous peoples, a form of colonialism that, according to Nagy-Zekmi, drew on orientalist stereotypes that had spread across Western culture.[19] Ignacio López-Calvo takes up a helpful middle position in this debate, reminding the reader that "prejudice and racism are still prevalent in many Orientalist aesthetic practices coming from Latin America,"[20] while also insisting that there are many instances where Latin American writers borrow elements from Asian cultures from "a position of respect and sometimes even veneration."[21] López-Calvo offers a salutary reminder of the need to be discerning in our approach to orientalism in the Spanish-speaking world: the simple truth is that not all Spanish or Latin American writers approach Asian cultures in the same way. Whereas some writers may be described as purveyors of stereotypes, others offer broad, open-minded, and enriching perspectives on the civilization of the other.

Paz wrote about the cultures of Asia, including that of India, with a passionate interest. His numerous writings about India are well informed, insightful, and eloquent. As we have seen, his focus shifted over the course of his career, moving from an overriding concern with what the East could teach the West to a preoccupation with what the West had contributed to the East. Paz's writings about India were certainly not immune to criticism, and frequent reservations have been put forward about his views of India. It is important to note, however, that Paz also has many admirers in India. In his writings about India, Paz repeatedly pondered the question of cultural contact itself. His lifelong interest in civilizations other than his own and in the interactions between civilizations tells us something important about how Paz saw himself. He was a profoundly Mexican author whose vocation was to be open to the world. And yet Paz's writings on India have been criticized and disqualified simply on the basis of the position from which he wrote. While it may indeed be the case that Paz was "a Westernised member of the Mexican elite," it is not at all clear that this fact about the author should in itself lead us to question "the suitability of his opinions . . . attempting to define downtrodden millions," or that it matters for an assessment of Paz's work that he had "little in common with the almost 90% of his country's population who lived in poverty in 1950."[22] Paz never viewed himself as a spokesperson for the downtrodden millions, whether of India or of Mexico. Indeed, his conception of the role of the intellectual did not involve the idea of being the "voice" for someone else. The suggestion that one has a right to speak only if one can credibly speak on behalf of others leads inevitably to the conclusion that one had better not speak at all. It is fortunate that Paz did not opt for this path.

CHAPTER 5
Psychoanalysis

In a 1975 interview with Claude Fell, Paz listed Marx, Nietzsche, and Freud as the three thinkers who had most influenced his intellectual outlook. One important feature that Marx, Nietzsche, and Freud have in common, and that surely appealed to Paz, is a certain methodological disposition, one that has come to be known as the hermeneutics of suspicion. In his conversation with Fell, the Mexican poet explains what this style of interpretation involves when he states that Freud taught him to practice criticism as a form of "autorrevelación de lo que escondemos" (self-revelation of that which we hide),[1] while Nietzsche showed him how to look for "lo que estaba detrás de las palabras como virtud, bondad, mal" (what was hidden behind words such as virtue, good, and evil).[2] In both cases, the interpreter of a certain set of phenomena seeks out what is concealed beneath the surface of things, indeed assumes that the truth of something is never obvious to the observer, but rather *needs to be unmasked*. Freud's concept of the unconscious and Nietzsche's idea of "genealogy" can both be seen as procedures for uncovering the hidden mechanisms or forces shaping individual or social phenomena. Although Paz does not explain the appeal Marx held for him as explicitly as he does the attraction he felt toward the other two thinkers, there is no doubt that the Marxist element in Paz entails the same type of interpretive maneuver as we observe in the Freudian and Nietzschean traces in his work. Consider, for example, Paz's reading of the Latin American Revolutions of Independence, and of the *Porfiriato*, with its focus on the relationship between social class and ideology, or what Marx would have called structure and superstructure. It is true that in Paz's case there is a twist to the analysis, a twist that complicates the Marxist model he is to some extent following. Whereas in Marx the ideology of a particular social class reflects the economic interests of that class, in Paz's reading of Mexico's nineteenth century the ideology of the ruling classes *does not match* their class background. In short, the leaders of the movement for independence expressed "modern" ideas, inspired by the French and American Revolutions, but in reality represented feudal economic interests,[3] whereas the ideologues of the Porfirio Díaz dictatorship celebrated the liberal ideals of science and progress, but in practice reinforced the social and economic power of the landholding classes.[4] In both cases, the ideologies of Mexico's ruling classes served not to disclose or express their economic interests, but to conceal them. Instead of revealing the relationship between social class and ideology, Paz reveals the *lack of relationship* between these two dimensions. But both the concepts Paz uses (social class and ideology) and the basic interpretive maneuver he applies to the historical data (excavating the truth that lies hidden behind the surface level of observable phenomena) owe much to the Marxist conception of the world.[5] Insofar as Paz practiced a hermeneutics of suspicion, he was a follower of the three eminent thinkers he mentioned in his interview with Fell.[6]

I would like to propose that for Paz the most important of the three thinkers mentioned was Freud. Compared to the other two, Nietzsche was far less of a presence in Paz's work. And even though there are probably more references in Paz's writings to Marx than to Freud, the Mexican poet's relationship with Marxist thought was highly critical and conflictive. For Paz, Marx frequently served as a guide-post, but he was also an important antagonist for much of his intellectual career. As we have just seen, he took from Marx a certain methodological approach. In addition, there are other Marxist echoes in Paz's work, such as the concern with alienation in modern society and an underlying utopianism. But for much of his career Paz was focused on refuting Marxist ideas. The critique of Marxism culminated in the 1980s in an attack on Marx as the inventor of an intrinsically dogmatic and authoritarian ideology.[7] Insofar as Paz came to regard Marxism as a manifestation of religious thinking, he concluded that it was a fundamentally anti-modern philosophy,[8] and he believed that as such it needed to be repudiated. Paz was often critical of Freud's ideas and, as we will see, his thought on certain topics occasionally took him in a completely different direction from that of the founder of psychoanalysis. However, there was never a rupture in his intellectual relationship with Freud of the kind that occurred with regard to Marx. In the intellectual autobiography he published toward the end of his life, Paz alludes to the importance of Freud's work in the intellectual milieu of 1930s Mexico City, in which he came of age.[9] Some of his most influential books, such as *El laberinto* and *Posdata*, are soaked in Freudian ideas. Furthermore, Paz continued to refer to Freud until the final phase of his career, as we see in his 1993 book on the topic of love, *La llama doble*.[10] It is clear that Freud—as well as other thinkers who followed in Freud's footsteps—exercised an important and enduring influence on Paz's writings.[11]

Paz resorted to Freudian ideas in a variety of contexts. Perhaps nowhere in the Mexican poet's work is the imprint of psychoanalysis as clear as in his books on national identity. Let us consider, to begin with, the case of *El laberinto*. In the book's first three chapters, the author describes certain key traits of the Mexican character. Paz organizes his account around the opposition between repression and liberation. The stage of repression is apparent in the Mexican's habit of wearing a mask, that is, of hiding his true self. The moment of liberation occurs during the typically Mexican tradition of the *fiesta*, which allows the members of the community to release their pent-up instinctual drives. The two stages in Paz's account are closely connected, for it is the act of repression (or masking) that eventually (and inevitably) provokes the explosion of the *fiesta*. It remains ambiguous, in Paz's account of the rhythms that define Mexican psychic and communal life, whether the *fiesta* ought to be seen as an authentic moment of liberation, or whether it represents a form of sublimation, that is, a deflection of the community's instinctual drives. It is clear, however, that the psychoanalytical concept of repression plays a key role in Paz's interpretation of the

Mexican character. Indeed, Paz later projects the notion of repression onto a historical plane when he depicts the Mexican Revolution as the inevitable explosion (or *fiesta*) that followed upon the repression (or masking) that characterized the *Porfiriato*.

In the book's fourth chapter, "Los hijos de la Malinche" ("The Sons of La Malinche"), Paz uncovers the historical roots of the contemporary Mexican's psychology. He goes back to the Conquest, framing it as a kind of family romance with strong Freudian elements. There are clear echoes in this chapter of Freud's writings on the Oedipus complex. Indeed, Paz's analysis of the origins of the Mexican character amounts to a re-writing of Freud's parricide/incest theme. Whereas in Freud's scheme the son feels erotically attracted toward his mother and spurns his father, in Paz's version, the Mexican, who takes the place of Freud's male child in his account of the Oedipus complex, reveres his father—whose symbol is Hernán Cortés—and rejects his mother—embodied in the figure of La Malinche, the indigenous woman who acted as Cortés's interpreter and eventually became his lover and the mother of their child. Here is how Paz puts it: "lo característico del mexicano reside, a mi juicio, en la violenta, sarcástica humillación de la Madre y en la no menos violenta afirmación del padre" (88; what characterizes the Mexican, in my opinion, is the violent, sarcastic humiliation of the Mother and the no less violent affirmation of the father). And yet, this passage only partly captures the nature of Paz's interpretation. It is important not to lose sight of the complexity of his reading, and how it shifts in the course of his discussion. Indeed, as we read on we realize that in the version of the Freudian family romance Paz puts forward in "Los hijos de la Malinche" the son not only affirms but also rejects the father-figure, and glorifies as well as humiliates the mother.

Paz explains that in the Mexican myth of origins the father is the macho, or what Paz calls "el Gran Chingón" (89), who neither protects his sons nor provides them with guidance and instead exercises power over them in a cruel and arbitrary fashion. His intention is not to care for and shield his sons, but to humiliate them. In Paz's view, one of the consequences of the father-figure's aggressive disposition is that the Mexican tends not to venerate

God the Father, who Paz describes as a "figura más bien borrosa" (a rather misty figure) in the Mexican imagination, but instead feels great devotion for "Cristo, el Dios hijo, el Dios joven" (91; Christ, the son of God, the youthful God), as well as other figures who represent the role of the victim, such as Cuauhtémoc, the last emperor of the Aztecs (92). There is a similar ambiguity in Paz's account of the role of the mother-figure in the Mexican family romance. We have already seen that the Mexican son spurns La Malinche. But La Malinche has a counterpart—the Virgin of Guadalupe—who offers protection and consolation. In Paz's words, she represents a "refugio a los desamparados" (refuge for the defenseless), "consuelo de los pobres" (consolation for the poor), "escudo de los débiles" (shield for the weak), and "amparo de los oprimidos" (93; shelter for the oppressed). In short, the Mexican projects onto the Virgin of Guadalupe all of his longings for love and for shelter from the harshness of life. And in order to fully understand the nature of the relationship between the son and the mother-figure in the Mexican imaginary, as Paz describes it, it is helpful to recall Roger Bartra's observation regarding "la profunda dimensión erótica y sexual de la Virgen en la cultura cristiana" (the profoundly erotic and sexual dimension of the Virgin in Christian culture).[12]

In sum, it appears that in Paz's account of the constitution of Mexican identity, both the mother-figure and the father-figure carry out dual and contrasting roles. The Mexican, in this account, suffers simultaneously from a conventional and a negative Oedipus complex, or what Freud calls a "complete Oedipus complex."[13] Such a notion entails recognizing, as Peter Rudnytsky puts it, that "sexual and aggressive impulses directed toward members of *both* sexes are inherent in the eternal triangle of the Oedipus complex."[14] This is exactly what we see in Paz's account of the family romance that stands at the origins of Mexican history: the male child feels erotically drawn to the mother, but also despises her, while the father inspires in him both hatred and devotion.[15]

Now, the reader of *El laberinto* may ask why the author resorts to a Freudian paradigm in his attempt to decipher the Mexican character.[16] Clearly, Paz's purpose is in the first place to describe, or rather to uncover, the hidden secret of Mexican identity. But the use of a psychoanalytical model adds a further dimension to Paz's reflections. The goal of psychoanalysis is not just to analyze but also to seek a cure. And that is exactly what Paz is pursuing in *El laberinto*: he wishes not simply to describe a condition, but to diagnose an illness, and to set the stage for healing. The therapeutic dimension of Paz's writings on Mexican identity cannot be overlooked in *El laberinto*; it is even more clearly present in *Posdata*, the 1970 essay in which Paz updated the ideas he had set out in the earlier book. Indeed, in *Posdata* he explicitly calls attention to the therapeutic goals of his work.

Posdata was a response to the tragic events that took place on October 2, 1968, in the Plaza de las Tres Culturas in Mexico City's Tlatelolco neighborhood. On that day, the Mexican government decided to crush the student movement that had emerged in Mexico in the course of the year, sending in military forces to massacre large numbers of people who had gathered as part of a peaceful demonstration in the center of the city.[17] In his essay, initially delivered as a lecture at the University of Texas at Austin, Paz sought to explain what had led the Mexican government to slaughter its own people.[18] In his search for answers, Paz takes the reader back to the distant past, specifically to Mexico's pre-Columbian era. This past is not immediately visible to present-day Mexicans; on the contrary, Paz describes it as a hidden dimension of reality that continues to exert a profound influence on the present. Speaking of the past as an entity that is "sumergido y reprimido" (109; submerged and repressed), "subterránea o invisible" (114; subterranean or invisible), and "enterrada e inconmovible" (152; buried and unshakeable), Paz evokes a concealed but powerful domain that can suddenly erupt in the present. And where does this idea of the relationship between past and present come from? At least part of Paz's inspiration comes from psychoanalysis. As he himself states: "El ejemplo del psicoanálisis me ahorra demorarme en una demostración fastidiosa: la persistencia de traumas y estructuras psíquicas infantiles en la vida adulta es el equivalente de la permanencia de ciertas estructuras históricas—o, más bien, *intrahistóricas*—en las sociedades" (64; The example of psychoanalysis spares me the need for a tedious demonstration: the persistence of childhood traumas and psychic structures in adult life is similar to the permanence of certain historical—or, better said, *intrahistorical*—structures in a society). In short, Mexico's pre-Columbian past occupies a place in the country's collective psyche that is analogous to the place of the unconscious in the individual psyche. Indeed, Paz repeatedly uses the word "inconsciente" (unconscious) to define the status of the past in Mexican society. This unconscious dimension of Mexican civilization suddenly and violently burst out into the open on October 2, 1968.

What are the principal elements of this subterranean history that appears to be controlling Mexico's fate? The first thing to note is that for Paz the Mexican past is tied to the Aztec empire. Other indigenous cultures are secondary in his account. In unveiling the secrets of the Aztec world, the Mexican poet zeroes in on the image of the pyramid, which he views as a symbolic representation of Aztec culture. What the pyramid evokes is, first of all, the idea of domination. According to Paz, the architectonic structure of the pyramid is an emblem of the hierarchical structure of Mexican society, from the Aztecs to postrevolutionary twentieth-century Mexico. The Aztecs had their tlatoanis; modern-day Mexicans have their all-powerful, albeit term-limited, presidents. The pyramid also evokes the Aztec practice of human sacrifice. As is well known, the pyramids were the stage upon which the Aztecs conducted their sacrifices, a key component of their religious rituals. In the Tlatelolco massacre, Paz sees a kind of modern-day revival of the ancient practice of human sacrifice, as well as a symptom of the hierarchical and oppressive nature of Mexican society. It is as if a latent content of the nation's civilizational unconscious had suddenly risen to the surface.

As I have already pointed out, Paz's interpretation of the Tlatelolco massacre has a therapeutic dimension as well as a descriptive one.[19] Paz argues that the past is still alive in modern-day Mexico. Referring to the Aztec period, he claims that "su fantasma nos habita" (its specter inhabits us).[20] His goal, then, is to expose this ghostly presence to the light of day. And in explaining the benefits that might derive from such an intellectual operation—that is, the act of bringing something hidden to light—Paz once again uses terminology drawn from the field of psychoanalysis. "Por eso creo" (That is why I believe), he writes, "que la crítica de México y de su historia—una crítica que se asemeja a la terapéutica de los psicoanalistas—debe iniciarse por un examen de lo que significó y significa todavía la visión azteca del mundo" (that criticism of Mexico and its history—criticism that resembles psychoanalytical therapy—must begin with an examination of what the Aztec vision of the world meant and still means).[21] Whereas in *El laberinto* Paz had focused on the impact of the Conquest on the Mexican imaginary, in *Posdata* he zeroes in on the country's Aztec heritage.[22] In both cases—though more explicitly in the later work—the Mexican author aims to lay bare certain collective myths that persist in the nation's unconscious and thereby to diminish their hold on contemporary Mexican society. This act of critical therapy via the method of historical criticism is designed to help forge a more open, a more rational, and therefore healthier community.

Paz's reading of the Tlatelolco massacre has been a frequent target of criticism. Indeed, it would not be an exaggeration to claim that in a career marked by controversy, *Posdata* provoked more controversy than any other work by Paz. The objections aimed at the book have focused largely on the link Paz establishes between the Tlatelolco massacre and Mexico's Aztec past. Paz's critics have dismissed the idea that responsibility for the events of 1968 might be traced back to the nation's pre-Columbian heritage. One might say that they have rejected Paz's psychoanalytic method, with its attempt to excavate a subconscious realm persisting under the surface of current events. The critics have demanded an interpretation focused not on the distant past but on the immediate context in which the massacre was perpetrated.

One of Paz's bluntest critics was Jorge Aguilar Mora.[23] In a widely-read polemic against Paz, Aguilar Mora offered an emphatic rebuttal of Paz's reading of the events of 1968: "Tlatelolco no es la encarnación de ningún mito, de ninguna figura de retórica histórica, no es ninguna actualización de ningún inconsciente mítico" (Tlatelolco is not the manifestation of a myth, nor of a historical rhetorical figure, it is not the actualization of a mythical unconscious).[24] For Aguilar Mora, the notion that there was an unconscious realm shaping the nation's historical development was simply a fiction concocted by Paz. Roger Bartra expressed a similar reservation, though he did so with a lighter touch than Aguilar Mora. In *La jaula de la melancolía*, (1987; *The Cage of Melancholy*) an overview of the tradition of Mexican writings on national identity, Bartra drew attention to the enduring influence in these writings of what he called "el mito del mexicano arcaico" (the myth of the archaic Mexican). In light of the power of this myth, it was not surprising that Paz, too, had resorted to the "arquetipo de la antigua barbarie azteca" (archetype of ancient Aztec barbarism) in explaining the Tlatelolco massacre.[25] According to Bartra, Paz had simply relied on a standard—and reductive—interpretation of Mexican culture. Xavier Rodríguez Ledesma developed a more extended rejoinder to the ideas Paz put forward in *Posdata*, arguing that Paz's reading was essentialist and deterministic, and that it absolved the Díaz Ordaz régime of responsibility for the events of October 2, 1968. According to Rodríguez Ledesma, Paz had argued that "el ser mexicano, sus actitudes y su sistema político, pueden explicarse por una esencia innata, expresión de nuestras más profundas y añejas raíces culturales" (the Mexican, his attitudes and his political system, can be explained by way of an innate essence that expresses our deepest and most ancient cultural roots). It was Rodríguez Ledesma's contention that the result of such a reading was that "el gobierno priísta de Díaz Ordaz queda exenta de culpa histórica ... ya que ... cualquier otro gobierno que hubiera ejercido el poder en el momento hubiera actuado de la misma forma, pues la encarnación del mito de la pirámide y de la piedra de los sacrificios apuntaba hacia allá inexorablemente" (The PRI government of Díaz Ordaz is absolved of historical guilt ... since ... any other government would have acted in the same way. The manifestation of the myth of the pyramid and of the sacrificial stone pointed inexorably in that direction).[26] Héctor Aguilar Camín expressed a similar dissatisfaction with Paz's explanatory model in a 2015 essay in which he looked back at his lengthy relationship (sometimes close, more often distant) with Paz: "Lo que nosotros queríamos, como deudos asumidos de la matanza de Tlatelolco, no era explorar la neurosis del gobierno, culpar el pasado azteca o explorar la vena sacrificial de nuestro origen. Queríamos una crónica de los hechos y unos responsables políticos" (What we were looking for, as we mourned the victims of the Tlatelolco massacre, was not an exploration of the government's neurosis, a blaming of our Aztec past, or an examination of the sacrificial streak we inherited from our origins. We were looking for a chronicle of the events and we wanted to know who bore political responsibility for what had happened).[27] In short, all of Paz's critics were posing the same question: why place the blame for the Tlatelolco massacre on the Aztecs? After all, the Aztec empire had collapsed many centuries ago.

It is striking to observe how uniform the complaints about *Posdata* have been. Domínguez Michael believes that Paz took note of the objections leveled at his interpretation of the Tlatelolco massacre and eventually abandoned the effort to read political events in a symbolical key.[28] Still, in a 1993 interview with Julio Scherer García, Paz both acknowledged that he had put forward an "interpretación arriesgada" (risky interpretation) of the events of 1968 *and* insisted that the interpretation was neither "insensata" (senseless) nor "carente de fundamentos" (baseless).[29] Evidently, Paz was eager to defend his approach, while also feeling somewhat uneasy about his psychoanalytical reading of the Tlatelolco massacre. Nevertheless, it is worth probing the discomfort this reading caused a little further. It should not, in my view, be accepted as the final word about *Posdata*. Paz's text was the object of many rebuttals that identified weaknesses in the text, yet the rebuttals had weaknesses of their own. An obvious problem with Paz's critics, as we will see, is that they tend to focus on a single aspect of *Posdata*, isolating it from the rest of the text.

Paz's critics claim that by blaming the Aztecs he absolves the Díaz Ordaz régime. But why should one argument exclude the other? It is perfectly possible to attribute the massacre to the persistence of certain archaic elements in Mexican culture *and* to point the finger at Díaz Ordaz and his henchmen for having ordered the massacre. Indeed, to focus only on Paz's discussion of the Aztec inheritance in present-day Mexico is to offer a very partial reading of *Posdata*. To get a better sense of the complexity of the text, and of Paz's intentions in writing it, it helps to turn to a letter Paz wrote on October 21, 1968 from New Delhi to his friend and translator Jean-Clarence Lambert, as he was mulling over his ideas for a book about the events of 1968 in Mexico. He notes that the book would develop its argument on three different levels:

> el social y político (la progresiva parálisis de la Revolución mexicana y la capacidad del sistema para adaptarse a las nuevas condiciones que él mismo ha creado en los últimos 10 años: una nueva clase media, un nuevo proletariado, y una nueva 'inteligencia'); es [*sic*] propiamente cultural (la separación entre el mundo oficial y la nueva literatura y arte de México); y finalmente el mítico (la presencia obsesiva del mundo azteca que para mí es la maldición de México).
>
> *the social and political level (the gradual paralysis of the Mexican Revolution and the capacity of the system to adapt to the new conditions it has created in the last ten years: a new middle class, a new proletariat, and a new "intelligentsia"); the properly cultural level (the breach between the official world and the new literature and art of Mexico); and finally the mythical level (the obsessive presence of the Aztec world, which for me is Mexico's curse).*[30]

Paz's outline of the work he was about to embark on makes it clear that the mythical interpretation does not take the place of a political reading; instead, the one exists *alongside* the other. There is no doubt that the section entitled "Crítica de la pirámide" ("Criticism of the Pyramid"), in which Paz develops his argument for the persistence of the Aztec past in contemporary Mexico, is the most eye-catching section of the book. But one should not overlook the fact that Paz spends many pages discussing the other topics he mentions in his letter to Lambert. These topics are an essential part of his search for an explanation for what happened in Mexico in 1968. It is simply inaccurate to suggest that Paz focused exclusively on Mexico's Aztec heritage in pinpointing responsibility for the Tlatelolco massacre.[31]

It is also wrong to claim that Paz interprets Mexican history in a single-mindedly deterministic fashion. His argument in *Posdata* clearly implies that the past shapes the present; it also suggests that the present constructs the past. In short, the relationship between past and present is not a one-way street; rather, it takes the form of a dialogue between the two poles. The active role of the present in giving shape to the past can be gleaned from Paz's discussion of Mexico's National Museum of Anthropology in the final pages of *Posdata*. An analysis of the lay-out of the museum shows that it was designed to exalt and glorify Aztec civilization at the expense of Mexico's other pre-Columbian civilizations. It depicts the Aztec empire as the culmination of everything that had gone before, an interpretation Paz explicitly rejects. The point, however, is that this is an interpretation that has been developed in present-day Mexico. Paz accuses his contemporaries of propagating a cult and of venerating a distorted image of the past. But this cult-like, worshipful behavior is the result of an active choice exercised in the present. Yes, there is an Aztec archetype underlying modern Mexican society, but it is an archetype that has been constructed within contemporary Mexican culture. "¿Por qué hemos buscado entre las ruinas prehispánicas el arquetipo de México?" (Why have we looked for Mexico's archetype among the pre-Hispanic ruins?), Paz wonders. "¿Y por qué ese arquetipo tiene que ser precisamente azteca y no maya o zapoteca o tarasco u otomí?" (And why should that archetype be Aztec rather than Maya or Zapotecan or Tarascan or Otomi?).[32] The point of these questions is, of course, to suggest that none of this was in any sense inevitable.

We have seen thus far that the psychoanalytical interpretation of the Tlatelolco massacre is neither meant to exclude other interpretations, nor intended to suggest that the sudden bursting forth of Mexico's subconscious past was determined in advance. Another important feature of Paz's reading of the Tlatelolco massacre that is often overlooked by his critics is that of the precise status of the subconscious in Paz's model. Paz's critics contend that the Mexican subconscious is a myth created by Paz, and they accuse him of being a mythifier. The problem with reading the world in mythical terms is that myths are taken to constitute timeless realities that block the possibility of bringing about change in the present. But Paz's concept of myth in *Posdata* does not at all imply such an impossibility. To get an idea of the status of myth in Paz's analysis of Mexican culture, as Paz himself sees it, it helps once again to turn to one of his letters, this time one that he wrote to Orfila. In this letter, Paz offers a response to the historian Gastón García Cantú, who had written a critical review of *Posdata*.[33] "Él cree" (He believes), Paz comments, "que yo postulo una interpretación mítica de México" (that I am postulating a mythical interpretation of Mexico). He goes on to explain that in actual fact his purpose had been the exact opposite: "No, para mí la 'crítica de la pirámide' es la crítica del mito y de sus fundamentos *inconscientes*" (On the contrary, for me to criticize the "pyramid" is to criticize a myth and its *unconscious* roots). In other words, Paz's goal was not to sustain a myth, but to critique it. In the letter to Orfila, he links his approach to the lessons he had learned from Marx and Freud:

> La crítica de la pirámide designa lo que Marx llamaba "la crítica del cielo," es decir, la ideología metafísica o mítica (generalmente religiosa) de una clase o de una sociedad. La crítica de la pirámide es, en términos de Marx, "la crítica de la conciencia *absurda* del mundo." Esa crítica (aquí interviene Freud) asume la forma de un *desciframiento* porque lo que llamaba Marx la "conciencia absurda del mundo" (religión, mito, etc.) generalmente no es consciente del todo y, además, se presenta siempre en forma de símbolos y no de conceptos.

> The criticism of the pyramid designates what Marx called "the criticism of heaven," that is, the metaphysical or mythical (and generally religious) ideology of a class or society. The criticism of the pyramid is, in Marx's terms, "the criticism of the absurd consciousness of the world." This criticism (here Freud comes in) takes the form of a deciphering because what Marx called the "absurd consciousness of the world" (religion, myth, etc.) is usually not fully conscious and, moreover, always presents itself in the form of symbols, not concepts.[34]

In short, the pyramid was not an unmovable structure within the Mexican mind; instead, it was a creation of that mind and a symptom of its false consciousness.[35] Paz's goal was not to entrap Mexicans in an oppressive myth, but to free them from it. He saw himself as a demythifier, not as a mythifier.[36]

The confusion surrounding the status of the unconscious in Paz's interpretation of Mexico is surely related to an ambiguity with regard to the nature of the unconscious itself. Steven Marcus has explained the complex location of psychoanalysis within the dominant intellectual trends of the modern world. On the one hand, one recognizes in Freud "an intellectual commitment and adherence to the idea of science,"[37] while on the other hand, the founder of psychoanalysis must be seen as "one of the last great legatees of the Romantic tradition in European thought."[38] In other words, Freud's scientific methodology was steeped in Enlightenment assumptions about the primacy of reason; however, his view of how the human mind worked amounted to a robust refutation of these same Enlightenment beliefs. Freud's emphasis on the primitive and archaic impulses that guide human behavior—that is, on its instinctual dimension—contradicts the Enlightenment conception of the individual as a fundamentally rational being. At the same time, psychoanalytic theory promotes a therapeutic practice that is geared toward the attainment of self-knowledge, and aims to cure individuals of their neuroses. From the point of view of its therapeutic aims, psychoanalysis inherits the Enlightenment belief in rationality and in human perfectibility. To use the concept of the unconscious, as Paz did, might signal an acknowledgment of the dark and uncontrollable dimension of the human mind. Or it might represent the first stage on the path to a more rational, enlightened existence.

Paz's writings on Mexican national identity echo the double orientation of psychoanalysis. On the one hand, the author of *El laberinto* and *Posdata* underscores the violent, instinctual qualities that are an inherent part of collective human psychology. On the other hand, he suggests that human beings have a capacity for criticism and self-analysis that allows them to overcome the harmful effects of their inner impulses. The simultaneous presence in Paz's text of these two perspectives explains why some of the Nobel Prize-winning author's critics accused him of promoting a mythical conception of Mexican identity, whereas Paz himself claimed that his intention in *Posdata* (and presumably in other works as well) had been precisely to *unmask* the cultural myths of his homeland by putting in practice "esa crítica de la ideología que Marx consideraba como la base de toda crítica" (that critique of ideology that Marx viewed as the basis of all criticism).[39] How could the readings of the same text have diverged so much? It was simply that Paz's critics focused on the first phase of Paz's discussion (the description of a cultural identity that might be equated with the construction of a myth), whereas Paz sought to draw attention to the second phase (the destruction of that myth through its analysis and critique).

Yvon Grenier has argued that a tension between liberalism and romanticism is one of the fundamental features of Paz's thought.[40] From the romantic tradition Paz inherits his exalted and sacralizing vision of the role of poetry in human life, his nostalgia for unified, organic communities, such as the ones he evokes in certain aspects of colonial society and of the *Zapatista* movement in *El laberinto*, and the critique of the excessive rationalism and materialism of the modern world. From the liberal tradition, Paz takes the belief in liberty, pluralism, and democracy. Of course, the romantics believed in freedom, too. Nevertheless, over time a deep tension emerged between the two currents of thought, at least in part owing to the fact that the individual freedoms promoted by liberal democratic societies were in practice often placed in the service of materialist and commercial interests that the romantics held in disdain. Paz was never able to reconcile the two intellectual inheritances that shaped him, and until the end of his life he continued to combine (sometimes awkwardly) a fervent defense of pluralism, freedom, and democracy with an equally impassioned excoriation of the Western societies where liberal values ruled, but where nihilism, a lack of spirituality, and a mindless consumerism were also prevalent.

My discussion of the role of psychoanalytic theory in Paz's essays on national identity confirms this double orientation of the Mexican poet's thought. The tension between romanticism and liberalism identified by Grenier as one of the defining features of Paz's intellectual profile echoes a key trait in Freud's work, namely the conflict between rationalism and irrationalism. In Freud's efforts to delve into the darkest corners of the human mind one sees a clear affinity with the romantic fascination with the imagination and dreams, with madness and creativity. At the same time, the therapeutic project advanced by psychoanalysis reflects the faith in science and progress that characterizes modern, liberal societies. In his appropriation of psychoanalytic theory, Paz shifted the emphasis from the individual to the community, for his interest was primarily in psychoanalyzing the Mexican nation. But in his relationship to the collective unconscious of his country, Paz manifests the same tensions we observe in Freud's thinking. On the one hand, Mexican national identity contains dark and irrational elements that can produce genuine horrors (as in the 1968 Tlatelolco massacre), as well as generate a unique creativity (as Paz suggests in his discussion of aspects of the Mexican character in *El laberinto*). On the other hand, and insofar as national identity is a kind of disease that has no place in an enlightened (liberal and democratic) society, psychoanalytic therapy (which in this case means critique, the intellectual's version of Freud's "talking cure") offers the path toward a cure.

In September and October 1968, as he was following the events in Mexico from faraway New Delhi, Paz found time to work on a book on a completely different topic. In a letter to Charles Tomlinson, dated September 25, 1968, he mentions several projects he has been working on. The list includes "un inmenso ensayo de cerca de 100 páginas sobre un tema que colinda con lo sublime y lo escatológico: la caca y el sexo" (a huge essay of close to one hundred pages on a theme that borders on the sublime and the scatological: poop and sex).[41] He would continue to work on this essay the following summer while living in the United States; it was published toward the end of 1969 in Mexico City by Joaquín Mortiz. The book in question was *Conjunciones y disyunciones*, surely one of Paz's most dazzling (and often dizzying) literary performances. Beginning as a review of Armando Jiménez's *Nueva picardía mexicana*,[42] the book soon launches into a broader meditation on the relationship between "la cara y el culo" (the face and the anus) in human life. From there we move on to an exercise in the comparative study of civilizations, with Paz contrasting attitudes to the dichotomy between what he calls *cuerpo* (body) and *no-cuerpo* (not body) in Eastern and Western cultures. His focus is initially on Tantrism, on the one hand, and Protestantism, on the other. Later in the discussion, he includes Daoism in his considerations. In the book's closing sections, Paz offers reflections on the sexual revolution in the West, about which he expresses skepticism, and more broadly on the meaning of 1968, which he celebrates. Like much of what Paz wrote, it is an extraordinarily erudite book. It is also a work steeped in the psychoanalytical culture of the period.

Conjunciones includes several references to Freud; however, the psychoanalytical thinker who presides over this work is Norman O. Brown, the author, most notably, of *Life against Death: The Psychoanalytical Meaning of History* (1959). Eli Zaretsky includes Brown, along with Herbert Marcuse and Wilhelm Reich, among the "utopian Freudians" who came to the fore in the 1960s.[43] With their rejection of the institution of the family, their celebration of "authenticity, expressive freedom, and play," and their critique of the "achievement ethic," these thinkers had a significant influence on the New Left.[44] Paz had read Brown with great interest a few years earlier. Indeed, in a letter to Orfila, written from Ithaca, New York, on May 3, 1966, he strongly recommended publishing a Spanish translation of Brown's best-known work: "No sé cuáles son sus proyectos editoriales. Me atrevo a proponerle algunos títulos. Se trata de libros que me han interesado en los últimos meses. En primer término *Life Against Death* de Norman O. Brown. . . . A mi juicio es una obra extraordinaria" (I don't know what your current publishing projects are. I will risk some recommendations. These are books that have interested me in recent months. In the first place, *Life against Death* by Norman O. Brown. . . . In my opinion, it is an extraordinary work).[45] It is clear from this comment that Brown had a profound impact on Paz. The work that most vividly registers this impact is *Conjunciones*, throughout which Paz engages with Brown's ideas.

What are Brown's key arguments, and how does Paz follow them, or depart from them? In *Life against Death*, Brown puts forward a theory of culture centered on the notion of sublimation. By sublimation, Brown means the "redirection" of sexual energy "toward new objects" (281).[46] Given the current organization of civilization, human beings cannot express their instinctual desires in an open and spontaneous fashion. They must repress their desires and seek what Brown calls "substitute-gratifications" (163). Human beings find these "substitute-gratifications" in the realm of culture, more specifically, through the creation of culture. Brown suggests that "if psychoanalysis is right, virtually the totality of what anthropologists call culture consists of sublimations" (135). This means that all of our higher mental activities, including our most elevated artistic and scientific pursuits, but also our more mundane endeavors, including work, are the result of a rechanneling of our sexual energies, a kind of aiming upward of our physical needs. A corollary of this view is that our highest achievements are a symptom of our alienation from ourselves, since they are, after all, substitute rather than genuine gratifications.

Brown argues that culture is the product of repression. Up to this point, he is in essence following Freud. But when he confronts the question of what to do about repression, he takes his argument in a completely different direction from that of the founder of psychoanalysis. Whereas Freud had concluded that repression was necessary for the survival of civilization,[47] Brown calls for the abolition of repression. To the extent that culture involves a redirection of our genuine needs and wants, which are rooted in the body, toward ostensibly higher endeavors, culture divorces us from our true nature. Brown sees this problem as becoming especially acute in the modern world with its exaltation of practical, utilitarian values. "Possessive mastery over nature and rigorously economic thinking," says Brown, "are partial impulses in the human being (the human body) which in modern civilization have become tyrant organizers of the whole of human life." The result is what he calls "abstraction from the reality of the whole body and substitution of the abstracted impulse for the whole reality" (236). According to Brown, it is imperative that human beings return to their bodies. If we could shed our "economical" style of thinking, the path would be open to establishing a relationship with the world that would be "erotic rather than anal (sadistic) in aim." Humans would seek "not mastery over but union with nature." Experience would be "based on the whole body and not just a part" (236). Recalling Freud's claims about the variegated and unrestrained nature of infantile sexuality, Brown argues that a liberated, unrepressed form of life "would be based on the polymorphous perverse body" (236). Elsewhere in *Life against Death*, Brown describes the life of "an unrepressed man" with the help of an explicitly Christian terminology: "In such a man would be fulfilled on earth the mystic hopes of Christianity, the resurrection of the body" (291). However, he departs from established Christian doctrine in envisioning a paradise not in the hereafter, but on earth.

Paz refers to Norman O. Brown on several occasions in *Conjunciones*, and does so in a consistently admiring manner. Indeed, at one point, he describes *Life against Death* as an "apasionante excursión" (30; enthralling excursion), which it surely is. However, whereas Paz hews closely to Brown's ideas about sexuality and culture, and about repression and sublimation, he differs from him in significant ways. As we have seen, Brown has been categorized as a "utopian Freudian." Paz is surely even more utopian than Brown. Like Brown (and Freud), Paz believes that culture is the product of sublimation. "No niego" (I do not deny), he states, "que el arte, como todo lo que hacemos, sea sublimación, cultura y, por tanto, homenaje a la muerte" (23; that art, like all that we undertake, is sublimation, culture and, therefore, an homage to death). Also like Brown, Paz believes that the key moment in our becoming-human was when the face separated from the genitals, that is, when we became erect creatures. Paz asserts that this separation "del sexo y el rostro" (of the genitals and the face) is not only what makes us human, it is also what condemns us "al trabajo, a la historia y a la construcción de sepulcros" (28; to labor, to history, and to the building of tombs). In short, to be human is both to flee from our authentic nature, and to create homages to the nature we have left behind. Paz further agrees with Brown's view that this syndrome, at bottom related to repression, is especially severe in the modern world. Toward the end of *Conjunciones* he describes—or more precisely, attacks—our world in the following terms: "el mundo moderno, el tiempo lineal, homólogo de las ideas de progreso e historia, siempre lanzado hacia el futuro; el tiempo del signo *no cuerpo*, empeñado en dominar a la naturaleza y domeñar a los instintos; el tiempo de la sublimación, la agresión, y la automutilación" (142; the modern world, the world of linear time, homologous with the ideas of progress and history, always launched toward the future; the time of the sign *not body*, convinced of the need to dominate nature and to control the instincts; the time of sublimation, aggression, and self-mutilation). In this passage, we recognize some of Paz's preferred ideas of the 1960s and 1970s, in particular the critique of progress and linear time. We also hear echoes of Brown's attack on a civilization built on the repression of the instincts. Unlike Brown, however, Paz does not believe that we have to wait for the abolition of repression to take place at some future point in time; on the contrary, he finds evidence of unrepressed life in the world around him, specifically in certain works of art and in certain religious and sexual practices.

As I stated earlier, much of *Conjunciones* focuses on the relationship between what Paz calls *cuerpo* and *no-cuerpo*. The conflict between the two is related to the clash between "el principio de realidad (represivo) y el principio de placer (explosivo)" (13; the [repressive] reality principle and the [explosive] pleasure principle). The inability to let pleasure reign, that is, the triumph of the reality principle over the pleasure principle, results in endless sublimation and the failure to live life fully and authentically. This problem is especially acute in Western culture, above all in its Protestant version, which is characterized, according to Paz, by its "horror . . . ante el cuerpo" (81; fear . . . of the body). Still, even within Western civilization, the division between *cuerpo* and *no-cuerpo* has at times been overcome. Paz acknowledges that art is a form of sublimation; however, he simultaneously insists that it is a different kind of sublimation, in which the body is not repressed: "el arte . . . es sublimación que quiere encarnar: regresar al cuerpo" (23–24; art . . . is a type of sublimation that seeks incarnation: the return to the body). As an example of this return to the body, Paz mentions Diego Velázquez's painting *Venus del espejo*, in which he observes a miraculous equilibrium between body and "not-body," the face and the sexual organs, the higher and the lower (19). He also provides a literary example of "la fusión de cara y sexo" (the melding of the face and the genitals) in *Libro de buen amor* by Juan Ruiz, Arcipreste de Hita, which Paz describes as "el libro del loco amor" (the book of mad love) in which "la escatología no es fúnebre ni el sexo es sangriento y dorado" (the eschatology is not funereal and sex is neither blood-soaked nor golden) and in which "no hay ni sublimación exagerada ni realismo exasperado" (36–37; there is neither exaggerated sublimation nor exasperated realism). In sum, for Paz, culture is not always and inevitably a symptom of our alienation from our bodies. In certain works of art, we encounter a celebratory and harmonious vision of the body.

The other realm in which Paz sees concrete instances of the reconciliation between the two poles of human existence, of the union, that is, between the body and what does not belong to the body, is in certain forms of Asian religious experience. In comparing the development of Christianity and Buddhism, Paz argues that whereas Christianity became increasingly detached from the body, Buddhism saw an evolution toward what he calls *corporeización* (embodiment) that is, an increasing value placed on the body and on bodily experience. In describing the cave sculptures at the Buddhist temple at Karli, Paz exclaims that "ninguna civilización ha creado imágenes tan plenas y cabales de lo que es el goce terrestre" (40; no civilization has created such full and complete images of the nature of earthly pleasure). The couples depicted in this monument are "ni dioses ni demonios sino seres como nosotros, aunque más fuertes y vivos. La salud que irradian sus cuerpos es natural: la solidez un poco pesada de las montañas y la gracia lenta de los ríos anchos. Seres naturales y civilizados: hay una inmensa cortesía en su poderosa sensualidad y su pasión es pacífica" (40; neither gods nor demons but creatures like us, although stronger and more alive. The state of health their bodies radiate is profoundly natural: the slightly heavy solidity of the mountains and the slow gracefulness of the wide rivers. Natural and civilized beings: there is an immense courtesy in their powerful sensuality and their passion is of a peaceful kind). What they represent for Paz is the union of nature and civilization, the two poles that, according to Freud, were necessarily and permanently in conflict with each other, and which, according to Norman O. Brown, might be reconciled with each other, but only at some unknown point in the future.

Paz finds what he calls "la más extrema expresión de la corporeización budista" (the most extreme expression of Buddhist corporealization) in Tantrism (61), and *Conjunciones* includes a lengthy discussion of the place of the body in this religious tradition, often in counterpoint with Protestant attitudes. Whereas Protestantism denies the body, Tantrism aims to reintegrate it into the totality of experience. "El tantrismo" (Tantrism), says Paz, "predica una experiencia total, carnal y espiritual" (65; advocates a total experience, bodily and spiritual). He goes on to provide an overview of some of the more extreme—and shocking—Tantric rituals, both alimentary and sexual, including the ingestion of excrement and copulation in public, and explains that the ultimate goal of such practices is "la conjunción de los signos *cuerpo y no-cuerpo*" (73; the conjunction of the signs of the *body* and the *not body*). In other words, it is a way of accepting rather than denying the body. Whereas Christianity regards physical love as essentially sinful, Tantrism offers a deeply sacramental approach to the realm of the erotic (80). It also makes possible a return to the more complete and fulfilling experience of sexuality both Freud and Brown associated with infancy. In discussing the Tantric practice of seminal retention, Paz notes that it implies "una erotización de todo el cuerpo, un regreso a los juegos y placeres infantiles que el psicoanálisis llama poliformes, pregenitales y perversos" (80; an eroticization of the entire body, a return to those childhood games and pleasures that psychoanalysis calls polymorphous, pregenital, and perverse). And he suggests, somewhat speculatively, that the Protestant equivalent of seminal retention is premature ejaculation, which results from the restriction of erotic experience to the genitals and leads to "frigidez en la mujer y placer frustrado en el hombre" (80; frigidity in the woman and frustrated pleasure in the man). In sum, Paz shares with Brown his extremely negative view of Protestant culture (which stands in for Western civilization as a whole), a negative view that focuses primarily on the repression of the body. But his years living in India had opened his eyes to other possibilities than those available in the West.[48] In this sense, Paz was, if not more utopian, at least more optimistic than Brown. As he surveyed the histories of the civilizations with which he came into contact, he discovered concrete examples of cultural practices that were not a symptom of our alienation from our bodies, but that suggested that culture and the body could exist in a state of dynamic equilibrium. His writings drew extensively on psychoanalytical concepts, but in the end Paz did not conform to the pessimism that was so prominent a feature of the psychoanalytical tradition.

In the preface to *La llama doble* (1993), Paz explains that the theme of love was a lifelong interest of his. His first poems, he says, were love poems, and since then the topic had appeared constantly in his poetry. He also traces a kind of prehistory of the book the reader holds in his hands. Paz mentions that in 1965, when he was living in India, inspired by the fact that he had recently fallen in love, he had proposed to write a book about the topic. But other obligations forced him to postpone his project. In the 1970s, he wrote an essay about the French utopian socialist Charles Fourier in which he developed some of his ideas about love,[49] but once again he was unable to move forward with the book he wanted to write. Finally, in late 1992, as he was going through his papers, he remembered his unfulfilled plan for a book about love. Unable to put the thought of the book aside, and overcoming his fear of being ridiculed for writing a book about love at his advanced age, Paz finally sat down and began to write. In just two months he produced a work of over two hundred pages. It was the product, he suggests, of an entire life devoted to thinking about the subject of love.[50] It was also a book in which Freud plays an important role, not surprisingly, given the long dialogue Paz had carried on with the founder of psychoanalysis. In *La llama doble* Paz draws on key Freudian concepts in his approach to the topics of sexuality, eroticism, and love. What is remarkable, however, is the distance he ends up establishing with respect to the psychoanalytical view of love.

Paz's concern is with the relationship among three different concepts: sexuality, eroticism, and love. He begins by capturing the interaction between the three dimensions with the help of a poetic image: "El fuego original y primordial, la sexualidad, levanta la llama roja del erotismo y ésta, a su vez, sostiene y alza otra llama, azul y trémula: la del amor" (7; The original and primordial fire, sexuality, lifts up the red flame of eroticism, which, in turn, sustains and raises up another flame, blue and glimmering: the flame of love). The image suggests a natural relationship among the three terms, as well as a movement from the lower to the higher levels. Still, the notions of "lower" and "higher" should not be taken to express a simple hierarchy, with the higher representing something superior to the lower, since the lower can stand for a primordial experience, while the higher represents a dimension that is derivative with respect to something else. This suggestion is picked up by Paz later on, in a sentence that also includes a Freudian resonance: "El erotismo y el amor" (Eroticism and love), he says, "son formas derivadas del instinto sexual: cristalizaciones, sublimaciones, perversiones y condensaciones que transforman a la sexualidad y la vuelven, muchas veces, incognoscible" (13; are forms that are derived from the sexual instinct: crystallizations, sublimations, perversions, and condensations that transform sexuality and turn it into something frequently unrecognizable). In introducing the psychoanalytical notion of sublimation, Paz appears to be putting aside the idea of continuity embodied in the image of the flame, introducing instead the idea that love and eroticism are deflections of sexuality, and that they may even work to repress it. Indeed, Paz himself makes the link with repression when he defines eroticism as "represión y . . . licencia, sublimación y perversión" (17; repression and . . . license, sublimation, and perversion).

However, as Paz develops his argument, he turns away from the psychoanalytical perspective. At one point, he offers a cogent summary of Freud's concept of erotic love. Although Paz does not explicitly reject Freud's point of view, it is clear that he does not share it. "Para Freud" (For Freud), Paz states, "las pasiones son juegos de reflejos; creemos amar a X, a su cuerpo y a su alma, pero en realidad amamos a la imagen de Y en X" (passions are mirroring games; we think we love X, her body and soul, but in actual fact we love the image of Y in X). He sums up the Freudian view as amounting to a "sexualismo fantasmal que convierte todo lo que toca en reflejo e imagen" (108; a phantasmic sexuality that turns everything it touches into a reflection and an image). Paz is here recalling Freud's contention that many of the features of the psychology of love in adult men are rooted in the need to repress—and at the same time to find an alternative outlet for—a mother-fixation inherited from infancy. Freud explains that in the realm of love "the ultimate object is never the original one but only a surrogate for it." The original object of what Freud calls "instinctual desire" is, after all, the mother, but this desire must be repressed. The result is the replacement of the original object "by an endless series of substitute-objects."[51] Men seek erotic love, but in reality their longing for their mother is never absent. Presumably, Paz is referring to this dynamic when he describes erotic attraction as having the quality of a mistake or a misidentification. Yet his own view, patiently explained in *La llama doble*, could hardly be further apart from the Freudian perspective.

The key elements in Paz's concept of love are the idea of the uniqueness of the beloved, the notion of choice, and the need for reciprocity. Throughout the book, he returns again and again to the claim that "el amor es una atracción hacia una persona única" (33; love is an attraction toward a unique person). This, in turn, is rooted in the Christian notion of the sanctity of each individual human being. Indeed, Paz himself (who was an atheist) draws attention to the Christian echoes in his argument about love: "Cada persona es única y por esto no es un abuso de lenguaje hablar de 'la santidad de la persona'. La expresión, por lo demás, es de origen cristiano. Sí, cada ser humano . . . encarna un misterio que no es exagerado llamar santo o sagrado" (95; Each person is unique and for that reason it is not an abuse of language to speak of "the sanctity of the person." This expression, incidentally, is of a Christian origin. Yes, each human being . . . is the incarnation of a mystery which it is not an exaggeration to describe as sacred). The idea that each person is unique constitutes the bedrock on which Paz's view of love is based; it takes him far away from the Freudian view of human beings as shaped by dark instinctual impulses. The next important concept in Paz's argument about love is that of choice. Although he does not deny the involuntary dimension in love, the idea, that is, that it originates in what he calls "un magnetismo secreto y todopoderoso" (34; a secret and all-powerful magnetism), Paz repeatedly emphasizes that "el amor es elección" (33; love is a choice). The idea of choice refers back to the concept of the unique individual at the heart of the experience of love, and is linked to the requirement that love should be exclusive, that is, offered to one person only. Finally, we note the importance of reciprocity: given the uniqueness, and even sanctity, of the individual, love cannot be genuine if it is forced upon the other. "La exclusividad" (Exclusiveness), says Paz, "requiere la reciprocidad, el acuerdo del otro, su voluntad" (117; requires reciprocity, the consent of the other, her willingness). By this point, the phantasmic quality of love described by Freud has been entirely dispelled, and Paz has decisively turned his back on the psychoanalytical tradition that had nourished him since the start of his literary career.

CHAPTER 6
Feminism

Octavio Paz regularly voiced his support for feminism. Indeed, his statements on the topic often went well beyond the expression of support or sympathy for the feminist cause, for Paz believed that the vast rebellion against women's subordination that occurred throughout the Western world in the second half of the twentieth century was the most important historical transformation to take place in his lifetime. Consider some of the statements Paz made about feminism over a period of many years. In *Corriente alterna*, he linked the women's liberation movement to the youth rebellion of the 1960s and declared that these two movements were perhaps "las dos grandes transformaciones de nuestra época" (175; the two great transformations of our era). A little over a decade later, in *El ogro filantrópico*, Paz explained why the feminist movement was so profoundly significant: "El movimiento de las mujeres expresa algo más profundo que una ideología—y de más alcance: quiere un cambio pero no tanto de los sistemas como de las relaciones humanas cualesquiera que sean los sistemas" (289; The women's movement is the expression of something deeper—and more far-reaching—than an ideology: it seeks a change not so much of the system, but in human relations, whatever the system may be). By the time of *Tiempo nublado*, Paz had come to the conclusion that the upheavals rocking the world starting in the 1960s had run their course. But he made an exception for the women's liberation movement: "este movimiento comenzó mucho antes y se prolongará todavía varias décadas. Es un proceso que pertenece al dominio de la 'cuenta larga.' Aunque su ímpetu ha decaído en los últimos años, se trata de un fenómeno que está destinado a perdurar y cambiar la historia" (15–16; this movement began much earlier and will persist for several more decades. It is a process that belongs to the *longue durée*. Although its impetus has declined in recent years, it is a phenomenon that is destined to last and to change history). Finally, in *Itinerario*, Paz notes that "el feminismo cambió muchas de nuestras actitudes tradicionales" (155; feminism changed many of our traditional attitudes). It is obvious that Paz is *celebrating* feminism for having brought about these changes. He views them as necessary and positive changes. Why, then, have feminist critics attacked Paz in so relentless a fashion? What has led them to portray someone who explicitly declared his support for feminism as a misogynist and a sexist?[1]

In Paz's voluminous writings, we can identify several works in which the social position of women is a central concern. The first work I will look at is *El laberinto*, a discussion of Mexican culture, history, and identity that includes a consideration of gender relations in contemporary Mexican society, an analysis of the place of La Malinche, the indigenous woman who acted as Hernán Cortés's interpreter during the Conquest of Mexico, in Mexico's national imaginary, and a meditation on the role of erotic love in human life. In each of these sections, feminist critics have found ammunition with which to attack Paz.[2] However, the most controversial parts of the book are those that depict the position of women in Mexican culture and society in the middle of the twentieth century. Feminist critics regard Paz's observations on this topic as deeply offensive. And Paz does indeed reproduce deeply offensive ideas about women in his discussion. But his feminist critics have made a very basic mistake in approaching Paz's ideas on the topic of women in Mexican society. Paz, as I will explain in more detail shortly, does not hold these offensive views about women himself. It is clear from his discussion that he is reporting on what others think. He is attributing misogynist views to the dominant Mexican culture, while distancing himself from these views. Articulating a viewpoint is not the same thing as endorsing it—a distinction Paz's feminist critics have failed to make.

Let us begin by reviewing the statements by Paz that caused offense, after which I will explain how the reader can know that Paz is *not* putting these statements forward as his own views on the topic. Here we have the author summarizing a stereotypical view of woman's role in society: "Prostituta, diosa, gran señora, amante, la mujer transmite o conserva, pero no crea, los valores y energías que le confían la naturaleza o la sociedad" (*El laberinto*, 39; As prostitute, goddess, great lady, or mistress, women transmit or preserve, but do not create, the values and the energy with which nature and society have entrusted them). From this perspective, women occupy a decidedly secondary position in the world: "En un mundo hecho a la imagen de los hombres, la mujer es sólo un reflejo de la voluntad y querer masculinos" (39; In a world made in man's image, women are merely reflections of masculine will and desire). Femininity, Paz concludes, "nunca es un fin en sí mismo, como es la hombría" (39; is never an end in itself, as is masculinity). Women, he says, "no tienen deseos propios" (40; do not have desires of their own). Perhaps even more shocking, to Paz's critics, is the fact that he appears to attribute women's weak and dependent role in society to their anatomy. In the context of a discussion of the ideal of masculinity in Mexican society (32), an ideal that requires that men adopt a closed and defensive posture in relation to their surroundings, Paz notes that Mexican women act as a negative counterpoint to this model of manliness: "Las mujeres son seres inferiores porque, al entregarse, se abren. Su herida es constitucional y radica en su sexo, en su 'rajada', herida que jamás cicatriza" (33; Women are inferior beings because when they surrender themselves, they open themselves up. Their wound is part of their constitution and dwells in their sex, in their "cut," which is like a wound that never heals). Is Paz truly suggesting that women are inferior beings and that their inferiority is the result of a feature of their anatomy? This is indeed the conclusion at which his feminist critics have arrived.

In actual fact, Paz is not voicing his own viewpoint in these passages. What he is attempting, instead, is to reconstruct the dominant perspective of his culture, while calling attention to the limitations of this perspective. His concern, in short, is not with defining womanhood, but with exposing the definition of womanhood that prevails in Mexican culture. So how does Paz indicate his distance from the views he reproduces in his text? He does this in several ways, most obviously by explicitly stating that the views he is describing are false. Consider, for example, the comment that follows upon a lengthy discussion of the Mexican woman's ostensibly passive nature: "Esta concepción" (This notion), Paz writes, referring to the notion that Mexican women are virtually dormant beings without desires or a will of their own, "[es] bastante falsa si se piensa que la mexicana es muy sensible e inquieta" (41; is very untrue when one recalls that Mexican women are very sensitive and restless). Or note Paz's response to his observation that women in Mexico are treated as instruments in the service of a particular goal: far from applauding such treatment he instead draws attention to the fact that the goals women are expected to serve have *not* been established by women themselves: "Fines, hay que decirlo, sobre los que nunca se le ha pedido su consentimiento" (39; Goals, it has to be said, for which her consent has never been requested). And take, as a final example, Paz's thoughts on the "respect" with which women are treated in Mexican society: "Quizás muchas preferirían ser tratadas con menos 'respeto' (que, por lo demás, se les concede solamente en público) y con más libertad y autenticidad. Esto es, como seres humanos y no como símbolos y funciones" (41–42; Perhaps many women would prefer to be treated with less "respect" [which, by the way, they only receive in public] and with greater freedom and authenticity. That is, as human beings and not as symbols or functions). In short, Paz clearly states that women are *not* treated as full human beings in Mexican society of his time, and notes that they are treated as "symbols" or "functions" instead. Nowhere in his writings does Paz indicate that *not* treating a class of people as full human beings is something he condones. On the contrary, the tendency to adopt an instrumental approach to the world (including other people) is for Paz one of the banes of modern existence.

Paz's explicit criticism of the way women are viewed and treated in Mexico shows that in *El laberinto* his goal is not to define womanhood but to analyze its cultural construction. His concern is with the creation of social myths and with denouncing these myths. One way in which Paz communicates his position to the reader is by consistently placing key concepts in his discussion in quotation marks. This makes it clear that Paz wants the reader to adopt a detached and critical perspective in relation to these concepts. They reveal not reality itself, but a certain construction of reality. The quotation marks indicate that Paz is "quoting" from the cultural text, rather than treating that text as a transparent window onto the real world. He is letting the reader know that this is the way people use the words he is quoting; it is not necessarily the way *he* would use them. Paz applies this technique to words such as "hombría" (32; masculinity), "rajarse" (33; open oneself up) and "rajada" (33; cut), "macho" (34), "decente" (39; decent), "sufrida" (39; long-suffering), and "mala mujer" (42; bad woman). Each time, the quotation marks amount to an invitation to the reader to question the way in which these concepts are used in Mexican culture.

Paz is analyzing an image of the feminine, not presenting a set of facts about it. To speak of an image, rather than of reality, is a way of relativizing the views we hold of the world. It is to make it clear that the image being discussed is just one among many possible perspectives one can adopt. Paz reinforces this message in his discussion of gender in *El laberinto* by repeatedly comparing Mexican perspectives on the feminine with the views found in other countries. Specifically, he contrasts Mexican images of femininity with the conceptions that prevail in Spain and the United States. By revealing that there are different points of view in different cultures, Paz undermines the tendency to see one's own viewpoint as absolute. The existence of alternatives suggests that each perspective is limited and relative.

However, Paz does not suggest that the Mexican point of view on femininity is simply one among many possibilities, and therefore somehow equally valid as any other position one might adopt. On the contrary, he makes it clear that he believes that the Mexican perspective is harmful. He does this by repeatedly evoking that which is missing from the Mexican perspective on womanhood. Paz notes that Mexican society stipulates how women should behave in certain situations. In conforming to pre-existent models of behavior, women lose the dimension of themselves that is "instintiva [y] personal" (39; instinctive [and] personal). There can be little doubt that Paz is troubled by how society deprives women of their deepest experiences. A few pages later, Paz once again observes how the Mexican conception of proper feminine behavior prevents women from finding their own inner truth: "Ser ella misma, dueña de su deseo, su pasión o su capricho, es ser infiel a sí misma" (40; To be herself, in command of her own desires, her passion or her whims, is to be unfaithful to herself). Paz, of course, wants the reader to grasp the irony: for a woman to be true to herself is, according to the dominant social norms of the era, to betray herself. For Paz, Mexican women are forced to live in an upside down world.

The clearest indication that Paz does not endorse the views about women which he discusses in *El laberinto* is provided by the overall context in which he presents the Mexican perspective on femininity. It is important to recall that the discussion of gender relations in Mexico appears in the second chapter of *El laberinto*, in which Paz reflects on what he refers to as the Mexican habit of wearing a mask, of concealing oneself. Paz explores different aspects of this "masking" behavior: among other things, he mentions the stoic comportment of Mexico's heroes, most notably Benito Juárez, and the people's love of what Paz calls "la Forma" (Form), revealed in the preference for order in the political realm and courtesy in personal interactions. The depiction of relations between men and women, with men expected to adopt a "closed" and "aggressive" stance toward others, and women depicted as "open" and "vulnerable," is part of this larger consideration of the role of masking in Mexican culture. Now, it is obvious that Paz is *not* an advocate of what he describes as the Mexican habit of wearing a mask. Nor is he offering a neutral description of a particular behavioral pattern. If anything, Paz appears to regard this type of behavior as symptomatic of a profound state of alienation. Throughout *El laberinto*, the author speaks of actions that are "instinctual," "spontaneous," and "free"—these are clearly the human qualities he applauds. It is equally clear that these qualities stand at the opposite pole from the type of behavior covered under the metaphor of "masking." To return now to the question of gender: if one understands that Paz is criticizing the Mexican habit of closing oneself off from the outside world, it should be clear that he is *also* criticizing the role assigned to women in Mexican society. After all, this role is an integral part of the larger problem of the mask. Paz's criticism of masking in Mexican social life feeds directly into a criticism of the victimization of Mexican women, for this victimization is an outcome of the preeminence of "masked," "closed," or "macho" behavior. To put it differently: if one believes that Paz endorses the definition of femininity he describes, then one must also believe that he endorses the definition of masculinity he presents in *El laberinto*. In short, one must take him to be defending "machismo." And yet this would be a completely implausible reading of Paz's account of gender relations in *El laberinto*. There is no evidence whatsoever in the text that he regards the aggressive, domineering, and self-protective behavior of the typical "macho" as something that men ought to aspire to.

Let us move on now to a different section of *El laberinto*, one that has also been read as indicative of Paz's objectionable views on gender relations: the discussion of La Malinche at the end of the book's fourth chapter, "Los hijos de la Malinche." In the opening chapters, Paz develops what we might call an ethnography of the Mexico in which he grew up. He describes characteristic customs and depicts the Mexican outlook on life. As we have seen, Paz pays extensive attention to what he views as the Mexican habit of concealing, or masking, one's inner being. He discusses the Mexican tradition of the *fiesta*, which he sees as providing Mexicans with an outlet for the emotions they repress in their day-to-day lives, and he considers the attitudes Mexicans adopt in relation to death. But Paz's aim is not simply to describe a particular cultural configuration; his ultimate goal is to assess and evaluate how Mexicans lead their lives, as well as to track down the historical roots of Mexican psychology. So what conclusions does he reach? Let us note, to begin with, that his evaluation of the Mexican character is highly negative. In "Los hijos de la Malinche," he offers the following diagnosis: "todo lo que es el mexicano actual . . . puede reducirse a esto: el mexicano no quiere o no se atreve a ser él mismo" (80; the Mexican's present existence . . . can be reduced to this: the Mexican does not want to be or does not have the courage to be himself). And what are the causes of this inability to live in harmony with oneself? For an answer to this question Paz goes all the way back to the Conquest of Mexico.

Paz views the Conquest as the moment in which the Mexican nation was born, and he reads it as a kind of family drama. In this drama, Cortés represents the father, while La Malinche occupies the role of the mother. On a symbolic level, their child, Martín Cortés, is the first *mestizo*, and also the first Mexican. Indeed, Cortés and La Malinche are the symbolic parents of all Mexicans. If Mexicans are the children of the conqueror and his mistress, their identity takes shape through the relationship they establish with their parents. According to Paz, as we saw in the previous chapter, the distinctive element in this relationship is the son's rejection of the mother-figure and identification with the father. And why, in Paz's opinion, do the Mexican sons denigrate their mother? They do so in the first place because she was violated by the Spanish conqueror. In short, she is victimized for having been a victim. But in addition to the disapproval showered upon La Malinche for being a rape victim, she is further disparaged for having allied herself with the Spaniards, that is, with the invading foreigners. The Mexican views her as a traitor to the nation. This, as Paz explains, is the origin of the word *malinchista* to describe someone who is susceptible to outside influences, and therefore is not a true patriot.

There can be little doubt that the image of La Malinche sketched by Paz is deeply derogatory. She is clearly the scapegoat of the national imaginary. But this is precisely the point: she is part of the Mexican national imaginary, not a product of Paz's own personal fantasizing. Feminist critics have a point when they take the Mexican poet to task for his androcentric view of Mexican national identity.[3] In his discussion of the family drama that has ostensibly given shape to the Mexican character, his focus is exclusively on the male child. An approach to national psychology that only takes account of approximately half of the country's population is indeed a drastically limited one. But where Paz's feminist critics have once again misread him is in assuming that his discussion of the figure of La Malinche in *El laberinto* represents his personal interpretation of Mexican history. Paz is not interpreting Mexican history; he is interpreting the interpretation of Mexican history that circulates in contemporary Mexican culture. He by no means subscribes to the dominant representation of La Malinche as a traitor to her country. On the contrary, the flow of his discussion makes it clear that the rejection of La Malinche (and thereby of the mother figure) is at least in part responsible for the psychological stress endured by the modern-day Mexican. The portrait of La Malinche in *El laberinto* is presented not as a factual report on the life of a specific historical person, but as a symptom of an unresolved identity conflict. If anything, Paz's discussion of the Malinche figure aims not to affirm her representation within Mexican culture, but to help overcome that representation.[4]

Many feminist critics speak as if Paz condones the scapegoating of La Malinche, as well as the hostile and aggressive conception of gender relations he describes in "Máscaras mexicanas." Nothing could be further from the truth, for Paz writes as a *critic* of these phenomena. The fact that Paz does not endorse the combative, hierarchical view of society inherent both in the ethos of the conquistadors and in contemporary *machismo* becomes even clearer when we contemplate the approach to the question of romantic-erotic love on which he expounds in the final chapter of *El laberinto*. In this chapter, labeled an appendix and titled "La dialéctica de la soledad" ("The Dialectic of Solitude"), Paz shifts from the ethnological and historical concerns that have predominated throughout the book to a focus on ontological questions. He describes a fundamental dialectic between solitude and communion, rupture and reunion that rules all of human life. Within this dialectic, love plays a key role, for it is the psychic force that compels individuals to seek to overcome the state of isolation in which they initially find themselves. Love, then, is "hambre de comunión" (213; a hunger for communion); it gives us access, even if only for an instant, to "[la] vida plena, en la que se fundan los contrarios" (213; the fullness of life, where contraries are fused together); it provides us with a vision of "un estado más perfecto" (213; a more perfect state). But genuine love also depends on freedom: again and again, Paz emphasizes the notion that love is the result of "[una] libre elección" (214; a free choice), and denounces the multitude of ways in which modern society places obstacles in the way of the free expression of our erotic preferences. It would be difficult to think of a more striking contrast than the one Paz establishes between the ideal version of love he depicts at the end of his book and the actual nature of gender relations in modern Mexico as he describes them in the second chapter of *El laberinto*. To describe love as "la revelación de dos soledades que crean por sí mismos un mundo que rompe la mentira social, suprime tiempo y trabajo y se declara autosuficiente" (216–17; the revelation of two solitudes who together create a world that breaks with society's lies, abolishes the realms of time and labor, and declares itself self-sufficient), as Paz does, represents a clear rejection of the *machista* values he had described earlier in the book. And yet numerous feminist critics have pegged him as a spokesperson for these values.

Like a true Romantic, Paz is deeply troubled by the constraints society places on the search for love. He claims that the existence of a panoply of rules and prohibitions, combined with the mistaken identification of love with marriage, makes "la elección amorosa . . . imposible en nuestra sociedad" (214; choice in matters of love . . . impossible in contemporary society). Paz's focus on the antisocial dimension of love leads him into a revealing misreading of a famous line from Marcel Proust's *À la recherche du temps perdu*. In the context of a discussion of how society pushes men to marry for convenience, rather than out of love, Paz quotes Swann's famous comment upon the conclusion of his love affair with Odette: "La frase de Swan [*sic*]: 'Y pensar que he perdido los mejores años de mi vida con una mujer que no era mi tipo', la pueden repetir, a la hora de su muerte, la mayor parte de los hombres modernos. Y las mujeres" (216; Swann's phrase: "And to think that I wasted the best years of my life on a woman who was not even my type," could be repeated, at the hour of their death, by the majority of present-day men. And women). Paz seems to be suggesting that Swann pursued Odette in order to conform to social expectations. But Proust is, in actual fact, putting his finger on something very different: from his perspective, Swann's wasting of his time with Odette points to the arbitrary, unpredictable, and irrational nature of love. It has to do with the vagaries of desire, not with the impositions of society. But that is exactly how Paz (mis)interprets the passage. Not that this misreading matters a great deal; what is important to understand is how Paz fits Swann's observation into his overall argument about love in the modern world. The reference to Proust is part of an attack on the modern world for making true love (which is rooted in free choice) unachievable.[5]

In the final chapter of *El laberinto*, there is a further surprise in store for the reader who believes that the author is a sexist. In the middle of his discussion of love, Paz suddenly alludes to the work of Simone de Beauvoir, whose path-breaking *The Second Sex* was published in 1949, just one year before the first edition of *El laberinto de la soledad* came out in Mexico. Consider the significance of this: Paz quotes from the work of a leading feminist almost immediately after the publication of her book denouncing the treatment of women in Western society. At the very least, it indicates an interest on Paz's part in feminism. You would not know this, however, from reading Paz's feminist critics, who never mention the Mexican poet's reference to *The Second Sex* in *El laberinto*.[6] What is more, Paz quotes de Beauvoir's work approvingly, using the French feminist's ideas in order to buttress his own argument.

Paz opens this section of his text with the bold claim that "en nuestro mundo el amor es una experiencia casi inaccesible" (213; in our world, love is an almost inaccessible experience). And why is this the case? Why is it impossible—or, at least, *almost* impossible—to experience love in modern society? Paz blames men for this situation, along with society. The problem with men is that they don't treat the women they supposedly love as full and autonomous human beings, turning them instead into "objects" or "instruments." Here is how Paz puts it: "Al convertir [a la mujer] en objeto, en ser aparte, y al someterla a todas las deformaciones que su interés, su vanidad, su angustia y su mismo amor le dictan, el hombre la convierte en instrumento" (214; In turning [women] into objects, into beings who exist in a separate realm, and in submitting them to all of the distortions dictated by his needs, his vanity, his anguish, and his love itself, men turn them into instruments). Now, anyone who has understood Paz's critique of modern society realizes that for Paz the act of turning another human being into an "object" or an "instrument" carries profoundly negative connotations. Equally pernicious is the act of imposing preconceived images on people—precisely what society does to women. "La mujer" (Women), Paz explains, "vive presa en la imagen que la sociedad masculina le impone" (215; are captives of the image imposed upon them by a male-dominated society). Women cannot be themselves, or express themselves, because they are forced to conform to "una imagen que le ha sido dictada por familia, clase, escuela, amigas, religión y amante" (214; an image that has been dictated by the family, social class, schools, friends, religion, and lovers). Throughout this section Paz is denouncing the way a masculinist society compels women to fit into a limited set of stereotypes. And he explicitly leans on the work of de Beauvoir to make his point: "la mujer es ídolo, diosa, madre, hechicera o musa, según muestra Simone de Beauvoir, pero jamás puede ser ella misma" (214; the woman is an idol, a goddess, a mother, a sorceress, or a muse, as Simone de Beauvoir has shown, but she can never be herself). And to be clear: Paz is *not* saying that women are inherently incapable of being themselves; he is arguing, like his feminist forerunner de Beauvoir, that the current masculinist social order *prevents* women from being themselves.

There is no clearer proof of Paz's interest in the contributions made by women writers to literature and culture, and of his concern with the position of women in society, than his decades-long commitment to studying and writing about the life and work of Sor Juana Inés de la Cruz. He devotes several pages to Sor Juana in the account he gives of colonial society in the fifth chapter of

El laberinto, describing her as a solitary figure who was ahead of her time, "una figura moderna" (125; a modern figure), as he puts it. According to Paz, two things above all else set her apart from the closed and repressive society in which she lived: her "defensa de la mujer" (defense of women) and her "afición por el pensamiento desinteresado" (125; commitment to disinterested thought). Around the same time, Paz received an invitation from José Bianco to write an article on Sor Juana for *Sur* on the occasion of the third centenary of the Mexican poet's birth.[7] This led to a more extended consideration of her life and work, subsequently reprinted in Paz's 1957 collection of essays *Las peras del olmo* (The pears of the elm tree).[8] In the early 1970s, as a visiting professor at Harvard University, Paz on several occasions taught a course on Sor Juana.[9] Paz's prolonged devotion to the study of Sor Juana's life and work culminated in 1982 with the publication of his monumental work of biography, history, and criticism, a 673-page volume entitled *Sor Juana Inés de la Cruz, o, Las trampas de la fe* (*Sor Juana, or, The Traps of Faith*).

It is obviously not possible to give a complete account of Paz's vast undertaking in his book on Sor Juana. Nor is that my goal here. Instead, I will highlight some aspects of the book that are relevant to an understanding of the Mexican author's relationship to feminism. Let me note, to begin with, that Paz offers an extraordinarily detailed account of Sor Juana's life and work and writes about her with deep admiration and sympathy. *Sor Juana* is most emphatically not the product of a mind that is inclined to disparage individual women, or that believes women ought to occupy a secondary role in society. On the contrary, the key themes in Paz's treatment of Sor Juana are clearly in harmony with the central preoccupations of feminist criticism. For one thing, Paz repeatedly draws attention to the fact that gender is a social construct and unambiguously rejects essentialist notions concerning the differences between men and women. He painstakingly shows how the social construction of gender in colonial Mexican society placed obstacles in the way of Sor Juana's flourishing as an individual and a writer. Indeed, Paz writes about the fiercely oppressive world in which Sor Juana lived with a mixture of indignation and sadness. Finally, it is clear that insofar as Sor Juana rebelled against the limits placed on her as a woman and an intellectual, Paz celebrates this rebellion.

Let me offer a little more detail on each of these aspects of Paz's approach to his topic. On the question of gender, Paz forcefully rejects the perspective of Ludwig Pfandl, an earlier Sor Juana critic, who, according to Paz, starts from the idea that there are "tipos biológicos fijos, inmutables" (fixed and immutable biological types) and assumes that "lo femenino y lo masculino son . . . categorías reacias a las realidades sociales e históricas" (*Sor Juana*, 93; the feminine and masculine are . . . categories that are resistant to social and historical circumstances). Paz's approach to gender is quite different, and much more in tune with contemporary feminist perspectives: "pienso que no hay tipos puros y que la gama de la intersexualidad es inmensa" (93; I do not believe in the existence of pure types and I am convinced that the range of intersexuality is immense). But what is most important to understand are the social and historical conditions within which gender is viewed and experienced. And the crucial point about colonial Mexican society, to which Paz returns again and again, is that it was "una civilización de hombres y para hombres" (94; a civilization of men and for men). Everything Sor Juana did or wrote has to be understood against the background of the male-dominated society in which she lived. There is no question that Sor Juana grasped—and rebelled against—the constraints she faced as a woman intellectual. As Paz puts it, "Los textos de Sor Juana dicen claramente que ella no creía que ser mujer fuese un impedimento natural: el obstáculo venía de las costumbres no de la condición femenina" (497; Sor Juana's writings clearly show that she did not believe that being a woman constituted a natural impediment: the obstacle was not the female condition but social customs). Or, as he explains in another passage of his book: "es indudable que [Sor Juana] vivió—mejor dicho: sufrió—con una lucidez poco común su condición de mujer. También es indudable que más de una vez se rebeló y se quejó" (397; there is no question that [Sor Juana] experienced—better said, suffered—her condition as a woman with an uncommon lucidity. Similarly, there is no question that she frequently rebelled against and complained about her situation). Paz sees in Sor Juana's work an anticipation of "el feminismo moderno" (159; modern feminism), a testimony of "su feminismo decidido" (394; her feminist convictions), and "una exaltación del espíritu femenino" (532; a celebration of the female spirit). If one places these comments alongside Paz's description of "machismo" as "una tiranía que ensombrece las relaciones entre el hombre y la mujer" (107; a tyranny that casts a shadow over relations between men and women), it surely becomes very difficult to portray him as a spokesperson for machista, antifeminist values.

There is one other aspect of Paz's study of Sor Juana that needs to be examined in the present context: his approach to the question of her sexual orientation. A number of critics have accused Paz of promoting a limited and degrading view of homosexuality.[10] Indeed, in at least one case the Mexican Nobel laureate has been charged outright with the expression of a "homophobic . . . cultural logic."[11] It is a surprising accusation to level at an author who throughout his career demonstrated a profound affinity for libertarian standpoints, and it can be countered not only by examining his discussion of Sor Juana's sexuality, but also by looking at the broader context of his work. Let us begin by refuting the notion that Paz is the spokesperson for some notion of "normality," a notion that, as we know, has been routinely used to make outcasts of individuals who do not conform to the dominant social conceptions of acceptable behavior.[12] Paz brings up the concept of "normality" on a number of occasions in his book on Sor Juana, and each time he makes it clear that he *rejects* such a concept, specifically when applied to notions of gender and sexuality. Two examples will suffice to make the point. First, in the context of a description of Sor Juana's comportment as a nun, which presents her as behaving pretty much like the majority of other nuns, Paz stops for a moment to dispel a misunderstanding that might arise in the reader. "No quiero decir" (I do not mean to suggest), he states, "que haya sido una 'mujer normal': no hay mujeres ni hombres normales, esa palabra no significa nada" (178; that she was a "normal woman": there are no normal women or men, the word "normal" has no meaning). Note that Paz argues that the idea of "normality" is inapplicable not only to Sor Juana, but to all people. He takes a similar approach later in the book in the second example I want to give here of how he handles the question of "normality." After dismissing the notion—advanced by other critics—that Sor Juana was a "neurotic" person, Paz makes the following observation: "Naturalmente, Sor Juana no era lo que se llama una persona 'normal.' ¿Quién lo es?" (578; Obviously, Sor Juana was not what one calls a "normal" person. But then: who is?). Critics who view Paz as the defender of a discriminatory notion of "normality" should at the very least ponder the explicit statements the author himself makes on this topic.

Paz adopted this position on "normality" consistently throughout his career. His repudiation of normative thinking fed into a tolerant and open-minded outlook on human sexuality. What could be clearer than his statement in the book he wrote late in life on love and eroticism that "el erotismo es singular y no desdeña ninguna anomalía" (erotic experience is always unique and it does not scorn any kind of anomaly)?[13] Or than his corresponding rejection—corresponding, that is, to the recognition of the variety of ways in which human sexuality expresses itself—of traditional prejudices against homosexuality? This rejection appears again and again in his work. Take, for example, his comments on Armando Jiménez's *Nueva picardía mexicana* in *Conjunciones y disyunciones*. In the midst of a generally laudatory discussion of Jiménez's book, Paz stops to complain about "la rusticidad y gazmoñería del sistema ético" (the coarseness and prudishness of the ethical system) that underlies the book. The flaw he identifies in the book resides principally in the expression of "supersticiones, prejuicios, inhibiciones" (superstitions, prejudices, inhibitions). And what are the main prejudices Paz repudiates? His answer to this question is very clear. More than anything else, he deplores "el machismo y sus consecuencias: la misoginia y el odio irracional a 'jotos' y 'maricones'" (machismo and its consequences: misogyny and the irrational hatred toward "faggots" and "queers").[14] Are these the words of someone who finds homosexuality "threatening"?[15] On the contrary, these are the words of a writer who understands that many people feel threatened by what is different from themselves, but who clearly rejects such feelings, denouncing them as the symptoms of an "irrational hatred."

Paz's not simply tolerant but openly sympathetic views of homosexuality are also clear from his writings about the gay poets he knew and admired. Consider the case of Luis Cernuda, the homosexual poet from Spain whom Paz first met in Spain in 1937 during the Spanish Civil War, and with whom he sustained a close friendship that lasted until Cernuda's death in 1963. In *La llama doble* Paz brings up Cernuda in the context of a discussion of the representation of homosexuality in literature. He begins by noting the traditional prohibition against homosexual themes in literature, observing, among other things, that this restriction was the cause of "la desgracia de Oscar Wilde" (the misfortune of Oscar Wilde) less than a century earlier. Even though "nuestras sociedades" (our societies) (presumably Paz is referring to Western societies) have become much more tolerant, the tendency has been to write about homosexual themes in a disguised fashion, as Proust did. At this point, Paz mentions Cernuda: "Algunos poetas modernos fueron más atrevidos y entre ellos destaca un español: Luis Cernuda. Hay que pensar en los años, el mundo y la lengua en que publicó Cernuda sus poemas para apreciar su denuedo" (Some modern poets were bolder and among them a Spanish poet stands out: Luis Cernuda. One needs to recall the years when he was writing, the world he lived in and the language in which he published his work in order to appreciate his bravery).[16] In short, Paz praises Cernuda for having written about homosexuality in an open and direct fashion in an era when it was extremely difficult to do so. Paz views this as an act of great courage on the Spanish poet's part. And if one believes that Paz, writing in the early 1990s, is not risking much by adopting an adamantly pro-gay position, one needs to recall that he had written about Cernuda's homosexuality in very similar terms approximately three decades earlier. Shortly after Cernuda's death in 1963, Paz wrote a long essay on the poet's work, an essay that included an eloquent and frank discussion of Cernuda's homosexuality. The

Mexican poet begins by noting that one cannot understand Cernuda's poetry "si se omite o atenúa su homosexualidad" (if one overlooks or downplays his homosexuality).[17] He then proceeds to acknowledge the risks Cernuda took in writing openly about his sexuality, especially in the context of a society "en la que el 'machismo' es una enfermedad continental" (in which 'machismo' is a continent-wide disease),[18] and concludes by describing Cernuda's defiance as a blow struck against all repressive norms and institutions: "Homosexualismo," Paz states, "se vuelve sinónimo de libertad" (Homosexuality becomes a synonym for freedom).[19] It is simply not possible to grasp Paz's position on the subject of homosexuality without taking into account the fact that he delivered a stirring defense not just of homosexual rights, but of the key role played by gay expression within the larger culture, even *before* the gay rights movement became a powerful force in Western societies.[20]

Having completed this brief detour through Paz's writings—the purpose of which has been to show that at key moments in his career the Mexican poet rejected homophobic viewpoints and celebrated gay poetic expression—we can now return to his book on Sor Juana, in order to consider the position he adopts on the controversial question of the Mexican nun's sexual orientation. To begin with, we may note that in one passage in the book, Paz adamantly rejects the notion that Sor Juana had a clear same-sex preference: "Pensar que ella sentía una clara aversión a los hombres y una igualmente clara afición a las mujeres es descabellado" (158; To think that she felt an aversion toward men and an equally strong preference for women is farfetched). Paz's forceful language has provoked strong criticism.[21] Still, in trying to adjudicate this issue we would do well to pose two broad questions, neither of which his critics address. First of all, we need to ask whether stating one's belief that a deceased person who has left no unambiguous statement concerning their sexual orientation is *not* homosexual should be taken as an indication of one's homophobia. Next, we need to look at the reasons Paz gives for believing that Sor Juana was not lesbian. Strangely enough, Paz critics do not bother to examine his arguments and simply assume that his statement that Sor Juana was not homosexual is proof of his homophobia.

In respect to the first argument, it is crucial to consider Paz's attitude toward homosexuality, as it expressed itself over the course of his entire lifetime. From the overview I provided earlier, it is clear that Paz was a strong critic of homophobia and a forceful supporter of gay liberation and artistic expression. Indeed, one could argue that his longstanding veneration of "subversion" in the arts led him to feel an instinctive sympathy for gay writers such as Luis Cernuda who fought against the inherited prejudices of his cultural milieu. In this context, it seems implausible to think that Paz would be expressing homophobic sentiments in his book on Sor Juana. To do so would go against the stand he had taken on homosexuality over a period of many years, and that he would continue to take in the years after the publication of his study of Sor Juana. What would explain such an unusual reversal? In fact, there is no need to try to explain it; a better solution is simply to reject the argument that Paz in his book on Sor Juana is contradicting his own explicitly stated support for gay rights.

It is, moreover, difficult to view Paz's actual arguments regarding Sor Juana's sexual orientation as the product of a homophobic outlook. The Mexican poet reaches his conclusions about Sor Juana on the basis of a painstaking reconstruction of the social, literary, and intellectual context informing her work. It is surely worth examining what factors he takes into consideration when assessing the question of whether Sor Juana was lesbian or not. Some facts, of course, are beyond question. We know that Sor Juana developed passionate friendships with several women over the course of her life, and that she addressed erotically charged poems to her female friends. But it is impossible to know with any certainty whether Sor Juana ever had an actual physical relationship with a woman (or a man, for that matter). In the course of his book, Paz adopts shifting perspectives on the question of the Mexican nun's sexuality. At times, he himself recognizes that it is simply impossible to attain firm knowledge about this topic. "Es vano tratar de saber cuáles eran sus verdaderos sentimientos sexuales" (158; It is a vain enterprise to try to understand what her true sentiments were), he states at one point. "Carecemos de datos y documentos" (287; We lack information and documentation), he notes elsewhere in his book, as a way of supporting his claim that on the topic of Sor Juana's sexuality one can only advance suppositions. Paz also describes Sor Juana's private life as concealing "una historia enigmática que . . . es imposible esclarecer enteramente" (302; an enigmatic story which . . . it is impossible to fully elucidate). And yet at other stages of his argument, he does make certain confident-sounding assertions about her sentimental and erotic life. There is no doubt, he says, that Sor Juana's affection for María Luisa Manrique, the vicereine of Spain, became so strong that it must be described as love (259). On the other hand, Paz claims that the impassioned sentiments Sor Juana expressed in her poetry about her female friends "no son sinónimos de lesbianismo" (146; are not synonymous with lesbianism). Elsewhere he repeats the argument against Sor Juana's lesbianism, although in a slightly different form, since he concedes that some of her most ardent poems may reveal Sapphic tendencies, albeit "en el sentido sublimado de la tradición platónica renacentista" (604; in the sublimated sense of the Renaissance Platonic tradition). There is one thing, though, about which Paz entertains no doubts whatsoever: Sor Juana's relationships with the women for whom she felt affection were entirely chaste (287).

One can legitimately ask why Paz so confidently claims to know that Sor Juana's relationships with her female friends were chaste when he himself has stated that it is impossible to know what Sor Juana's true feelings were, or what transpired between her and her friends. Even so, it is worth looking at the factors he takes into account in advancing his argument. In essence, Paz tries to refute the argument that Sor Juana's poetry reveals that she was having a sexual relationship with the vicereine by emphasizing that the relevant poems should not be read as confessional (since the notion of confessional poetry was completely foreign to Sor Juana's era), and should be placed in the context of certain dominant literary codes instead. Paz notes, for example, that "la tradición poética y retórica poseía un vocabulario y unas figuras para nombrar el cuerpo femenino" (299; the rhetorical and poetical tradition possessed a store of words and figures of speech to describe the female body); this, in combination with the absence of a similar vocabulary for speaking about male bodies, might explain why Sor Juana's poems include descriptions of the body of her female addressee. The Mexican nun was availing herself of existing poetic conventions rather than expressing the truth about her feelings. Paz also points out that inherited poetic forms allowed for the expression of gratitude to be given an erotic coloration. Sor Juana often expressed gratitude to certain female friends of hers who were her social superiors. The language she used to do so sometimes carried an erotic charge. An understanding of the poetic conventions of the period allows one to see that this did not necessarily point to the existence of an actual sexual relationship. Most important for Paz is the fact that Sor Juana was part of a Neoplatonic intellectual tradition in which the soul occupies a pre-eminent position. According to Paz, Sor Juana's writings about her female friends were infused with this Neoplatonic outlook. The conclusion Paz draws from this element of Sor Juana's work is that her poems express amorous feelings that are Platonic in nature, and not rooted in an actual sexual relationship. It is certainly possible to disagree with Paz's arguments. However, they deserve to be taken seriously, rather than brushed aside as homophobic.

So far in this chapter I have examined Paz's writings on two important female figures from Mexican history: La Malinche and Sor Juana. I have also looked at his treatment in the final chapter of *El laberinto* of the theme of romantic-erotic love as an element in human life in general. In closing this chapter I want to take up the matter of love again, as it was one of the core themes of his literary oeuvre. Paz wrote a great number of poems about love, in addition to which he discussed it at length in essayistic works such as *Conjunciones y disyunciones*, "¿Por qué Fourier?," and, most notably, in *La llama doble*, a stunningly ambitious work about the status of love and eroticism in Western civilization, covering the entire span of Western history, from Greek and Roman antiquity until the present day. Insofar as Paz was wont to draw analogies between love and other human creations, primarily poetry, the topic of love came up in many other writings as well, even if they were not primarily about love, eroticism, or human sexuality. In my discussion of *El laberinto* I showed that the Mexican poet clearly expressed his concern with women as subjects, and drew on the feminist thought of Simone de Beauvoir in order to articulate his own ideas about the fate of love in modern society. The final chapter of *El laberinto* offers ample evidence with which to counter the accusation that Paz was interested in women only as objects. The same can be said of *La llama doble*.

To illustrate my point I will highlight two key aspects of Paz's book on love and eroticism, a book that was clearly the product of a lifetime of reflection on the topic. First, I will look at Paz's account of the role of women in the evolution of both the idea and practice of love in Western civilization; then I will briefly examine Paz's highly personal descriptions of the experience of love itself. With regard to the first point, it is crucial to understand that the freedom and autonomy of women is a central theme in the story Paz wishes to tell. Indeed, he goes so far as to suggest that in the absence of this element, there would be no story at all. "La emergencia del amor es inseparable de la emergencia de la mujer" (72; The emergence of love is inseparable from the emergence of women), he states at one point, adding that "No hay amor sin libertad femenina" (73; There is no love without freedom for women). He repeats the same point almost verbatim a few pages later: "la historia del amor es inseparable de la historia de la libertad de la mujer" (78; the history of love is inseparable from the history of women's freedom). At several stages of the historical narrative he presents in *La llama doble*, Paz gives examples of how the conquest by women of more freedom and autonomy for themselves had as its corollary a flourishing of the experience of love. In the ancient world, in the cities of Alexandria and Rome, Paz finds premonitions of modern attitudes toward love and eroticism. According to Paz, a "revolución invisible" (invisible revolution) takes place in these new urban settings, one that gave women more power over their own lives (54). Their freedom is to a large extent the freedom to choose whom to love: "son mujeres libres . . . porque en una medida desconocida hasta entonces tienen albedrío para aceptar o rechazar a sus amantes. Son dueños de su cuerpo y de su alma" (56; they are free women . . . because to an unprecedented degree they now have the freedom to accept or reject their lovers. They are in command of their bodies and souls). The rise of courtly love in twelfth-century France is also closely tied to the improvement in the status of women. Paz notes how the codes of courtly love, in placing the woman in the superior position and making the man her vassal, overthrew the traditional hierarchy of the sexes and adumbrated a new role for women in society: "la elevación de la mujer fue una revolución no sólo en el orden ideal de las relaciones amorosas sino en el de la realidad social" (94; the elevation in the status of women constituted a revolution not only within the ideal world of romantic relations but also in the realm of social reality). And in the modern era, what Paz calls "la creciente independencia de la mujer" (135; women's increasing independence) was intimately connected to the new emphasis on romantic love as a cornerstone of one's personal life. In sum, Paz underlines again and again that the liberation of women was a precondition for the emergence in our world of a certain conception of love. Now, it is of course possible to disagree with Paz's historical narrative. But the accuracy of that narrative is not our main concern in the present context. What matters are the values expressed through this narrative. The question we need to ask is what experiences Paz places in a positive light. After reading *La llama doble* the reader is left in no doubt whatsoever that Paz values women's freedom.

To value female emancipation is to reject male domination. Nowhere in *La llama doble* does Paz suggest that his ideal image of love or sex involves an aggressive male lording it over a passive female. On the contrary, his definition of love and eroticism revolves continuously around notions of transparency, reciprocity, and fusion. In a series of poetically charged passages in *La llama doble*, Paz defines erotic love as a "vuelta a la naturaleza reconciliada" (28; return to a harmonious nature), "la conjunción del sujeto y del objeto" (143; the union of subject and object), "la experiencia del regreso al origen" (143; the experience of a return to the origins), "el descubrimiento de la unidad de la vida" (144; the discovery of the unity of all life), and "lugar de reunión" (145; a space of reunion). And just to be clear: Paz does not state or assume that the discovery of this place of reunion or the experience of reconciliation with nature implies the erasure of one's partner. On the contrary, his attempts to evoke the experience of love always involve a profound sense of mutuality. Consider how he concludes one especially exalted passage on what it feels like to love another person: "Es una atracción por un alma y por un cuerpo; no una idea: una persona. Esa persona es única y está dotada de libertad; para poseerla, el amante tiene que ganar su voluntad. Posesión y entrega son actos recíprocos" (210; It is an attraction toward a soul and a body; not an idea: a person. That person is unique and is endowed with freedom; to possess the beloved, the lover has to earn their will. Possession and surrender are reciprocal acts). In his writings on love, Paz constantly resorts to paradoxes: in love, one loses oneself and finds oneself, the body of one's lover is irreducibly different yet fused with one's own body; when making love, the body becomes utterly palpable yet mysteriously evanescent. The paradoxes are a way of hinting at how the experience of love exists at the limits of the expressible. They are also Paz's method for pointing toward the ultimate paradox of love, in which two people are at the same time one person. And to reiterate: they are one person in Paz's view not because the male has conquered the female, but because the two lovers in the encounter have voluntarily and reciprocally erased the boundaries of their being. One can agree or disagree with Paz's perspective on the topic; what one cannot claim is that he is a spokesperson for "machista" values.

Paz's feminist critics have focused on a small number of passages from his work. Mostly, they have discussed a few sections from *El laberinto*. They have read these passages without reflecting in detail on Paz's rhetorical strategy and without relating them to other parts of the book. Nor have they examined the overall arc or orientation of Paz's career. The feminist misreading of the passages on Mexican gender relations in *El laberinto* and on the figure of La Malinche comes into clear focus when we consider Paz's explicit statements in support of feminism over the course of his long career, as well as his descriptions of erotic love as an escape from domination rather than an exercise in domination. Anyone who examines the feminist reception of Paz's work notes that the same charges have been leveled at him over and over again.[22] The purpose of this chapter has been to try to set the record straight and to counter what unfortunately has become a commonplace reading of Octavio Paz's conception of gender. About Paz's feminist critics one can state the following: the fact that they fight for a just cause does not mean that they always have a sense of justice.

CHAPTER 7

The Left

Numerous controversies swirled around Paz throughout his career, particularly in the final decades of his life, following his return to Mexico in the wake of his resignation as ambassador to India. There is no doubt that the most intensely debated topic has been the question of Paz's relationship to the Left. It was an issue that Paz repeatedly addressed in essays and interviews, and that his critics have pondered at length. In examining the existing interpretations of Paz's political ideas, one notes that they can be situated in relation to two sets of oppositions. In the first place, there is the question of whether to stress continuity or rupture. Was there an underlying consistency in Paz's thinking—in particular with regard to his evaluation of leftist ideas—or was his career marked by a decisive rupture with the Left? The second opposition has to do with the question of how Paz's political positions are evaluated. Are they applauded or rejected? Do commentators on his career view the evolution of his thinking in a favorable or unfavorable light? Clearly, both oppositions allow for shades of opinion, as well as the possibility of an intermediate position, somewhere in between the positive and negative readings of Paz's politics, and recognizing both rupture and continuity in the evolution of his ideas.

One critic who places the question of rupture versus continuity at the heart of his study of Paz's career is Fernando Vizcaíno. At the outset, Vizcaíno formulates the key questions about Paz's political thought that he will attempt to answer: "¿cuál es su continuidad? ¿cuáles son sus momentos de ruptura?" (What are its elements of continuity? Where can we locate moments of rupture?).[1] But he has difficulty deciding which element—rupture or continuity—ultimately predominates. And insofar as he sees moments of rupture in Paz's career, he also has difficulty determining exactly when the key breaks occurred. One of the versions of the story developed by Vizcaíno has Paz distancing himself from the Left in the late 1930s. The Molotov-Ribbentrop pact and the assassination of Trotsky in Mexico City left Paz deeply shaken, setting in motion a process of disillusionment with the Left. According to Vizcaíno, however, "la ruptura no sería total hasta principios de los años cincuenta, cuando Paz denunciaría los campos de concentración soviéticos" (the break would not be complete until the early 1950s when Paz denounced the Soviet concentration camps).[2] But contrasting with this interpretation, centered on a *total* rupture with the communist ideal that supposedly takes place in the early 1950s, Vizcaíno puts forward an alternative reading that divides Paz's career into three periods, which he calls the phases of his "youth," his "maturity," and his "fin de siècle." During his youthful years, Paz supports socialism and revolution. In his maturity, "trás . . . el asesinato de Trotsky . . . y durante el tiempo de los testimonios de Víctor Serge, de Solyenitsin, de Kruschev, Gorbachov y muchos más, el camino aún es el socialismo pero a éste se arriba, ya no a través de la revolución, sino por medio de la democracia" (after . . . the assassination of Trotsky . . . and during the time of the testimonies of Victor Serge, Solzhenitsyn, Khrushchev, Gorbachev, and many more, the path still leads to socialism, not through a revolution, but by democratic means).[3] Instead of a clear break with the Left around 1950, we now have a single mature phase in Paz's career, running from Victor Serge, who was already a subject of controversy in 1935, when writers and intellectuals argued over his case at the International Congress of Writers for the Defense of Culture in Paris,[4] to Gorbachev, who came to power in 1985. The period of maturity culminates in 1989 with the collapse of Communism in Eastern Europe. After this, according to Vizcaíno, a new period begins: "el mundo es otro y Paz reinicia su diálogo con la historia" (the world has changed and Paz renews his dialogue with history).[5] What the content of this new dialogue with history might be is not stated. Given the lack of precision in Vizcaíno's account of the turning points in Paz's career, it is perhaps not surprising to observe that alongside the rupture-centered reading the author presents an alternative interpretation focused on the continuity in Paz's thinking. According to this point of view, the Mexican poet's "preocupaciones fundamentales" (fundamental concerns) have remained the same throughout his career. They are "la democracia y la modernidad" (democracy and modernity).[6] What has also remained the same was to whom Paz addressed his arguments: "Desde los años cincuenta la izquierda aparece como el gran interlocutor de Octavio Paz" (Since the 1950s, the Left has been Octavio Paz's principal interlocutor).[7]

Guadalupe Nettel has a more explicit focus on the continuity in Paz's political positions. Like many others, she sees Paz's 1951 article on the David Rousset affair as a key moment in his career: "El artículo ... constituyó también la primera manifestación de la postura política que Paz mantendría hasta el final de sus días, a saber: simpatía por los ideales socialistas y oposición virulenta a los regímenes totalitarios" (This article ... was the first expression of the political posture Paz would maintain until the end of his days: sympathy for the ideals of socialism and virulent opposition to all totalitarian regimes).[8] She argues that Paz's thinking was characterized by "una serie de motivos recurrentes: la defensa de la libertad de expresión, de las libertades individuales y de la democracia frente a los totalitarismos" (a series of recurring themes: the defense of freedom of expression, of individual liberties, and of democracy in the face of totalitarian ideologies).[9] Occasionally, however, Nettel highlights the changes in Paz's political outlook. She notes, for example, that over the course of his career he shifted from being a dissident of the Left to being a dissident, plain and simple.[10] She also notes that by the early 1980s Paz was identifying as a liberal, adding, however, that it took him a long time to openly embrace the label.[11]

Yvon Grenier stresses the continuity in Paz's thinking, and he explicitly disagrees with critics who are prone to identifying breaks in his career. "The case can be made," Grenier suggests, "that the magnitude of Paz's purported 'turn' from the 'Left' to the 'Right' is often exaggerated, probably for two reasons. First, there is a tendency to exaggerate Marx's influence on Paz's thought, especially on the young Paz. Secondly, the exceptional consistency of Paz's political views over these turbulent decades is not fully appreciated."[12] For Grenier, the underlying element in Paz's thinking is "a genuine devotion to the principle of freedom." Testimony to this devotion to freedom is the fact that "he started writing critically about communist dictatorships as early as the late 1930s."[13] Another commentator who focuses on the consistency in Paz's political outlook over the course of his career is Alberto Ruy Sánchez. The consistency can be seen in the Mexican poet's longstanding opposition to totalitarian regimes, which, according to Ruy Sánchez, "[está] presente en sus escritos desde los años cincuenta y en su formación desde los cuarenta" (is reflected in his writings from the 1950s onward, and is part of his development as a thinker since the 1940s).[14] Jaime Sánchez Susarrey, too, argues for continuity; however, he focuses on a narrower time period. In his overview of political and intellectual debates in Mexico from 1968 to 1992, he claims that it was not Paz who changed during these years, but his enemies. Paz was a staunch upholder of liberal, pluralistic values all along; his opponents on the Left took much longer to turn into supporters of democracy.[15]

As a rule, when observers of Paz's career emphasize the continuity in his political thought, they do so in order to applaud him. It is not just that consistency is seen as something worthy in itself; rather, Paz's early adherence to the ideal of freedom constitutes evidence of his clear-sightedness, as well as his ethical probity, in recognizing and being willing to speak out against the crimes committed in the name of Communism throughout the twentieth century. As we know, vast numbers of writers and intellectuals took far longer to understand the bankruptcy of Communist ideology (and many have still not understood it). The continuity in Paz's thinking means, among other things, that he was ahead of his time. Nevertheless, there are exceptions to this tendency to view continuity in a positive light. Take, for example, the work of Jorge Aguilar Mora, one of Paz's best-known—and most persistent—antagonists. In his 1976 doctoral dissertation, defended at the Colegio de México and subsequently published in book form by Editorial Era in Mexico City, Aguilar Mora argued that a conservative ideology was already in evidence in *El laberinto*, Paz's first published book-length essay. This conservatism persists throughout Paz's work; it is evaluated negatively by Aguilar Mora.[16]

Most of Paz's critics from the Left take a different approach from Aguilar Mora's. They see his career in terms of rupture rather than continuity. This allows them to distinguish a good Paz from a bad Paz. The good Paz was a leftist; the bad Paz abandoned his leftist ideals and ended up siding with the Right. Critics differ as to when the break took place, although it is common to zero in on the 1970s as a crucial moment in the poet's ideological transformation. A typical approach is that of Raymond Leslie Williams: he sees a change taking place in the 1970s, with Paz as a supporter of the Left before then, and as "fundamentally reactionary" in his politics and political alliances afterward.[17] Enrique González Rojo also believes that Paz was on the correct side, politically speaking, until the late 1960s; however, his thinking took a wrong turn at some point after that. Focusing his criticism on Paz's support for the Salinas presidency, González Rojo argues that there is "una gran diferencia entre la postura crítica, anti-gobierno en 1969 y su actitud servil, partidario en 1989–1990" (a big difference between Paz's critical, anti-government position in 1969 and his fawning, supportive attitude in 1989–1990).[18] In a 1979 review of Paz's *El ogro filantrópico*, Héctor Aguilar Camín, who would later become the Mexican poet's ally in the fight for liberal, democratic values in Mexico, complained about what he described as a "proceso de simplificación y derechización" (process of simplification and of turning to the Right) in Paz's thinking. He contrasted the conservatism of Paz's outlook in the 1970s with his defense of socialist ideals in his 1951 essay about the Soviet concentration camp controversy.[19] Xavier Rodríguez Ledesma, for his part, shares Aguilar Camín's distaste for the overall direction of Paz's political thinking and also views *El ogro* as a crucial text in the Mexican poet's shift away from a pro-socialist outlook. Rodríguez Ledesma divides Paz's career into three periods. The first phase covers the 1930s, during which time Paz felt a clear affinity for Marxist thought. A process of disillusionment with Communist revolutions began in the 1940s; however, this did not lead him to reject Marxism *in toto*. On the contrary, during this middle phase of his career, Paz criticized the Left—in particular Stalinism—but he did so from a socialist perspective. Finally, in the late 1970s, around the time of the publication of *El ogro*, there is a definitive rupture with Marxism. For Rodríguez Ledesma this marks a step backward, not a step forward. He speaks dismissively of what he calls a "furor antimarxista" (anti-Marxist fury) that takes possession of the poet in the final phase of his career.[20]

Enrique Krauze is undoubtedly the most forceful exponent of an interpretation of Paz's intellectual trajectory that couples an emphasis on rupture with a favorable assessment of Paz's political evolution. He claims that Paz's reading of Alexander Solzhenitsyn's *The Gulag Archipelago* (1973) had a decisive impact on his understanding not just of the Soviet Union, but of Communist revolutions in general, and of the ideology that undergirded them. It is a theme Krauze has returned to repeatedly over the course of his own long career as a student of Paz's life and work. In a 1986 essay published in the American journal *Salmagundi*, Krauze writes that Paz "arrived at his definitive vision of the Soviet state" after reading *The Gulag Archipelago*. From that moment on, Krauze continues, the Mexican poet "dedicated a good part of his public effort to counterprophecy: to denounce the USSR, its satellites and sympathizers." According to Krauze, Paz's reading of Solzhenitsyn led him to a complete rejection of Marxist-Leninist ideology, which henceforth he would view as "not only a historical explanation contradicted by the facts, but as a morality of imposture and intolerance, a Jesuit policy and an unfulfilled prophecy."[21] In 2011, in a long essay on Paz titled "El poeta y la Revolución" (The poet and the Revolution), Krauze returned to the days in late 1973 and early 1974 when Paz was reading Solzhenitsyn, linking this reading to Paz's meeting around the same time in Cambridge, Massachusetts, with the Russian poet Joseph Brodsky, who for Paz represented, in Krauze's words, "la realidad del escritor perseguido en la URSS" (the reality of the writer who has suffered persecution in the Soviet Union).[22] According to Krauze, reading *The Gulag Archipelago* was Paz's Kronstadt.[23] It was the event that opened his eyes to the true nature of the Soviet regime. Finally, in 2014, at an event held in Mexico City to commemorate the centenary of Paz's birth, Krauze reiterated his view that the encounter with *The Gulag Archipelago* was a decisive moment in Paz's career, what Krauze, on this occasion, calls a *parteaguas* (watershed moment).[24] The break is, of course, celebrated, for it meant that Paz had finally come to see the truth about the Soviet system.

Unlike Krauze, Christopher Domínguez Michael and Armando González Torres underline the gradual nature of the changes in Paz's relationship with the Left. González Torres uses terms such as "alejamiento" and "distanciamiento" (distancing) to describe how Paz's views of the Left shifted over time.[25] González Torres's choice of words suggests a process rather than a sudden break. He also casts doubt on the notion that Paz experienced a definitive rupture with the Left; he does so by stressing Paz's continued adherence until the end of his life to ideas or attitudes that were inimical to conservative or rightist thought. "Paz conservó siempre" (Paz never abandoned), he notes, "una retórica antiburguesa de origen romántico y existen múltiples aspectos de su pensamiento inasimilables al pensamiento de derecha" (an anti-bourgeois rhetoric of Romantic origins, and there are many aspects of his thought that cannot be reconciled with rightist ideology).[26] Domínguez Michael, too, underlines the drawn-out nature of Paz's debate with the Left. He clearly approves of Paz's gradual jettisoning of many of his leftist views, but he insists that the process—"[un] sinuoso proceso de desaprendizaje" (156; a sinuous process of unlearning)—was slow.[27] And like González Torres, he believes that Paz continued to hold on to certain leftist convictions until the end of his life (367). And yet Domínguez Michael also zeroes in on certain moments of rupture in Paz's career. Consider some of the statements he makes about Paz's ideological positions in the late 1970s and early 1980s. By 1977 or 1978, he claims, Paz "consideraba irrecuperable a la izquierda" (378; believed that the Left was beyond hope). In 1979, around the time of the publication of *El ogro*, "la ruptura política definitiva de Paz con la izquierda mexicana se estaba consumando sin remedio" (391; Paz's definitive political rupture with the Mexican Left was taking place without any possibility of turning back). Domínguez Michael picks up the notion of unlearning again and suggests that the process was complete by the time Paz wrote his first essay about *The Gulag Archipelago* in 1974 (404). Finally, he describes Paz's disagreement with the Left with regard to the Central American conflicts of the 1980s as "otro punto de no retorno" (429; another point of no return). In short, the emphasis on gradual change exists alongside the identification of moments of rupture in Paz's political outlook.

Now that we have explained how different critics evaluate the shifts in Paz's ideological outlook, and at what points in time they occurred, if at all, it will be helpful to examine specific episodes in Paz's career to see what adjustments might need to be made to the existing accounts of the evolution of the Mexican poet's political thought. A key moment according to several critics, as we have seen, took place in the 1970s when Paz read Solzhenitsyn's *The Gulag Archipelago*. Krauze argues that Paz's reading of Solzhenitsyn's monumental work was a watershed moment in his life. There is no doubt that Krauze is correct in suggesting that Paz's encounter with Solzhenitsyn's work had a profound impact on him. Nevertheless, his account simplifies a complicated story. Whereas Krauze presents Paz's reading of *The Gulag Archipelago* as the moment at which the Mexican poet reached a definitive understanding of the nature of the Soviet Union, in reality Paz's ideas about the Communist nation, and in particular about the Marxist-Leninist ideology on which it was founded, continued to evolve in the years after 1973. Indeed, there were differences in emphasis and perspective even between the two major essays Paz wrote in response to the publication of *The Gulag Archipelago*. It is important to note, furthermore, that even though Solzhenitsyn had a decisive impact on Paz's views of the Soviet Union and of Marxism-Leninism, there were profound differences in outlook between the two men, in particular concerning the questions of modernity, religion, and nationalism. A close look at the two essays in which Paz records his response to Solzhenitsyn's work, "Polvos de aquellos lodos," which appeared in the March 1974 issue of *Plural*, and "Gulag: Entre Isaías y Job," first published in *Plural* in December 1975, will allow us to pinpoint where Paz agreed with Solzhenitsyn and where he disagreed with him, and to identify the nuances and contradictions of an intellectual encounter that was undeniably of crucial importance to the Mexican poet's intellectual development.[28]

In his essays on Solzhenitsyn, Paz expresses his admiration for the Russian author, singling out the clarity and integrity of his vision and his passion for speaking the truth. The essence of Solzhenitsyn's achievement, according to Paz, is to have offered a *"testimonio*—en el antiguo sentido de la palabra: los mártires son testigos—del sistema represivo fundado en 1918 por los bolcheviques" (*El ogro*, 248; *testimony*—in the ancient sense of the word: the martyrs give *testimony*—of the repressive system founded in 1918 by the Bolsheviks). Paz notes that "el temple del escritor, la hondura de sus sentimientos y la rectitud y entereza de su carácter despiertan espontáneamente mi admiración" (247; the author's fortitude, the depth of his feelings, and the strength and integrity of his character provoke a spontaneous admiration in me). He views Solzhenitsyn as a daunting moral exemplar whose work stands as a powerful rebuke to the many twentieth-century writers and intellectuals who closed their eyes to the crimes committed in the name of Communism. At the end of his first essay on *The Gulag Archipelago*, Paz somberly notes that "muy pocos entre nosotros podrían ver frente a frente a un Solyentizin" (261; there are very few among us who could look a man like Solzhenitsyn in the eye). In short, Paz views his Russian colleague as a man of extraordinary moral and intellectual stature.

More than anything else, his reading of *The Gulag Archipelago* allows Paz to clarify and deepen his understanding of the nature of the Soviet system. Looking back at the David Rousset affair of a quarter of a century earlier, Paz is proud of the fact that he had not allowed the dominant faction in intellectual life of the period (which was not sympathetic to Rousset) to cloud his view of the topic. Upon reading Rousset's report, he had immediately understood the urgency of denouncing the existence of concentration camps in the Soviet Union, and with that aim in mind he had prepared a text about the camps for publication in the Argentine journal *Sur*. Yet at the same time he notes that he now believes that the explanation he gave in 1951 for the existence of the camps was wrong. At the time of the Rousset affair, he had been convinced that the camps served an economic purpose; by 1974, thanks to his reading of Solzhenitsyn, he has come to understand that the primary function of the camps was political and psychological.[29] They were, he writes, "una institución de *terror preventivo*" (243; an institution of *preventive terror*) designed to force the country's entire population to live "bajo la amenaza de internación" (244; under the threat of internment). The second error Paz believes he is now in a position to correct is the idea that "los campos de concentración soviéticos eran una tacha que desfiguraba al régimen ruso pero no constituían un rasgo inherente al sistema" (242; while the Soviet concentration camps were a stain that disfigured the Russian regime, they were not an inherent feature of the system). Surely the most significant aspect of the Mexican poet's response to Solzhenitsyn is his reconsideration of his earlier view that the camps were a *perversion* of Marxist ideology. He now speaks of the need for "una revisión de la herencia autoritaria del marxismo" (a reconsideration of the authoritarian heritage of Marxism), adding that this rethinking of the Marxist inheritance "debe ir más allá de Lenin e interrogar los orígenes hegelianos de Marx" (245; must go beyond Lenin in order to interrogate the Hegelian origins of Marxist thought). In short, it has become imperative to investigate the extent to which Marx himself was responsible for what was done in his name by his twentieth-century followers.

Yet it is precisely in relation to this issue that significant differences between Paz and Solzhenitsyn come to light. Although Paz acknowledges that "en el marxismo había tendencias autoritarias que venían de Hegel" (in Marxism there were authoritarian tendencies that derived from Hegel), he immediately adds that Marx "nunca habló de dictadura de un Partido" (252; never spoke of the dictatorship of a single party). This was, he claims, a new element introduced by Lenin. The essence of Leninism, according to Paz, is to be found in "la concepción de un partido de revolucionarios profesionales que encarna la marcha de la historia" (252; the notion of a party of professional revolutionaries that embodies the march of history). And it is this idea that started the process that ultimately led to Stalinism. That Paz wishes to distinguish Marx from Lenin becomes even clearer later in the same essay when he once again acknowledges the validity of the charge that there is an authoritarian strain in Marx's thinking, but immediately reminds the reader that "los gérmenes de libertad que se hallan en los escritos de Marx y Engels no son menos fecundos y poderosos que la dogmática herencia hegeliana" (259; the seeds of liberty in the writings of Marx and Engels are no less fertile and powerful than the dogmatic Hegelian inheritance). Indeed, the Mexican poet wishes to go even further in his defense of Marx, claiming that "el proyecto socialista es esencialmente un proyecto prometeico de liberación de los hombres y los pueblos" (259; the socialist project is essentially a Promethean project of human liberation). Toward the end of the essay, in a passage in which he explores the differences between Stalinism and Nazism, Paz ends up reviving the very idea of the lack of relationship between Stalinism and Marxism which he had earlier wished to refute. "El stalinismo" (Stalinism), he states firmly, "fue la perversión de la gran y hermosa tradición socialista" (260; was a perversion of the grand and beautiful socialist tradition). At this stage of Paz's thinking, there are clear traces of a pro-Marxist position. Indeed, he would not abandon his defense of the utopian strain in Marxist thought until several years later. Solzhenitsyn, on the other hand, never expresses the kind of defense of Marxism we see in Paz's essays of the 1970s.[30]

A second area of disagreement between the two men emerges when we compare their views of modernity. Paz explains that he feels an affinity with Solzhenitsyn because he sees him as a critic not just of Russia and of Bolshevism, "sino de la edad moderna misma" (248; but of the modern age itself). Solzhenitsyn was renowned not only for his attacks on Soviet Communism, but also for his searing critiques of the liberal democracies of the West. In "Polvo de aquellos lodos," Paz refers to the aversion Solzhenitsyn felt toward the West's "racionalismo y su democracia materialista de comerciantes sin alma" (247; rationalism and its materialistic democracy of soulless shopkeepers). The Mexican poet, too, had long harbored profound reservations about Western society. And yet by the 1970s, he had made the defense of the values of freedom and democracy the main theme of his political writings.[31] He had become a proponent of modernity, as well as its critic. This set him apart from his Russian colleague. Paz remarks that his admiration for Solzhenitsyn does not imply "adhesión a su filosofía" (247; adherence to his philosophy), and explains that the author of *The Gulag Archipelago* criticizes the modern world "desde supuestos distintos a los míos" (248; from assumptions that are different from mine). To understand how Paz differed from Solzhenitsyn, one might consider the Mexican poet's perspective on the Russian dissident movement: besides Solzhenitsyn, key figures in this movement were Roy Medvedev, who criticized the Soviet system from a Marxist-Leninist perspective, and Andrei Sakharov, who did so from a liberal, Westernizing standpoint. There can be little doubt that Paz was most sympathetic to the position occupied by Sakharov.[32] In sum, Paz's commitment to key elements in the liberal, Western tradition distanced him from Solzhenitsyn. In an odd way, Paz was both more Marxist and more liberal than Solzhenitsyn.

And yet there is a further element to the dialogue between Paz and Solzhenitsyn that needs to be taken into account, one that complicates our view of Paz as a staunch spokesman for democracy during the 1970s. As we have seen, Paz was more liberal in his outlook than Solzhenitsyn. At the same time, however, he was sympathetic to the Russian thinker's nationalist and anti-Western stance. Paz had always insisted on the need to acknowledge the role played by local culture and tradition in society and politics. But what if these forces *contradicted* the principles of liberty and democracy? This is precisely the puzzle that emerges when Paz and Solzhenitsyn join hands in their defense of the uniqueness of the cultural traditions of their respective nations. Paz notes that the Russian thinker would accept a nondemocratic regime in his country, as long as this regime matched "la imagen que se hizo el pensamiento tradicional del soberano cristiano, temeroso de Dios y amante de sus súbditos" (255; the traditional idea of the Christian sovereign, fearful of God and loving toward his subjects). Paz describes Solzhenitsyn's viewpoint as "una visión más bien realista y honda de la historia de su patria" (255; a profound and realistic vision of the history of his native land). And he urges his fellow Spanish Americans to make a similar effort at "sobriedad y realismo" (255; sobriety and realism) in confronting the world they live in. After all, the Hispanic and Russian traditions have one important feature in common: "ni ellos ni nosotros tenemos una tradición crítica porque ni ellos ni nosotros tuvimos realmente algo que se pueda comparar a la Ilustración y al movimiento intelectual del siglo XVIII en Europa" (254; neither they nor we possess a critical tradition because neither they nor we truly had something comparable to the Enlightenment and to the intellectual movement of eighteenth-century Europe). What to do about the missing Enlightenment was an enduring concern for Paz. At times, his solution was to turn himself into a one-man Enlightenment. In "Polvos de aquellos lodos," he sketches a different course, suggesting, somewhat surprisingly, a turn away from Enlightenment values.

Paz's reading of Solzhenitsyn leads him to call for "un pensamiento político propio" (255; a political thought of its own) for Spanish America. But the defense of a political thought that emerges out of Spanish America's specific circumstances does not necessarily imply support for a liberal democratic system. Indeed, Paz suggests that democracy as it is understood and practiced in the West may not be the best political system for Spanish America. Paz puts forward two reasons for his skepticism about democracy. In the first place, democracy has failed in its place of origin. Paz argues that "el fracaso de las instituciones democráticas, en sus dos versiones modernas: la anglo-sajona y la francesa, nos deberían impulsar a pensar por nuestra cuenta y sin los anteojos de la ideología de moda" (255; the failure of democratic institutions in their two modern versions: the Anglo-Saxon and the French, ought to push us to think for ourselves and to remove the blinders of fashionable ideologies). The second problem is that Western democratic institutions are not necessarily transportable to other parts of the world. Political institutions should, in Paz's view, match the conditions of the place where they are implemented, a principle that has not always been followed in Latin America. In sum, Paz appears here not as a defender, but as a critic of democracy.

Let us consider each of these arguments against democracy in more detail. The argument against Western democracy is surprising, given Paz's reputation as a staunch believer in liberal democracy. Nevertheless, there can be no question that in his first essay on Solzhenitsyn he takes a position *against* democracy, or at the very least against what we might call *actually existing* democracy. Paz argues that the greatest threat the West faces at this moment in time is the turn of bourgeois society toward "el totalitarismo burocrático" (265; bureaucratic totalitarianism). Indeed, he believes that both East and West are confronting the same process of bureaucratization (which Paz repeatedly associates with totalitarianism). The reason is that at bottom the nations of the Communist bloc and the democracies of the West are not that different from each other: both sides are part of the wider twentieth-century phenomenon of industrial society.[33] And it is industrial society that bears within itself the seeds of totalitarianism. For Paz, the bureaucratic state is the great evil of the contemporary world and he emphasizes that it is a phenomenon that exists on both sides of the post-war ideological divide. Looking to the West, he sees it reflected in "las grandes empresas transnacionales y otras instituciones que son parte de las democracias de Occidente, como la CIA norteamericana" (266; large multinational corporations and other institutions that are part of the democratic West, such as the CIA in the United States). If Paz rejects the Soviet Union, but also repudiates the capitalist democracies of the West, what alternative does he see? At this point, he limits himself to stressing the need to find other options: "si la libertad ha de sobrevivir al Estado burocrático, debe encontrar una alternativa distinta a la que hoy ofrecen las democracias capitalistas" (266; if freedom is to survive the bureaucratic state, it needs to find an alternative that is different from the one offered by the capitalist democracies). One thing, however, is clear: in condemning both parties to the Cold War in equal measure, Paz was adopting a position that was clearly at odds with his image as a pro-Western Cold Warrior.[34]

What about the second argument against democracy? Here the problem appears to be not that Western democracy has failed in Europe and the United States, but that its principles are inapplicable in Latin America. We know that the struggle between modernity and tradition in Mexico was one of Paz's most persistent preoccupations. Paz was a constant defender of the idea of tradition. But what if tradition embodied noxious values? Paz was clear-eyed about this possibility, and in "Polvos de aquellos lodos" he emphasizes that he is by no means an uncritical worshiper of the past. "No siento nostalgia alguna" (I do not feel any nostalgia), he asserts, "por el Tlatoani o por el Virrey, por la Culebra Hembra o por el Gran Inquisidor; tampoco por su Alteza Serenísima, por el Héroe de la Paz o por el Jefe Máximo de la Revolución" (255; for the Tlatoani or the Viceroy, for the Female Serpent or the Grand Inquisitor; nor for His Serene Highness, for the Hero of the Peace or for the Maximum Leader of the Revolution). In short, Paz does not care for his continent's authoritarian tradition. But at the same time he believes that Latin Americans should not deny or repress the past: "esos nombres grotescos o temibles designan unas realidades y esas realidades son más reales que nuestros códigos" (255; these grotesque or fearful names designate something real, and that reality is more real than our law books). Sounding more like José Martí in this passage than like, let's say, Enrique Krauze, Paz claims that native cultural and political traditions have a more powerful hold on us than ideas and institutions imported from other countries. At this point, we should recall that Paz began this excursus in his essay with the observation that Solzhenitsyn would support a nondemocratic regime in his native country, provided that this regime was somehow true to his country's traditions. Is Paz suggesting that he too might support a nondemocratic regime in Mexico? He does not state this outright. But he does not reject the idea either.

His reading of Solzhenitsyn prompts Paz to think about much more than just the nature of the Soviet Union. We have seen that Paz diverged from the Russian thinker on the question of Marxism, which the Mexican poet continued to regard in a somewhat favorable light. Paz's feelings about Solzhenitsyn's criticism of the Western democracies were mixed: although he sympathized with the Russian author's denunciations of the West's materialism and lack of spirituality, Paz's outlook was ultimately more liberal and secular. Paz and Solzhenistyn converged again on the topic of national identity, which they both regarded as crucial to understanding the world they lived in. But it is precisely around the question of nationalism that a new split emerges between the two thinkers. Toward the end of "Polvos de aquellos lodos," Paz taxes Solzhenitsyn with overlooking the most important feature of the current world situation: the rise of the Third World. Solzhenitsyn reads global politics exclusively in terms of the clash between East and West. What he does not see is that "el siglo de la disintegración y liquidación del sistema imperial europeo ha sido también el del renacimiento de viejos países asiáticos, como China, y el del nacimiento de jóvenes naciones en África y en otras partes del mundo" (267; the century of the disintegration and the liquidation of the European imperial system has also been the century of the rebirth of the old Asian nations, such as China, and the birth of young nations in Africa and other parts of the world). Paz believes that the Russian thinker's arrogance prevents him from acknowledging "los sufrimientos de los pueblos humillados y sometidos por Occidente" (267; the suffering of the nations that have been oppressed and humiliated by the West). And it leads Solzhenitsyn to misunderstand the Vietnam War, which he sees as the outgrowth of an imperial struggle, rather than as a war of national liberation, which is what it was according to Paz (268). In a sense, Solzhenitsyn's Russian nationalism blinded him to Third-World nationalism.[35]

In examining Paz's intellectual trajectory in the years after his 1971 return to Mexico, his enemies on the Left have focused on the fervor and persistence with which Paz denounced the Soviet Union and its ideological allies. Seeing an anti-communist warrior, they branded him a reactionary.[36] Paz's supporters, in the meantime, emphasize the passion he brought to the defense of democracy. They see a man who helped pave the way for the renewal of the spirit of democracy in Mexico in the 1980s and 1990s. Both sides to the debate have tended to simplify a complicated story, in which we see Paz responding in nuanced ways to a variety of ideological crosscurrents. My view is that Paz remained much further to the Left in his political opinions of the mid-1970s than either his antagonists or his defenders acknowledge. His criticism of some elements of Marxist ideology did not prevent him from praising other elements. His denunciation of the Soviet Union did not place him squarely in the "free world" camp; indeed, he remained a strong critic of US imperialism and of what he saw as the spiritual flaws of Western liberal democracies. Finally, his criticism of the authoritarian tradition in Latin American politics did not turn him into a skeptic of Third World revolutions in general. On the contrary, he remained a strong supporter of the struggle for national liberation in colonized nations, even if this struggle was led by Communists, as in the case of Vietnam.

In the 1980s, the Salvadoran Civil War and the Sandinista Revolution in Nicaragua dragged Central America into what turned out to be one of the final episodes of the Cold War. The sudden interest of the superpowers (especially the United States) in Central America led the world to train its spotlight on the region for a few brief years. Given Paz's highly critical views of how Communist regimes had evolved in different parts of the world over the course of the twentieth century, it is not surprising that he entered the war of ideas surrounding events in Central America in this period. Indeed, Paz joined forces with other members of the *Vuelta* group to denounce what he saw as the anti-democratic orientation of the leftist forces in the Central American struggles.[37] Paz's criticisms of the Sandinista regime were not received kindly on the Left.

THE LEFT 169

Antagonism to Paz from the Mexican Left had been mounting for a long time, and it reached a kind of climax in October 1984 in the wake of a speech Paz delivered in Frankfurt, Germany, where he had gone to receive a literary prize. Paz's comments about the Sandinistas provoked leftist demonstrators to march on the US embassy in Mexico City chanting "Reagan rapaz, tu amigo es Octavio Paz" (Rapacious Reagan, Octavio Paz is your friend). The demonstrators also burned an effigy of Paz, in a symbolic attack on the man the Left seemed to view as its greatest enemy.[38] Was this the moment, then, at which Paz definitively became a man of the Right?

In actual fact, Paz's ostensible rupture with the Left at this point in time took place mostly in the minds of the leftists themselves. The Left had boxed itself into an inordinately schematic view of the debate on Central America, in particular the intellectual battle over the Sandinista regime. Leftist commentators saw only two possible positions: either you supported the Sandinistas or you did not; if you did not, it was automatically assumed that you were siding with Reagan's Nicaragua policies. From this perspective, to be a critic of the Sandinistas *and* a critic of US interventionism in Latin America was simply not an option. But it was precisely a black-and-white, Manichaean approach of this kind that Paz resisted. A review of his publications on the Central American crises of the 1980s, and of discussions of the topic of other authors published by Paz in *Vuelta*, reveals that the defense of democracy for all Central American countries was consistently combined with criticism of the role played by the United States in the region.[39]

One story that was tracked in *Vuelta* over the course of several years was the conflict that pitted the Sandinista government against *La Prensa*, an opposition newspaper. In November 1981, *Vuelta* reprinted an editorial from *La Prensa* by its two editors-in-chief Pablo Antonio Cuadra (also known as a poet) and Pedro J. Chamorro Barrios, in which they attacked the restrictions placed on their newspaper by the Sandinista government.[40] As the Nicaraguan crisis worsened over the next few years, *Vuelta* continued to monitor *La Prensa*'s embattled situation. In January 1983, Paz's journal published an editorial Cuadra wrote for *La Prensa*, which the Sandinista government had censored.⁴¹ In August 1985, Cuadra contributed a long essay in which he chronicled Sandinista censorship of the press. When in 1986 the Nicaraguan government decided to close down *La Prensa*, *Vuelta* published first an unsigned editorial,⁴² and subsequently an article by Gilles Bataillon,⁴³ both of which argued that the Sandinista regime's actions had severely undermined its own legitimacy. The constant attention to the suppression of press freedom had the effect of framing the Nicaraguan conflict as a struggle of the forces of democracy against a repressive single-party state. But the unrelenting criticism of a revolutionary Latin American regime, a regime, moreover, that had incurred the wrath of the Reagan administration, led leftists to the conclusion that Paz and his collaborators at *Vuelta* had become rightists and supporters of US imperialism.

In actual fact, Paz and others writing for *Vuelta* repeatedly distanced themselves from the Reagan administration's policies in Central America and frequently drew attention to the sorry history of relations between the United States and Latin America. It is worth noting that *Vuelta* first registered the turmoil in Nicaragua in a March 1978 article by Donald Castillo, in which the author emphasizes the broad nature of the Nicaraguan opposition to the dictator Anastasio Somoza, but also offers a chronicle of the numerous acts of aggression perpetrated by the United States against Nicaragua in both the nineteenth and twentieth centuries. On the occasions when Paz himself addressed the situation in Nicaragua, he consistently criticized the role played by the United States in the region. In an essay titled "América Latina y la democracia," first published in *Vuelta* in June 1982 and subsequently included in *Tiempo nublado*, Paz states that "los Estados Unidos han sido uno de los mayores obstáculos con que hemos tropezado en nuestro empeño por modernizarnos" (the United States has been one of the principal obstacles we have encountered in our efforts to modernize ourselves), and notes furthermore that "los Estados Unidos han sido, en América Latina, los protectores de los tiranos y los aliados de los enemigos de la democracia" (in Latin America, the United States has been the protector of tyrants and the ally of the enemies of democracy).⁴⁴ In the same essay, Paz observes that the Nicaraguan Revolution appears to be headed down the same path as earlier revolutions that ended in "la petrificación totalitaria" (totalitarian petrification).[45] Yet in view of the disastrous history of US interventions in the region, it is clear that for Paz any attempt on the part of the United States to meddle in Nicaragua must be opposed. In the published version of his Frankfurt speech, which appeared in *Vuelta* in November 1984, Paz again offered harsh criticism of the US role in Latin America: "Los Estados Unidos no inventaron ni la fragmentación ni las oligarquías ni los dictadores bufos y sanguinarios pero se aprovecharon de esta situación, fortificaron a las tiranías y contribuyeron decisivamente a la corrupción de la vida política centroamericana" (The United States did not invent the fragmentation of our countries, nor the oligarchies, nor the clownish and bloodthirsty dictators, but they took advantage of this situation, they bolstered the tyrannies, and contributed decisively to the corruption of political life in Central America).[46] In yet another contribution to the Central America debate of the 1980s, an essay titled "Contrarronda: México, Estados Unidos, América Central, et cetera," published in *Vuelta* in October 1987, Paz once again explained that support for democracy in the region did not translate into support for the United States: "En México la defensa de la democracia es la defensa de la herencia de Hidalgo, Morelos, Juárez y Madero. Así, no debe confundirse con la defensa del imperialismo norteamericano ni con la de los regímenes conservadores militares de América Latina" (In Mexico, the defense of democracy is the defense of the heritage of Hidalgo, Morelos, Juárez, and Madero. It must not be confused, therefore, with the defense of North American imperialism, nor with that of Latin America's conservative military regimes).[47] Paz's antagonists on the Left simply ignored statements of this kind, or brushed them aside as insincere or irrelevant. My view is that Paz's statements about the Central American crisis have to be taken at face value: he opposed the support given by the Left to an undemocratic regime, but what the Left did not want to acknowledge was that Paz shared its hostility toward American foreign policy in the region.[48] The Mexican poet was not an enemy of the Left per se; he was merely a critic of the authoritarian and anti-democratic Left. He continued to identify with a moderate, social democratic Left.[49] And contrary to what the demonstrators outside the US embassy in October 1984 chanted, Paz was not Reagan's friend.

Given the force and persistence with which he had denounced Marxist-Leninist regimes, it is not surprising that Paz was pleased when the Berlin Wall fell in November 1989 and a wave of peaceful revolutions toppled Eastern Europe's Communist governments. With the aim of reflecting on the new situation in the world (and no doubt gloating a bit over the defeat of his ideological enemies), Paz organized an international colloquium in Mexico City in late August and early September 1990 titled *La experiencia de la libertad* (The experience of liberty). Prominent intellectuals from around the world attended, including Daniel Bell, Irving Howe, and Leon Wieseltier from the United States; Cornelius Castoriadis and Jean-François Revel from France; Peter Sloterdijk from West Germany; Michael Ignatieff from Canada; Lucio Colletti from Italy; Hugh Thomas and Hugh Trevor-Roper from Great Britain; Jorge Semprún from Spain; José Guilherme Merquior from Brazil; Jorge Edwards from Chile; Mario Vargas Llosa from Peru; Carlos Franqui from Cuba; Juan Nuño from Venezuela; Adam Michnik, Czeslaw Milosz, Leszek Kolakowski, and Bronislaw Geremek from Poland; Valtr Komárek from Czechoslovakia; János Kornai, Agnes Heller, and Ferenc Fehér from Hungary; Norman Manea from Rumania; Vitaly Korotich, Nikolai Shmelev, and Tatyana Tolstaya from what was still the Soviet Union; and Rolando Cordera, Arnaldo Córdova, Adolfo Sánchez Vázquez, Carlos Monsiváis, Héctor Aguilar Camín, Luis Villoro, and Carlos Castillo Peraza from Mexico. Paz and Krauze moderated the majority of the sessions. The participants represented a wide variety of viewpoints, and debated each other vigorously throughout the colloquium. Nevertheless, across a wide swath of the Mexican press responses to the event were extremely negative, with leftist commentators using terms such as "right-wing," "reactionary," "capitalist propaganda," and even "fascistic" to describe the orientation of the meeting.[50] Was there any justification for such characterizations?

There is no question that someone with Marxist-Leninist sympathies would have felt uncomfortable listening to many of the participants in Paz's colloquium. Jorge Semprún, himself a former Communist, declared that the failure of Communism was "el acontecimiento más importante del siglo" (the most important event of the century).[51] The British historian Hugh Trevor-Roper dismissed Marxist ideology as "una construcción artificial que carece de toda validez" (an artificial construction that is completely lacking in validity).[52] Paz, for his part, noted that virtually everyone at the colloquium was in agreement that Marxism had lost its relevance to the contemporary world and was now simply part of the *history* of philosophy. A handful of the Mexican participants insisted that the failure of "actually existing" socialism in Eastern Europe ought not to be interpreted as a sign of the failure of Marxist ideology per se. The philosopher Adolfo Sánchez Vázquez reminded the audience of what he called "el carácter emancipatorio del pensamiento de Marx" (the emancipatory nature of Marx's thought),[53] while the historian and political scientist Arnaldo Córdova argued that the Eastern European regimes were not in fact socialist, and that their collapse had no implications for an understanding of socialism as a political project.[54] This was not, however, a majority point of view. The Hungarian economist János Kornai affirmed that "hasta cierto punto las ideas de Marx son responsables del sistema, tal como éste evolucionó en el régimen comunista" (up to a certain point, Marx's ideas are responsible for the system as it evolved under Communist regimes),[55] while Paz himself also took up the old question of the roots of Communism's failure and insisted, on this occasion, that they could be traced back to Marx and Hegel.[56] The Greek-French thinker (and former Trotskyist) Cornelius Castoriadis blamed the degeneration of the Russian Revolution on, among other things, "la concepción marxista de la historia" (the Marxist conception of history).[57] In sum, anti-Marxist viewpoints received ample expression at the *La experiencia de la libertad* colloquium.

Alongside the attacks on Marxist ideology and the historical record of "actually existing" socialism, there was frequent praise at the colloquium for the free-market economic system. Semprún stated the issue as follows: "pensando en aquello que Sartre decía: que el marxismo era el horizonte irrebasable de nuestro tiempo, yo digo un poco en broma que la economía de mercado es el horizonte irrebasable de nuestro tiempo" (thinking of what Sartre said: that Marxism was the unsurpassable horizon of our era, I claim, a little jokingly, that the free-market economy is the unsurpassable horizon of our era).[58] Mario Vargas Llosa, too, spoke with conviction about the benefits of capitalism: "El sistema capitalista, representado por las democracias occidentales, es hoy en día el que ha llevado más lejos la cultura de la libertad y de la justicia social en el mundo" (The capitalist system, in the form of the Western democracies, is nowadays the system that has done the most to advance the culture of liberty and of social justice in the world).[59] The speakers from the Soviet Union and Eastern Europe also expressed their firm belief that a free-market economy would bring great benefits to their countries. Still, it is impossible not to note the strong reservations about capitalism voiced by many colloquium participants. Irving Howe stated that "en mi ciudad, Nueva York, el triunfo del capitalismo coincide con la descomposición parcial de la civilización" (in my city, New York, the triumph of capitalism coincides with the partial breakdown of society).[60] The Mexican historian and novelist Héctor Aguilar Camín questioned whether countries with weaker economies were in fact in a position to "elegir con total libertad su integración a este nuevo mundo y a esta nueva economía global" (decide, in a completely free way, how to become integrated into this new world and this new global economy).[61] Paz noted that the principle of the free market did not work in certain areas, such as that of culture. He also addressed some of the dangers that flowed from the triumph of capitalism, such as the loss of spirituality and the celebration of mindless consumerism.[62] The most scathing attacks on the capitalist system came from Castoriadis, who, like Paz, seemed deeply concerned about the spread of consumerist values and the decay of culture. What was Western democratic capitalism all about, according to Castoriadis? "Yo digo" (I say), he announced with noticeable alarm, "que el contenido concreto de esta sociedad es: consumismo y Madonna" (that the specific content of this society is: consumerism and Madonna).[63]

No one at the colloquium came to the defense of Madonna or consumerism. Still, several participants expressed their surprise at the battering handed out to free-market capitalism. As former Communist Lucio Colletti observed somewhat sarcastically, "hemos presenciado el derrumbe de la economía nacionalizada o estatizada, del monopolio político de la economía. A todo esto nosotros respondemos con una crítica a la economía de mercado" (we have witnessed the collapse of state-controlled or nationalized economies, of the political monopoly over the economy. To all of this we respond with a critique of the free-market economy).[64] The French philosopher and journalist Jean-François Revel also seemed irritated by the anti-capitalist tendencies of many of the speakers. He offered the following assessment of the flow of the discussion at the colloquium: "gran parte del día de ayer más bien oímos un enjuiciamiento de la economía de mercado, del capitalismo, del liberalismo y de la democracia política, según los esquemas del marxismo más clásico" (for much of the day yesterday we heard judgments being passed on the free-market economy, on capitalism, on liberalism and political democracy, from the most classical of Marxist perspectives). Revel was much less forgiving than many of his colleagues in judging the fate of socialism: "La mitificación del socialismo duró mucho tiempo; se pretendía que sus quiebras crónicas no probaban que el socialismo no pudiese funcionar. ¡Era la única creación de la mente humana que reclamaba semejante privilegio!" (The mythification of socialism lasted a long time; it was assumed that its chronic failures did not mean that socialism was unworkable. It was the only creation of the human mind that claimed this kind of privilege!)[65] He had a point, of course, but in this debate much depended on how one defined "socialism."

According to Vargas Llosa, "hay países que de socialistas sólo tienen el nombre, como España y Francia" (there are countries that are socialist in name only). He explained that these countries have governments "que se llaman socialistas, pero que no son socialistas, dado que no cumplen con la premisa básica del socialismo: el control total de la economía por el Estado" (that call themselves socialist, but that are not in fact socialist, given that they do not comply with the basic premise of socialism: complete control of the economy by the state).[66] The Peruvian novelist also praised Margaret Thatcher for having triumphed over "una tradición socialista-democrática que había hecho crecer cada vez más el intervencionismo estatal y, de esta manera, había desmovilizado a la sociedad" (a democratic socialist tradition that had allowed state intervention to increase more and more, and had resulted in the demobilization of society).[67] But neither Vargas Llosa's very narrow definition of socialism nor his starkly pro-capitalist and anti-socialist perspective were shared by many of the participants. It was far more common at the meeting to view capitalism and socialism as poles on a sliding scale, with increased intervention of the state in the economy inclining a society toward the socialist pole. Several participants identified themselves explicitly as socialists, but no one (apart from Vargas Llosa) seemed to think that being a socialist meant being an advocate for *total* control of the economy by the state. Irving Howe offered a sketch of what he called "una sociedad democrática socialista" (a democratic socialist society) that involved fiscal measures to reduce inequality, a strong safety net, government investment in health and education, democratization of the workplace, and so on. He called not for a rejection of the free market, but for a combination of capitalist and socialist principles leading to something he called "socialismo de mercado" (market socialism).[68] Other participants, most notably Bell and Castoriadis, expressed a concern with creating more humane and egalitarian societies. On several occasions, Swedish social democracy was upheld as a model of the desirable society.

In the ongoing debate on the relationship between the state and the market, Paz tended to adopt a moderate, middle-of-the-road position. "Creo no equivocarme" (I do not think I am mistaken), he stated, "si digo que la mayoría de nosotros está a igual distancia del Estado-patrón y del *laissez-faire* absoluto" (if I say that the majority of us are equally distant from the owner state as we are from complete *laissez-faire*).[69] Pursuing the same line of thought, the Mexican poet observed that "así como el Estado debe tener límites, también la propiedad privada debe tenerlos; en muchos casos, por razones de utilidad social" (there should be limits on the state, as there should be on private property; in many cases, for reasons of social utility).[70] On other occasions, as has already been noted, Paz launched into fierce denunciations of the spiritual crisis of Western civilization, a crisis he attributed to the very capitalist system he hoped would remedy some of Mexico's ills. In short, a variety of viewpoints were advanced by the participants in the colloquium, and even by the organizer of the colloquium himself.[71]

The colloquium's critics, however, saw things differently. The Mexican economist Rolando Cordera complained about what he regarded as the overall drift of the discussion: "se rechaza *in toto* la intervención del Estado, se propone como panacea al mercado, se habla de mercado libre sin calificarlo" (state intervention is completely rejected, the market is put forward as a panacea, people talk about the free market without any qualification).[72] Feeling that he had not been given enough time to develop his ideas during the colloquium session in which he had been invited to participate, Arnaldo Córdova took to the pages of the Mexico City daily *Uno más uno* to criticize what he described as "los excesos retóricos de todos los participantes en su defensa del mercado y, por consecuencia, del capitalismo totalmente liberado de la tutela y la intervención del Estado" (the rhetorical excesses of all the participants in their defense of the market and, consequently, of a capitalism completely freed of any kind of state intervention).[73] One can only imagine how long-time leftists such as Howe and Castoriadis, or even classical liberals like Merquior and Vargas Llosa, might have reacted to being portrayed as proponents of an unfettered capitalism and of the complete demolition of the state.[74]

What did it mean to be on the Left in 1990? In the wake of the uproar caused among leftist intellectuals in Mexico by the colloquium *La experiencia de la libertad*, Paz took to the pages of *Vuelta* to address this question. "Las palabras cambian sin cesar de significado" (Words are constantly changing their meanings), he observed. What had once been considered characteristics of the Left, such as critical thinking or an opposition to "la moral tribal" (tribal thinking), were now labeled rightist by people who identified as leftist. Paz's recommendation was to ignore categories such as Left and Right, and to focus instead on "las actitudes, las ideas y las opiniones" (attitudes, ideas, and opinions).[75] Paz's frustration was perhaps understandable, and the idea that certain political labels were losing their usefulness was widespread at the time.[76] Nevertheless, an attempt to locate Paz on the political spectrum may be helpful, provided, of course, that one avoids simplification.

Paz was opposed to authoritarianism, and he was a critic of repressive regimes of all types. He persistently criticized the Left (especially the Latin American Left) for its weak record on the defense of freedom and democracy, and for refusing to acknowledge the economic failure of Communist societies. Paz was a proponent of Mexico's modernization, and he believed that a liberal democratic form of government, combined with a more free-market approach to the economy, were the best way for his country to achieve progress. At the same time, he was a sharp critic of the capitalist system, which he saw as spiritually impoverished and harmful to a society's cultural development. If one looks at the vast and varied network of intellectuals he associated with at this point of his career, one sees classical liberals, left liberals, social democrats, numerous former Marxists, and thinkers of various other stripes. Among the guests at *La experiencia de la libertad*, there were not many genuine conservatives or rightists. Carlos Castillo Peraza was the only Mexican thinker associated with conservatism who participated in Paz's colloquium. It is also important to note that throughout the colloquium Paz expressed an internationalist, cosmopolitan, and multiculturalist outlook, even while recognizing the importance of tradition and national identity in shaping societies. In short, Paz's political views had a complex, layered quality to them. They continued to include leftist ingredients, even as he was being reviled by most of his leftist colleagues in the Mexican intellectual world.

CHAPTER 8
Conservatism

Paz was often labeled a conservative, or even a reactionary, but there has been little in-depth exploration of what exactly this might mean.[1] In some respects, it is clear that the label does not fit Paz. Here we have an author who was close to the Communist party at the beginning of his career and continued to laud certain aspects of Marxist thought well into the 1970s. He displayed an affinity for the counter-culture in the 1960s, expressed support for social democratic politicians in the 1980s, and regularly denounced capitalism in the 1990s, even after he had thrown his weight behind the free-market reforms promoted by the Salinas government in Mexico. Furthermore, he never ceased celebrating the Mexican Revolution, or at least certain strands within the Revolution. If this combination of positions represents conservatism, surely the vast majority of conservatives would not support it. It is important to note, moreover, that the view of Paz as a conservative thinker did not emerge toward the end of his career; on the contrary, it was widely held in the 1970s, when Paz was regularly citing Marx in his writings.[2]

Commentators who call Paz a conservative do not use the label in a neutral sense. In almost every single instance, to describe the Mexican poet as a conservative thinker is a way of denouncing him. One ought not to be surprised by this, since for almost the entire span of Paz's career, the Left dominated the Mexican intellectual world. One consequence of this tilt to the Left is that scholarly attention to conservative ideology has been scant, and mostly hostile. Indeed, it is not unusual for commentators to regard the conservative tradition in Mexican thought as an unpatriotic and anti-Mexican intellectual and political tendency, and to view it, as a result, as essentially illegitimate.[3] This, in spite of the fact that prominent conservative thinkers of the nineteenth century, such as Lucas Alamán, and of the twentieth, such as José Vasconcelos, were strongly anti-American and viewed themselves as true patriots. Another common way of disparaging conservative ideology is to depict it as lacking in ideas, or to charge it with using ideas in order to mask self-interested goals.[4] Indeed, there was a period in Paz's career when he himself regularly criticized conservatism in exactly these terms. Paz's essays from the 1970s, collected in *El ogro filantrópico*, are littered with disdainful observations about conservative political positions, including charges that conservatives have nothing to contribute to the Mexican political debate, that they have no ideas, that they are only interested in making money, and that they have no vision for the nation.[5] In short, even as critics on the Left were branding Paz a conservative, Paz was echoing the Left's denigration of conservatism.[6]

Clearly, a degree of misunderstanding played a role in Paz's falling out with the Left. This does not mean, however, that there were no real differences between Paz and large sectors of the Left, since there clearly were. A good example would be the debate surrounding the true nature of the Soviet Union. Whereas Paz was relentlessly critical of the repressive features of the Soviet system, many leftist intellectuals in Mexico continued to voice support for the Soviet Union until the very end. It also does not mean that there was no overlap at all between Paz's ideas and the conservative tradition in Mexican intellectual thought. Paz was a complex thinker with varied interests and broad sympathies. The protean quality of Paz's thought helps explain why he occasionally gravitated toward conservative ideas. In this chapter, I will explore Paz's affinity for conservatism from two different angles. First, I will look at his writings on the colonial period in Mexican history. Throughout his career, Paz penned extended meditations on the different periods in Mexican history; in doing so, he offered remarkably sympathetic portrayals of the society of New Spain, a period usually celebrated by conservatives and disparaged by liberals and leftists. Next, I will examine Paz's rapprochement in the 1980s and 1990s with the PAN, Mexico's conservative party, long dismissed by Paz, but viewed in a more favorable light by the Mexican poet in the final decade and a half of this life.[7]

In Mexico, as elsewhere, ideology and historiography have always been closely intertwined. Different factions in the nation's political struggles have sought to impose not only a social, political, and economic vision for the country, but also an interpretation of Mexico's past.[8] Given Mexico's racial heterogeneity, and the profound upheavals the country has experienced in the course of its history, it is not surprising that the various versions that have been put forward of Mexico's past are strikingly divergent. Questions surrounding the place of the country's indigenous heritage in the construction of Mexican nationhood, or how to evaluate the Spanish Conquest and the colonial era that ensued, have been answered in sharply contrasting ways. Important currents within Mexican historiography have sought to integrate the various components of the nation's heritage—whether conceived of in terms of racial groups or historical periods—into a cohesive narrative. Yet the opposite tendency, that is, the portrayal of particular elements within the country's past as inimical to the definition of its nationhood, has remained remarkably resilient throughout Mexican history, resulting in deeply contentious debates about national identity.

During the fight for independence in the early nineteenth century, and in the early years of Mexico's life as an independent nation, it was not uncommon for writers and historians to depict the break with Spain as a return to the nation's roots in the pre-Columbian era, with the corollary that the colonial period was viewed as an aberration, that is, as a part of the nation's past that had to be rejected in its entirety.[9] Conservative historians such as Lucas Alamán reacted forcefully against the indigenist reading of Mexican history, arguing that only the Hispanic, colonial inheritance could provide a solid foundation for Mexican nationhood.[10] The dispute between indigenist and Hispanist readings of the nation's past was repeated in the decades after the Mexican Revolution of

1910.[11] There were, of course, other readings in addition to these two influential interpretations, both of which emphasized the ruptures between different stages of Mexican history. Attempts to draw out the continuity between different periods, or to identify bridges between different ethnic groups, resulted in readings of Mexico as an essentially *mestizo* nation.[12] But the emphasis on rupture and conflict remained strong.

Paz was himself a deeply knowledgeable student of Mexican historiography, and with the way in which the different interpretations of the Mexican past advanced divergent views of Mexican national identity. In the opening pages of his book on Sor Juana, a book that begins with a lengthy reconstruction of the world in which Sor Juana lived and worked, Paz offers a succinct overview of two widely discussed interpretations of Mexican history. In the first—the indigenist—the pre-Columbian era is viewed as the foundation of the Mexican nation. The colonial period is seen as a period of darkness; with Independence, Mexico recovers its true self. This reading assumes that there were profound rifts between the three stages of the nation's history. The second interpretation offers a more gradualist view of Mexico's past. It relies on agricultural and biological metaphors, and depicts Mexico as a nation that grows over time, with the different stages of the past representing the phases in the nation's process of maturation.[13]

It is worth noting that Paz does not mention a third influential interpretation of Mexican history. I am referring to the conservative view, according to which the foundations for Mexican nationhood were laid after the Conquest, during the colonial period, a view that implies that the pre-Columbian era was irrelevant and had nothing of value to offer in the construction of a new nation. Paz himself placed a very high value on Mexico's indigenous roots. In this regard, his position was very distant from that of Mexico's conservative thinkers. "Los indios son el hueso de México, su realidad primera y última" (The Indians are the essence of Mexico, the nation's first and final reality), Paz once wrote.[14] His emphasis on *Zapatismo* as the most authentic and fruitful strain within the Mexican Revolution also reveals Paz's indigenist side, since Zapata was celebrated for his fidelity to Mexico's indigenous traditions. Yet Paz's indigenism did not result in a rejection of the colonial period in Mexican history. On the contrary, over the course of his career Paz authored many eloquent pages on the subject of colonial culture and society, revealing on occasion a perhaps surprising convergence with the conservative perspective on Mexican culture and identity.[15]

Paz's most sustained meditation on colonial Mexico appears in *El laberinto de la soledad*. But prior to writing *El laberinto*, Paz had already offered some reflections on New Spain in an early essay entitled "Americanidad de España," and he would return to the topic later in his career, most notably in several essays included in *El ogro filantrópico* and in his book on Sor Juana. All of Paz's writings on the colonial period in Mexican history are marked by a nonpolemical stance; he criticizes colonial society, yet at the same time he recognizes elements in it that are of great value and that are, moreover, fundamental to an understanding of Mexican nationhood. Such an approach is already in evidence in "Americanidad de España," a brief essay Paz wrote in 1938, not long after his return from Spain. Paz acknowledges what he calls "la realidad atroz de la vida colonial" (the atrocious nature of life in the colonial period) and its responsibility for the existence of a "fuerte corriente antiespañola" (strong anti-Spanish currents) in Mexican culture (153).[16] But his aim is to counter this current and he does so in two ways. In the first place, he points out that the Spanish themselves suffered under the same regime of "crueldad, injusticia, rapacidad y usura" (153; cruelty, injustice, rapacity, and usury) as the one that held sway in New Spain. Thanks to the Spanish Civil War, it has now become clear, Paz suggests, that there are in effect "two Spains," and that Mexico should feel solidarity with the Spain that is battling Francoism, which he sees as the ideological heir to the colonial regime. Secondly, Paz argues that Spain brought things of a positive nature to the New World and that the colonial enterprise cannot be reduced to "[el] régimen económico de encomenderos, clero y Corona" (153; the economic regime of *encomenderos*, clergy, and the Crown). And what is the inheritance from the colonial period that modern-day Mexico should continue to cherish and fight for? Here is how Paz explains it: "Desde el siglo XVI, al otro día del desembarco y de la fundación de municipios, nacieron en México dos cosas: la Nación y la Democracia" (154; In the sixteenth century, soon after the Spanish disembarked in the New World and began founding towns, two things were born in Mexico: the Nation and Democracy). In short, the two key ideals of the present moment in Mexico were implanted there during the colonial period. "La obra de España en América todavía no termina" (154; The work of Spain in America is not yet finished), says Paz. The anti-Spanish stance that characterizes the major political currents in Mexico is rooted in a misunderstanding.[17]

Paz produced a fuller and more complex account of the colonial period in chapter 5 of *El laberinto*, "De la conquista a la colonia" ("From the Conquest to the Colony"). In this text, Paz approaches the society and culture of New Spain from two opposite points of view. He begins by offering a strikingly favorable assessment of the colonial era, and then switches to a more negative perspective. What are the elements of the colonial period that Paz finds attractive? First, he lauds the sheer solidity of the social structure implanted by the Spanish state in the New World: "la solidez del edificio social que construye" (110; the solidity of the social edifice it built). It is, Paz adds, "un orden hecho para durar" (110; an order designed to last). But besides the durability of the colonial order—and surely connected to it—is the fact that, for Paz, the social structure of this period offers a picture of coherence, harmony, and interconnectedness. All of the different components of colonial society are tied together in an integrated whole, without conflict between them. It is, according to Paz, "una sociedad regida conforme a principios jurídicos, económicos y religiosos plenamente coherentes entre sí que establecían una relación viva y armónica entre las partes y el todo" (110–11; a society governed according to juridical, economic, and religious principles that were coherently linked together and that established a vibrant and harmonious relationship between the parts and the whole). It is worth recalling that in his critique of the *Porfiriato*, which Paz develops in the next chapter of *El laberinto*, he zeroes in on the *lack of harmony* between the different components of Mexican society during the late nineteenth century. Paz stresses, among other things, the profound gap separating the ideologies—imported from abroad—informing the actions of the Mexican elites under the *Porfiriato* and the country's social realities. The result is that disjunction and incongruity characterize Mexican society of the period. In this regard, it is clear that for Paz the tradition-bound society of the colonial period offers a far more appealing model to contemplate than the modernizing one of the late nineteenth century.

In his attempt to define Mexico's colonial period, Paz regularly resorts to biological imagery. We have already seen that he speaks of a vibrant relationship among the different components making up Mexican society, suggesting that a society can be regarded as a living organism. What makes this type of relationship possible is, according to Paz, Catholicism, which he describes as "el centro de la sociedad colonial" (111; the heart of colonial society). Paz explains that Catholicism's orientation toward the afterlife infuses society with a "fe viva" (living faith) which, in turn, sustains, "como la raíz al árbol" (like the root of a tree), other cultural and economic forms (111). In short, Catholicism provides colonial society with a sense of wholeness and coherence, making it resemble a form of life. "Gracias a la religión" (Thanks to religion), says Paz, "el orden colonial no es una mera superposición de nuevas formas históricas, sino un organismo viviente" (111; the colonial order is not a mere overlay of new historical structures, but rather a living organism). Note, once again, the implied contrast with other periods in Mexican history, such as the *Porfiriato*, which Paz will condemn for its inauthenticity and lack of organic wholeness. In comparison, the colonial period is looked upon much more favorably by the author of *El laberinto*. Note, as well, the echo in this passage of the conservative conception of society as an entity that grows slowly over time, in a manner that is understood to be natural. Parallel to this idea of society as an organic whole, conservatives typically reject the attempt to modify society in accordance with abstract blueprints.[18] In his reflections on New Spain, Paz appears to subscribe to the conservative view of how a society works.

In his discussion of New Spain, Paz devotes much attention to the place of the indigenous population in colonial society. He insists that it is not his intention to cover up the mistreatment of the native peoples of the Americas at the hands of the Spanish colonizers. Nevertheless, Paz argues that the Catholic Church offered a kind of home to the colony's indigenous population. Somewhat surprisingly, he describes the Church as an open order. What he means by this is that Catholicism is "un orden universal, abierto a todos los pobladores" (111; a universal order, open to the entire population). Insofar as the Catholic Church is open to everyone, it is an inclusive rather than an exclusive institution. Paz notes that baptism in the Church allows the Indians to find "un lugar en el mundo" (a place in the world) and to belong to "un orden vivo" (112; a living order). In short, standing at the heart of the Mexican poet's account of the colonial period is the notion of *participation*. The indigenous peoples witnessed the destruction of their civilization at the hands of the Spanish invaders. The Catholic Church, however, made it possible for them to renew their ties to the world, and to feel part of a larger whole. In this regard, Spanish colonization in the New World compares favorably with that of the British. Paz notes that the sense of belonging felt by the indigenous population in New Spain "fue despiadadamente negada a los nativos por los protestantes de Nueva Inglaterra" (112; was ruthlessly denied to the native inhabitants by the Protestants of New England).[19] It is worth highlighting the fact that Paz's defense of colonial society is carried out in the name of the segment of the population that was relegated to the lowest rung of the social order.[20]

After developing an eloquent defense of the colonial order, Paz shifts his perspective. In the closing section of "De la conquista a la colonia," the author of *El laberinto* highlights not the strengths, but the weaknesses of the society of New Spain. Yes, Catholicism offered a refuge to a native population that had been dispossessed of its beliefs and traditions; the problem, however, was that the Catholic Church was too rigid, requiring a passive rather than an active engagement on the part of its followers. In Paz's words, it reduced "la participación de los fieles a la más elemental y pasiva de las actitudes religiosas" (116; the participation of the faithful to the most elemental and passive of religious attitudes). It did not demand "una participación creadora" (116; a creative participation). As a result, the Catholicism of Mexico's colonial period was characterized by a "relativa infecundidad" (116; a relative lack of fecundity). "Religión y Tradición" (Religion and Tradition), Paz concludes, "se nos han ofrecido siempre como formas muertas, inservibles, que mutilan o asfixian nuestra singularidad" (116; have always been presented to us as dead and unusable forms that mutilate or asphyxiate our singularity). Note the shift that has taken place in Paz's argument: in the first section of his discussion of the colonial period, he had stressed that New Spain was imbued with *life*; now, in a strikingly different approach, he portrays the same society as essentially *dead*. In discussing the reign of Charles II, he describes religious belief during this period as being characterized by "la petrificación de unas creencias que habían perdido toda su frescura y fertilidad" (119; the petrification of beliefs that had lost all their freshness and fertility). The opposition between what is living, which Paz associates with terms such as fecundity, fertility, and creativity, and what is dead, linked to notions of petrification and asphyxiation, is one of the organizing principles of Paz's writing. In "De la conquista a la colonia," he applies first one set of concepts to Mexico's colonial period, and then another, describing it from two diametrically opposed points of view.

Paz closes his discussion of the colonial period in *El laberinto* by stating that Mexico had no choice but to break with Spain. There was no other way out of the paralysis in which colonial society found itself. New Spain was, according to Paz, "un orden sin salida" (an order without an exit), and as such its rule had to be overthrown (127). This was an idea that Paz would return to in the reflections he develops on the colonial period in several essays of the 1970s.[21] In an essay contrasting the United States and Mexico, he notes that "la tradición de Nueva España . . . no ofrecía elementos ni principios que pudieran servir para resolver el doble problema al que la nación se enfrentaba: el de la vida independiente y el de la modernización" (the tradition of New Spain . . . did not offer elements or principles that could help resolve the dual problems facing the nation: that of independence, on the one hand, and modernization, on the other).[22] In short, colonial society did not offer a fruitful path forward. And yet Paz continues in these years to depict New Spain in favorable terms. In his 1975 interview with Claude Fell, he repeats the idea that colonial society offered Mexico's indigenous population a place within the social order and a meaningful vision of the world: "el catolicismo les da una visión del mundo y del trasmundo; les da un estatuto y les ofrece el cielo; los bautiza, es decir, les abre las puertas de un orden distinto" (Catholicism gives them a vision of the world and the afterworld; it gives them a legal status and offers them access to heaven; it baptizes them, that is to say, it opens the door to a different order).[23] In the same interview, he compares colonial society favorably with twentieth-century Mexico. "La sociedad novohispana de los siglos XVII y XVIII" (Colonial society of the seventeenth and eighteenth centuries), he proposes, "es un todo mucho más perfecto y armónico que la sociedad mexicana de la primera mitad del siglo XX" (constitutes a far more perfect and harmonious whole than Mexican society of the first half of the twentieth century).[24] And he criticizes modern-day Mexicans for having ignored and even disdained their country's colonial past, describing it as "una tradición admirable" (an admirable tradition).[25] In short, Paz continued to see the colonial period as somehow both obsolete and exemplary.

Paz develops yet another extended meditation on the society of New Spain in the opening chapters of his 1982 study of the life and work of Sor Juana Inés de la Cruz. He prefaces his discussion of Sor Juana's life and work with several chapters on the society in which she grew up. In his treatment of colonial society, much more extensive and detailed in this work than in any of his previous approaches to the topic, Paz repeats some of the same themes we have seen before. Still, the overall emphasis is somewhat different, especially in comparison with the pages devoted to colonial society in *El laberinto*. Paz is interested in the nature of the colonial regime, which, following Max Weber's terminology, he defines as patrimonialist.[26] He also discusses New Spain's economic system, depicting it as mercantilist and dominated by large landowners. Religion and the Catholic Church play an important role in his account of colonial society, but he pays far less attention to the religious experience of the indigenous population. What was a key idea in *El laberinto*—that Catholicism gave the native peoples of colonial Mexico a sense of belonging and connectedness—is here mentioned only in passing.[27] In the opening sections of *Sor Juana*, far more emphasis is placed on the Church as a hierarchical and orthodox organization that stifled the creativity of colonial society. This view of the role of religion in the colonial period leads into Paz's conclusion, which echoes the conclusion of the pages he devoted to New Spain in *El laberinto*. He depicts New Spain as a closed and, in some sense, immobilized society, in which change could only come through a rupture with the past. This, indeed, is what happened with Mexico's achievement of its Independence at the beginning of the nineteenth century. Still, for Paz the break with New Spain was necessary and inevitable, if also profoundly damaging and traumatic. "México cambió" (Mexico changed), he claims, "y ese cambio fue un desgarramiento, una herida que aún no se cierra" (and that change was a tearing apart, a wound that has still not healed).[28]

To compare Independence to a wound suggests that something of value was lost in Mexico's transition from colonial status to nationhood. Such a point of view links Paz to the conservative tradition in Mexican intellectual life. Nineteenth-century conservatives such as Alamán believed that the foundation of Mexican national identity was to be found in the society of New Spain. Paz did not believe that the colonial period offered the *only* basis on which to build a productive sense of nationhood, as was the case with many conservatives, some of whom went so far as to deplore the movement for independence itself.[29] But neither did Paz share the wholesale rejection of the colonial period found among indigenist and liberal thinkers. This feature of Paz's thinking in itself places it in the orbit of conservative ideology. One cannot offer a defense of the colonial period without sharing certain conservative presuppositions about the nature of society. This is clear from the very terms in which Paz seeks to explain colonial society, for his words echo an organicist and communitarian outlook that has typically been a feature of conservative thought. His description in *El laberinto* of colonial society as a living organism has an unmistakably Burkean ring to it. But there are also clear differences between Paz and his conservative predecessors in Mexico. For one thing, Paz adopts the perspective of Mexico's indigenous population, and underlines their sense of participation in a larger whole. Conservative thinkers such as Alamán, Carlos Pereyra, and Vasconcelos also value a shared sense of community, but they pair their communitarianism with an emphasis on authority and hierarchy. This is something we do not find in Paz. Moreover, conservatives celebrate the evangelization of the Indians, their inclusion in the Catholic Church, but they also frequently express disdain for the achievements of indigenous civilization, to the point of coming across as frankly racist.[30] Paz, on the other hand, combines respect for both civilizations, the pre-Columbian and the colonial. In short, there are clearly traces of conservative thinking in Paz's writings on Mexico's colonial period, but Paz can by no stretch of the imagination be described as an orthodox conservative.

In 1997, in the first direct elections for mayor of Mexico City, Paz voted for Carlos Castillo Peraza, the PAN candidate.[31] How did the Nobel laureate evolve from being a PAN critic in the 1970s to a PAN voter in the 1990s? Paz's views about the PAN began to shift in the wake of the 1982 nationalization of Mexico's banks by the PRI government, and the protracted economic malaise that followed. In his numerous comments about the PAN from these years onward, Paz repeatedly emphasized the party's democratic credentials. It was clear that he had many disagreements with the party, but he admired its commitment to the democratic process. At a time when the country was undergoing a long and difficult transition to democracy, it is surely understandable that Paz would focus on this particular issue above all others. In surveying the political panorama of the 1980s and 1990s, Paz was especially concerned with identifying political forces that he believed would assist the country's transition to democracy, rather than impeding it. In 1990, in a conversation with Braulio Peralta, Paz stated the following: "Creo en la democracia; hay que votar por ella" (I believe in democracy; one must vote for it).[32] Around this time, he also often said that he no longer believed in the distinction between Left and Right.[33] Paz's notion of a post-ideological period was no doubt overstated, but it was shared by many others in the early 1990s. It was part of a significant concern with giving priority to the strengthening of democracy itself. This, more than anything else, explained Paz's vote for Castillo Peraza.

In a widely read 1985 article calling for an end to the PRI's monopoly on political power, Paz underlined the important role the PAN was in a position to play in accelerating the transition to democracy. For there to be democracy, the country needed political parties that could compete with the PRI. Paz drew attention to an encouraging element in the political landscape of the mid 1980s: "la existencia de distintos partidos políticos independientes. Mejor dicho: de un partido, el PAN, y de varios grupos que tienden a serlo sin conseguirlo aún" (the existence of independent political parties. Better said: of one party, the PAN, and of various other groups that are trying to become independent parties but have not quite achieved it).[34] In short, the PAN offered the best hope for forcing an opening up of the political system, as it already constituted an independent political entity that was well positioned to compete with the PRI. In addition, Paz commended the PAN for the perspective from which it assailed the Mexican political system. "La crítica política del PAN al sistema" (The PAN's criticism of the system), he wrote, "ha impresionado favorablemente a la opinión pública pues está fundada en los principios democráticos" (being rooted in democratic principles, has made a favorable impression on public opinion).[35] He would return to this point in an article he wrote for the Mexico City newspaper *La Jornada* in the wake of the contested presidential election of 1988, in which the PAN had won a far greater number of votes than ever before, even though it ended in third place. Paz argued that the PAN owed its success to its defense of democratic values. He noted furthermore that the PAN had been much more successful in ridding itself of its past authoritarian tendencies than the Left in shedding its dogmatism.[36] It was a revealing contrast, suggesting that for Paz the PAN had more democratic credibility than the Left, which, under the leadership of former PRI politician Cuauhtémoc Cárdenas, had come very close to ousting the PRI from power that year. Paz made a similar point in a 1990 conversation with Braulio Peralta. Referring to the PAN, and drawing an implicit contrast with the Left, he stated that "ellos sí hicieron una autocrítica de sus orígenes autoritarios. Han sido mucho más democráticos que los otros partidos" (they undertook a self-criticism of their authoritarian origins. They have been far more democratic than the other parties).[37] A few years later, commenting on the 1994 presidential election, Paz once again praised the PAN for its support of the democratic process. "Sus credenciales democráticas son intachables" (Their democratic credentials are impeccable), he said.[38] In short, Paz was sympathetic toward Mexico's conservative party, but what he most praised was its commitment to liberal values.

Numerous commentators have drawn attention to the irony of Mexico's conservative party becoming the party of change during the country's transition to democracy. Soledad Loaeza puts it best: "A finales del siglo XX las fuerzas políticas que la historia identificaba con el conservadurismo y la tradición se apropiaron de la bandera del cambio y llevaron a la Presidencia de la República a Vicente Fox" (At the end of the twentieth century, political forces that had been identified with conservatism and tradition took over the banner of change and carried Vicente Fox to the presidency of the Republic).[39] How did this happen? To answer this question, it is helpful to recall a number of salient features of the history of the PAN. Throughout the decades of PRI hegemony, the PAN played the role of a loyal opposition, consistently participating in elections in which the party had no chance of winning. In this way, it paradoxically both helped legitimize the ersatz version of democracy imposed by the PRI and established its credentials as a party committed to bringing about change by electoral means. As Loaeza observes about the PAN, "la defensa del voto y del cambio por la vía electoral era parte integral de su identidad" (the defense of voting rights and of change by electoral means were integral elements of the party's identity).[40] As the need to democratize Mexico gained increased favor throughout Mexican society in the final decades of the twentieth century, the PAN's commitment to democracy helped it secure an increasingly wide base of support.

Another element of the PAN's identity was its anti-statism. It is important to note that the PAN was founded in 1938, in explicit opposition to President Lázaro Cárdenas's leftist policies. These policies included efforts at redistribution of the nation's resources, and entailed the strengthening of the state. The PAN was especially alarmed by the government's efforts to establish greater control over the country's educational system. In the early 1980s, certain actions by the PRI government, combined with a shift in the international environment, helped to create an opening for the PAN. President José López Portillo's decision to nationalize the banks, which he announced on September 1, 1982, only three months before leaving office, provoked widespread opposition, not only because it did not appear to be an economically sound move, but also for the authoritarian manner in which the decision was made. López Portillo's actions came to be regarded by many as a symptom of the country's excessively presidentialist and statist governing system. Around the same time, many countries, including the United States under Ronald Reagan and the United Kingdom under Margaret Thatcher, were seeing a turn away from economic policies that stressed the role of the state and a move toward the free-market policies that came to be known as "neoliberalism."[41] In such a context, it is perhaps not surprising that a party that combined a commitment to democratization with a critique of the statism and presidential authoritarianism of the PRI governments should have garnered increasing support from the electorate over the subsequent decades, culminating, as we have seen, in the election of the PAN candidate Vicente Fox to the presidency in July 2000.[42]

Paz did not live to see Fox elected president, and we do not know how he would have voted in 2000. Still, as we have already seen, he had a highly favorable view of the democratic credentials of the party Fox represented. Furthermore, Paz had already made it clear in a 1986 interview with the French journalist and author Jean-François Revel that he sympathized with the anti-statist posture of Mexico's conservative party.[43] Another aspect of Paz's political outlook that might account for his rapprochement with the PAN was the gradualist approach to political change for which he became an increasingly strong advocate in the final decades of his life. At key moments during Mexico's political transition of the late twentieth century, Paz expressed a wish for prudence and moderation on the part of the country's main political actors. In the wake of the contested presidential election of 1988, in which there was widespread evidence that the PRI had committed fraud to help its candidate win, and the results of which were contested by the opposition, Paz voiced his opinion that the intransigence of the opposition might lead to "otro estallido" (another explosion), comparable to the one that had taken place in 1968.[44] He reminded his readers that since the publication of *Posdata* in 1970 he had consistently defended the view that "la salida hacia formas más plurales y democráticas de convivencia debería ser pacífica y gradual" (the move toward more plural and democratic forms of coexistence had to be gradual and peaceful).[45] What this meant in August and September of 1988 was that the opposition should abandon its demand that the elections be annulled, and take satisfaction in the fact that the country was making great strides in the process of democratization, reflected in the fact that opposition parties had achieved ample representation in the Chamber of Deputies for the first time in modern Mexican history. The emphasis on a gradualist approach could not be clearer.[46]

Paz struck a similar note after the 1994 presidential election. The *Zapatista* uprising in January of that year, as well as the assassination of the PRI's presidential candidate, Luis Donaldo Colosio, in March, had left the country deeply shaken. Once again, the PRI candidate, Ernesto Zedillo, who had been selected to replace

Colosio, won, this time in an election that was widely viewed as fair. In the Mexican electorate's decision to return the PRI to power for six more years, Paz saw a confirmation of his views about the best way to conduct the nation's transition to democracy. "El país quiere cambiar" (The country wants to change), he noted, "y esta voluntad de cambio explica la abundancia de votantes; asimismo, teme al desorden y odia a la violencia" (and that desire for change explains the abundance of voters; at the same time, the country also fears disorder and detests violence). He added that the results of the election revealed two complementary thrusts among the voters: "la voluntad de cambio y el anhelo de seguridad" (the desire for change and the longing for security).[47] In short, the transition away from the anti-democratic hegemony of the PRI would take place over an extended period of time, and it might even involve relying on the PRI to provide stability as the nation entered an uncertain era. In 1997, this time writing in the wake of the legislative and local elections of July 6, Paz once again drew attention to the gradualist political values he had come to espouse. "Lo que necesitamos para asegurar nuestro futuro" (What we need to secure our future), he claimed, "es moderación, es decir, *prudencia*, la más alta de las virtudes políticas según los filósofos de la Antigüedad" (is moderation, that is, *prudence*, which, according to the philosophers of Antiquity, is the highest of all political virtues).[48] Earlier, I suggested that there was a paradoxical element to Paz's sympathy for the PAN: he applauded Mexico's conservative party for its staunch support for liberal democratic values. His defense of gradualism and prudence brings Paz closer to traditional conservative values.

As we have seen, Paz often expressed a favorable view of the PAN in the 1980s and 1990s. However, he invariably combined his praise for the PAN with a reminder of his profound differences with Mexico's conservative party. Paz occasionally mentioned his reservations about the PAN's political program, which he criticized for being too vague,[49] as well as his disappointment at the party's failure to extend its reach into Mexico's rural areas.[50] But his main complaint about the PAN centered on the party's positions on certain social issues. In "PRI: Hora cumplida," Paz pointed out that the PAN seemed blind to many of the country's problems. Primary among these problems was the challenge of rapid population growth, which the country had been facing for several decades. "Los problemas sociales y culturales del país son más vastos" (The social and cultural problems of our country are vaster), Paz stated, "y sobre algunos de ellos, como el demográfico, la posición del PAN es insatisfactoria" (and with regard to some of them, such as the demographic one, the PAN's position is unsatisfactory).[51] In a 1984 conversation with Braulio Peralta, he made the same point. After repeating his usual praise for the party's commitment to democracy, Paz emphasized his differences with the PAN: "hay cosas, desde luego, que no puedo compartir, con las que no puedo estar de acuerdo con el PAN. Por ejemplo: uno de los grandes problemas de México es la natalidad. Y ellos están contra el control de la natalidad: yo estoy a favor de ese control, sin excluir la despenalización del aborto" (of course, there are positions held by the PAN that I am unable to share or agree with. For example: one of Mexico's greatest challenges is the birthrate. And the PAN is opposed to birth control. I support it, without excluding the legalization of abortion).[52] In his article on the 1994 presidential election, he once again drew attention to his disagreements with the PAN on social issues. "Discrepo" (I differ), Paz affirmed, "en varios puntos de importancia—educación, control de natalidad y otros—del ideario del PAN" (on several important issues—such as education, birth control, and other issues—with the ideology of the PAN).[53] In sum, Paz praised the PAN for supporting democracy, and he believed that the party had a key role to play in Mexico's transition away from what was in effect a one-party state. However, he combined his support for the party's liberalism with criticism of its failure to adopt sufficiently liberal positions in the realm of social and cultural issues.

The PAN's conservative positions on birth control and abortion rights were intimately linked to the party's Catholic identity. Paz himself was an atheist, a fact that helped to explain his repudiation of important aspects of the PAN's social and cultural orientation. And yet, even as the question of religion divided Paz from the PAN, it also provided a bridge between the poet and Mexico's conservatives. We have already seen that an understanding of Catholicism was central to Paz's investigation into Mexican identity in *El laberinto*. He took up the issue of religion in Mexican history again in a 1988 conversation with Castillo Peraza, the PAN politician with whom Paz appears to have developed a close relationship in the final decade of his life.[54] Paz began the interview by describing himself as a pagan, but immediately acknowledged that it was absurd to describe oneself in such a way "cuando uno ha nacido dentro de una sociedad católica, en la que los valores en los que se cree son cristianos o son consecuencia del cristianismo" (153; when one was born into a Catholic society, in which the values that are upheld are Christian or a consequence of Christianity).[55] In short, Paz recognized that the country's Catholic traditions were integral to his own identity, even though he did not adhere to Catholic doctrine. Later in the conversation, Paz explained why he believed religion had played such an important role in his country's history. The key was to be found in the colonial period. It was not that he overlooked Mexico's indigenous heritage. "En el ser del mexicano está el pasado prehispánico indígena" (155; The pre-Hispanic indigenous past is part of the Mexican's identity), he observed. But the change brought about in Mexico's identity by the Catholic Church went deeper. "La gran revolución que se ha hecho en México" (The greatest revolution undertaken in Mexico), he claimed, "la más profunda y radical, fue la de los misioneros españoles" (155; the most profound and radical revolution, was the one brought about by the Spanish missionaries). What revolution was Paz referring to? The Mexican poet phrased it as follows: "hicieron que un pueblo cambiara de religión" (155; they made a people change their religion). In comparison, modernity and its ideology of liberalism had had far less of an impact on Mexican identity. Paz went on to suggest that this was precisely what he had discovered in the process of writing *El laberinto* almost forty years earlier. It was a discovery about Mexico, but also about himself: "Esta obra mía es un intento de diálogo con mi ser de mexicano y en el centro de ese diálogo está la religión" (155; That book is an attempt at a dialogue with my Mexican self and at the heart of that dialogue stands religion). In sum, Paz must have felt drawn toward the PAN's Catholic identity, in spite of the fact that this identity translated into specific policy positions that he repudiated.

CHAPTER 9

Poetics

One of Paz's most persistent endeavors as a writer was the defense of poetry. Whether through explorations of the nature of poetry itself, as in *El arco y la lira*; discussions of the work of poets he admired, as in the essays collected in *Cuadrivio* (1964; Quadrivium); or histories of the Western poetic tradition, as in *Los hijos del limo*, Paz sought to convince his readers of the irrevocable value of poetry. Indeed, it is clear that for Paz poetry was the highest human calling. This was not, however, a widely shared point of view, for in reality, in the modern world, poetry appeared to have become a largely peripheral activity. In the face of such hostility—or indifference—poets of the modern era such as Paz have felt compelled to put tremendous effort into explaining the importance of their work. Hence the need to write not just poetry, but defenses of poetry as well. Deeply aware of the circumstances in which modern poets found themselves, and of the imperatives arising out of those circumstances, Paz threw himself with great verve into the task of explaining why poetry was a thing of such great value to human life. In the opening pages of *La otra voz*, one of the final books of his long career, he described himself as one more in a long line of champions of poetry. "Estas páginas" (These pages), he observes, "no son sino una variación, una más, de esa *Defensa de la Poesía* que, hace más de dos siglos, escriben incansablemente los poetas modernos" (8; are one more version of that *Defence of Poetry* which for more than two centuries modern poets have been tirelessly writing). To say that Paz was indefatigable in his advocacy of poetry would be no exaggeration.

Paz approaches the defense of poetry from a variety of perspectives. One of the principal arguments he puts forward in poetry's favor is that it is an autonomous phenomenon. Why is this important? In what sense is an argument about the autonomy of poetry also an argument about its value? In trying to answer this question one must understand, first and foremost, that to claim that poetry exists in an autonomous realm is to emphasize that poetry does not depend on—or serve—something outside of itself. If the purpose of poetry were, let us say, the betterment of humanity, our central concern would be not poetry, but the betterment of humanity. If we were to find other—more effective—avenues for securing this betterment, we would be justified in giving priority to those avenues, rather than poetry, in the pursuit of our goal. To make poetry ancillary to something else is to diminish it. To place it in a subservient role is to reduce its importance. In brief, the best defense of poetry is to assert that it is an autonomous enterprise, done for its own sake. It finds its justification in itself, not in something other than itself.

Paz states the argument for poetry as an autonomous realm in an especially emphatic way in the opening pages of *El arco*, the Mexican poet's most sustained examination of the nature of poetry. In doing so, he is making it clear that the idea of poetic autonomy is one of the foundational elements of his entire theory. Many of the other ideas he will develop follow from this first axiom. "Cada poema" (Every poem), Paz claims near the beginning of *El arco*, "se ostenta como algo diferente e irreductible" (14–15; presents itself as something different and irreducible).[1] The claim is repeated several times over in the next few pages. "Cada creación poética es una unidad autosuficiente" (15; Every poetic creation is a self-sufficient whole), he states. "Cada poema es un objeto único" (17; Every poem is a unique object), he adds a few pages later. He describes the poem as "algo que se cierra sobre sí mismo, universo autosuficiente" (69; something that closes in on itself, a self-sufficient universe). Again and again, Paz emphasizes the poem's separateness from other phenomena, its uniqueness. A poem, he says, must be thought of as "un ejemplar aislado, que no se repetirá jamás" (18; an isolated specimen, which will never be repeated). If the poem were repeatable, that is, if one could produce identical, interchangeable poems at will, it would no longer be self-sufficient or autonomous. It would become part of a class of phenomena, rather than a unique entity in its own right. Such a view of the poem bears implications for each and every word used in a poetic text, for if each individual poem is unique, irreducible, and self-sufficient, not a single word can be altered in a poem without destroying the whole of which that word is a part. "El poema" (A poem), Paz states, "está hecho de palabras necesarias e insustituibles" (45; is made up of necessary and irreplaceable words).

We will see that in *El arco*, and elsewhere, Paz combines strong claims about the autonomous nature of the poetic artifact with a completely different set of claims that would appear to negate that autonomy. But I will leave that topic for later. First, it will be necessary to examine some of the implications of the idea of poetic autonomy. What ideas about the nature of poetry flow from the key concept of the poem's autonomous status? To begin with, one might draw attention to the theme of the poem as having a life of its own. "Cada obra" (Every work), Paz claims in *El arco*, "tiene vida propia" (16; has a life of its own). The idea of the poem's resemblance to a biological organism comes up repeatedly in Paz. "El poema es una totalidad viviente" (45; A poem is a living totality), he asserts elsewhere in *El arco*. In the prologue to the anthology of Mexican poetry Paz edited for the UNESCO in 1952, he proposes that "todo poema es un organismo de significaciones internas, irreductibles a cualquier otro decir" (every poem is an organism made up of internal meanings, irreducible to any other expression).[2] In an essay on the Mexican poet Juan José Tablada, Paz explains that Tablada's poems "nos enseñaron a considerar el poema como un todo viviente, como un organismo animado" (taught us to view a poem as a living whole, as an organism infused with life).[3] In short, all poems are like living organisms; however, some poems, such as Tablada's, are especially successful at drawing the reader's attention to this feature of poetry.

Paz uses biological metaphors when speaking about poetry in order to highlight poetry's status as an independent, autonomous entity. These metaphors also serve to focus attention on another one of poetry's key traits: its concreteness. The idea of the poem's concreteness is related both to the conception of the poem as an object in the world, rather than a mirror held up to the world, and to the slightly different notion that poetry provides the reader with an extraordinarily vivid and immediate apprehension of the world. In the first case—when we speak of a poem as an object rather than a representation of something or as a mode of communication—the point is to emphasize its status as part of reality, rather than as an entity that stands at a remove from reality. In the second case, the poem is still regarded as a vehicle for representing an aspect of reality; it is simply that it offers an immediacy so exceptional that it is as if the object being represented rises up in front of us in all its specificity. Sometimes the idea is that the poem is not related to anything outside itself, as when Paz suggests that "el poema no tiene objeto o referencia exterior" (the poem has no external reference or object).[4] Sometimes it is that the representation offered in a poem is so vivid that the gap between the poem and the world has virtually disappeared. It is as if the poem has become one with the object it represents. Paz often expresses the latter idea with the help of a famous phrase by Antonio Machado, who once said that poetry "no representa, sino presenta" (does not represent, but makes present). Paz quotes this suggestive line more than once in his work. Elaborating on Machado's view, he suggests that "el poeta no describe la silla: nos la pone enfrente" (the poet does not describe a chair: he places it before us).[5] Poetry offers a different mode of apprehending the world, one that is not abstract but concrete, not distant but immediate. In Paz's view, poetry offers a direct knowledge of the world, unlike what we observe in other epistemological systems: "A la inversa de lo que ocurre con los axiomas de los matemáticos, las verdades de los físicos, o las ideas de los filósofos, el poema no abstrae de la experiencia" (Contrary to what happens with the axioms of the mathematicians, the theories of the physicists, or the ideas of the philosophers, a poem does not abstract from experience).[6] When Paz lauds his favorite poets, he often draws attention to their love of concreteness. Consider, for example, the following words of praise he reserves for the poetry of Ramón López Velarde: "Tenía una aversión natural por los sistemas y a las ideas prefería las cosas" (He had a natural aversion to systems and he preferred things to ideas).[7] It is things that matter, whether it is the poem as thing, or the poem as that which puts things in front of us in all their intense vividness.

"No ideas but in things," William Carlos Williams famously wrote in *Paterson*. Did he mean that only a thing could communicate an idea? Or was he opposed to ideas *tout court*? To Paz, who had obviously read Williams even if he did not engage with him in as sustained a manner as he did with other American poets, such as T. S. Eliot and Ezra Pound, the idea often seemed to be that poetry should not contain ideas at all, and that it should spurn all modes of discourse related to the presentation of ideas, such as interpretation, explanation, instruction, or argument. Let us consider, to begin with, what Paz says about interpretation. For the poem to be autotelic, that is, centered on itself rather than on something extraneous to it, implies that it is immune to interpretation. To interpret a text means to translate the words of a poem into a different set of words that ostensibly convey the poem's meaning. It means, to put it a little differently, to extract the ideas contained in a poem and place them in front of the reader in an entirely different form. According to Paz, however, such an operation is impossible, for to interpret a poem is not to communicate its meaning, but to allow its meaning to escape. Why is this so? It is because the meaning of a poem is entirely bound up with its words, and does not consist in the ideas behind the words. Once one changes the words, the original meaning of the words vanishes. Using the concept of the image as a stand-in for that of poetry itself, here is how Paz puts it in *El arco*: "La imagen se explica a sí misma. Nada, excepto ella, puede decir lo que quiere decir" (The image explains itself. Nothing, except the image, can explain what it wants to say).[8] He goes on to explain what it means to describe a poem as an "irreducible" phenomenon: it means that it exists in itself and for itself and cannot be transposed into any other terms. It cannot be summarized in the form of an idea. "Las imágenes" (Images), says Paz, "son irreductibles a cualquier explicación e interpretación" (are irreducible to any kind of explanation or interpretation).[9] Once you interpret the poem, you destroy it. Again, the suggestion is that the poem is an object added to the world, not an idea about the world. "Toda imagen poética" (Every poetic image), Paz claims, "es inexplicable, simplemente es" (exists beyond explanation, it simply is).[10] The statement that a poem "simply is" may well remind the reader of the American poet Archibald MacLeish's well-known dictum that "a poem should not mean/But be." Indeed, Paz must have been familiar with MacLeish's proposition, since he echoes it even more closely in a comment he makes on the work of the abstract expressionist painter Jackson Pollock. "Los cuadros de Pollock" (Pollock's paintings), he writes, "no significan, son" (do not signify, they simply are).[11] It was much easier, of course, to make this claim about a painting (or about music) than about art forms that use language, for words cannot easily be shorn of their signifying dimension. Yet, as we have seen, Paz makes the claim about poetry, too.

While readers should refrain from interpreting poetry, poets should resist the temptation to use their poems for the purposes of explanation or instruction. In some sense, poetry should remain entirely free of content. In describing the nature of what he calls poetic revelation, Paz insists that this revelation, contrary to what the word might suggest, does not disclose anything. "Esta revelación" (This revelation), he claims in *El arco*, "no es un saber de algo sobre algo, pues entonces la poesía sería filosofía" (is not a knowledge of something about something, for in that case poetry would be philosophy).[12] Note once more the stress on distinguishing poetry from other forms of discourse, that is, on affirming its autonomy. That the concept of autonomy entailed strictures on what was acceptable for a poem to do is clear from the types of value judgments Paz makes in his discussions of the work of other poets. Again and again, we see that Paz prefers the kind of poem that is not too explicit about what it is trying to say. He does not like didactic poetry. Poetry that appears to have designs on the reader is forcefully rejected. Paz's aesthetic preferences emerge from his discussions of the works of individual poets. In an essay on Blanca Varela, he states—admiringly—that "su poesía no explica, ni razona" (her poetry does not explain or argue).[13] In an otherwise favorable review of the work of Marco Antonio Montes de Oca, Paz expresses his disapproval of those moments in Montes de Oca's poetry "cuando predica, cuando filosofa" (when he preaches, when he philosophizes).[14] Elizabeth Bishop is praised because her poetry "no nos enseña nada" (does not teach us anything).[15] Going into a little more detail as to what should be excluded from poetry, Paz explains that the work of Emilio Adolfo Westphalen "no está contaminada de ideología ni de moral ni de teología" (is not infected with ideology or morality or theology).[16] About Carlos Pellicer, he says, "no razona ni predica: canta" (he does not argue or preach: he sings).[17] In an early essay on López Velarde, Paz points to the damage that is done when poetry is harnessed to a purpose that is not poetry itself. He speaks of "la tentación del poema cívico" (the lure of the civic poem) from which the poet from Zacatecas suffered. But he is cheered by López Velarde's success in evading this temptation: "Canta en voz baja y evita la elocuencia, el discurso y las grandes palabras" (he sings in a quiet voice and avoids eloquence, speeches, and big words).[18] In sum, Paz rejects the type of poetry that overlaps too much with other types of discourse, as well as poems that are turned toward the outside world, serving a purpose extraneous to the inherent purpose of poetry itself.

The attack on the kind of poetry that reasons, instructs, explains, and preaches helps us understand why Paz so often expressed hostility toward politically committed poetry. Such poetry went against its own nature, as Paz understood it. In a passage from *El arco*, he describes the risks run by poets who place themselves at the service of political interests. "Los partidos políticos modernos" (Modern political parties), Paz explains, "convierten al poeta en propagandista y así lo degradan" (degrade the poet by turning him into a propaganda machine). For what does a propagandist do? "El propagandista" (The propagandist), he observes, "disemina en la 'masa' las concepciones de los jerarcas. Su tarea consiste en trasmitir ciertas directivas, de arriba para abajo" (disseminates the ideas of the leaders among the "masses." His task is to transmit certain instructions, from the top down).[19] Given what we know by now about Paz's poetics, we immediately grasp what he finds objectionable about the poet's role in this endeavor. Clearly, the poet has lost his independence when he obeys the needs of a propaganda machine. He follows a political agenda, not his own creative inspiration. He disseminates and transmits ideas formulated by someone else, in the service of a goal that stands apart from the goals of poetry. The poet, in sum, has become a conduit for something to which he himself has not given shape; his work has given up its autonomy.

We have seen that Paz dislikes discursive poetry, that is, poetry that reasons and explains. Similarly, he spurns poetry that conveys a message. One might say that political poetry offers an extreme version of the kind of poetry that is focused on content more than anything else. What matters in political poetry are the ideas expressed, not the poem in itself. And for Paz, this is the wrong way to approach poetry. The work of art, he explains in an essay on Boris Pasternak, "no es un proyectil" (is not a projectile).[20] The image of the projectile suggests both the notion of taking aim at something, that is, of having a clear focus or purpose, and that of a weapon used in a battle. Such a goal-oriented and belligerent view of art is entirely alien to Paz, who prefers the idea of art's purposelessness. Note, however, that whereas Paz often voices the notion that political poetry is too much focused on its usefulness, he also occasionally develops a slightly different idea, which is that political poetry only touches the surface of human existence. "La poesía" (Poetry), he argues in *El arco*, "vive en las capas más profundas del ser, en tanto que las ideologías y todo lo que llamamos ideas y opiniones constituyen los estratos más superficiales de la conciencia" (40–41; emerges from the deepest layers of our being, whereas ideologies, ideas, and opinions represent the most superficial level of consciousness). The idea is now not so much that the poet stands apart from the rest of humanity, but that he or she is more deeply immersed in human experience than, let us say, people pursuing a political agenda. As we saw earlier, political parties demand of the poet that he or she convey certain ideas to the people; the poet, however, has a natural connection with the people that goes beyond the need to transmit messages to the masses. According to Paz, "la relación entre el poeta y su pueblo es orgánica y espontánea" (41; the relationship between the poet and the people is organic and spontaneous). In sum, Paz leaves us with two different images: one of the poet as an isolated individual crafting unique poetic objects; the other of the poet as someone immersed in his or her community. What the two images have in common, however, is a rejection of the idea of the poet as someone who serves a political goal.

Paz's views on the nature of poetry have implications for how we *read* poetry. In essence, Paz's position is that if poetry is an autonomous phenomenon, we should read poetry as poetry, not as something else. What this something else might be becomes clear in a passage from *El arco* in which Paz describes the kind of approach to poetry that he repudiates. It is an approach that focuses not on the poem itself, but on aspects external to it. Paz begins by explaining that with the death of God (or the decline of religion), we now turn to other concepts to explain the world to ourselves. "El lugar de Dios" (The place of God), he suggests, "y de la antigua naturaleza poblada de dioses y demonios lo ocupan ahora seres sin rostro: la Raza, la Clase, el Inconsciente (individual o colectivo), el Genio de los pueblos, la Herencia" (163; and of the ancient conception of a natural world that is peopled with gods and demons has been taken over by faceless beings: Race, Class, the (individual or collective) Unconscious, the Genius of a people, Heredity). What does this have to do with poetry? Clearly, if we as humans are shaped by factors such as race, class, the unconscious, and so on, then poetry must be shaped by these forces, too. If this is the case, critics will need to look outside of the poem in order to understand it. From this point of view, "el poeta es un médium por cuyo intermedio se expresan, en cifra, el Sexo, el Clima, la Historia o algún otro sucedáneo de los antiguos dioses o demonios" (163; the poet is a conduit for the coded expression of other forces, such as Gender, Climate, History, or some other substitute for the ancient gods or demons). Paz concedes that looking at poetry in this way might have some value. But he insists that the external perspective on poetry is insufficient. In brief, such a perspective cannot answer a key question: "¿cómo se transforman esas fuerzas o realidades determinantes en palabras? . . . Para los psicoanalistas la creación poética es una sublimación; entonces, ¿por qué en unos casos esa sublimación se vuelve poema y en otros no?" (163; how do such forces or deterministic factors become translated into words? . . . For the psychoanalysts, poetic creation is a form of sublimation; if that is indeed the case, how does that sublimation turn into poetry in some cases and not in others?) Only an approach to poetry that reads poems as poems, and not as the conduit for external forces, can avoid the trap Paz identifies when he poses these questions.

Paz reflected on the question of critical methodology again many years later in "Cuantía y valía," an essay from *La otra voz*. He reiterates the same reservations he had expressed about extra-textual approaches to poetry in *El arco*, but now writes against the background of resurgent historical and political approaches to literature in the 1980s. He begins by complaining about critics and theorists who have decided to apply the methods of the natural and social sciences to the study of art and literature. "Olvidan" (They forget), he notes, "que realidades distintas piden métodos y criterios distintos" (94; that different aspects of reality need to be studied with different methods and criteria). Changes in society are not sufficient, Paz suggests, to explain changes in artistic expression, which follow laws of their own. Literature should be read as literature, not as something else. Paz proceeds to summarize the working method of the typical politically oriented critic. "Primero" (First), he explains, "se reduce la obra a mero documento social; en seguida, se afirma que el texto no dice lo que dice. Mejor dicho, el texto oculta una realidad social y política. Descubrir esa realidad es la misión del crítico" (95; the work is reduced to a mere social document; next, the argument is made that the text does not say what it says. Better said, the text conceals a set of social and political facts. The critic's mission is to uncover those facts). This digging beneath the surface of a text to uncover its hidden motivations—motivations generally of a suspect nature—amounts to what has been called a hermeneutics of suspicion. Interestingly, Paz himself was an advocate of this type of approach at earlier stages of his career, although one might say in his defense that he applied this interpretive method to sociocultural phenomena rather than literary texts. However that may be, in "Cuantía y valía" he refers to the postcolonial interpretation of Shakespeare's *The Tempest* as an example of the kind of reading he repudiates. "*La Tempestad*" (*The Tempest*), he explains, "se transforma en un espectáculo de fuegos de artificio que encubren con sus luces la infame realidad: el nacimiento del imperialismo moderno.... El texto es un tejido de engaños; al destejerlo, el crítico desenmascara al autor mentiroso, cómplice de las tiranías y de las opresiones" (95; is transformed into a fireworks display that covers up a shameful reality with its flashing lights: the birth of modern imperialism. The text is a web of deceit; in taking it apart, the critic unmasks the author, revealing his dishonesty, as well as his complicity with the forces of tyranny and oppression). It is understandable that someone like Paz, who venerates literature, would react with irritation at readings that seek to make authors from the past—even, or especially, the most revered ones—complicit with horrendous historical crimes. He deplores the condescending attitude many critics adopt toward the past, as if literary works were no more than chapters from "la historia de las supersticiones humanas" (95; the history of human superstitions). The solution, he argues, is to read literature as literature, not as something else. To the academics who had accumulated immense cultural power in the second half of the twentieth century, Paz offered the following advice: "tienen que reaprender a leer los poemas como textos poéticos, no como documentos sociales o psicoanalíticos" (114–15; they need to learn anew to read poems as poems, not as social or psychoanalytical documents).

Paz was a strong advocate of the idea of poetic autonomy, and yet he was also a critic of the selfsame idea. Sometimes the criticism is more implicit than explicit, but it is real nevertheless. Consider, for example, that whereas in *El arco* Paz presents the idea of autonomy as a fact about poetry, in other essays he discusses it as a historically situated perspective on poetry. In *Corriente alterna*,

Paz offers the following, highly compressed account of how the idea of the "work of art" and the corresponding notion of "aesthetic contemplation" emerged at a specific moment in time: "Desde la disgregación del catolicismo medieval, el arte se separó de la sociedad. Pronto se convirtió en una religión individual y en el culto privado de unas sectas. Nació la 'obra de arte' y la idea correlativa de 'contemplación estética.' Kant y todo lo demás" (73; Ever since the disintegration of medieval Catholicism, art became separate from society. Soon it turned into an individual religion and into the private cult of certain sects. "The work of art" was born and along with it the idea of "aesthetic contemplation." Kant and all that.) By presenting the idea of aesthetic autonomy as part of a historical narrative, Paz relativizes the phenomenon in question. If the notion of the autonomous work of art requiring a special type of attention emerges under specific historical conditions, then it is understood that the idea of autonomy can also die out or fade away. Indeed, this is exactly what Paz predicts will happen. "La época que comienza" (The era that is now beginning), he prophesizes, "acabará por fin con las 'obras' y disolverá la contemplación en el *acto*. No un arte nuevo: un nuevo ritual, una fiesta—la invención de una forma de *pasión* que será una repartición del tiempo, el espacio y el lenguaje" (73; will finally bring to an end the idea of the "work" and will replace contemplation with *action*. Not a new art: a new ritual, a *fiesta*—the invention of a form of passion that will amount to a new distribution of time, space, and language). No one reading this passage is likely to conclude that Paz deplores this development; on the contrary, one immediately senses his excitement at the transformation awaiting in the future. In sum, if the autonomy of poetry depends on particular circumstances, and if, moreover, such autonomy can be superseded by something that appears to be more valuable or meaningful, then poetic autonomy is not as absolute a phenomenon as we might have thought. It is more a feature of the history of poetry than of poetry itself.

Paz offers a more extended meditation on the limitations of the ideal of poetic autonomy in a remarkable 1973 essay on the subject of crafts titled "El uso y la contemplación" (Use and contemplation).

The goal of this essay is to situate the realm of crafts in relation to art on the one hand, and mass-produced objects on the other. Not surprisingly, Paz prefers craftsmanship to mass production. More surprisingly, in the comparison between crafts and art, the former comes out on top. Paz begins by explaining that crafts belong to a world prior to the separation between the realms of the useful and the beautiful. It is this split, where beauty is transformed into "un valor aislado y autosuficiente" (7; an isolated and self-sufficient value), that accounts for the invention of the museum and the rise of the religion of art. "La religión del arte" (The religion of art), he explains, "nació ... de las ruinas del cristianismo" (7; was born ... from the ruins of Christianity). What this new religion inherited from the old religion was "el poder de consagrar a las cosas e infundirles una suerte de eternidad" (7; the power to consecrate objects and to infuse them with a kind of eternity). In short, the realm of aesthetic contemplation offers a new experience of the sacred in a world without God.[21] The museum is the institution that buttresses this new conception of art: "los museos son nuestros templos y los objetos que se exhiben en ellos están más allá de la historia" (7; museums are our temples and the objects they exhibit exist in a realm beyond history). Paz explains the status of art in the modern world in terms that are by now thoroughly familiar to anyone acquainted with his work. "Para nosotros" (For us), he explains, "el objeto artístico es una realidad autónoma y autosuficiente y su sentido último no está más allá de la obra sino en ella misma" (10; the aesthetic object is an autonomous and self-sufficient entity and its deepest meaning exists in itself, not in something outside itself). But the very fact that he presents this way of viewing the art work as a historical phenomenon, that is, as an idea that emerges at a specific moment in time, and for concrete historical reasons, makes this view appear relative. Paz approaches the theme of artistic autonomy from a detached perspective. Instead of defending the idea of autonomy, he is analyzing it.

In "El uso y la contemplación," Paz goes a step further in questioning the notion of artistic autonomy. It is not just that he places the concept in a historical context; he also shows how it has led art into a dead end. How did this happen? Paz suggests that the rise of the religion of art—linked to the idea of its autonomy—provoked an inevitable reaction. Dada, which attacked art itself, was a good example of this reaction against the enthronement of art. But what was the result of this assault on art? Paz believes that in focusing on art itself, that is, in making art its central subject, the attack on art merely strengthened it. "Nuestros museos" (Our museums), he notes, with a hint of irony, "están repletos de anti-obras de arte y de obras de anti-arte" (10–11; are filled with anti-works of art and works of anti-art). In short, the institution of art, which goes hand in hand with the idea of artistic autonomy, absorbs the attacks on it, and ends up being sustained rather than undermined by them. The other part of this story to which Paz calls our attention is the transformation of art into an intellectual argument. When artworks turn into vehicles for debating the nature of art, they can no longer be understood unless the viewer is familiar with the ideas behind them. The risk, in other words, is "quedarse con el concepto y sin el arte, con la *trouvaille* y sin la cosa" (11; is to be left with the concept instead of the art, with the *trouvaille* instead of the thing itself).[22] A key figure in this development was, of course, Marcel Duchamp, on whom Paz wrote not just one, but two books.[23] Paz is convinced that Duchamp managed (mostly) to sidestep the danger he was courting; his followers, however, have been less successful. Art now finds itself in an impasse: "La religión artística moderna gira sobre sí misma sin encontrar la vía de salud: va de la negación del sentido por el objeto a la negación del objeto por el sentido" ("El uso," 12; The modern religion of art spins around itself without finding a way out: it goes from the negation of thought by the object to the negation of the object by thought). What Paz is describing is, in essence, a crisis of the idea of aesthetic autonomy.

The Mexican poet's celebratory description of the world of crafts draws out all that has been lost by art in its pursuit of autonomy. Earlier we saw that one of the key elements of the autonomous work of art was its concreteness. As art turned more and more in on itself, becoming more than anything else a reflection on art, it allowed the quality of concreteness to slip away. Paz rediscovers it in the work of the artisans. "La artesanía" (Crafts), he suggests, "es una presencia física que nos entra por los sentidos" (13; are a physical presence that enter through the senses). Our relationship with crafts is corporeal, he says, in contrast to our relationship with mass-produced objects, which is functional, and with art, which is semi-religious. "En verdad" (In truth), Paz adds, "no es una relación, sino un contacto" (15; it is not a relationship, but a form of contact). Crafts open the door to a fuller and healthier awareness not only of our physical existence, but also of time. To explain this point, Paz once again contrasts the work of the artisans with that of artists, on the one hand, and industrial designers, on the other. "El artista moderno" (The modern artist), he writes, "está lanzado a la conquista de la eternidad y el diseñador a la del futuro; el artesano se deja conquistar por el tiempo" (17; seeks to conquer eternity while the designer seeks to conquer the future; the craftsman allows himself to be conquered by time). The artisan does not seek to escape from time, but to unite with it. All this leads to a more concrete and more humane relationship to the world. "La artesanía" (Crafts), Paz proclaims in the final sentences of his essay, "es el latido del tiempo humano" (23; are the beating heart of human time). Implicitly, the Mexican poet is suggesting that in its pursuit of the ideal of purity, art has lost the connection that artisanship offers.

As a final example of how Paz not only defended the autonomy of art, but also questioned it, let us turn now to the pages he devoted in *Los hijos del limo* to the work of the French poet Pierre Reverdy. What were the key traits of Reverdy's poems, and why did they provoke reservations in Paz? In Paz's discussion of Reverdy, we encounter many of the themes which, as we saw earlier, flow out of the idea of poetic autonomy. "Reverdy," Paz claims, "tiende a convertir cada poema en un objeto" (176; tends to turn every poem into an object). One of the central presuppositions of Reverdy's aesthetics is "la idea de un arte que no sea imitación de la realidad" (177; the idea of an art that is not a copy of reality). As part of these efforts to turn the poem into an autonomous object, Reverdy eliminated a series of elements that made poetry appear dependent on something outside of itself. Paz speaks of the removal from Reverdy's poems of narrative, biography, and history (177). But what did this purification of the poetic realm achieve? Paz seems to admire Reverdy's rigor, but his assessment of his poetry is ultimately unfavorable. "El poema" (The poem), he says, "es un espacio cerrado en el que no ocurre nada, no pasa nada, ni siquiera el tiempo" (177–78; is a closed space in which nothing happens and nothing transpires, not even time). The French poet's work was so pure that it ended up being sterile. "Reverdy," he argues, "es uno de los poetas más intensos de este siglo; también es uno de los más monótonos" (178; is one of the most intense poets of this century; he is also one of the most monotonous). In the end, Reverdy's work serves as an example of how the pursuit of autonomy has drained poetry of its interest.

Paz's deliberations on poetic autonomy and its associated themes place him squarely in the tradition of romantic/symbolist aesthetics.[24] There are surely many reasons why Paz felt drawn to this particular view of art. An important consideration must have been the fact that defending the idea of poetic autonomy was a way of defending poetry itself. Denying such things as poetry's usefulness, its referential dimension, or its capacity for conveying content were, perhaps paradoxically, ways of elevating its importance by not making it dependent on external considerations. But Paz seems to have simultaneously understood that cutting poetry off from anything outside itself might also have a crippling effect on the status of poetry. This explains why, alongside the defense of poetic autonomy one finds in Paz's work, as I have just demonstrated, a critique of the idea of poetic autonomy. It also explains why he often switches to a completely different justification for poetry and art. On the one hand, the theme of poetic autonomy leads Paz into a position reminiscent of Oscar Wilde's famous notion that "art has no influence upon action." On the other hand, the Mexican poet frequently puts forward the idea not that art is disconnected from action, but that it *is* action, and not that art is remote from life, but that art and life are, or will be, at some point in the future, fused into a single whole. I will proceed now to examine this alternative thread in Paz's defense of poetry, giving a sense of the multifaceted nature of his poetics.[25]

The question of the transformative effect of poetry on society stood at the center of Paz's reflections on poetry. It maintains, throughout his work, an uncomfortable relationship with the utterly different idea that poetry existed in an autonomous realm, entirely separate from social, historical, and political considerations.[26] Paz introduces the topic of poetry's impact on the world at the very beginning of *El arco*, indeed even before the book as such gets off to a start. In his preface, Paz wonders whether writing poetry—and trying to define what it is—is, in actual fact, a worthwhile enterprise. "¿No sería mejor," he inquires, "transformar la vida en poesía que hacer poesía con la vida?" (7; Would it not be better to transform life into poetry than to make poetry out of life?) He sets this question aside for the bulk of the book, as he explores different aspects of the nature of poetry, but he returns to the theme of turning life itself into a form of poetry toward the end of *El arco*. In the concluding paragraphs of a chapter titled "Ambigüedad de la novela" (Ambiguity of the novel), he notes that the modern novel has become increasingly poetic, a development he reads as a triumph for poetry. And what does this triumph point toward, according to Paz? It signals, he says, a new stage in the relationship between literature and the world. He envisions "una aventura entre todas desesperada y extrema: la poesía no encarnará ya en la palabra sino en la vida. La palabra poética no consagrará a la historia, sino que será historia, vida" (231; a desperate and extreme adventure: poetry will not be embodied in words, but in life itself. The poetic word will not serve to consecrate history; instead it will *be* history, life itself). In the next chapter, "El verbo desencarnado" (The disembodied word)—the book's last chapter, if we leave aside the epilogue and appendices—Paz explains more in detail what he means by this.

One can imagine many ways in which poetry might transform life. Paz explicitly ties the idea of the poeticization of the world to the concept of revolution. Indeed, the complicated relationship between poetry and revolution is a question he addresses repeatedly over the course of his career. In "El verbo desencarnado" he suggests that the project of revolution is closely intertwined with that of modern poetry. "La sociedad revolucionaria" (A revolutionary society), he claims, "es inseparable de la sociedad fundada en la palabra poética" (236; is inseparable from a society founded on the poetic word). In short, to be truly revolutionary, a society must be rooted in poetry, and the goal of poetry becomes, at bottom, to bring about a revolution in society. According to Paz, "la empresa poética coincide lateralmente con la revolucionaria" (236; the poetic enterprise coincides laterally with the revolutionary enterprise). It is hard to imagine a more exalted view of poetry.[27] From this perspective, it is the handmaiden of revolution, which is itself the highest goal and the endpoint of human history. But the revolution is nothing unless it involves the enthronement of poetry at the center of all social activity.[28]

Paz goes on to provide a historical overview of this particular conception of the relationship between poetry and society. He begins with Blake's prophecy of a world in which poetry reigns supreme. "La sociedad poética, la nueva Jerusalem" (the poetic society, the New Jerusalem), says Paz, summarizing Blake, "se perfila por primera vez, desprendida de los dogmas de la religión y de la utopía de los filósofos. La poesía entra en acción" (238; becomes visible for the first time, freed of the dogmas of religion and the utopias of the philosophers. Poetry jumps into action). Next he mentions Friedrich Schlegel's call to "vivificar y socializar la poesía, hacer poética la vida y la sociedad" (239; vivify and socialize poetry, to make life and society poetic), and Novalis's dream of a society that is "un poema viviente" (240; a living poem). Paz's narrative concerning the poeticization of the world—or, better said, the dream of the world's poeticization—culminates in the twentieth century with the surrealists, a group with which Paz had become informally affiliated, and whose leader, André Breton, he befriended, after he settled in Paris in 1945.[29] Paz places surrealism firmly in the romantic tradition. "El programa surrealista" (The surrealist program), he affirms, "no es distinto al proyecto de Federico Schlegel y sus amigos: hacer poética la vida y la sociedad" (244; is no different from the project of Friedrich Schlegel and his friends: to make life and society poetic). Paz eloquently summarizes the revolutionary ideals the surrealists were committed to: not only the conviction that "todos podemos ser poetas" (we can all be poets), but, more profoundly, "la transformación de los hombres en poemas vivientes" (246; the transformation of human beings into living poems). It is precisely at this point, however, that the Mexican poet's argument takes a different turn, as he takes stock of whether the revolutionary transformation of the world prophesied by a long line of poets, from the romantics to the surrealists, has in any sense been fulfilled.[30]

Paz, who has up until this point discussed the idea of a communion through poetry in hopeful and even exalted terms, now speaks bluntly of the failure of the revolutionary dream. He begins by explaining once more what the dream consisted of. "La nueva sociedad comunista" (The new communist society), he states, "sería una sociedad surrealista, en la que la poesía circularía por la vida social como una fuerza perpetuamente creadora" (248; would be a surrealist society, in which poetry would circulate in society as a perpetually creative force). What happened to this grand aspiration? According to Paz, the dream crashed into reality. On the one hand, there was the utopia envisioned by the poets; on the other hand, there was an actually existing Communist society—the Soviet Union—the reality of which bore no relation whatsoever to the hopes of the revolutionaries. Putting his finger on the degeneration of the egalitarian dream into a totalitarian nightmare, Paz speaks of "el culto a los jefes" (the cult of the leaders), "los guardianes de los libros santos" (the guardians of the sacred texts), and "[la] casta de teólogos e inquisidores" (248; the caste of theologians and inquisitors). The new society ended up being as oppressive as the old society, if not more so. And what did the poets do when faced with this situation? The Mexican poet's concluding assessment of the situation of poetry in the mid twentieth century—and of its purpose and justification—is ambiguous. On the one hand, he offers a sobering evaluation of where the romantic/surrealist project has left us. Breton may continue to proclaim that the revolution and surrealist poetry are twinned together, but in reality, says Paz, "su acción en el campo de la realidad ha sido esporádica y no ha llegado a influir en la vida política" (249; his actions in the real world have been sporadic and have not succeeded in influencing political life). He goes on to note that the idea on which the surrealist endeavor was predicated has simply failed to materialize. "La poesía" (Poetry), he states starkly, "no ha encarnado en la historia" (250; has not become incarnate in history). And yet, at the same time, he cannot abandon the dream that has infused poetry since the romantic era. This dream offers, after all, one of the most powerful avenues for asserting the crucial importance of poetry in the modern era. "El poema futuro" (The poem of the future), Paz proclaims, as he brings *El arco* to a close, "para ser de veras poema, deberá partir de la experiencia romántica" (250; in order to be a true poem, must take the experience of Romanticism as its point of departure). In sum, the promise of a society in which poetry is the supreme activity has not been fulfilled, and has no appearance of becoming fulfilled. Yet that promise cannot be cast aside. The defense of poetry would appear to depend on it.

With the passing of time, Paz jettisoned his surrealist/revolutionary ideals and developed a more modest defense of poetry. Given the exalted and even extreme nature of the earlier defenses, this was perhaps the only direction in which he could develop. An important factor in Paz's evolution was the increasingly clear failure of the revolutionary dream, of which he had been such a fervent advocate in the earlier stages of his career, and whose foundering he had already registered in *El arco*. By the 1980s, the revolution was no longer the aimed-for or long-anticipated culmination of the historical process. It was now, in Paz's eyes, part of the problem rather than the solution. A changing world, along with the springing up of new political ideas, led to a rethinking of the function of poetry. Paz himself formulated the problem that needed to be addressed in several essays from this period. In "Poesía, mito, revolución" (Poetry, myth, revolution), Paz sketches the new historical conjuncture in which the West finds itself, with the waning of the myth of revolution and the rise of liberal democracy. He asks what the role of poetry might be under these new circumstances. "¿Cuál puede ser la contribución de la poesía en la reconstitución de un nuevo pensamiento politico?" (68; How can poetry contribute to the forging of a new kind of political thought), he wonders.[31] In "La otra voz," an essay Paz wrote in December 1989, not long after the fall of the Berlin Wall, he poses a similar question. Again, he begins by noting the collapse of what he calls "las crueles utopías" (the cruel utopias) into which the modern era's revolutionary hopes had been transformed, as well as the triumph of the free-market model. But he worries about the place of poetry in a capitalist society. "Hoy las artes y la literatura" (Today, literature and the arts), he states, "se exponen a un peligro distinto: no las amenaza una doctrina o un partido político omnisciente sino un proceso económico sin rostro, sin alma y sin dirección" (125; are exposed to a different danger: not the threat of a doctrine or an omniscient political party, but of a faceless and soulless economic process that advances without any sense of direction).[32] He goes on to pose the following question: "En esta vuelta de los tiempos, ¿cuál podría ser la función de la poesía?" (135; What might be the function of poetry in these changing times?).

Paz does not mention the idea of poetic autonomy in these essays. On the contrary, he adopts a frankly functionalist approach, asking how poetry might be of use in helping shape a new social and political order. Nor does he allude to the surrealist idea of the poeticization of all of life. Clearly, Paz has set aside the deeply utopian ideals he had expressed earlier in his career. So what alternative does he provide? In "Poesía, mito, revolución," Paz suggests that poetry offers not new ideas, but insight into what he calls "la terrible antigüedad y la no menos terrible juventud de las pasiones" (68; the terrifying antiquity and the no less terrifying youthfulness of our passions). He goes on to associate the realm of human passions with what he calls "la otra voz" (the other voice). And what does this *other* voice express? "Es la voz" (It is the voice), says Paz, "del poeta trágico y la del bufón, la de la solitaria melancolía y la de la fiesta, es la risotada y el suspiro, la del abrazo de los amantes y la de Hamlet ante el cráneo, la voz del silencio y la del tumulto, loca sabiduría y cuerda locura, susurro de confidencia en la alcoba y oleaje de multitud en la plaza" (68; of the tragic poet and of the buffoon, of solitary melancholy and of the *fiesta*, of the burst of laughter and the sigh, of the lovers' embrace and of Hamlet contemplating the skull, it is the voice of silence and of tumult, of insane wisdom and sane madness, of secret whispers in the alcove and of the swell of the multitude in the plaza). The enumeration the Mexican poet provides here seems designed to capture the sheer heterogeneity of human experience, and the endless contrasts and paradoxes that characterize it. The role of poetry is to call the reader's attention to the multiple dimensions of human life that are ignored or suppressed in modern society, to enrich and give depth to our otherwise impoverished lives. One gets the sense from this passage that, for Paz, poetry is no longer charged with changing life, but with making it more nuanced and more complete.

In "La otra voz," Paz provides a more extended answer to the question of what the function of poetry might be in the late twentieth century. He returns to the association between poetry and the "other voice," suggesting that this voice expresses "realidades y aspiraciones más profundas y antiguas que las geometrías intelectuales de los revolucionarios y las cárceles de conceptos de los utopistas" (130–31; truths and aspirations that are older and more profound than the intellectual geometries of the revolutionaries and the conceptual prison-houses of the utopians). But he also approaches the role of poetry in the modern world from a slightly different perspective. In this other thread running through "La otra voz" the idea is no longer that poetry brings to light a subversive, buried dimension of experience, but that it helps to strengthen the social bond. How does Paz reach this conclusion? Again, in developing this part of the argument, he begins by sketching the historical context informing the contemporary poetic enterprise. To evoke this context he goes back to one of the foundational events of the modern era: the French Revolution. Paz notes that three central ideals of the French Revolution—liberty, equality, and fraternity—are still the building blocks of modernity. He argues, however, that fraternity is the most important ideal of the three. "Sólo la fraternidad" (Only fraternity), he claims, "puede disipar la pesadilla circular del mercado" (129; can dissipate the circular nightmare of the market). And how can poetry promote the goal of fraternity? It does so, Paz suggests, through its very nature. At this point, the Mexican poet returns to an idea he had exposed at length in his earlier work: the notion that the poetic imagination is essentially of an analogical nature.[33] "Todas las formas poéticas" (All poetic forms), he argues, "y todas las figuras de lenguaje poseen un rasgo en común: buscan y, con frecuencia, descubren semejanzas ocultas entre objetos diferentes" (and all figures of speech have one thing in common: they search for and often discover resemblances among disparate objects). He goes on to describe the poem as "un pequeño cosmos animado" (a small animated cosmos) and an "espejo de la fraternidad cósmica" (mirror of cosmic fraternity).[34] What poetry does, in sum, is to show us how to relate, in a spirit of community and solidarity, with the universe. It provides a model of connectedness and, as such, helps sustain life and keep chaos at bay. It neither withdraws into an autonomous realm, nor invades the whole of life; instead, it offers an image of how to make a better world.

CHAPTER 10

Octavio Paz as a Literary Character

Narrative works featuring historical authors as characters abound in Western literature.[1] Perhaps the most popular subject of such works has been William Shakespeare, who appears as a character in an astonishing number of fictions and films, including, of course, Jorge Luis Borges's "Everything and Nothing" and "Shakespeare's Memory."[2] Borges himself has been a frequent subject of fictional representations,[3] as have other Latin American writers such as Sor Juana Inés de la Cruz,[4] José Martí,[5] and Carlos Fuentes.[6] Octavio Paz, too, has enjoyed intense interest on the part of his fellow authors, primarily in Mexico, but occasionally in other countries as well. In some of these works he appears under his real name; in others, his identity is disguised behind an invented name. In the latter cases, we are dealing with *romans à clef*. Paz does not occupy the role of protagonist in any of the narrative works in which he appears, although he is an important character in many of them. In other narratives he is limited to small parts, appearing in a handful of scenes or episodes, or being referred to occasionally by the narrator. The frequency of his appearances in Mexican novels and short stories tells us something about how large Paz has loomed in the Mexican literary imagination, while the fact that non-Mexican authors too have included the Mexican Nobel laureate in their fictional works is surely a reflection of his international stature.

There are many reasons why writers are drawn to the motif of the author as a literary character. It allows them to come to terms with their precursors, to address literary and artistic themes, and to raise issues surrounding the problem of representation. It is interesting to note, however, that the authors who have included portrayals of Paz as a literary character in their works have tended not to focus on questions of literary inheritance, artistic vocation, or representation; instead, they have been concerned primarily with the question of cultural prestige and power. Fictional portrayals of Paz often draw attention to his role as a protagonist—sometimes generous and attentive, more often fearsome and domineering—of Mexican cultural life. While some authors concern themselves with Paz's ideas, many are interested above all in the power he wielded within the literary world. There are a number of fictional representations of Paz that depict his private life, but the dominant tendency has been to write about the Mexican poet and essayist's public persona. This overall orientation tells us something about Paz; it surely also points to a significant feature of the Mexican literary world to which he belonged.

A writer who knew Paz well and occasionally depicted him in his work was Carlos Fuentes.[7] The two had met in Paris in 1950, at a time when Paz had just published two of the most important books of his career, *El laberinto de la soledad* and *Libertad bajo palabra* (Freedom under oath). The meeting with Paz had a profound impact on Fuentes, who was just twenty-one years old and had not yet published his first book. Years later he would vividly evoke the effect of Paz's books on him: "My friends and I had read those books aloud in Mexico, dazzled by a poetics that managed simultaneously to renew our language from within and connect it to the language of the world."[8] Paz's ideas about Mexican identity, culture, and history left an unmistakable imprint on the work of his younger friend, as any perusal of the torrent of books Fuentes would begin to publish a few years later will easily confirm. Given Fuentes's fascination with Paz, and the deep admiration he felt for him, it is not surprising that he included portraits of his friend in some of his works, beginning with his first novel, *La región más transparente* (1958; The most transparent region, published in English as *Where the Air Is Clear*), in which one of the main characters, Manuel Zamacona, is a Mexico City intellectual with a clear resemblance to Fuentes's friend.

Fuentes himself dismissed the notion that there was a connection between Zamacona and Paz. In a letter to the editor published in *Saturday Review*, Fuentes stated firmly that to associate the one with other, as the critic José Vázquez Amaral had done in his review of the English translation of *La región*, constituted "a gratuitous identification, and one which I flatly deny."[9] A few years later, in an interview with Luis Harss, Fuentes adopted a less definitive posture, stating merely that Zamacona was a composite of different Mexican intellectuals of the period.[10] Still, the echoes of Paz's ideas in Zamacona's historical and philosophical meditations were so difficult to avoid that one critic was led to debate whether the reminiscences of Paz's work in Fuentes's novel might not constitute a form of plagiarism.[11] Paz, for his part, appears not to have liked the novel. In his review of *La región*, Vázquez Amaral reported that Paz had described Fuentes's novel as "an ambitious work in the worst possible sense."[12] In a March 30, 1959, letter to José Bianco, the Mexican poet offered a more detailed account of his feelings about the novel, and about Fuentes as a person. "A mí también me asombró su novela" (I, too, was surprised by his novel), he informs his correspondent. "Le tenía estimación, lo quería, creía en él. ¿Cómo era posible que hubiera escrito *eso*? Pero *eso*—y esa fue mi segunda sorpresa—tuvo un gran éxito. Mis sentimientos frente a Fuentes son ambiguos: fue amigo mío, muy amigo, después de la novela, dejé de verlo; ahora nos hemos vuelto a ver. No puedo evitar quererlo; no puedo evitar que me irrite . . . y me defraude" (I respected him, I felt affection for him, I believed in him. How could he have written *that*? But *that*—and this was my second surprise—turned out to be a big success. I have mixed feelings about Fuentes: he was my friend, a very good friend, but after he published his novel I stopped seeing him; now we have started to see each other again. I can't help feeling affection for him; I can't help feeling irritated by him . . . and disappointed).[13] Paz does not specifically address the possibility that Fuentes may have wanted to portray him in his novel; what is clear, however, is that the publication of *La región* provoked at least a temporary rift between the two authors.

Through Zamacona, Fuentes alludes to the overwhelming preoccupation with the question of national identity among Mexican intellectuals of the 1940s and 1950s. The vogue for writing about Mexico was reflected not only in the publication of Paz's *El laberinto*, but also in the constitution of the Hiperión circle of intellectuals, who initiated a series of conferences and book publications on the topic of Mexican identity.[14] Like Paz and the members of the Hiperión group, Zamacona is an avid practitioner of what had come to be labelled as *la filosofía de lo mexicano* (the philosophy of Mexicanness) and in a scene early in the novel we see him laboring over an essay on Mexican identity. In *El laberinto*, Paz had famously described Mexican identity in terms of a Freudian-style family romance, and Zamacona undertakes something similar in the essay he writes in *La región*. "El padre permanece en un pasado de brumas" (The father remains in a misty past), he claims, "objeto de escarnio, violador de nuestra propia madre" (an object of scorn, the rapist of our own mother).[15] Although Paz never suggests in *El laberinto* that the symbolical father of today's Mexican is a vague, misty figure (on the contrary, he clearly identifies the Spanish conquistador as the father), the need to reject the paternal figure connects Zamacona's reading of Mexican identity to the one put forward by Paz. Zamacona proceeds to elaborate on the resentment the Mexican feels toward his symbolical father: "El padre consume lo que nosotros nunca podremos consumar: la conquista de la madre. Es el verdadero macho, y lo resentimos" (The father consummates what we will never be able to consummate: the conquest of the mother. He is the true macho and we resent him for it).[16] Compare Zamacona's comments to Paz's description of the father as an aggressive, wrathful figure, and as, among other things, a violent conqueror of women: "Este aspecto—Jehová colérico, Dios de ira, Saturno, Zeus violador de mujeres—es el que aparece casi exclusivamente en las representaciones populares que se hace el mexicano del poder viril" (This aspect—furious Jehovah, wrathful God, Saturn, Zeus the rapist of women—is the aspect that appears almost exclusively in the popular representations of masculine power in Mexico).[17] Note, furthermore, that for Paz one of the keys to understanding the psychology of the Mexican is his feeling of being "fruto de una violación" (the product of a rape).[18] This is exactly the element that Zamacona brings to the fore in his discussion of the Mexican character. This does not mean that the two versions of Mexico's family romance are identical. In the version Fuentes presents in *La región* through the story of Zamacona, it turns out that the father (Federico Robles) is of indigenous descent, whereas the mother (Mercedes Zamacona) is a criolla. Paz, by contrast, associates the father with the Spanish conquistador and the mother with the indigenous woman. But the two versions share an emphasis on the mother's violation by the father.

In his ruminations on Mexico, Zamacona develops ideas about the country's history that are highly reminiscent of those expressed by Paz in *El laberinto*. In the essay he writes near the beginning of the novel, Zamacona introduces the theme of "la imitación extralógica" (69; extra-logical imitation), a theme he further explores later in the novel in a conversation with Robles (Manuel's father, though neither is aware of this fact about their relationship). The idea of extra-logical imitation derives from the work of the French nineteenth-century thinker Gabriel Tarde; it is used by Zamacona to propose a reading of Mexican history as a series of efforts to import political and economic models from Europe. All these efforts end in failure and frustration, because the European models do not make a good fit with the Mexican situation. As Zamacona explains to Robles, "siempre hemos querido correr hacia modelos que no nos pertenecen, vestirnos con trajes que no nos quedan, disfrazarnos para ocultar la verdad" (279; we have always wanted to chase after models that do not belong to us, dress up in clothes that do not fit, put on a mask in order to hide the truth). Although the masking of reality seems to be a constant throughout Mexican history, for Zamacona the *Porfiriato* best exemplifies this phenomenon: "¿No ve usted al porfirismo tratando de justificarse con la filosofía positivista, disfrazándonos a todos?" (279; Do you not see the *Porfiriato* trying to use positivist philosophy to justify itself, and as a result disguising all of us?) This reading of Mexican history—and of the *Porfiriato* in particular—is extremely close to the one Paz develops in the sixth chapter of *El laberinto*, "De la Independencia a la Revolución." Paz, too, quotes Tarde's concept of extra-logical imitation and uses the *Porfiriato* to illustrate it (*El laberinto*, 88). There is an unbridgeable distance, he argues, between the ideology adopted by the Díaz regime, with its emphasis on science and progress, and the actual social forces, essentially feudal in nature, sustaining the regime. The result of this breach between ideology and reality is that Mexican society during the *Porfiriato* becomes characterized by simulation and inauthenticity. Paz speaks of the positivist ideology adopted by the Porfirian regime as a "disfraz" (144; disguise), prefiguring the metaphor of the mask also used by Zamacona.

In the historical narrative developed by Paz and Fuentes (with Zamacona as his mouthpiece), the Mexican Revolution is interpreted as an explosive (and redemptive) response to the denial and repression of Mexico's true character during the *Porfiriato*. But whereas Zamacona's reading of the *Porfiriato* hews very closely to the model put forward in *El laberinto*, his explanation of the Revolution adds some new ingredients to Paz's reading of this period of Mexican history. Paz describes the Revolution as a profound act of self-discovery on the part of the Mexican nation. The Revolution, he writes, "es un hecho que irrumpe en nuestra historia como una verdadera revelación de nuestro ser" (148; is an event that bursts forth in our history like a true revelation of our being). It is, he adds, "un movimiento tendiente a reconquistar nuestro pasado, asimilarlo y hacerlo vivo en el presente" (160; a movement that attempts to reconquer our past, assimilate it, and bring it to life in the present). The view of the Revolution as a revelation of the nation's true identity is a centerpiece of Zamacona's reading of his country's past, too. "La Revolución" (The Revolution), he says, "nos descubre la totalidad de la historia de México" (brings to light the totality of the history of Mexico).[19] But whereas Zamacona's notion of the Revolution as involving a removal of the country's mask echoes Paz's comments, his description of what is uncovered once the mask is ripped off takes us in a different direction than *El laberinto*. Paz merely states that the Revolution is a kind of revelation; Zamacona, on the other hand, provides more information on exactly what it is that stands revealed when the Revolution erupts. Paz suggests that Mexico is something *deep*; hence the images of immersion and penetration into a zone of interiority. The Mexican Revolution "es un movimiento del ser . . . que se adentra en su propia intimidad" (160; is a movement of our being . . . that plunges into our own innermost recesses). It is "una súbita inmersión de México en su propio ser" (162; a sudden immersion of Mexico in its own being). But he doesn't say very much about what one discovers once one probes these depths. For Zamacona, by contrast, Mexico is essentially *plural*. The Revolution uncovers Mexico's true identity, but it does so by making visible the totality of the country's varied past: "en la Revolución aparecieron, vivos y con el fardo de sus problemas, todos los hombres de la historia de México" (everyone who has existed in the course of Mexican history came to life during the Revolution, bearing the burden of their problems).[20] In short, Zamacona follows Paz in reading the Mexican Revolution in psycho-cultural terms, but he offers a different interpretation of exactly what the Revolution exposes about Mexico.[21]

The parallels between Zamacona's ideas about Mexican history and identity and those expressed by Paz suggest that Fuentes very likely did have his friend in mind when he wrote his first novel. Indeed, Fuentes establishes a link between his character and the author of *El laberinto* not only through the echoes of his ideas, but also by having Zamacona appear at one point in the novel with a copy of *El laberinto* under his arm. But the divergences between Zamacona and Paz also suggest that Fuentes's character is a composite of different traits, with Paz providing some but not all of the elements of his characterization. Given that many of Zamacona's ideas are expressed by Fuentes himself in his essays, we could say that Zamacona is a combination of Paz and Fuentes. Now, if we accept the notion that Zamacona is based at least in part on Paz, the question we must ask is what this portrait reveals about Fuentes's relationship with Paz at this stage of his career. In answering this question, it is important to note that Zamacona is among the most likeable characters in *La región*. If we compare him with the other leading characters of the novel, we see that Zamacona, unlike Rodrigo Pola, is not an opportunist, nor does he possess the sinister qualities of Ixca Cienfuegos. Furthermore, he is much more thoughtful and less self-serving in his interpretation of Mexico's current situation than the blustery Federico Robles. In short, if this is a portrait of Paz in the 1950s, it is a largely sympathetic one. Still, one cannot help but notice that Zamacona, who dies in a random incident, murdered by a man in a cantina who had taken offense at the way Zamacona had looked at him, is, in the end, a somewhat ineffectual figure.[22]

Fuentes used Paz as a model again in "La desdichada," a short story that is part of the collection *Constancia y otras novelas para vírgenes* (1990; *Constancia and Other Stories for Virgins*). The story is set in the 1930s and describes the friendship between Toño and Bernardo, two students at Mexico City's Escuela Nacional Preparatoria (National Preparatory School), who share a small apartment in the center of the city. Bernardo becomes enamored of a mannequin in a wedding dress he discovers in a nearby store display, and one day Toño brings the mannequin, without the wedding dress, back to their apartment. A strange kind of *ménage à trois* develops between the two young men and the wooden mannequin. Among the several themes Fuentes develops in the story is that of literature, for the two young men are aspiring writers. In a 1998 essay about his friendship with Paz, written shortly after the poet's death, Fuentes stated that the idea for the story had come from an anecdote he had heard from José Alvarado, who had been close to Paz in the 1930s.[23] Fuentes also explained that "el papel de Bernardo corresponde a un retrato imaginario del joven Octavio" (Bernardo's role amounts to an imaginary portrait of the young Octavio).[24] In his portrait of Paz as a young artist, Fuentes zeroes in on his ideas about literature, contrasting Bernardo's view of the poet as a visionary with Toño's desire to write what he calls "la poesía de los bajos fondos" (poetry of the slums).[25] Bernardo, borrowing Toño's words, expresses the difference as follows: "Toño sonríe y me dice que soy un romántico; espero que el arte, la belleza y hasta el bien desciendan de la altura espiritual. Soy un cristiano secular que ha sustituido al Arte con A mayúscula por Dios con d minúscula. Toño dice que la poesía está en las vitrinas de las zapaterías" (Toño smiles and tells me I am a romantic; I cherish the hope that art, beauty, and even the good will descend from the spiritual heights. I am a secular Christian who has substituted Art with a capital A for God with a lower-case g. According to Toño, poetry can be found in the window displays of the shoe stores).[26] The reader who is at this point reminded of Pablo Neruda is clearly on the right track, for Bernardo himself mentions the Chilean poet later in the same passage. One gets the sense that the author sides with Neruda's aesthetic of the concrete and the everyday rather than with Paz's ivory tower approach; nevertheless, "La desdichada" offers a not at all unsympathetic portrait of the young Octavio.

Fuentes's long (and complicated) friendship with Paz had come to a definitive end with the publication in *Vuelta* of a fiercely critical piece on Fuentes by Paz's collaborator Enrique Krauze.[27] Given this background, it is striking to note the affectionate tone of Fuentes's depiction of Paz in "La desdichada," a story that came out only two years after the rupture between the two authors. In writing about his former friend, Fuentes came across as generous and forgiving. Still, Fuentes got his revenge on Paz almost two decades later, in his novel *Adán en Edén* (Adam in Eden) (2009), one of the last books of his long career. In this new version, Paz is far from being the ineffectual figure he was in *La región*. Indeed, in *Adán en Edén* Fuentes zeroes in on the widespread notion of Paz as the "pope" of Mexican culture. The Paz character in the novel is named Maximino Sol, with the surname surely designed to suggest that this is a man who regards the universe as revolving around himself, an overblown self-conception also alluded to by his first name. It is worth noting that Sol appears in only one chapter. Since the episode it describes has no effect on the plot of the novel, the reader may well suspect that Fuentes had a set-piece about Paz on hand, and decided somewhat arbitrarily to insert it into this novel. Maximino is depicted as a physically unimpressive man:

"Su cuerpo pequeñín y regordete se veía apretado por el chaleco de rayas grises, y la papada le colgaba un tanto por encima del nudo de la corbata" (41; his small and chubby body fit tightly in a gray-striped coat, and his double chin hung slightly over the knot of his tie).[28] He comes across as pedantic and censorious. To converse with Maximino Sol is to find oneself in a "salón de clase perpetuo" (42; a perpetual classroom). His judgments of his fellow Mexican writers are singularly ungenerous: "Sol comenzó por despacharse, uno por uno, a los escritores de su generación, de generaciones anteriores y, aun, de generaciones más jóvenes que la suya" (42; Sol began by dismissing, one by one, the writers of his own generation, of previous generations and even of younger generations than his own). His rejection of every single other writer is, of course, a way of elevating himself. Thoroughly disagreeable character that he is, Maximino nevertheless lords it over the Mexican literary field: "ejercía una especie de tiranía fascinante sobre la literatura mexicana" (40; he exercised a fascinating kind of tyranny over Mexican literature). Fuentes's slashingly satirical depiction of Paz in *Adán en Edén* reveals how his perspective on his erstwhile friend and mentor had changed over time.[29]

Whereas Fuentes portrayed Paz first as a young, aspiring intellectual, and later as an established figure in Mexico's literary world, Luis Guillermo Piazza depicts the Mexican poet and essayist at an intermediate stage in his career, when he has already acquired a certain status as a writer, but has not yet come to occupy a central position in the Mexican literary field. In his 1967 novel *La mafia*, Piazza offers a satirical portrait of Mexico City's hip cultural scene of the mid-sixties, packaged in a highly experimental narrative form. The novel uses the technique of the collage, juxtaposing the interior monologues of an anxious narrator trying to figure out what kind of book to write; letters from prominent writers such as Carlos Monsiváis (also referred to as "CM" or "monsi") and Carlos Fuentes (whose name is often written as "carlosfuentes," as if he were a brand more than a person); glossaries of terms that will help the reader navigate the world of Mexico City's cultural avant-garde; descriptions of book presentations, art gallery openings, roundtables, film screenings, and other social gatherings of the city's cultural elite; gossipy meditations on who is "in" and who is "out" in the literary world; pseudo-erudite disquisitions à la Borges on abstruse historical topics; and visual materials including a series of drawings by Mexican artist José Luis Cuevas as well as several reels of small black-and-white Kodak photos of partying Mexico City literati (one recognizes Carlos Fuentes in many of the pictures, as well as Gabriel García Márquez, José Donoso, and others). The novel touches on numerous themes having to do with Mexico City's cultural life, and includes chapters titled "Los viajeros" (The travelers), in which the narrator talks about the many foreign writers who alight in the city in search of a taste of the exotic, especially writers from the United States such as Tom Wolfe, James Purdy, Jack Kerouac, and William Burroughs, and "Los acabados" (The finished ones), in which the phenomenon of the burnt-out writer is discussed. The narrator also refers to several key concepts that circulated among the members of the artistic avant-garde of the period, including Susan Sontag's polemic "against interpretation," the idea of the "página en blanco" (the blank page) (echoing Mallarmé), and the rejection on the part of Boom writers such as Fuentes and Mario Vargas Llosa of the regionalist novel. It is not clear whether the author genuinely believes in the existence of a "mafia" that controls the city's cultural life; what is clear, however, is that Piazza thinks that the literary world is characterized by an absurd pretentiousness, a great deal of posturing, and a very human but at the same time somewhat laughable hunger for recognition. In *La mafia*, the avant-garde is stripped of its ethical and political dimensions and exposed as a cultural movement that is fixated on the question of what is in fashion and what is not.[30]

 The author of *La mafia* bombards the reader with the names of well-known figures in Mexico City's literary and art worlds. Octavio Paz is not among the most frequently mentioned of these figures, but he does make several appearances in the novel. The references provide the reader with a perspective on the poet's standing in Mexico City's trend-setting cultural circles of the 1960s. Let us recall, to begin with, that Paz was living in India at the time, and indeed his distance from what is happening in Mexico is a constant theme in the mentions he receives in the novel. The first reference to Paz appears early in the novel in a section that addresses the escapist fantasy of the city crafted by a long line of foreign authors: "Para ellos Mexico City es lo otro, el Mal, el libre pecado, la liberación familiar, Henry Miller en un París mestizo, la fascinación del horror" (37; For them, Mexico City is the Other, Evil, the freedom to be sinful, liberation from the family, Henry Miller in a *mestizo* Paris, the fascination of horror).[31] Immediately after evoking this distorted vision of the city, the narrator introduces two prominent Mexican authors—Paz and Fuentes—who, he seems to suggest, similarly contemplate Mexico from a distance. "Por curioso que parezca" (Strange as it may seem), he writes, "Octavio Paz y Carlos Fuentes atisbaban a Mexico City, la recreaban desde aquí con miras a tenerla así presente en la nostalgia" (37; Octavio Paz and Carlos Fuentes kept an eye on Mexico City, they recreated the city from here with the goal of holding on to it in their nostalgia). Two notions can be extracted from this sentence. First, it is significant that Paz and Fuentes observe (or catch a glimpse of) "Mexico City" rather than "la Ciudad de México." The implication seems to be that they are depicting the foreign construct more than the actual city. Second, these authors create an image of the city specifically in order to cherish it as part of a nostalgic sentiment, a sentiment that by definition implies a certain distance from the object one is contemplating. The idea that the narrator wishes to draw a parallel between the way Paz sees Mexico and the perspective of the foreigners who have written about the country is reinforced when he compares a comment by the Mexican poet after a visit to a Mexico City brothel ("son las prostitutas más horrendas del mundo"; they are the most hideous prostitutes in the world) to "un juicio de Graham Greene en los peores momentos de su rabia por la persecución religiosa" (37–38; a judgment by Graham Greene in the worst moments of his rage at religious persecution).

    In his next appearance in the novel, Paz is again paired with Fuentes. In a chapter titled "Las cartas" (The letters), Piazza reproduces a series of letters written from abroad by Mexican authors, including several missives from Fuentes, who is traveling in Italy. On two occasions, Fuentes mentions that Paz has been visiting. From Rome, he writes the following: "Ayer pasó por Roma Octavio Paz, brillantísimo, joven, dueño de una visión mundial de las cosas. Alegría gigantesco de verlo y hablar con él" (54; Yesterday Octavio Paz passed through Rome; incredibly brilliant, young, in possession of a global perspective on things. It was a tremendous joy to see him and talk with him). Writing from Amalfi, the Mexican novelist continues to praise his older colleague: "Incluyo un artículo sobre Paz en Roma. Me dejó panting el poeta: ¡qué brillo, qué energía, qué vigencia, qué visión ecuménica sin par en el continente vacío! Paz no sacrifica, incluye; no se contenta, indaga; no reduce, ensancha; no acepta, corresponde" (55; I enclose an article about Paz in Rome. The poet left me panting: such brilliance, such energy, such relevance, such an unparalleled ecumenical vision of the empty continent! Paz does not sacrifice anything, he includes; he is not complacent, he explores; he does not reduce, he amplifies; he does not accept, he corresponds). If this passage sounds like an excellent imitation of Fuentes's breathless writing style, it is because Piazza is not in fact mimicking Fuentes, but quoting directly from a letter his Mexican colleague wrote to him from Amalfi on February 18, 1966.[32] With regard to Paz, these passages highlight his expansive, cosmopolitan vision. They also draw attention to the fact that it is Fuentes who, in a sense, is promoting Paz, even though he was considerably younger than his poet friend. As Domínguez Michael reminds us, in these years Fuentes occupied a more prominent place in Mexico's cultural world than Paz, who did not acquire his dominant position in the country's intellectual life until after his definitive return to Mexico in 1971.[33]

Interestingly, Paz's return to Mexico, or rather the rumors of his return, are mentioned on several occasions toward the end of *La mafia*. In a chapter that begins with yet another allusion to Fuentes ("Estamos aquí y aquí nos tocó estar, Región más Aparente") (140; We are here and this is where we are fated to be, the Most Apparent Region), the narrator refers in passing to Paz's possible return to Mexico: "y Paz que cada seis meses se corría el rumor de que estaba por llegar y formaría su propia mafia" (141; and Paz and every six months a rumor went around that he was about to return and that he would start his own mafia). On the final page of the novel, the narrator registers an anonymous voice that alludes to the same possibility: "cuando vuelva Paz" (when Paz returns), the voice says inconclusively. In short, Piazza portrays Paz as someone on the sidelines of the Mexican cultural field, yet as an important figure nevertheless. Fuentes promotes him excitedly, and the cultural world seems to await his return and to expect that he will claim a central role—even to the extent of creating his own mafia—within this world. Some would claim that this is exactly what happened when Paz returned to Mexico and founded first *Plural* (1971–76) and then *Vuelta* (1976–98), surely the most important cultural magazines to appear in Mexico during the final decades of the twentieth century. But in Piazza's 1967 depiction Paz comes across as a somewhat distant, enigmatic figure.

Perhaps no other contemporary author has reflected in his fiction as frequently on the question of Paz's dominant role in the Mexican cultural world as Enrique Serna. The narrator of his story "La vanagloria" (Vainglory) is a poet from the provincial city of Torreón who sends one of his books to Paz, and, much to his surprise, receives an encouraging (though not uncritical) response from the great man of letters. The narrator is a marginal figure even in the small cultural world of the city where he lives, and he tries to use the letter from Paz to boost his prestige among his fellow writers. The literary field in Torreón appears to be a harshly competitive environment, divided into a "círculo de los artistas rechazados o marginados" (3; group of rejected or marginalized artists),[34] to which the narrator belongs, on the one hand, and a small group of successful writers, "ganadores recurrentes de premios y becas" (3; repeated winners of prizes and grants), on the other. The narrator has nothing but contempt for the latter group; he regards its members as bad poets who, through their "club de elogios mutuos" (club of mutual praise), have managed to get their hands on "los botines más codiciados de la subvención pública a las bellas letras" (3; the most coveted spoils from the trough of state subsidies to the arts).

Indeed, using an image that crops up regularly in Serna's writings on Mexico's cultural world, he describes them as a kind of mafia (5). Yet in spite of his disdain for the successful writers of his city, the narrator wants what they have, and for a while it appears that the letter from Paz will generate the recognition he longs for. He invites the entire literary world of Torreón—friends and enemies alike— to a celebration at his home, where he promises to show everyone the letter from Paz. Unfortunately for the narrator, his young daughter, whom he deeply loves, but also resents for tying him to a domestic world that seems at odds with his romantic dreams of literary glory, defaces the letter with a thick black marker, leaving it completely unreadable. It is too late to cancel the party, and, of course, none of the guests believes the narrator's story. Everyone thinks he is lying about having received a laudatory letter from Mexico's Nobel laureate. The narrator's expected triumph turns into a thorough humiliation.

The narrator had been hoping to use Paz's letter to apply for a Guggenheim fellowship (5). Prodded by his wife, he decides to contact the poet to request a new letter. But Paz is difficult to track down. The narrator obtains the poet's phone number, but whenever he calls, he is told that Paz is away, doing the things that important writers do, such as giving a lecture in New York (9), or recording a TV program (11). The narrator decides to write Paz a letter, but in the meantime fate intervenes: a fire destroys Paz's apartment, and soon after the poet is diagnosed with cancer. Under the circumstances, the narrator concludes that it is too much to expect a reply to his letter. Shortly thereafter, he reads in the paper that Paz, together with President Ernesto Zedillo and novelist Fernando del Paso, will be attending an event to celebrate the creation of a cultural foundation named after the Nobel laureate. The narrator rushes down to Mexico City, arriving in Coyoacán in time to hear Paz's speech, which he finds so prodigiously beautiful and well constructed that he compares it to "una catedral suspendida en el aire" (15; a cathedral suspended in the air). But when the narrator tries to approach Paz, a security guard detains him and ejects him from the gathering.

The narrator of "La vanagloria" describes Paz as a "mago de la palabra" (13; magician of the word), and compares him to a "Sumo Pontífice" (17; high priest). When he receives the poet's letter, he declaims every word "como si rezara el Credo" (16; as if he were reciting the Creed). It is obvious that we as readers are meant to laugh at the sacred aura that attaches to Paz in Serna's story. Toward the end of his story, the narrator himself insists that "La poesía era un reino spiritual, no una corte con reyes y chambelanes" (17; Poetry was a spiritual domain, not a court with kings and chamberlains), which happens to be a very Pazian idea. The irony, of course, is that the promoter of the idea of poetry as a higher calling at the same time sits at the center of a literary system that revolves around petty rivalries and a selfish and mean-spirited struggle for prestige. Is Serna's Paz aware of this? Is he responsible for the way his name is used for base purposes? Paz is somehow the mover of the system, while at the same time remaining outside of its web. When the narrator finally receives a brief letter from Paz, he unexpectedly decides not to share it with anyone, thus stepping out of the futile cycle of pride and resentment that had until then entrapped him. This is Paz's paradoxical role in Serna's narrative: the man who embodies vainglory also shows how to escape it.

"La vanagloria" was not first time Serna had offered a satirical portrait of the Mexican literary field in the final decades of the twentieth century.[35] Nor was it the first time that he had mentioned Paz in his fiction. His novel *El miedo a los animales* (1995; *Fear of Animals*) is a murder mystery set against the background of Mexico's cultural world, which Serna depicts as a fiercely competitive and fundamentally fraudulent environment. Indeed, literary quality appears to be the last thing that matters in this world, which is powered almost exclusively by mutual favors. Throughout the novel, Serna suggests that there is little difference between the world of letters and the world of crime, since both are dominated by mafias. The novel is set in 1994, a turbulent year in Mexican history, marked not only by the *Zapatista* uprising in Chiapas, but also by a series of high-profile (and still unresolved) assassinations, including the assassination of presidential candidate Luis

Donaldo Colosio. Serna deliberately hints at a parallel between the dark goings-on in the world of politics and the equally shadowy operations of the literary field. 1994 was, of course, a year of high visibility for Paz, as he waded into the debate on the *Zapatista* uprising, and was forced to confront the collapse of his hopes for the Salinas administration, whose efforts to liberalize the Mexican economy Paz had supported. Paz is not the main focus of Serna's satire, but there are several references to him in *El miedo*, with his name repeatedly linked to the hierarchical nature of the Mexican literary field. In this field, there are marginal writers who belong to "[el] lumpen literario" (the literary lumpenproletariat), as the narrator of "La vanagloria" puts it,[36] on the one hand, and successful writers who win awards and fellowships and work their way up the state cultural apparatus, usually through their skill at self-promotion, on the other. The latter group, according to the narrator of *El miedo*, likes to frequent "cocteles y ceremonias para gente bonita, donde la intelectualidad cortesana le bebía los alientos a Octavio Paz" (cocktail parties and ceremonies for beautiful people, where intellectual lackeys fawned over Octavio Paz).[37] In short, the Mexican intellectual world resembles a court, with Paz as its undisputed monarch.[38]

The Mexican novelist, short-story writer, and art critic Juan García Ponce maintained a close association with Paz for much of his career. In the 1950s, Paz and García Ponce were involved in some of the same cultural initiatives in Mexico City, such as the *Revista mexicana de literatura*, a literary journal of which the chief editors were Emmanuel Carballo and Carlos Fuentes, and Poesía en Voz Alta (Poetry Out Loud), a theater group. García Ponce later served on the editorial boards of *Plural* and *Vuelta*, and frequently published his work in the two journals. Still, from the late 1980s onward, a certain distance began to grow between the two men, with García Ponce disapproving of what he regarded as Paz's political turn to the Right.[39] The apparent chill in the relations between the two men may account for García Ponce's ambivalent portrait of Paz in his 1993 novel *Pasado presente* (The present past). On the one hand, García Ponce draws attention—in a strikingly nonresentful way—to Paz's prestige in the Mexican cultural world of the 1950s and 1960s. On the other hand, he zeroes in on some of the great poet's foibles, such as his weakness for attractive women, including the wife of one of the main characters in *Pasado presente*, a man named Lorenzo, who is based on García Ponce himself.

Although John King intriguingly describes *Pasado presente* as a "lyrical, nostalgic evocation of the moment of the late fifties and sixties,"[40] what stands out in the novel is the detached, slightly monotonous, and largely nonjudgmental tone with which García Ponce depicts the erotic and artistic pursuits of his characters. The almost clinical perspective from which the action is observed allows the author unobtrusively to pinpoint what drives his characters. *Pasado presente* evokes key cultural initiatives of the period, referring to some of them by their actual names, such as the Centro Mexicano de Escritores and the Dirección de Difusión Cultural at the UNAM, and to others with fictional names, as is the case with the *Revista mexicana de literatura*, which in the novel turns into the *Revista del Valle de México*, and Poesía en Voz Alta, which García Ponce renames Espacio Poético (Poetic space). The novel also portrays many leading figures from Mexico's cultural world of the period, generally disguising them behind fictional names. Carlos Fuentes, for example, is easily identifiable as Adalberto Arroyo, the inordinately ambitious young author of a collection of short stories titled *Los días sin rostro* (The faceless days), an obvious reference to Fuentes's first book, *Los días enmascarados* (The masked days).[41] Other figures depicted in the novel include Emmanuel Carballo, Salvador Elizondo, Jaime García Terrés, Luisa Josefina Hernández, Juan Soriano, and Paz.

The Paz figure in the novel is named César Salazar. When he first appears in the novel, he has just returned from a sojourn in Europe, bringing with him an aura of knowledgeability, well-connectedness, and even glamor. "César era muy guapo" (César was very handsome), the narrator explains, "con ojos verdes, un perfil perfecto, enterado como nadie en este país de todos los movimientos poéticos de vanguardia, amigo personal de los creadores del surrealismo, amante de la pintura y un gran poeta él mismo" (129; with green eyes, a perfect profile, knowledgeable like no one else about all the avant-garde poetic movements, a personal friend of the founders of surrealism, a lover of painting, and a great poet in his own right). César plays a dynamic role in Mexico City's cultural circles of the period, contributing to various initiatives with his writings, but also with his ideas and his support. It is clear that his younger colleagues are eager to win his admiration. When a writer named Hugo (based on Salvador Elizondo) wins the prestigious Premio Villaurrutia for one of his novels, the reader understands that his satisfaction is enhanced by the fact that César Salazar served on the jury for the award (308). As is the case with many other literary depictions of Paz, the emphasis in *Pasado presente* is very much on the poet's powerful position within the Mexican intellectual world.

César is a promoter of up-to-date cultural trends, surely an important element of his prestige. Some of his ideas, however, may have consequences that are uncomfortable for his friends. At one point in the novel, we learn that César likes to talk about the virtues of the surrealist notion of *l'amour fou* (244). But what does this mean in practice? When Lorenzo separates from his wife Carmenchu, César is seen lending advice and assistance, although perhaps with a self-interested twist. He attributes the break between his friends to "problemas 'espirituales' en vez de psicológicos" ("spiritual" problems rather than psychological ones) and then tries to solve Carmenchu's spiritual problems by "invitándola a bailar" (259; asking her to dance with him). The diagnosis seems overblown and the remedy does not seem to match the nature of the problem, as César himself sees it. Most likely what is truly at work here is that César finds Carmenchu attractive. César's reputation as an adventurer in the realm of love leads Hugo to suspect that his girlfriend Geneviève may have had an affair with César, a suspicion he cannot let go of in spite of Geneviève's denials. In sum, César Salazar is an important and influential figure in Mexico City's intellectual circles, as portrayed in García Ponce's *Pasado presente*, much admired by his younger colleagues, and yet viewed as a perhaps not entirely trustworthy character.

Among the many literary representations of Paz that focus on his powerful position within Mexico's cultural world, Roberto Bolaño's portrayal of the Mexican poet in his 1998 novel *Los detectives salvajes* (*The Savage Detectives*) is surely one of the most noteworthy. The novel describes a group of young poets who wish to overthrow the literary establishment in 1970s Mexico. They call themselves the "real visceralistas" (real visceralists) and their goal is to revive the avant-garde spirit of the 1920s. Octavio Paz may have been an avant-garde poet himself during his youth, but for this younger group of writers he has come to embody the institution of literature and as such he represents the enemy they are fighting against.[42] Their hostility is so intense that they go so far as to hatch a plot to kidnap the renowned poet. Bolaño offers a memorable portrait of Paz as a kind of dictator who lords it over a calcified literary system; nevertheless, his portrayal of Paz is more complex and ambiguous than has generally been recognized.[43] Although it is true that Bolaño mocks Paz's status within the literary world, as well as some of his ideas about literature, his portrayal also has an affectionate quality to it. It is surely a mistake to describe the novel's criticism of the Nobel prize-winning poet as "virulent."[44] Such a comment misses the layered, nuanced quality of Bolaño's view of Paz. This is especially clear in the famous chapter—narrated by Paz's secretary—describing the poet's enigmatic encounter in Mexico City's Parque Hundido with Ulises Lima, a member of the "real visceralista" group.

    To understand Bolaño's view of Paz it is essential to reflect on the narrative devices he uses to depict him. What, for example, is the effect of describing Paz from the point of view of his secretary, a woman named Clara Cabeza? Clara narrates the roughly ten-page-long episode centering on the great Mexican poet in a tone that is at times admiring, at times mildly uncomprehending, and at times subtly disdainful. She marvels at her employer's fame, as we can see from her almost reverential discussion of his correspondence: "le escribían de los cuatro puntos cardinales y gente de toda clase, desde otros Premio Nobel como él hasta jóvenes poetas ingleses o italianos o franceses" (501–2; they wrote to him from the four cardinal points, people of all kinds, from Nobel Prize winners like himself to young English or Italian or French poets).[45] But while Clara may be awestruck by Paz's literary importance, she also calls attention (inadvertently or not) to his self-importance. What to think, for example, of the fact that Paz keeps the occasional letters that he receives in Chinese in a file marked "marginalia excentricorum" (502)? Clara may be a diligent and respectful assistant to the great poet, but this does not prevent her from expressing puzzlement over some of his actions. She cannot understand, for example, why Paz insists on keeping letters that have not even merited a reply from him. "Había que clasificarlas y guardarlas" (They needed to be classified and filed away), she explains, "vaya a saber por qué, yo de buen gusto las hubiera arrojado a la basura" (502; who knows why, if it were up to me I would have tossed them in the trash). Clara is not only dismissive of the poet's archiving habits, she is also less than impressed by some his literary ideas. Speaking of "la otredad" (otherness), one of the core concepts of Paz's literary oeuvre, she nonchalantly mentions that it is a topic that she has thought about a great deal, but that unfortunately "no he logrado averiguar de qué se trata" (503; I haven't been able to find out what it's all about). Her failure to understand Paz may reflect Clara's limited education; more likely, Bolaño wishes to make a point about what he regards as the fuzziness of Paz's ideas. The fact that the put-down is placed in the mouth of a character who seems to like her employer and evinces no animus against him makes it all the more effective. And yet at the same time, the criticism does not seem to detract from the fondness Clara appears to feel for her boss.

Throughout Clara's narration, Paz comes across as a vulnerable and basically likeable character. One senses that Clara wants to put in a good performance as Paz's secretary, not just out of a sense of pride in her work, but also because of the affection she feels for her employer. She makes sure that he takes his medication on time, and in many ways shows that she is an absolutely loyal employee. When Paz asks her whether she trusts him, she assures him that she trusts him "más que . . . nadie" (507; more than anyone). Very revealing is the attentive and affectionate manner in which Clara narrates the story of Paz's encounters with Ulises Lima in the Parque Hundido. On the first day Clara drives him to the park, she notices his "aire ausente" (absent-mindedness) when he gets into the car with her, and upon their return home a few hours later she mentions that after the walk in the park, and the enigmatic first meeting with Lima, Paz has become more lively and cheerful, "más vivaracho" (more peppy), as she puts it (505). The next day, when the silent encounter between the two poets— one famous, the other obscure—repeats itself, Clara once again notes the meeting's effect on Paz: "Le brillaban los ojos, esos ojos tan bonitos que tiene" (506; His eyes were sparkling, those lovely eyes of his). When Paz mentions that Lima was part of a group of poets that had announced a plan to kidnap him, although no one really knows for what reason, whether as a political gesture or as a joke, or perhaps out of resentment toward Paz's fame and success, Clara responds in a characteristically empathetic way. "La gente acumula mucho rencor gratuito" (People accumulate a lot of gratuitous rancor), she comments (507). Does Clara care for Paz, carry out his wishes, and sympathize with him merely because he is her employer and she depends on him for her livelihood? Surely the hierarchical relationship between the two characters cannot be ignored in assessing Clara's portrait of Paz. But just as surely her affection for him seems genuine.

A notable feature of Clara's narrative is that she never seems to fully understand the story she herself is telling. The section of the novel dealing with Paz's encounter with Lima is full of revealing omissions. Clara cannot explain why Paz wants her to take him to the Parque Hundido, and on the drive she describes him as engaged in strange and unintelligible mumbling (504). She has no explanation for the odd behavior of the two poets, who for several days in a row walk past each other in the park, exchanging glances, but without speaking. She does not know why her employer asks her to make a list of Mexican poets born after 1950. The meetings between Paz and "el desconocido" (the stranger) in the Parque Hundido fill her with apprehension. Fortunately, everything turns out well, and Paz and Lima end up having a long conversation, described by Clara as "distendida, serena, tolerante" (510; relaxed, serene, tolerant). But as she winds up her narrative, she repeatedly emphasizes that she is still in the dark as to the significance of what she observed. She wants to ask Paz for more information about "nuestra pequeña aventura" (our little adventure), but in the end she desists: "Las cosas habían ocurrido tal como habían ocurrido y si yo, que era el único testigo, no sabía lo que había pasado, lo mejor era que siguiera en la ignorancia" (510; Things had happened the way they had happened and if I, as the only witness, did not know what had happened, it was better to remain in a state of ignorance). One day, with Paz away lecturing at an American university, Clara returns to the Parque Hundido. Nothing happens, but when she leaves the park she feels happy. The closing words of Clara's testimony once again draw attention to the state of *not knowing* in which she so often seems to find herself: "me sentía feliz, aunque no me pregunten por qué pues no sabría decírselo" (511; I felt happy, but don't ask me why because I would not be able to tell you).

How might this narrative strategy—in which the teller of the story consistently fails to come to conclusions about things, and envelops even simple events in a cloud of ambiguity—influence our understanding of how Bolaño wishes to portray Paz in his novel? First, let me point out that the inconclusiveness of Clara's story is consistent with the open-ended, fragmentary, even somewhat aimless presentation of the narrative throughout *Los detectives salvajes*. The effect of this style of storytelling is to counter a dogmatic or definitive approach to the world. In Bolaño, everything is suffused in an aura of uncertainty. Many critics think that the Chilean author forcefully rejects Paz and everything he stands for. Surely it cannot be denied that the portrait of the Mexican poet in *Los detectives salvajes* includes satirical elements. But to assume that Bolaño's aims were purely polemical fails to take into account the disposition of his narrative, which, as we have seen, inclines toward a state of uncertainty. It is not that Paz disappears as a character into a fog of epistemological doubt, for Clara's description of her employer is full of recognizably human elements. But Bolaño vigorously blocks attempts on the part of the reader to pin Paz down.[46]

Federico Vite's *Fisuras en el continente literario* (2007; Fissures in the continent of literature) takes Bolaño's *Los detectives salvajes* as its point of departure, reintroducing Paz alongside his secretary Clara Cabezas, but imagining a kidnapping that actually takes place, rather than remaining in its planning stages. The man responsible for Paz's kidnapping is a police commander named Ojeda who cherishes literary ambitions. Ojeda is writing a novel and has decided that he wants Paz to revise it for him, and help him get it published. Vite's Paz picks up on well-known details of the poet's personality, such as his fondness for *The Simpsons* and his dislike of Gabriel García Márquez. The Paz of Vite's novel also possesses the same inflated sense of his own importance as Bolaño's, as is evident from the manner in which he addresses his kidnapper. "La Comunidad Europea lo hundirá en la cárcel" (The European Community will put you in jail), he threatens, adding for good measure that "hasta el presidente de la República debe estar buscándome" (62; even the President of the Republic is probably looking for me).[47] But Vite's Paz is above all a man of great cunning, for he decides that commander Ojeda's novel has considerable literary value, and ends up stealing it in order to publish it under his own name. He also appears to use his connections in the circles of power to have Ojeda dispatched to Portugal with some kind of diplomatic appointment. The themes of Vite's novella are not very well worked out: on the first page of the text, the story of Paz's literary theft is taken to signify that "la literatura es un asunto de muchísimas personas" (9; literature is a matter involving a lot of people), but this idea seems to fall by the wayside later on and in the end we are left not with a reflection on the communal nature of authorship, or the intertextual dimension of any literary work, but with a portrait of the ruthless way in which power is exercised in the literary world.

A not very favorable portrayal of Paz can be found in Heriberto Yépez's *A.B.U.R.T.O.* (2005), a novel revolving around the March 1994 assassination of the PRI presidential candidate Luis Donaldo Colosio. Yépez reconstructs the life of Mario Aburto, the man who confessed to killing Colosio at the conclusion of a campaign rally in a working-class neighborhood in Tijuana, depicting the ostensible assassin's humble beginnings in the state of Michoacán, his move to the border city of Tijuana, his work in a maquiladora, his frustrated love affairs, and his eclectic readings in literature, philosophy, and social science. Yépez does not resolve the mystery that still surrounds the Colosio assassination; what he does, instead, is to reconstruct the cultural milieu out of which Aburto emerged. As part of his evocation of Mexico in the early 1990s, Yépez includes sketches of major figures of the period including Carlos Salinas de Gortari, who served as president of Mexico from 1988 to 1994, and whom the narrator refers to condescendingly as "Carlitos," Subcomandante Marcos, leader of the EZLN (*Ejército Zapatista de Liberación Nacional*), who also receives somewhat mocking treatment in the novel, and Octavio Paz. Paz appears near the beginning of the novel in the company of his wife, watching a TV game show in which the young Mario Aburto is participating. Mario is about to suffer a devastating humiliation when he loses all his winnings in one fell swoop as a result of an all-or-nothing gamble, but Paz is delighted to recognize in young Mario an example of his theories about the Mexican character. When his wife points out that Mario's actions illustrate Paz's theories about the role of the *fiesta* in Mexican life, Paz explodes with joy: "En la cara de Octavio se trazó una gran sonrisa y en ese mismo segundo saltó de la cama, abriendo los brazos y piernas, ¡yupi!, reventando de regocijo su apretada piyama" (A huge smile appeared on Octavio's face and in that same second he jumped up from the bed, stretching his arms and legs, whoopee!, his excitement almost ripping his tight-fitting pajama).[48] The narrator also claims that Paz stole his ideas about the Mexican character from Samuel Ramos, and further suggests that the Nobel-prize-winning poet suffers from a massive inferiority complex which not even his vast consumption of all the cultures of the world can do anything to assuage.[49] In short, Paz is portrayed as an immature, tormented man, who reflects the flaws of Mexican culture, rather than diagnosing them. It is worth noting, however, that when a few years later Yépez himself wrote a book-length essay on the Mexican national character his ideas on the subject owed a considerable debt to Paz, whose work on Mexican identity he discusses in a balanced and non-polemical fashion.[50]

In his 2015 novel *De puño y letra* (Written by hand), Luis Arturo Ramos places a character based on Paz in the context of a detective story. The plot begins with the novel's protagonist, Bayardo Arizpe, a minor poet who earns a living as a private eye and rare books seller, arriving at the home of the widow of the recently-deceased poet Orlando Pascacio, in whose name one immediately recognizes a reference to Octavio Paz.[51] In his portrayal of Pascacio, Ramos follows the familiar theme of the poet as a kind of *caudillo* of the Mexican literary world, a man with so much influence that it is said that even the President of the nation is aware of his every gesture: "Afirman que cuando Pascacio estornudaba, el Presidente en turno llamaba por teléfono para decirle 'Salud'" (40; It is said that whenever Pascacio sneezed, whoever was President at the time would call him on the phone to say "cheers").[52] Pascacio has a reputation as a formidable critic of Mexican poetry; however, until now he has exercised his unforgiving judgment only on the poets of the past: "de todos era sabido ... que Orlando Pascacio se negaba, en público como en privado, a comentar la obra de algún poeta vivo ... a pesar de que se desgajara en elogios o pulverizara el trabajo de aquellos cuya obra ya alcanzaba, en términos legales, el dominio público: es decir, más de cincuenta años de muertos" (20; everyone knew ... that Orlando Pascacio refused, either in public or in private, to comment on the work of any poet who was still alive ... even though he would praise or destroy poets whose work had entered, in a legal sense, the public domain: that is, being dead for more than fifty years). During his meeting with Pascacio's widow, Bayardo learns that the poet has left behind a manuscript in which he discusses the work of Mexico's most important contemporary poets. The posthumous publication of this work, titled *De puño y letra*, is expected to cause a big stir in the Mexican literary world. As it turns out, the manuscript has disappeared from Pascacio's apartment, and his widow has decided to hire Arizpe to get it back. In pursuing the case of the missing manuscript, Bayardo makes various discoveries about Pascacio's private life, as well as about the envy and ambition that fuel Mexico's republic of letters. Ramos combines the theme of literary power with a meditation on the problem of authenticity and inauthenticity in the contemporary world. The novel's title, which alludes to a work written by hand, as well as to the broader idea of something that is a true reflection of who one is, evokes an older world of direct human contact, in contrast to the new world of cell phones, computers, and other dehumanizing technologies. Interestingly, the novel combines a satirical outlook on Pascacio's (excessive) cultural power with a kind of defense of his right to have his voice heard. This is what Arizpe accomplishes (spoiler alert!) when he locates not only Pascacio's missing manuscript but also a set of recordings of the deceased poet reading from his posthumous book. In his description of this voice, Ramos no longer seems to be suggesting that there is something illegitimate about the power it expresses; on the contrary, there is a kind of awe in listening to it: "la voz de Orlando Pascacio llenó el espacio con la grandilocuencia del mar en tiempo de huracanes.... Bayardo sorprendió al poeta en medio de una alocución cuyo origen fincaba en ningún sitio para remontar luego al infinito. Era voz, simplemente voz... cuya incorpórea presencia quedaba validada por el simple hecho de existir" (275; Orlando Pascacio's voice filled the air with the grandeur of the sea during a hurricane.... Bayardo encountered the poet in the middle of an oration that seemed to originate from nowhere and then rise up to the infinite. It was a voice, simply a voice... whose disembodied presence was validated through the simple fact of existing).

All of the literary representations we have looked at thus far focus on Paz as a public figure. Elena Garro, who was married to Paz for more than two decades, and had a child with him, offers a more personal look at Paz in her writings, without omitting an interest in his public persona. Garro drew literary inspiration from her troubled marriage; she also used her novels to get revenge on her former husband. *Testimonios sobre Mariana* (1981; Testimonies about Mariana) is a *roman à clef* describing the life of a Latin American couple and their daughter in post-war Paris. Mariana is an enigmatic, beautiful, almost dream-like woman, who is married to Augusto, a prominent archaeologist and cultural functionary in an unnamed international organization. No one understands why Mariana and Augusto are married to each other, since they have utterly different ways of viewing the world, and clearly do not get along. Both engage in extramarital affairs. Indeed, Mariana seems to exercise a powerful attraction over many of the men she meets, and she becomes involved first with a wealthy South American dandy named Vicente, who is married to an older woman named Sabina, and later with a mysterious millionaire named Barnaby. Mariana becomes pregnant by Vicente, but has an abortion. Augusto, for his part, also becomes sexually involved with other women, something he makes no effort to conceal. All of this takes place in a decidedly upper-class setting: the characters in *Testimonios* are always dining in the finest restaurants, staying in luxurious hotels, and taking leisurely trips around the European continent. But Mariana is a deeply unhappy woman, with her husband mostly to blame for her misfortunes.

Augusto is an almost comically disagreeable character. First and foremost, he is depicted as a shamelessly tyrannical husband. When Mariana offers an opinion on a topic Augusto is discussing over dinner with Sabina, he rudely instructs her to be quiet. "La orden cayó en la mesa como un manotazo desagradable" (5; The command fell on the table like a frightful thump), comments Vicente, who is one of the novel's three narrators.[53] Augusto is constantly reprimanding Mariana in public, or humiliating her. He has an extremely low opinion of his wife's intellectual abilities, insisting at one point that she is incapable of thinking: "Mariana es muy inútil, es penoso convivir con ella, no piensa" (37; Mariana is a useless woman, it is painful to live with her, she doesn't think). He complains about her love of luxury and her lack of practical sense. Even though Augusto has a profoundly domineering personality, he somehow makes it seem that Mariana is the one who controls *him*. At one point, he explains that he would be happy living in an attic devoting himself to his studies, but his obligations to Mariana and their daughter make that impossible: "Mariana y la niña me encadenan al dinero, a lo cotidiano y a la vida artificial" (406; Mariana and the girl chain me to money, to the quotidian, and to an artificial life). In short, in this version, the woman is blamed for tying the man to earthly preoccupations. In the course of the novel, Augusto's animosity toward his wife becomes increasingly sinister. Indeed, Vicente is convinced that Augusto is intent on destroying Mariana. It is no wonder that Mariana is deeply afraid of him. And yet she cannot escape his clutches.

In addition to describing Augusto's behavior as a husband, the novel also zeroes in on his professional life. Augusto has scaled the heights of his field thanks to a series of brilliant studies of the Egyptian archaeological site of Karnak. He is also a powerful cultural bureaucrat. He enjoys his position and his reputation, and he does not hesitate to signal his importance by surrounding himself with the trappings of worldly success. "Por la mañana encontré a Augusto en su impecable despacho rodeado de prestigio, teléfonos y fotografías" (265; In the morning I found Augusto in his impeccable office surrounded by prestige, phones, and photographs), says the narrator of the second part of the novel, Augusto's secretary Gabrielle. Even while cultivating the image of a successful man of the world, Augusto is a follower of the progressive, left-wing ideologies that were in vogue in the post-war era. "Augusto tenía fama de ser un revolucionario, no sólo en materia arqueológica, sino en política" (435; Augusto was reputed to be a revolutionary, not only in the field of archaeology, but in politics, too), one of the novel's narrators informs us. Elsewhere in the novel he is described as "un radical de izquierda" (a radical leftist) who reserves a special hatred for the United States (117), and is fond of predicting the end of capitalism (200). The novel also depicts—without explanation—Augusto's conversion later in life to supporter of the dissident movement in the Soviet Union. As Vicente explains when Augusto comes to deliver a series of lectures in the South American country where he lives: "Él se había identificado con Solzhenitzin, había hecho causa común con ellos, ya que sufría del totalitarismo político de su país" (161; He had identified with Solzhenitsyn, and had expressed his solidarity with the dissidents, since he himself suffered under the political totalitarianism of his country). It is clear that politics is central to Augusto's intellectual endeavors.

Whatever his political preferences may be at any given moment, Augusto is depicted in *Testimonios* as a hypocrite. Vicente notes that Augusto's revolutionary talk does not match his life-style: "El lujo del restaurante contradecía las palabras de Augusto" (118; The luxury of the restaurant contradicted Augusto's words). He also suspects that Augusto's professed identification with Alexander Solzhenistyn is mere posturing, since he has just received an appointment as director of his country's Museum of Archaeology. How can Augusto presume to be a dissident in the mold of Solzhenitsyn when the authorities in his home country are showering him with honors? Worst of all, however, is the contradiction between his ostensible outlook on life and the way he treats his wife. Augusto is a follower of Jean-Paul Sartre, and talks all the time about freedom and responsibility. He is also closely involved in the primitivist cultural currents of the period: "Unido a un grupo de sociólogos buscaba en las culturas desaparecidas la vida colectiva del hombre primitivo, sus costumbres sexuales y sus hábitos eróticos, como ejemplo a seguir por el hombre occidental" (442; Together with a group of sociologists he searched for the collective life of primitive man in vanished cultures, his sexual customs and erotic habits, as examples to be followed by Western man). In short, Western man needs to reinvigorate his decadent culture by looking at the much freer way of life experienced in primitive societies. But Augusto seems blithely unaware of the contradiction between his celebration of human freedom and his constant denial of that same freedom to Mariana, who feels like a prisoner in her marriage (95).

Augusto, of course, is based on Paz, while Mariana is Garro's portrait of herself. Vicente is Adolfo Bioy Casares, with whom Garro had an affair when their paths crossed in Paris, while Sabina is Silvina Ocampo, the Argentine author who was married to Bioy. Mariana's other love interest, Barnaby, is based on the Mexican writer and filmmaker Archibaldo Burns, while a character named Pepe alludes to José Bianco, the Argentine author and longtime editor of the cultural magazine *Sur*, with whom both Paz and Garro had enduring friendships. Garro's decision to make Augusto an archaeologist seems very apposite, not only because Paz aspired as a young man to become an archeologist,[54] but also because as a vocation it echoes Paz's deep preoccupation with unearthing the past. Paz, of course, served in his country's diplomatic service in Paris, whereas Augusto works for an international organization; still, Garro's purpose seems to be to draw attention to her former husband's worldly ambition. Paz's political beliefs were indeed on the Left in the years immediately after World War II, although he was already becoming a critic of the Soviet régime, and of the intellectuals who supported it. This is an aspect Garro does not develop. Another important fact about her husband that Garro leaves out of her novelistic recreation of her marriage is the fact that Paz was a poet. Indeed, as we know, he was a poet who worked in the romantic and symbolist traditions. It is an element of Paz's persona that does not fit Garro's conception of the character of Augusto, who is an authoritarian, striving, and self-centered man without an iota of poetic sensibility. In short, Garro offers a vivid and memorable portrait of her former husband during a certain period of their life together, but it is obviously only in part a depiction of Paz.[55]

Garro offers another fictional representation of her marriage to Paz in her posthumously published novel *Mi hermanita Magdalena* (1998; My little sister Magdalena).[56] The story begins with an account of seventeen-year-old Magdalena's impulsive marriage in Mexico City to a much older man named Enrique, the novel's Paz figure. Apparently, Magdalena had approached the wedding ceremony binding her to Enrique as a kind of joke, and initially she returns to her parents' home as if nothing had happened. Her new husband, however, takes a different view of the matter, showing up at Magdalena's house a few days later, and whisking his wife off to Paris. All of this is narrated by Magdalena's sister Estefanía, who describes her sibling's marriage as a catastrophe that causes the entire family's ruin.[57] Estefanía soon heads off to Paris herself, to help her sister, who has by now left her husband, and is living alone in a hotel as she waits for her divorce proceedings to advance. No one seems to know exactly what Enrique does for a living. He claims that he is in the import-export business, but the two girls suspect that he is actually involved in something shadier. As we know, Garro lived in Paris with Paz and their daughter in the late 1940s and early 1950s, but the action of *Mi hermanita* takes place in 1961, in the midst of the Algerian crisis. The turbulent political atmosphere of the period provides a fitting backdrop for the novel, which is filled with dark intrigue; indeed, there is a suggestion that Enrique may be involved in the arms trade. Like Augusto in *Testimonios*, Enrique has an ugly, tyrannical streak, but unlike Augusto he is not an intellectual. If anything, he is an actor, a con man, and a somewhat mysterious man of the world. When he arrives in Paris with his young wife, he pretends to be a Mexican aristocrat, and spends huge sums of money. He likes expensive restaurants, dresses elegantly, and is fond of flirting with women. Magdalena and Estefanía spend most of the novel gripped by a sense of persecution, but this does not prevent them from spending an enjoyable few summer months in the lakeside Swiss town of Ascona, where Magdalena becomes involved with three men at the same time. One character notes that Magdalena is very popular with the opposite sex, something that seems to provoke a feeling of envy in her sister. The figure of the husband, or ex-husband, in *Mi hermanita* appears to be less closely tied to Paz than the Augusto of *Testimonios*. Still, there is no doubt that *Mi hermanita* reflects how Garro saw her marriage to Paz.[58]

Some critics have read Garro's *romans à clef* about her marriage with Paz as feminist works.[59] According to this argument, *Testimonios* and *Mi hermanita* offer critiques of patriarchal society, and depict the catastrophic consequences for women of a culture that sustains inequality in gender relations. To read the novels in this way is to suggest that they are not about a single marriage, or about one husband's bad behavior. In other words, the feminist reading suggests that the novels are not simply attacks on Paz, but rather explorations of broader social issues. Moving from the particular to the general is of course a standard interpretive move. And there is indeed something entirely plausible about reading the representation of a tyrannical husband as standing in for the larger social problem of patriarchy. And yet, there are elements in Garro's novels that contradict the political message feminist critics see in them. For one thing, the narrators of *Testimonios* and *Mi hermanita* do not themselves make the leap from the particular case to the general problem. They never explicitly make the point that the problems of the female protagonists of the novels should be seen as part of a larger social issue rather than simply as the result of an individual misfortune. It is, of course, possible that Garro wants her readers to identify the broader theme themselves, rather than spelling it out for them. But what, then, to make of the fact that both novels revolve almost obsessively around the power of attraction exercised by the female protagonists over a series of male suitors? What would explain Garro's concern with depicting female characters who are the center of male attention? The nature of the plots of *Testimonios* and *Mi hermanita* gainsays the feminist message about female autonomy some critics see in these novels, and suggests that these texts are focused more on finding the right man than on denouncing all men. It also suggests that in creating the characters of Augusto and Enrique, Garro was indeed concerned first and foremost with depicting Paz, not with criticizing the patriarchy.[60]

Garro was not alone in mining her Parisian sojourn for literary material. One of the South American intellectuals she met in Paris was the Argentine author and editor José Bianco, who became close to both Garro and Paz when he lived in Paris in the late 1940s and early 1950s, and maintained a lengthy correspondence with both of them after his return to Buenos Aires.[61] Bianco's novel *La pérdida del reino* (1972; The loss of the kingdom) narrates the life of an Argentine critic, journalist, and aesthete named Rufino (Rufo) Velázquez, focusing on his friendships, his love affairs, and his frustrated literary ambitions. The fourth and final section of the novel is set in post-war Paris, where Rufo falls in love with an enchanting Argentine woman named Laura Estévez, who is married to a wealthy Mexican named Horacio. In an odd twist, it turns out that Laura is having an affair with Néstor Sagasta, a childhood friend of Rufo who is also residing in Paris. Laura is a woman of uncommon attractiveness, glamorous but natural and spontaneous at the same time. When Rufo first meets her on a visit to a museum, he describes her as "una jovencita rubia, envuelta en pieles muy lujosas del mismo color y brillo de su pelo suelto" (296; a young blonde woman wrapped in luxurious furs that had the same color and shine as her loosely-worn hair). But what he most likes about her is that she is "simpática, original" (303; likeable, original). He finds her to be "tan ajena a cualquier convencionalismo, tan delicada, tan refinada, y a la vez con un fondo alegre, popular" (306; so indifferent to conventionality, so delicate, so refined, and at the same time with a simple, cheerful heart). Laura is also fortunate to have a kind and tolerant husband. To Rufo, Laura and Horacio are an utterly charming couple, who are more like a brother and sister than a husband and wife (310). Horacio treats his wife's lover Néstor as if he were a member of the family (310), and cultivates a cordial yet somewhat detached attitude toward people in general (320). Bianco's concern in *La pérdida* was much more with Garro (Laura) than Paz (Horacio), yet his portrait of Paz as a man of serene temperament who treats his wife in an accepting and magnanimous fashion is clearly of interest to the present study, as it offers a very different impression of the Mexican poet than we find in most of the literary portrayals we have examined.

The vast majority of literary portrayals of Paz have been penned by Mexican authors, or by authors who lived in Mexico for most of their life, as was the case of Luis Guillermo Piazza, or spent a formative period of their life there, as we see with Roberto Bolaño. Bianco, is not, however, the only non-Mexican writer to have included Paz as a character in a work of fiction. In his 2014 novel, *Los huesos olvidados* (2014; The forgotten bones), the Spanish author Antonio Rivero Taravillo tells the story of a Spanish woman in her late fifties who goes in search of information about her father, a man named Juan Bosch, whom she has never known. Bosch's parents had emigrated from Spain to Mexico in 1913 when their son was still an infant, and Juan had remained there until 1932. In that year, he was deported by the Mexican government for his political activities, which were deemed illegal since he was not a Mexican citizen.

Back in Spain, Bosch finds work in a textile factory in Barcelona and becomes active in left-wing political circles. During the Spanish Civil War, which breaks out in 1936, he joins the POUM (*Partido Obrero de Unificación Marxista*), an independent, anti-Stalinist Communist party. Bosch fights against the Fascist rebels on the Asturias front, but also gets caught up in the internecine struggles on the Left in Civil War Spain. He is last seen in October 1937, after which he disappears, presumably a victim of the persecution unleashed by Spain's pro-Moscow official Communist Party.

Bosch was, of course, a real person, known to literary critics and historians as a friend of Octavio Paz in the late 1920s and early 1930s. Indeed, Paz describes him as an important influence on his early political ideas. In an intellectual milieu dominated by Communist ideas, Bosch, who was a little older than Paz, introduced his friend to the libertarian philosophical tradition.[62] A few years after Bosch's return to Spain, Paz received a report that his friend had been killed on the battle-front in Asturias, whereupon he wrote a poem to honor Bosch's memory. One can imagine the poet's surprise, then, when, in October 1937, during his sojourn in Spain, Paz recognized his old friend in the audience at a poetry reading in Barcelona. Paz and Elena Garro, who had joined her husband on his journey to Spain, subsequently had a furtive meeting with Bosch, who expressed fear for his life at the hands of his political enemies, and asked for help in escaping Spain. But even though Bosch promised to contact his Mexican friends the following day, he was never heard from again.[63]

Los huesos mixes real events with imaginary ones, historical and invented characters. Very little is known about Bosch outside out of what Paz and Garro relate in their writings about this period. Rivero Taravillo undertakes to fill the gaps in our knowledge about Bosch's life, and invents a story about a brief love affair Bosch has with a militiawoman, who gives birth to a daughter whom Bosch will never know. Also fictional is the story of the daughter, named Encarnación Expósito, who travels to Mexico City almost sixty years later in search of information about her father. Although Encarnación is a made-up character, she meets some real people during her stay in Mexico, including Paz and Garro. Paz, who is now old and sick, and living in a hotel after a fire has destroyed his apartment on the Paseo de la Reforma, is eager to talk about Bosch, but oddly enough has misremembered his old friend's first name, which he mistakenly takes to have been "José," both in his writings and in his conversation with Encarnación, when in fact, as Encarnación points out, his name was "Juan." Standing corrected, Paz is described as "contrariado" (annoyed) by the realization "que su memoria ... flaqueaba a veces" (26; that is memory ... sometimes faltered).[64] Much later in the novel, the theme of memory is taken up again when Encarnación happens upon an interview with Paz in the Spanish daily *ABC*. She is deeply moved by the poet's final words in the interview: "La memoria es la gran fabricante de fantasmas" (56; Memory is the great manufacturer of ghosts). One might conclude, then, that Paz is brought into the novel at least in part in order to voice certain ideas about the difficulty of remembering the past, or, to put it differently, of distinguishing the real from the imaginary.

The theme of memory intersects in *Los huesos* with the theme of politics. While the novel recognizes that our understanding of the past is uncertain and fragile, it nevertheless insists on the importance of remembrance. From the pursuit of an accurate reconstruction of the events that took place during the Spanish Civil War, resulting in Bosch's disappearance and that of innumerable others, the novel extracts a difficult political lesson. Here we have Encarnación explaining how the story of Bosch fits into the memory wars that have raged in Spain in recent decades:

> Debió de sucederle [a Bosch] lo que a tantos que murieron traicionados en la retaguardia, los que no nutren las estadísticas y serán olvidados cuando se empiece a hacer justicia y afloren las fosas y cadáveres ocultos y silenciados. Los huesos olvidados, Antonio. Cambiarán las tornas y los que fueron despachados con el calificativo de rojos serán honrados, al tiempo que los 'muertos por Dios y por España' se sumirán en las sombras, carentes de los homenajes de cuyo monopolio han gozado hasta hace poco. Pero de

Bosch y de otros como él, ¿qué se hará? Su memoria es incómoda para unos y para otros. En una guerra entre Caín y Abel, es como si fueran el bando del tercer hijo de Adán y Eva, el tal Set, del que nadie habla nunca. (171)

What happened [to Bosch] must have happened to so many like him who were betrayed and died in the rearguard, all those who are left out of the statistics and will be forgotten once justice is done and the graves and the hidden and silenced corpses begin to appear. The forgotten bones, Antonio. The world will change and those who were dispatched with the label 'reds' attached to them will now be honored, whereas those who 'died for God and Spain' will be relegated to the shadows, deprived of the tributes on which they had a monopoly until a short while ago. But what will we do with Bosch and others like him? His memory is a nuisance for both sides. In a war between Cain and Abel, it is as if he were on the side of Adam and Eve's third son, this guy called Set, whom no one ever talks about.

Encarnación draws attention to the schematic and often one-sided manner in which "memory" has been promoted in Spain. During the Franco régime, only those who died fighting for the rebel side were honored. After the transition to democracy, a new narrative emerged, one that gave the impression that only the Francoists had committed atrocities, and that the only victims of the Spanish Civil War were the Republicans.[65] Through the protagonist of his novel, Rivero Taravillo counters these reductive interpretations of the past, reminding his readers that many of the victims on the Republican side were victims not of Francoist, but of Stalinist persecution.

Rivero Taravillo's perspective on the Spanish Civil War and on how to remember it is one that Paz would no doubt have sympathized with. Bosch was an important figure in Paz's intellectual itinerary. In the first place, as Paz himself has pointed out, Bosch introduced him to an intellectual tradition—that of libertarianism—that would become central to his own political identity. Secondly, Bosch's fate during the Spanish Civil War stood as a warning of the dangers of a certain brand of politics. The encounter with Bosch in Barcelona helped open Paz's eyes to the violent repression carried out in the name of the Communist ideal. It was a key stage in his disillusionment with the Left. By going back to Bosch, and making Paz an important part of the story, Rivero Taravillo highlights preoccupations held by the Mexican poet. In short, this is a sympathetic portrait of Paz. It avoids the satirical perspective so common in depictions of Paz the intellectual, drawing attention to his ideas and his relationship to the past, rather than zeroing in, as so many Mexican writers do, on his status and power within the Mexican intellectual world.

Paz is treated far less sympathetically in the work of Colombian novelist Fernando Vallejo. *Entre fantasmas* (1993; Among ghosts), which includes several references to the Mexican poet, consists of a single lengthy monologue written in the author's signature misanthropic style. In the course of the novel (if that is the right term) the narrator rages against Colombia (his native country), Mexico (his adopted land), Fidel Castro and the Cuban Revolution, numerous Mexican presidents, most notably José López Portillo, for whom he reserves a special loathing, rich people and poor people, blacks and indigenous people, God and the Catholic Church—in short, it is clear that he detests just about everything and everyone, with the possible exception of dogs. "La humanidad entera" (The entire human race), the narrator proclaims at one point, "no vale un solo momento de dolor de un perro" (97–98; is not worth a single moment of a dog's suffering).[66] At several stages of his monologue, the narrator aims his venom at prominent figures in the Mexican cultural world, including Octavio Paz. The Mexican poet is depicted as a man with an unseemly hunger for praise and recognition, provoking the narrator to address him in a somewhat condescending manner: "No hay remedio para la vejez, Octavio, házme caso; la fama y los homenajes no son remedio, son paliativos. Remedio lo que se dice remedio no hay. O sí: la muerte" (34; There is no remedy for old age, Octavio, just listen to me; fame and tributes are not remedies, they are palliatives. A remedy as such does not exist. Or, actually, yes it does: death). When the narrator reports Paz's death, he offers the following thoroughly sarcastic homage to the deceased poet: "Se nos fue Paz el transparente, el mallarmeano Paz, el honesto Paz, el incorruptible Paz. . . . El articulado Paz, el conmiseratorio, el subterfúgico, el conspicuo, el inescrutable, el impertérrimo, el polirredento, ay, ay" (30–31; Paz has left us, the transparent Paz, the mallarméan Paz, the honest Paz, the incorruptible Paz. . . . The well-spoken Paz, the commiserative, the subterfugian, the conspicuous, the inscrutable, the undaunted, the polyredeemed, alas, alas). What is Vallejo getting at with this long list of glowing adjectives (some of them invented)? One might note that all of the adjectives point to the poet's elevated sense of himself, and to his idealistic view of the world, an outlook that provokes unrestrained scorn on the narrator's part. It is worth recalling that Paz had a deeply spiritual view of existence, and that he repeatedly rejected philosophies that offered a diminished or disparaging view of human capabilities. Consider Paz's rejection of Sartre's view of humankind as *une passion inutile*,[67] or his assertion, in an essay on the Belgian poet Henri Michaux, that "el hombre no es una criatura mediocre. Una parte de sí . . . está abierto al infinito" (man is not a mediocre creature. One part of him . . . is open to the infinite).[68] In short, Paz's perspective on life was utterly different from Vallejo's. It is not surprising, therefore, that the Colombian novelist made the Mexican poet a target of his mockery.[69]

Another Colombian novelist who wrote about Paz is Héctor Abad Faciolince. In *El olvido que seremos* (2006; *Oblivion: A Memoir*), an autobiographical novel about his relationship with his father, Abad Faciolince briefly evokes the Mexican cultural world of the late seventies, in which Paz, of course, played a central role. The year is 1978; the novelist's father has been appointed cultural attaché in the Colombian embassy in Mexico City. Abad Faciolince, who has just turned nineteen, joins his father, spending nine months in the Mexican capital, immersing himself in the city's literary life. He expresses great admiration for many of the Mexican writers whose work he becomes acquainted with during this period of his life, including Juan Rulfo, Paz, and José Emilio Pacheco. Abad Faciolince devours Paz's poetry and essays, but he is less impressed by the person behind the work. A meeting with the famous poet proves impossible to arrange: "(Paz) tenía actitud de Pontífice y no veía a nadie sino que había que pedirle audiencia con tres meses de anticipación" (Paz had the attitude of a high priest who was not available to meet with anyone unless you requested an appointment three months in advance).[70] This comment leads into some reflections on how it is better to be happy than famous. The novelist clearly thinks that Paz made the wrong choice in this regard.

The depictions of Paz as a literary character are as noteworthy for what they leave out as for what they include. The author as literary character is an ideal device for examining literary issues such as the nature of artistic inspiration, the stages of the writing process, or the interaction between life and art. The device also lends itself to explorations of the vexed relations between fiction and reality. However, such issues are rarely, if ever foregrounded, in the many narrative works that include Paz as a character, whether under his own name or an invented one. The overwhelming emphasis in these writings is on Paz's public persona, particularly on his dominant role in the Mexican cultural world. Numerous authors have been intrigued by the possibilities of approaching the Paz phenomenon through works of fiction rather than conventional criticism or commentary. But it is striking to note the extent to which these writers have been concerned with questions of cultural power and prestige—that is, with the social dimension of literature—and have sidestepped the artistic and epistemological themes often raised in the author-as-character genre of writing. The texts explored in this chapter offer rich and informative, and often also amusing, perspectives on the life and character of Mexico's most famous twentieth-century author. And yet one cannot help wonder about the narrowness of the overall focus, with its relentless emphasis on status, the struggle for recognition, and the hierarchical nature of the literary field. One thing is certain: there is plenty of room for different and innovative approaches to depicting Paz as a literary character.

Notes

INTRODUCTION

1. Paz highlights Neruda's role in bringing him to Spain in a 1977 interview on Spanish television. See Octavio Paz, "A fondo," interview by Joaquín Soler Serrano, Televisión Española, 1977, video, 0:48:10–0:49:32, www.rtve.es/alacarta/videos/a-fondo/Octavio-paz-fondo-1977/1349841. He offers a slightly different account of who was responsible for extending the invitation to come to Spain in *Itinerario*, his 1993 intellectual autobiography. He again mentions Neruda, but places more emphasis on the role played by the Spanish poet Arturo Serrano Plaja. See Octavio Paz, *Itinerario* (Mexico City: Fondo de Cultura Económica, 1993), 56–58. For a study of the relationship between Paz and Neruda in the 1930s, see Daniel Solomon Cooper, *The Roots of Transformation: Octavio Paz and the Militant Americanist Awakening of Pablo Neruda* (PhD diss., University of California, Los Angeles, 2018).
2. On the Rousset affair, see Tony Judt, *Past Imperfect: French Intellectuals, 1944–1956* (Berkeley: University of California Press, 1992), 113–15.
3. See Octavio Paz, "David Rousset y los campos de concentración soviéticos," *Sur* 197 (March 1951): 48–76. This text includes documents related to the Rousset affair, as well as extensive commentary by Paz. Years later, Paz acknowledged that he had received help from Elena Garro in preparing the article for *Sur*. See Paz, *Itinerario*, 97.
4. For a collection of the reports Paz wrote as a diplomat in France, see Froylán Enciso, *Andar fronteras: El servicio diplomático de Octavio Paz en Francia (1946–1951)* (Mexico City: Siglo XXI, 2008).
5. For excellent studies of Paz's journals, see John King, *The Role of Mexico's* Plural *in Latin American Literary and Political Culture: From*

Tlatelolco to the Philanthropic Ogre (New York: Palgrave MacMillan, 2007); and Malva Flores, *Viaje de* Vuelta*: Estampas de una revista* (Mexico City: Fondo de Cultura Económica, 2011). On *Plural* and *Vuelta*, it is also worth consulting Adolfo Castañón, *Tránsito de Octavio Paz (Poemas, apuntes, ensayos)* (Mexico City: El Colegio de México, 2014), 490–557.

6. For Paz's relationship to France and to French culture, see Philippe Ollé-Laprune and Fabienne Bradu, ed., *Una patria sin pasaporte: Octavio Paz y Francia* (Mexico City: Fondo de Cultura Económica, 2014).

7. See Fabienne Bradu, *Permanencia de Octavio Paz* (Madrid: Vaso Roto Ediciones, 2015); Adolfo Castañón, *Tránsito de Octavio Paz*; Christopher Domínguez Michael, *Octavio Paz en su siglo* (Mexico City: Aguilar, 2014); Enrique Krauze, "Octavio Paz: El poeta y la revolución," in *Redentores: Ideas y poder en América Latina* (Mexico City: Random House Mondadori, 2011), 135–295; and Guillermo Sheridan, *Poeta con paisaje: Ensayos sobre la vida de Octavio Paz 1* (Mexico City: Ediciones Era, 2004); *Habitación con retratos: Ensayos sobre la vida de Octavio Paz 2* (Mexico City: Ediciones Era, 2015); and *Los idilios salvajes: Ensayos sobre la vida de Octavio Paz 3* (Mexico City: Ediciones Era, 2016).

8. See *Zona Octavio Paz*, https://zonaOctaviopaz.com.

9. Gabriel Zaid, "Un espíritu excepcional," in *Octavio Paz sin concesiones: 15 miradas críticas*, eds. César Cansino, Omar M. Gallardo, and Germán Molina Carrillo (Puebla: Benemérita Universidad Autónoma de Puebla / Grupo Editorial Mariel, 2016), 19.

10. Armando González Torres offers the following perspicacious assessment of this aspect of Paz's intellectual profile: "Después del 68 Paz pudo haber reinado con afabilidad y pasar sus años mexicanos, como hacen muchos, contemporizando con todos, apoyando las causas rentables del momento, coqueteando con las supuestas izquierdas y aceptando premios—eso sí, con el ceño fruncido—, provenientes de las supuestas derechas. Sin embargo, rechazó adaptarse a los reflejos condicionados de la intelectualidad de su época y ejerció una beligerancia incómoda, a ratos excesiva, a ratos pedante, al final de cuentas ejemplar. Porque Paz tomó posturas frente a los principales acontecimientos de su tiempo, pero no lo hizo desde las pretensiones de una certeza histórica, o de una ciencia superior, sino desde un punto de vista enraizado en el parecer personal y la mirada moral" (After 1968 Paz could have reigned in an affable manner and spent his years in Mexico, as many do, being accommodating with one and all, supporting whatever causes seemed advantageous at the time, flirting with

the ostensible Left and accepting prizes—with a furrowed brow, of course—from the ostensible Right. Nevertheless, he chose not to obey the conditioned reflexes of the intellectual world of his era and instead adopted an uncomfortably combative stance that was at times excessive, at times pedantic, but in the final account exemplary. For Paz took a stand on the principal issues of his time, but did so not from the point of view of some historical absolute, or a superior science, but from a perspective that was rooted in personal conviction and an ethical outlook). See Armando González Torres, "Comerse al mundo: Octavio Paz y los peligros de la vocación," in *Aire en libertad: Octavio Paz y la crítica*, ed. José Antonio Aguilar Rivera (Mexico City: Fondo de Cultura Económica, 2015), 148. The English translation is mine as are all subsequent translations from Spanish to English throughout this book, including translations of quotations from Paz.

11. See Gabriel Wolfson, ed., *Se acabó el centenario: Lecturas críticas en torno a Octavio Paz* (Puebla: UDLAP, 2015).
12. For a detailed study of Paz's literary style, see Eliana Albala, *El estilo ensayístico de Octavio Paz* (Mexico City: Centro de Investigación y Docencia en Humanidades del Estado de Morelos / Juan Pablos Editor, 2015).
13. The best example of this approach in Paz criticism is Rubén Medina, *Autor, autoridad y autorización: Escritura y poética de Octavio Paz* (Mexico City: El Colegio de México, 1999).
14. See Maarten van Delden and Yvon Grenier, *Gunshots at the Fiesta: Literature and Politics in Latin America* (Nashville, TN: Vanderbilt University Press, 2009), 233.
15. In the preface to *Corriente alterna*, Paz explains that the fragment as a form of writing is the best way to capture "esta realidad en movimiento que vivimos y que somos" (the reality in movement that we experience and that defines us). See Octavio Paz, *Corriente alterna* (Mexico City: Siglo XXI, 1967), 1.

CHAPTER 1

1. See Octavio Paz, "Rebelión, revuelta, revolución," in *Corriente alterna*, 147–52. For Paz, rebellion is individualistic, solitary, and spontaneous; he sees it as being related to love and art. Revolution, on the other hand, is abstract and intellectual and seeks a wholesale transformation of the world. Revolution is oriented toward the future, and it is related to philosophy and politics.
2. See Paz, *Itinerario*, 46.

3. See Octavio Paz, *Los hijos del limo: Del romanticismo a la vanguardia* (Barcelona: Seix Barral, 1974).
4. In his account of the beginnings of Paz's career as a writer, Guillermo Sheridan stresses what he calls the young man's "vocación de poeta rebelde" (vocation of a rebellious poet). See Guillermo Sheridan, *Poeta con paisaje*, 163. Adolfo Castañón, for his part, draws attention to the young Octavio's preference for "la política revolucionaria, insurgente contestaria respondona de 'izquierda'" (the revolutionary, insurgent, critical, subversive left-wing politics) he learned from his father, Octavio Paz Solórzano, a lawyer and journalist who served as Emiliano Zapata's representative in Los Angeles during the Mexican Revolution. See Adolfo Castañón, *Tránsito de Octavio Paz*, 51. Fabienne Bradu underlines the same quality in Paz when she writes "Si algo fundamental nos enseñó Octavio Paz es la virtud y la salud de la rebelión" (If there is one fundamental thing Octavio Paz taught us it is the value of rebellion). See Fabienne Bradu, *Permanencia de Octavio Paz*, 90.
5. Kevin Hillstrom explains that the term *pachuco* originated as "a hostile slang term for rough, uneducated Mexican workers from El Paso, Texas, and Ciudad Juarez, Mexico, who migrated to California in the 1920s and 1930s," adding that "over time, California-born Mexican Americans started using the term when referring to any Hispanic who was rude, vulgar, or a troublemaker." However, in spite of the derogatory connotations of the word, some Mexican American youths began to "voluntarily" identify as *pachucos*, and to develop a "perverse pride in behaving in ways that shocked or outraged the society that kept them at arm's length." See Kevin Hillstrom, *The Zoot Suit Riots* (Detroit: Omnigraphics, 2013), 47–48. It is interesting to note that Hillstrom quotes Paz in his discussion of the *pachucos*.
6. For negative commentary on Paz's depiction of the *pachuco* in *El laberinto*, see Jorge Aguilar Mora, *La divina pareja: Historia y mito en Octavio Paz* (Mexico City: Ediciones Era, 1978), 42; José Vicente Anaya, "Plagios de Paz en *El laberinto de la soledad*," in *Versus: Otras miradas a la obra de Octavio Paz*, ed. José Vicente Anaya (Zacatecas: Ediciones de Medianoche, 2010), 59–60; Carlos Blanco Aguinaga, "El laberinto fabricado por Octavio Paz," in *De mitólogos y novelistas* (Madrid: Ediciones Turner, 1971), 11; Debra A. Castillo, "Octavio Paz's Bread and Mole," *Hispanófila* 178 (December 2016): 155; Javier Durán, "Border Crossings: Images of the Pachuco in Mexican Literature," *Studies in Twentieth Century Literature* 25, no. 1 (Winter 2001): 143–46; Arturo Madrid-Barela, "In Search of the Authentic Pachuco: An Interpretive Essay,"

Aztlán 4, no. 1 (Spring 1973): 35–38; and José Quiroga, *Understanding Octavio Paz* (Columbia: University of South Carolina Press, 1999), 70.
7. Octavio Paz, *El laberinto de la soledad, Posdata y "Vuelta a* El laberinto de la soledad*"* (Mexico City: Fondo de Cultura Económica / Colección Popular, 1993). *El laberinto* was first published in 1950 and reprinted in a revised and expanded edition in 1959. The paperback version of *El laberinto* from which I will be citing is based on the 1959 edition.
8. Paz hit back at one of his critics—Carlos Blanco Aguinaga—in a June 15, 1973, letter to Carlos Fuentes in which he reports on a lecture he had recently delivered at the University of California, San Diego, where Blanco was on the faculty. "El salón estaba repleto" (The room was full), Paz reports, "y tuve que responder a muchas impertinencias. Por fortuna, salí con bien. Tu viejo conocido, Blanco, con rabia celtíbera pero vocabulario de un marxismo cavernícola digno de un teólogo de Las Urdes [sic], fue el que azuzó en contra mía a una cofradía chicana de la cual es confesor y 'chaman.' Me recibió con un artículo en la revista *Aztlán* contra *El laberinto* y su influencia desmoralizadora en la guerrilla chicana. ¡Pobre Blanco: como no pudo ser el virrey de Chalchicomala, quiere ser el tlatoani de San Diego, Cal.!" (and I had to respond to many impertinent comments. Fortunately, I came out unscathed. Your old acquaintance Blanco, with Celtiberian fury and a cavemanlike Marxism worthy of a theologian from Las Urdes [sic], incited the Chicano brotherhood, of which he is the confessor and 'shaman,' against me. He welcomed me with an article in the journal *Aztlán* in which he speaks out against *The labyrinth* and its demoralizing influence on the Chicano insurgency. Poor Blanco! He failed to become the Viceroy of Chalchicomala, so now he aspires to be the tlatoani of San Diego, California!). See Octavio Paz to Carlos Fuentes, 15 June 1973, *Plural* Editorial Files, Box 1 Folder 44, Manuscripts Division, Department of Rare Books and Special Collections, Princeton University Library.
9. Marco Luis Dorfsman suggests that *El laberinto* is not a work about "understanding" Mexican identity. "It is instead," he proposes, "a presentation of the fact that the question of identity itself is a problem." See Marco Luis Dorfsman, *Heterogeneity of Being: On Octavio Paz's Poetics of Similitude* (Lanham, MD: University Press of America, 2015), 15.
10. Enrico Mario Santí states that it is not possible to understand Paz's portrayal of the *pachuco* without taking into account what he calls "el carácter prototípico de esta figura en relación con el mexicano en

general" (the prototypical nature of this figure in relation to the Mexican in general). See Enrico Mario Santí, "Introducción a *El laberinto de la soledad*," in *El acto de las palabras: Estudios y diálogos con Octavio Paz* (Mexico City: Fondo de Cultura Económica, 1997), 172.

11. Jorge Capetillo-Ponce comments on the universalizing thrust of Paz's depiction of the *pachuco*: "It is a testament to the overall ambience of *The Labyrinth* . . . that as we read about the *Pachuco* he takes on for us the quality of any marginalized, isolated human being living in any part of the world." See Jorge Capetillo-Ponce, "The Walls of the Labyrinth: Mapping Octavio Paz's Sociology through Georg Simmel's Method," in *Octavio Paz: Humanism and Critique*, ed. Oliver Kozlarek (London: Transaction Publishers, 2009), 166.

12. In her discussion of what she calls the "semantic registers" of *El laberinto*, Annick Lempérière notes the frequency with which Paz resorts to a religious vocabulary in his book on the Mexican character. Lempérière states that the only type of vocabulary that appears with even greater frequency in Paz's essay is that which is associated with the nation. She also observes that the figure of the *pachuco* is strongly linked to the realm of the sacred and adds that the paucity of religious terminology in the chapter of *El laberinto* devoted to masks indicates that religion is *not* associated with inauthenticity. See Annick Lempérière, *Intellectuels, etat et société au Mexique: Les clercs de la nation (1910–1968)* (Paris: L'Harmattan, 1992), 261–62.

13. David Brading believes that what is most memorable about *El laberinto* is "la gran exuberancia con la que celebró la singularidad de México y con que enfatizó lo mucho que el país y sus habitantes diferían de la pobre, superficial civilización industrial, la cual encontraba su representación más eficaz en los Estados Unidos" (the tremendous exuberance with which he celebrated Mexico's uniqueness and with which he drew attention to how much the country and its inhabitants differed from the barrenness and superficiality of industrial civilization, of which the United States was the most effective representative). See David A. Brading, *Octavio Paz y la poética de la historia mexicana* (Mexico City: Fondo de Cultura Económica, 2002), 69–70.

14. Over the course of his career, Paz offered numerous illuminating reflections on *El laberinto*. On several occasions, the Mexican poet mentions that when he first encountered the *pachucos* in Southern California, he felt a profound sense of identification with them. In one retrospective essay, Paz writes the following: "Me reconocí en los *pachucos* y su loca rebeldía contra su presente y su pasado. Rebeldía

resuelta no en una idea sino en un gesto" (I recognized myself in the *pachucos* and their crazy rebellion against their present and their past. A rebellion that resolved itself not in an idea but in a gesture). See Octavio Paz, "Cómo y por qué escribí *El laberinto de la soledad*," in *Itinerario*, 27. Among the commentators who have recognized this sense of identification with the *pachuco* on Paz's part is the Brazilian critic Silviano Santiago. "Octavio Paz," he observes, "se redescubre mexicano identificándose con la figura del conciudadano americanizado por excelencia—el *pachuco*" (Octavio Paz rediscovers his Mexicanness thanks to his identification with the figure of his thoroughly Americanized fellow citizen—the *pachuco*). See Silviano Santiago, *Las raíces y el laberinto de América Latina*, trans. Mónica González García (Buenos Aires: Ediciones Corregidor, 2013), 35.

15. From the letters Paz wrote from Berkeley to his wife Elena Garro, who had remained in Mexico City, it is clear that the author of *El laberinto* felt a deep empathy for the Mexican population living in the United States. Note the following passage from a letter dated November 27, 1944, in which Paz begins by complaining about feeling lonely and being overworked, but concludes with a powerful expression of compassion for the Mexican *braceros* working in the United States in those years: "tu no sabes lo que es realmente estar solo en un país extraño. En el consulado me va muy mal; trabajo mucho—porque nadie trabaja, y me tratan (no los hombres, sino las brujas oficinistas) como a un perro o a un office-boy. En general salgo una hora más tarde—y lo hago no por espíritu burocrático sino porque quiero que den buenos informes a México y porque me da pena ver a los pobres braceros, LITERALMENTE DESAMPARADOS" (you don't know what it is like to be alone in a foreign country. Things are not going well for me at the consulate; I work very hard—because no one works, and they treat me (not the men, just the witches who work in the office) like a dog or an office-boy. Usually, I leave the office an hour late—and I do so not because I have a bureaucratic spirit but because I want the consulate to send good reports to Mexico and because I feel sorry for the poor *braceros*, LITERALLY DEFENCELESS) (emphasis in original). See Octavio Paz to Elena Garro, 27 November 1944, Box 11, Folder 22, Elena Garro Papers, C0827, Manuscripts Division, Department of Rare Books and Special Collections, Princeton University Library.

16. What is most significant about these books is that they portray the rebel as a hero. For Wilson, the "outsider" is someone who "stands for the Truth," and consequently cannot live "in the comfortable, insu-

lated world of the bourgeois." See Colin Wilson, *The Outsider* (New York: Jeremy P. Tarcher / Putnam, 1982), 13, 15. For Camus, the act of rebelling is a way of creating meaning in an otherwise absurd world. See Albert Camus, *L'homme révolté* (Paris: Gallimard, 1951), 23. For an excellent discussion of the figure of the antihero in twentieth-century literature, and of how the antihero is in fact a hero, see Murray Roston, *The Search for Selfhood in Modern Literature* (New York, Palgrave, 2001). For an informative account of the romanticized vision of the rebel in postwar American culture, see Grace Elizabeth Hale, *A Nation of Outsiders: How the White Middle Class Fell in Love with Rebellion in Postwar America* (New York: Oxford University Press, 2011).

17. Octavio Paz, *Posdata* (Mexico City: Siglo XXI, 1970), 100–101.
18. For a discussion of Paz's links with Romanticism, see Yvon Grenier, *From Art to Politics: Octavio Paz and the Pursuit of Freedom* (Lanham, MD: Rowman & Littlefield, 2001), 54–62.
19. Octavio Paz, *Conjunciones y disyunciones* (Mexico City: Joaquín Mortiz, 1969).
20. Conversely, a careful reading of Paz's depiction of the *pachuco* in *El laberinto* helps us understand why Paz felt an affinity for the rebels of the 1960s. Silviano Santiago draws attention to the link between the *pachuco* of Paz's *El laberinto* and the subversive movements of the 1960s. See Silviano Santiago, *Las raíces y el laberinto*, 60–1.
21. Octavio Paz, "A fondo—Octavio Paz," interview with Joaquín Soler Serrano (Televisión Española, 1977), video (1:06:25–1:06:31).

CHAPTER 2

1. Octavio Paz, "Chiapas, ¿nudo ciego o tabla de salvación?," in *Obras completas*, vol. 14 (Mexico City: Fondo de Cultura Económica, 2000), 254.
2. Octavio Paz, "El nudo de Chiapas," in *Obras completas*, vol. 14 (Mexico City: Fondo de Cultura Económica, 2000), 247.
3. Paz, "Chiapas," 248.
4. Octavio Paz, "Octavio Paz. De la revolución a la crítica," interview by Enrique Krauze, in *Luz espejeante: Octavio Paz ante la crítica*, ed. Enrico Mario Santí (Mexico City: Ediciones Era, 2009), 687.
5. Paz, *Itinerario*, 37.
6. Paz, *Itinerario*, 100.
7. One critic who has recognized the oscillation in Paz's views of the phenomenon of twentieth-century revolutions is Rafael Rojas. "La

idea de la Revolución en Paz" (The idea of the Revolution in Paz), he writes, "parece moverse pendularmente de la asunción al rechazo y del rechazo a la asunción, escenificando el desdoblamiento de su escritura al calor de la historia" (appears to move in pendular fashion from support to rejection and from rejection to support, revealing the oscillations of his writing under the pressure of history). See Rafael Rojas, *La polis literaria: El boom, la Revolución y otras polémicas de la Guerra Fría* (Mexico City: Penguin Random House / Taurus, 2018), 24.
8. Octavio Paz, *La otra voz: Poesía y fin de siglo* (Barcelona: Seix Barral, 1990), 58.
9. Paz, *Corriente alterna*, 183.
10. Paz, *Corriente alterna*, 212
11. Paz, *Tiempo nublado*, 27–28.
12. Leszek Kolakowski, "The Death of Utopia Reconsidered," in *Modernity on Endless Trial* (Chicago and London: University of Chicago Press, 1990), 138.
13. Isaiah Berlin, "The Decline of Utopian Ideas in the West," in *The Crooked Timber of Humanity: Chapters in the History of Ideas* (London: John Murray, 1990), 48.
14. Anthony Stanton, introduction to *El laberinto de la soledad* by Octavio Paz, ed. Anthony Stanton (Manchester: Manchester University Press, 2008), 31. For a helpful discussion of Paz's interpretation of the Mexican Revolution, see also Omar M. Gallardo, "Octavio Paz: Poética y política de la revuelta mexicana," in *Octavio Paz sin concesiones: 15 miradas críticas*, ed. César Cansino, Omar M. Gallardo, and Germán Molina Carrillo (Puebla: Benemérita Universidad Autónoma de Puebla / Grupo Editorial Mariel, 2016), 215–35.
15. For a discussion of the topic of the real nation versus the legal nation in the Latin American intellectual tradition and in particular in the work of Carlos Fuentes, see Maarten van Delden, "The Real Nation and the Legal Nation," in *Carlos Fuentes, Mexico, and Modernity* (Nashville, TN: Vanderbilt University Press, 1998), 169–96.
16. In his very thorough study of the image of Zapata in twentieth-century Mexican culture, Samuel Brunk suggests, unfairly in my view, that Paz's depiction of Zapata in *El laberinto* "suited the (Mexican) state." He also notes, more convincingly, that "Paz's picture of Zapatismo as a backward-looking Indian uprising is debatable." See Samuel Brunk, *The Posthumous Career of Emiliano Zapata: Myth, Memory, and Mexico's Twentieth Century* (Austin: University of Texas Press, 2008), 135, 259. The conservative dimension of the *Zapatista* revolution has

been underlined by many historians, most notably John Womack Jr., who opens his pathbreaking study of Emiliano Zapata and his movement with the following statement: "This is a book about country people who did not want to move and therefore got into a revolution." See John Womack Jr., *Zapata and the Mexican Revolution* (New York: Vintage Books, 1968), ix. Following in Womack's footsteps, Enrique Florescano notes that the goals of the *Zapatista* uprising in Morelos "tenían una dimensión local y un contenido conservador" (had a local dimension and a conservative content). See Enrique Florescano, *El nuevo pasado mexicano* (Mexico City: Ediciones Cal y Arena, 1991), 82.

17. Max Parra, *Writing Pancho Villa's Revolution: Rebels in the Literary Imagination of Mexico* (Austin: University of Texas Press, 2005), 33–35.
18. Frank Tannenbaum, *Peace by Revolution: An Interpretation of Mexico* (New York: Columbia University Press, 1933), 115.
19. Tannenbaum, 116, 118.
20. Tannenbaum, 187.
21. Alfonso Reyes, "Pasado inmediato," in *Obras completas*, vol. 12 (Mexico City: Fondo de Cultura Económica, 1983), 185.
22. Octavio Paz, *El ogro filantrópico: Historia y política, 1971–1978* (Mexico City: Joaquín Mortiz, 1979), 128.
23. Paz, *Itinerario*, 251.
24. Paz, *El laberinto*, 204.
25. Paz, *El laberinto*, 187.
26. Paz, *Posdata*, 147.
27. Paz, *Posdata*, 39.
28. Paz, *El ogro*, 65.
29. Paz, *El ogro*, 106.
30. Paz, *Itinerario*, 36.
31. Paz, *El ogro*, 130.
32. Paz, *Itinerario*, 32.
33. Paz, *El laberinto*, 204.
34. Paz, *Posdata*, 56.
35. Paz seemed to make an exception for the presidency of Lázaro Cárdenas, claiming that "la obra de Cárdenas consuma la de Zapata y Carranza" (the work of Cárdenas completes that of Zapata and Carranza). See *El laberinto*, 167–68.
36. Paz, *El laberinto*, 195.
37. Paz, *Posdata*, 55–56.
38. Paz, *Itinerario*, 35.
39. Later critics who have explored Latin American cultural production from the perspective of the themes of disjunction, incongruity, or

the sense of being out of place, include Carlos Alonso and Roberto Schwarz. Alonso claims that "In Spanish America the appropriation of the discursive modalities of metropolitan modernity have had to contend with the absence of its material antagonist in its midst, or more precisely, with its phantasmatic presence as the always distant and assumed reality of the metropolis." There is a clear echo here of Paz's notion of the disjunction between ideology (what Alonso calls "discourse") and socio-economic structure (the "material antagonist" in the quotation from Alonso). See Carlos Alonso, *The Burden of Modernity: The Rhetoric of Cultural Discourse in Spanish America* (New York: Oxford University Press, 1998), 32. Roberto Schwarz's concept of "misplaced ideas" can also be seen as part of this tradition of inquiry into Latin American modernity. The starting-point for Schwarz's investigation into Brazilian culture is the observation that "Since the last century educated Brazilians . . . have had the sense of living among ideas and institutions copied from abroad that do not reflect local reality." See Roberto Schwarz, *Misplaced Ideas: Essays on Brazilian Culture* (New York: Verso, 1992), 9. Neither Alonso nor Schwarz mentions Paz.

40. Paz, *Posdata*, 76.
41. Paz, *Corriente alterna*, 200.
42. Paz, "De la revolución a la crítica," interview by Enrique Krauze, 683–84.
43. Octavio Paz, *Pequeña crónica de grandes días* (Mexico City: Fondo de Cultura Económica, 1990), 71.
44. Paz, *Pequeña crónica*, 70.
45. Paz, *Pequeña crónica*, 71.
46. Paz, *Pequeña crónica*, 73.
47. Ángel Gilberto Adame, ed., *Octavio Paz en 1968: El año axial. Cartas y escritos sobre los movimientos estudiantiles* (Mexico City: Penguin Random House / Taurus, 2018), 44.
48. Octavio Paz and Arnaldo Orfila Reynal, *Cartas cruzadas* (Mexico City: Siglo XXI, 2005), 164–65.
49. Adame, *Octavio Paz en 1968*, 51.
50. Adame, *Octavio Paz en 1968*, 65.
51. Adame, *Octavio Paz en 1968*, 80.
52. Adame, *Octavio Paz en 1968*, 114.
53. Paz, *Posdata*, 35.
54. "El movimiento del 68" (The 1968 movement), says Álvarez Garín, "desafiaba y combatía las formas despóticas de control y de gobierno del régimen priísta. Pero no se planteó nunca combatir la existencia de ese gobierno. En otras palabras, en ninguno de los posibles niveles de decisión nos propusimos derrocar al gobierno" (challenged and

fought against the despotic forms of control and of governing used by the PRI regime. But it never considered combating the existence of that regime. In other words, at no stage of our decision-making did we ever propose to overthrow the government). See Raúl Álvarez Garín, *La estela de Tlatelolco: Una reconstrucción histórica del Movimiento estudiantil del 68* (Mexico City: Grijalbo, 1998), 164–65.
55. Álvarez Garín, 199.
56. Luis González de Alba, *Los días y los años* (Mexico City: Ediciones Era, 1971), 36–38.
57. Jorge Volpi, *La imaginación y el poder: Una historia intelectual de 1968* (Mexico City: Ediciones Era, 1998), 83.
58. Volpi, *La imaginación*, 418.
59. Adame, *Octavio Paz en 1968*, 206.
60. Adame, *Octavio Paz en 1968*, 206–7.
61. Adame, *Octavio Paz en 1968*, 207.
62. Adame, *Octavio Paz en 1968*, 207.
63. Consider, for example, the following observation Paz made in 1997 about the student movement: "En 1968 comenzó a reaparecer en la superficie histórica un estado de espíritu que había permanecido semioculto: la parte más activa y pensante del país estaba cansada de la hegemonía del PRI y de su complemento, el sistema presidencialista. Pero los dirigentes del movimiento estudiantil fueron insensibles a este anhelo democrático: ellos querían la revolución social" (In 1968 we saw the reappearance on the surface of history of a state of mind that had remained half hidden until then: the country's most active and thoughtful sectors were tired of the hegemony of the PRI and of its complement, the presidentialist system. But the leaders of the student movement were deaf to the call for democracy: what they wanted was a social revolution). See Adame, 248.
64. Paz, *Corriente alterna*, 176.
65. Paz, *El laberinto*, 231. It is interesting to note that Lysander Kemp, in his translation of *El laberinto*, speaks of a nightmare in which "the torture chambers are endlessly repeated in the mirrors of reason." His version misses the sense that reason *is responsible* for the creation of the torture chambers. See Octavio Paz, *The Labyrinth of Solitude*, trans. Lysander Kemp (New York: Grove Press, 1985), 212.
66. Paz, "El nudo," 245.
67. See Grenier, *From Art to Politics*, passim.
68. For an incisive critique of Paz the romantic, see José Antonio Aguilar Rivera, "Vuelta a Paz," *Nexos*, 1 January 2014, www.nexos.com.

mx/?p=15722. Interestingly, Aguilar Rivera proposes that Paz's romanticism is reflected in his continued adherence to the myth of the Revolution: "Nunca dejó de anhelar una revolución que prometiera restaurar la comunión, la fraternidad, la virtud, el amor y la Verdad" (He never stopped yearning for a revolution that would restore community, brotherhood, virtue, love, and Truth). For Aguilar Rivera's views on Paz, see also José Antonio Aguilar Rivera, *La geometría y el mito: Un ensayo sobre la libertad y el liberalismo en México, 1821–1970* (Mexico City: Fondo de Cultura Económica, 2010), 137–40.

69. The concept of "expressive individuation" is coined by Charles Taylor in his work on modern selfhood. See Charles Taylor, *Sources of the Self: The Making of the Modern Identity* (New York: Cambridge University Press, 1989), 376.

CHAPTER 3

1. Octavio Paz and Alfonso Reyes, *Correspondencia (1939–1959)*, ed. Anthony Stanton (Mexico City: Fondo de Cultura Económica, 1998), 117.
2. Paz, *El laberinto*, 210. This passage has been criticized for how it erases history and thus downplays the differences between powerful and less-powerful nations. See, for example, Blanco Aguinaga, "El laberinto," 5–25.
3. Paz and Reyes, *Correspondencia*, 117.
4. Octavio Paz, "El caracol y la sirena (Rubén Darío)," in *Cuadrivio* (Mexico City: Joaquín Mortiz, 1965), 49.
5. Paz, "El caracol y la sirena," 50.
6. Paz, *Corriente alterna*, 201.
7. Paz, "El caracol y la sirena," 50.
8. Paz, *Corriente alterna*, 159.
9. Octavio Paz, "México y Estados Unidos: Posiciones y contraposiciones," in *Tiempo nublado* (Barcelona: Seix Barral, 1986), 141.
10. Paz, "México y Estados Unidos," 141.
11. A number of critics have expressed reservations about Paz's reliance on stark binary oppositions in his approach to the relationship between Mexico and the United States. Debra Castillo, for example, notes that "the 'two civilizations' concept sets up Paz's argument for other binaries as well, since Paz, while deploring the category errors of stereotyping, in his own work consistently finds himself drawn to the clean differentiations of perfectly balanced and oppositional myth." See Castillo, "Octavio Paz's Bread and Mole," 155. According

to Jesús Silva-Herzog Márquez, Paz's discussions of the differences between Mexico and the United States are marred by an identity-focused approach that clashes with his frequently critical perspective on nationalist thinking. For Silva-Herzog Márquez, Paz's insistence on "la distancia infranqueable entre los dos países" (the unbridgeable divide between the two countries) resulted in "una lectura frigorífica de la historia" (a frozen reading of history). See Jesús Silva-Herzog Márquez, "Sílabas enamoradas," in *La idiotez de lo perfecto: Miradas a la política* (Mexico City: Fondo de Cultura Económica, 2006), 185.

12. For an account of Paz's time in Berkeley, see Guillermo Sheridan, "Cartas de un Hijo Pródigo (a Octavio G. Barreda)," in *Habitación con retratos*, 92–99. For Paz's newspaper articles on the San Francisco Conference, see Octavio Paz, *Crónicas truncas de días excepcionales*, ed. Antonio Saborit (Mexico City: UNAM, 2007).

13. In a prefatory note to *Posdata*, Paz observed that "si América Latina vive un período de revueltas y transformaciones, los Estados Unidos atraviesan por otro no menos violento y profundo: la rebelión de los negros y los chicanos, la de los jóvenes y las mujeres, la de los artistas y los intelectuales" (whereas Latin America is living through a period of revolts and transformations, the United States is experiencing no less violent and profound upheavals: the rebellions of blacks and chicanos, of women and the young, of artists and intellectuals). See Paz, *Posdata*, 15–16.

14. At an April 1995 gathering of Nobel laureates in Atlanta, Paz offered some reflections on the end of the idea of the melting pot in the United States, and the emergence of an alternative view of how the nation's many racial and ethnic groups might live together. "Es claro" (It is clear), he states, "que la idea del crisol no bastaba para enfrentar los problemas del siglo XX. Los Estados Unidos se han convertido no sólo en un estado pluralista sino también en un país multicultural . . . se enfrentan ustedes a la creación de un nuevo tipo de cuerpo político, casi diría un nuevo tipo de civilización: multicultural y multirracial" (that the idea of the melting pot was insufficient to deal with the problems of the twentieth century. The United States has become not only a plural state but also a multicultural nation . . . you are dealing with the creation of a new type of body politic, I would almost say a new type of civilization: multicultural and multiracial). See Czeslaw Milosz, Octavio Paz, Claude Simon, and Derek Walcott, "Particularismos, universalismo, literatura," *Vuelta* 235 (June 1996): 8.

15. Paz, *Pequeña crónica*, 44.

16. Paz, "México y Estados Unidos," 139–40.
17. Paz, *Pequeña crónica*, 13.
18. Paz, *Pequeña crónica*, 159.
19. Paz, "México y Estados Unidos," 152–53.
20. Paz, "México y Estados Unidos," 154.
21. Octavio Paz, "El espejo indiscreto," in *El ogro*, 59.
22. In talking about nations and civilizations, Paz continued to favor botanical imagery throughout his career. Note, for example, the following description of the United States in an essay from 1990: "es un retoño de la civilización europea transplantado a nuestro continente; aquí arraigó y se convirtió en una planta distinta" (it is a sprout of European civilization that was transplanted to our continent; here it took root and became a different kind of plant). See Paz, *Pequeña crónica*, p. 40.
23. Octavio Paz, "¿Poesía latinoamericana?" in *El signo y el garabato* (Mexico City: Joaquín Mortiz, 1973), 160.
24. In linking Protestantism with capitalism, Paz is following the thesis Max Weber had put forward in *The Protestant Ethic and the Spirit of Capitalism*. Paz does not refer to Weber when discussing the interrelatedness of religion and economics in the United States; on the other hand, in his analyses of Latin American culture and society, the Mexican poet regularly uses another important concept developed by Weber—that of patrimonialism. Consider, for example, his observation in "El espejo indiscreto" that "La monarquía española es un ejemplo de régimen patrimonialista" (The Spanish monarchy is an example of a patrimonialist regime), to which he adds "También lo han sido (y lo son) sus sucesores, las 'repúblicas democráticas' de América Latina" (Its successors, the 'democratic republics' of Latin America, have also been (and still are) patrimonialist). See "El espejo indiscreto," in *El ogro*, 58. For a discussion of the idea of patrimonialism in Paz's approach to Latin American culture and society, see Roberto Hozven, *Octavio Paz: Viajero del presente. Otra vuelta* (Mexico City: Fondo de Cultura Económica, 2014), 31–40, 61–5.
25. Paz, "México y Estados Unidos," 151.
26. Paz, "México y Estados Unidos," 151.
27. Paz, *El laberinto*, 22.
28. Paz, *El laberinto*, 74–5.
29. Paz, "México y Estados Unidos," 148.
30. Paz, *El laberinto*, 27.
31. Paz, *El laberinto*, 28.

32. The idea that American individualism leads, paradoxically, to a loss of individuality was developed in an especially eloquent fashion by Tocqueville in the opening chapters of the second volume of *Democracy in America*. See Alexis de Tocqueville, *Democracy in America*, two vols. trans. Henry Reeve, ed. Francis Bowen (Mineola, NY: Dover Publications, 2017), 1–13. There are numerous other echoes of Tocqueville in Paz's writings on the United States, including the ideas, put forward by Paz in "México y Estados Unidos," of American materialism, the American focus on work, the religious origins of American society, and the great spatial mobility of the American people. Paz mentions Tocqueville several times in his 1980 essay "La democracia imperial," alluding, among other things, to the French diplomat's comments on how democracies are constitutionally incapable of developing an effective foreign policy. See Octavio Paz, "La democracia imperial," in *Tiempo nublado* (Barcelona: Seix Barral, 1986), 42. Jacques Lafaye calls Paz "un Tocqueville mexicano" (a Mexican Tocqueville). See Jacques Lafaye, *Octavio Paz en la deriva de la modernidad* (Mexico City: Fondo de Cultura Económica, 2013), 126.
33. Paz, *El laberinto*, 28.
34. Paz, *El laberinto*, 22.
35. Paz, "La democracia imperial," 38.
36. Paz, "México y Estados Unidos," 153.
37. Paz, "La democracia imperial," 38.
38. Paz, "La democracia imperial," 37.
39. Paz, "La democracia imperial," 37.
40. There is a long line of French writers—from Tocqueville to Jean Baudrillard—who view the United States as a country existing outside of history. It is a tradition of thought on which Paz surely nourished himself, and which Paz in turn bolstered. Consider the fact that Baudrillard cites Paz in his book on the United States. See Jean Baudrillard, *Amérique* (Paris: Le Livre de Poche, 1986), 80. Dominique Jullien offers a helpful discussion of the *topos* in French literature of the United States as an anti-historical nation. See Dominique Jullien, *Récits du Nouveau Monde: Les voyageurs français en Amérique de Chateaubriand à nos jours* (Paris: Nathan, 1992), 143–81.
41. Octavio Paz, "La mesa y el lecho," in *El ogro*, 212.
42. Paz, "México y Estados Unidos," 146.
43. Paz, "México y Estados Unidos," 153–54.
44. Paz, *El laberinto*, 57.
45. Paz, *El laberinto*, 77.

46. Paz, "México y Estados Unidos," 150.
47. Paz, *El laberinto*, 66. John Mander suggests that an interesting argument in *El laberinto* about how "If the Mexican understands death better than the North American, he also understands life better than the pragmatic Anglo-Saxon" becomes derailed when Paz explains the advantages of being murdered by a Mexican. He speaks of "the potential danger, even silliness" of Paz's thinking on this topic. See John Mander, *Static Society: The Paradox of Latin America* (London: Victor Gollancz, 1969), 64.
48. Paz, "México y Estados Unidos," 149.
49. Claudio Veliz places Paz's approach to the differences between Mexico and the United States in the tradition of Latin American *arielismo*, a reading of which the best-known exponent is no doubt José Enrique Rodó. Thinkers in this tradition establish a contrast between Latin American spirituality and US American materialism. There is some truth to Veliz's suggestion; however, Paz's reading of Mexican culture goes well beyond the standard *arielista* motifs and takes into account topics such as the relationship to the body or attitudes toward death that are not treated by Rodó in his essay *Ariel*. See Claudio Veliz, *The New World of the Gothic Fox: Culture and Economy in English and Spanish America* (Berkeley: University of California Press, 1994), 10.
50. Octavio Paz, *In/mediaciones* (Barcelona: Seix Barral, 1979), 46.
51. Octavio Paz, *Sor Juana Inés de la Cruz, o, Las trampas de la fe* (Mexico City: Fondo de Cultura Económica, 1982).
52. See Xavier Rodríguez Ledesma, *El pensamiento político de Octavio Paz: Las trampas de la ideología* (Mexico City: Plaza y Valdés, 1996), 217, and José Joaquín Brunner, *América Latina: Cultura y modernidad* (Mexico City: Grijalbo, 1992), 50.
53. Paz, "México y Estados Unidos," 143.
54. Richard Morse, *New World Soundings: Culture and Ideology in the Americas* (Baltimore, MD: Johns Hopkins University Press, 1989), 106.
55. Morse, 155.
56. Morse, 147.
57. In a passage from *El arco y la lira*, Paz suggests that France, not the United States, embodies a "normal" historical development. "En el resto de Europa" (In the rest of Europe), he writes, "parece que la historia ha procedido a saltos, rupturas e interrupciones; en Francia, al menos desde el siglo XVIII hasta el primer cuarto del XX, todo parece que fue hecho a su hora: la Academia prepara la Enciclopedia, ésta la Revolución, la Revolución el Imperio, y así sucesivamente. España,

Italia, Alemania y la misma Inglaterra no poseen una historia tan fluida y coherente" (one gets the impression that history has proceeded through leaps, ruptures, and interruptions; in France, at least from the eighteenth century until the first quarter of the twentieth century, everything appears to have been carried out in a timely fashion: the Academy paves the way for the Encyclopedia, which does the same for the Revolution, and the Revolution leads into the Empire, and thus successively. Spain, Italy, Germany, and even England do not possess such a fluid and coherent history). Although the country chosen to represent historical normality varies, the conceptual opposition undergirding Paz's argument, contrasting coherence and rupture, the aleatory and the purposive, the organic and the inorganic, remains the same. See Octavio Paz, *El arco y la lira: El poema, la revelación poética, poesía e historia*, 2nd ed. (Mexico City: Fondo de Cultura Económica, 1967), 228–29.

58. Paz, *El laberinto*, 77.
59. Paz, *Pequeña crónica*, 57.
60. For a more extended exploration of Paz's ambivalent stance with regard to modernity, see my chapter "The Incomplete End of Modernity of Octavio Paz," in Van Delden and Grenier, *Gunshots at the Fiesta*, 115–36.
61. Paz, *Posdata*, 74–75.
62. Paz, *La otra voz*, 129.
63. Paz, *La otra voz*, 125.

CHAPTER 4

1. See Octavio Paz, *Vislumbres de la India* (Mexico City: Seix Barral, 1995), 5–26, for an account of the poet's journey to India and his first impressions of the subcontinent.
2. For Paz's stay in Japan, see Aurelio Asiain, "Octavio Paz en Japón, Japón en Octavio Paz," in *Japón en Octavio Paz*, ed. Aurelio Asiain (Mexico City: Fondo de Cultura Económica, 2014), 16–33.
3. Domínguez Michael, *Octavio Paz en su siglo*, 225.
4. Robero Cantú, "Points of Convergence: Ancient China, Modernity, and Translation in the Poetry and Essays of Octavio Paz, 1956–1996," in *Alternative Orientalisms in Latin America and Beyond*, ed. Ignacio López-Calvo (Newcastle: Cambridge Scholars Publishing, 2007), 2.
5. Raleigh Trevelyan, "One Nation under Many Gods," review of *In Light of India* by Octavio Paz, translated from the Spanish by Eliot Weinberger, *New York Times Book Review*, 30 March 1997, 25.

6. For a negative assessment of Paz's sympathy for the British, his emphasis on Western influences in India's history, and his secularist viewpoint, see Vasant G. Gadre, "*Vislumbres de la India*: Viciadas por el prisma del pensamiento occidental de Octavio Paz," *Ciberletras* 5 (August 2001), www.lehman.cuny.edu/ciberletras/v05/gadre.html. Gadre writes from the perspective of a Hindu nationalist. For a discussion of the topic that is more favorable to Paz, see Fabienne Bradu, "Octavio Paz en perpetua ruptura," *Literatura mexicana* 19, no. 2 (2008): 123–30.

7. In alluding to the role of the West in shaping Gandhi's outlook, Paz is following a standard theme in scholarship on the leader of the fight for Indian independence. For example, in his biography of Gandhi, Douglas Allen writes the following: "In England Gandhi is for the first time exposed to many Western ethical, social, political, economic, legal and constitutional writings, priorities and values, and experiential ways of being in the world. Many of these he later rejects as false, illusory, superficial, violent, immoral and anti-spiritual, but some of these Western experiences provide him with lasting skills and values, including his critiques of much of traditional hierarchical India." See Douglas Allen, *Mahatma Gandhi* (London: Reaktion Books, 2011), 30–31. Not all scholars, however, depict the influence of British culture on Gandhi in such a positive light. Yasmin Khan, for example, stresses not the emancipatory dimension of the lessons Gandhi learned in London, but the coerciveness of the imperial relationship. "The idea of London as the centre of the world," Khan notes, "had percolated into the thinking of colonized subjects." The implication is clearly that the mythical status attributed to London is a symptom of a colonized mind-set. Khan also observes that "the power of the imperial myth" was such that for a very long time Gandhi could not help but view the world "through the inevitable framework of British imperial rule." Again, the emphasis is on how the imperial relationship has a distorting effect on Gandhi's outlook. See Yasmin Khan, "Gandhi's World," in *The Cambridge Companion to Gandhi*, eds. Judith M. Brown and Anthony Parel (Cambridge: Cambridge University Press, 2011), 18–19, 21. Clearly, Paz's perspective is closer to Allen than Khan.

8. For a scholarly account that lends support to Paz's discussion of the role of Nehru's British education in forging his intellectual outlook, one may consult Judith M. Brown's biography of the Indian leader. Among other things, Brown highlights Nehru's "exposure to the serious study of science" at Cambridge, as well as the extent to which Nehru's idea of India emphasized the need to "embrac[e] the modern

world." See Judith M. Brown, *Nehru: A Political Life* (New Haven and London: Yale University Press, 2003), 39, 189.

9. Paz is not alone in crediting British imperialism with helping to pave the way for Indian independence and democracy. Niall Ferguson argues that "India, the world's largest democracy, owes more than it is fashionable to acknowledge to British rule," mentioning, among other things, "the institutions of parliamentary democracy," which, he suggests, would not have been adopted "without the influence of British imperial rule." See Niall Ferguson, *Empire: The Rise and Demise of the British World Order and the Lessons for Global Power* (New York: Basic Books, 2003), 326, 358. A forceful rebuttal of the idea that British rule in India had beneficial consequences is provided by the Indian diplomat, novelist, and politician Shashi Tharoor. He argues that the British systematically expropriated Indian wealth, destroyed native political institutions, carried out a divide and rule strategy of domination, and practiced extensive racial discrimination against the native population. Tharoor strongly disagrees with the idea that the British "instilled in their Indian subjects the spirit of democracy and the rule of law." See Shashi Tharoor, *Inglorious Empire: What the British Did to India* (London: Hurst & Company, 2016), 40. Tharoor's argument has, in turn, received some rebuttals of its own. For critiques of *Inglorious Empire*, see Charles Allen, "Who Owns India's History: A Critique of Shashi Tharoor's *Inglorious Empire*," *Asian Affairs*, 49, no. 3 (2018): 355–69, and Tirthankar Roy, review of *Inglorious Empire* by Shashi Tharoor, *Cambridge Review of International Affairs*, 31, no. 1 (2018): 134–38. Allen lends support to Paz's idea that European modernity—or in Allen's account, the ideals of the Enlightenment—helped to change India for the better, whereas Roy argues that the record of the British Raj was much more mixed in both economic and political realms than is acknowledged in Tharoor's black-and-white presentation of Indian history.

10. The postcolonial scholar Gauri Viswanathan offers a very different approach to the role of education within the British imperial enterprise. Focusing on the discipline of English studies in the British Indian curriculum, she argues that the teaching of English in India "served to strengthen Western cultural hegemony" and was part of a larger project of "social and political control." Whereas Paz sees an imperial project that undermines itself, Viswanathan sees a project of domination hiding behind the mask of a benevolent undertaking. See Gauri Viswanathan, *Masks of Conquest: Literary Study and British Rule in India* (New York: Columbia University Press, 1989), 2, 3.

11. See Octavio Paz, "Dos apostillas: Asia y América," in *Puertas al campo* (Mexico City: UNAM, 1966), 141–54. The critic who has written most in depth about this aspect of Paz's thinking is Erik Camayd-Freixas. See his "Introduction: The Orientalist Controversy and the Origins of Amerindian Culture," in *Orientalism and Identity in Latin America: Fashioning Self and Other from the (Post)Colonial Margin*, ed. Erik Camayd-Freixas (Tucson: University of Arizona Press, 2013), 1–18.
12. Octavio Paz, "El arte de México: Materia y sentido," in *In/mediaciones* (Mexico City: Seix Barral, 1979), 55.
13. Paz, "El arte de México," 56.
14. Paz's ideas about the historical "solitude" of pre-Columbian civilizations, and his use of this feature of the pre-Columbian world as an explanation for the Spanish conquest of the New World, are reminiscent of the interpretation of the Conquest put forward by the French-Bulgarian philosopher and semiotician Tzvetan Todorov. Todorov focuses his analysis on the modes of interpretation and communication prevailing among the civilizations that entered into contact with each other in the Americas in the early sixteenth century. In Todorov's view, the Spanish owed their victory in the Conquest of the New World to their better interpretive and communicative skills, which were in turn rooted in their understanding of the concept of cultural otherness, something the indigenous inhabitants of the Americas lacked, however sophisticated their civilizations may have been in other respects. See Tzvetan Todorov, *The Conquest of America: The Question of the Other*, translated by Richard Howard (New York: Harper & Row, 1984). It is clear that Paz was interested in Todorov's approach to the Conquest. In August 1979, he published an essay by Todorov on the topic in *Vuelta*—essentially, an advance of the book that was to come out a few years later. In October 1992, to mark the quincentenary of Columbus's voyage to the Americas, *Vuelta* published the text of a round-table discussion on the Conquest, in which the participants were Paz, Todorov, and Ignacio Bernal. The round-table had taken place at the *Instituto Francés de América Latina* in Mexico City on April 21, 1980. Although Paz notes some differences of opinion with Todorov, he is generally in agreement with his French colleague. Interesting from the point of view of the present chapter is the fact that Paz, in the course of a description of some of the distinctive features of the Mesoamerican world-view, draws a sharp contrast with Indian civilization. "A ningún indio de la India" (To no Indian person in India), he states, "se le ocurrió jamás pensar que los persas, los griegos, los escitas, los kushanes, los hunos blancos, todos los pueblos que, desde

el siglo V a. de C., han invadido a la India fuese un pueblo de dioses, superhombres o divinidades" (would it ever have occurred that the Persians, the Greeks, the Scythians, the Kushans, the white Huns, that is, all of the peoples who since the fifth century BC invaded India, were gods, supermen, or divinities). See Octavio Paz, Ignacio Bernal, and Tzvetan Todorov, "La Conquista de México: Comunicación y encuentro de civilizaciones," *Vuelta* 191 (October 1992): 12.

15. Octavio Paz, "El uso y la contemplación," in *In/mediaciones* (Mexico City: Seix Barral, 1979).
16. See Edward Said, *Orientalism* (New York: Pantheon Books, 1978).
17. Julia A. Kushigian, *Orientalism in the Hispanic Literary Tradition: In Dialogue with Borges, Paz, and Sarduy* (Albuquerque: University of New Mexico Press, 1991), 3.
18. Kushigian, 3.
19. Silvia Nagy-Zekmi, "Buscando el Este en el Oeste: Prácticas orientalistas en la literatura latinoamericana," in *Moros en la costa: Orientalismo en Latinoamérica*, ed. Silvia Nagy-Zekmi (Madrid and Frankfurt: Iberoamericana/Vervuert, 2008), 11–21.
20. Ignacio López-Calvo, introduction to *Alternative Orientalisms in Latin America and Beyond*, ed. Ignacio López-Calvo (Newcastle upon Tyne: Cambridge Scholars Publishing, 2007), viii.
21. Ignacio López-Calvo, introduction to *One World Periphery Reads the Other: Knowing the "Oriental" in the Americas and the Iberian Peninsula*, ed. Ignacio López-Calvo (Newcastle upon Tyne: Cambridge Scholars Publishing, 2010), 4.
22. Alejandro González-Ormerod, "Octavio Paz's India," *Third World Quarterly* 35, no. 3 (2014): 531, 539, 533.

CHAPTER 5

1. Octavio Paz, "Vuelta a *El laberinto de la soledad*," interview by Claude Fell, in Paz, *El laberinto*, 326.
2. Paz, "Vuelta," interview by Claude Fell, 347.
3. Paz, *El laberinto*, 131–32.
4. Paz, *El laberinto*, 141–42.
5. For a different view, one that holds that Paz's debt to Marx is not all that significant, see Yvon Grenier, "Socialism in One Person: Specter of Marx in Octavio Paz's Political Thought," in Oliver Kozlarek, ed., *Octavio Paz: Humanism and Critique* (Bielefeld: Transcript Verlag, 2009), 47–64.

NOTES TO PAGES 102–103   285

6. In his study of the work of Claude Lévi-Strauss, Paz offers a helpful account of the key influences that shaped the Belgian-French anthropologist's thought. "Lévi-Strauss," Paz explains, "ha aludido en varias ocasiones a las influencias que determinaron la dirección de su pensamiento: la geología, el marxismo y Freud. Un paisaje se presenta como un rompecabezas: colinas, rocas, valles, árboles, barrancos. Ese desorden posee un sentido oculto; no es una yuxtaposición de formas diferentes sino la reunión en un lugar de distintos tiempos-espacios: las capas geológicas. Como el lenguaje, el paisaje es diacrónico y sincrónico al mismo tiempo: es la historia condensada de las edades terrestres y es también un nudo de relaciones. Un corte vertical muestra que lo oculto, las capas invisibles, es una 'estructura' que determina y da sentido a las más superficiales. Al descubrimiento intuitivo de la geología se unieron, más tarde, las lecciones del marxismo (una geología de la sociedad) y el psicoanálisis (una geología psíquica). Esta triple lección puede resumirse en una frase: Marx, Freud y la geología lo enseñaron a explicar lo visible por lo oculto" (On several occasions, Lévi-Strauss has referred to the influences that shaped the direction of his thought: geology, Marxism, and Freud. A landscape looks like a puzzle: hills, rocks, valleys, trees, ravines. Beneath this disorder there is a hidden meaning; a landscape is not the mere juxtaposition of different forms, but rather the coming together in one place of various times and spaces: the geological strata. Like a language, the landscape is simultaneously diachronic and synchronic: it is the compressed history of the geological eras and it is also a knot of relationships. A vertical cut shows that what is hidden, the invisible strata, is a "structure" that determines and gives meaning to what is on the surface. To the intuitive discovery of geology were later added the lessons of Marxism (a geology of society) and psychoanalysis (a geology of the psyche). This triple lesson can be summarized in one sentence: Marx, Freud, and geology taught him to explain the visible via the hidden). It is not difficult to see that what Paz states in this passage about Lévi-Strauss helps us to understand key characteristics of his own thought. See Octavio Paz, *Claude Lévi-Strauss, o, El nuevo festín de Esopo* (Mexico City: Joaquín Mortiz, 1967) 11.
7. See Paz, *Tiempo nublado*, 27.
8. See Paz, *Sor Juana*, 602.
9. Paz, *Itinerario*, 49–50.
10. Adolfo Castañón notes that "el ascendiente de la obra de Sigmund Freud sobre Octavio Paz no cabe ser soslayado" (the influence of the

work of Sigmund Freud on Octavio Paz cannot be sidestepped), and adds that in the Mexican poet's *Obras completas* "el nombre del fundador del psicoanálisis aparece mencionado explícitamente, por lo menos, 90 veces" (the work of the founder of psychoanalysis is explicitly mentioned on at least ninety occasions). See Castañón, *Tránsito de Octavio Paz*, 205.

11. For previous discussions of the role of psychoanalysis in Paz's writings, see Thomas Mermall, "Octavio Paz: *El laberinto de la soledad* y el sicoanálisis de la historia," *Cuadernos americanos* 156 (Jan.-Feb. 1968): 97–113; Santí, "Introducción a *El laberinto de la soledad*," 123–231; Rubén Gallo, *Freud's Mexico: Into the Wilds of Psychoanalysis* (Cambridge, MA: MIT Press, 2010), 92–108; Bruno Bosteels, *Marx and Freud in Latin America* (New York: Verso Books, 2012), 180–86; and Domínguez Michael, *Octavio Paz en su siglo*, 167–75.

12. Roger Bartra, *La jaula de la melancolía: Identidad y metamorfosis del mexicano* (Mexico City: Grijalbo, 1987), 206.

13. Sigmund Freud, *The Ego and the Id*, trans. Joan Riviere (London: Hogarth Press, 1927), 42.

14. Peter L. Rudnytsky, *Freud and Oedipus* (New York: Columbia University Press, 1987), 39.

15. Both Gallo and Santí discuss the Oedipal framework of Paz's reading of the Mexican family romance in "Los hijos de la Malinche." Santí draws attention to the psychoanalytical reach of Paz's interpretation and offers the following description of the three participants in the national myth of origins: "el padre Violento, la madre humillada, y el hijo angustiado por su origen conflictivo" (the Violent father, the humiliated mother, and the son whose conflictive origin causes him anguish). See Santí, "Introducción a *El laberinto de la soledad*," 194. Gallo goes into more detail, and emphasizes the fact that Paz *rewrites* the Freudian model: "Paz borrowed the concept of a collective Oedipus complex from *Moses and Monotheism*, but then transformed Freud's patriarchal model into a matriarchal one. Freud praised the virtues of paternal authority—the source of reason, ethics, and conscience—but Paz emphasizes the importance of the maternal—a rich realm of myths, sensuality, and pre-Columbian traditions." See Gallo, *Freud's Mexico*, 98. I agree with Gallo's suggestion that Paz rewrites Freud's family romance, although my interpretation of *how* he rewrites it is obviously different. In my view, the importance of the maternal dimension in *El laberinto* emerges more from Paz's account of the role of the Virgin of Guadalupe in Mexican culture, than from the link with pre-Columbian traditions.

16. Blanca García Monsiváis argues that unlike Samuel Ramos, who in *El perfil del hombre y la cultura en México* (1934) based his interpretation of the Mexican character on a specific psychological theory (that of Alfred Adler), Paz eschewed a "procedimiento definitivo" (definitive method) and "un marco disciplinario" (a disciplinary framework) in his approach to the topic, offering instead "una serie de interrogantes, cuestionamientos" (a series of interrogations and questions) in his exploration of Mexican identity in *El laberinto*. I agree with García Monsiváis about the open-ended qualities of Paz's writing. But she overstates the degree to which Paz frees himself from all theoretical paradigms. See Blanca García Monsiváis, *El ensayo mexicano en el siglo XX: Reyes, Novo, Paz, desarrollo, direcciones y formas* (Mexico City: Universidad Autónoma Metropolitana, Unidad Iztapalapa, División de Ciencias Sociales y Humanidades, 1995), 131.
17. Discussions of the massacre generally present it as having taken place on the night of October 2, 1968. Elena Poniatowska, for example, gave her widely-read testimonial about the massacre the title *La noche de Tlatelolco*. Luis González de Alba, a student leader who was present at the massacre, has vigorously contested this presentation of the events of October 2. He made his point clear when he titled his final book on the massacre *Tlatelolco, aquella tarde* (Tlatelolco, that afternoon). See Elena Poniatowska, *La noche de Tlatelolco* (Mexico City: Era, 1971) and Luis González de Alba, *Tlatelolco, aquella tarde* (Mexico City: Ediciones Cal y Arena, 2016).
18. The exact number of victims is still unknown.
19. David Brading suggests that Paz saw himself as a prophet or a sorcerer more than as a therapist. See Brading, *Octavio Paz y la poética de la historia mexicana*, 37.
20. Paz, *Posdata*, 134.
21. Paz, *Posdata*, 134–5.
22. An important source for Paz's ideas about the civilization of the Aztecs is Laurette Séjourné's *Pensamiento y religión en el México antiguo*. Séjourné was a French-Mexican archaeologist who was married to Arnaldo Orfila Reynal, the director first of the Fondo de Cultura Económica and later of the Siglo XXI publishing house, with whom Paz conducted a lengthy correspondence in the 1960s. Paz acknowledges his debt to Séjourné in one of this letters to Orfila. Writing from Paris on January 2, 1969, he praises Séjourné for being "una de las primeras en ver el carácter verdadero de la hegemonía azteca—los 'nazis' del mundo pre-colombino" (one of the first to grasp the true character of the hegemony of the Aztecs—the "Nazis" of the pre-Columbian world).

See Paz and Orfila Reynal, *Cartas cruzadas*, 196. Paz was drawing on Séjourné's depictions of Aztec civilization as representing "la barbarie absoluta" (absolute barbarism) and on her definition of the Aztec regime as "un Estado totalitario cuya existencia estaba basada sobre el desprecio total de la persona humana" (a totalitarian state whose existence was based on a total contempt for the dignity of human life). See Laurette Séjourné, *Pensamiento y religión en el México antiguo* (Mexico City: Siglo XXI, 1957), 19, 21. What Paz overlooks in his letter to Orfila is the fact that Séjourné combined condemnation of the "barbarism" and "totalitarianism" at the root of Aztec religious practices with praise for the high level of cultural achievement reached by the Aztecs. This, no doubt, is what led Orfila to make the following comment in a letter to Paz: "en nuestra casa, desearían discutirle su opinión sobre la influencia azteca en la barbarie contemporánea" (Laurette and I feel inclined to question your views on the Aztec influence on the present-day barbarism). See Paz and Orfila Reynal, *Cartas cruzadas*, 193.

23. Paz and Aguilar Mora met in Paris in late 1968. Many years later, Aguilar Mora provided a brief account of the several conversations he had in a Parisian hotel room with the exiled poet. Aguilar Mora had witnessed the Tlatelolco massacre, and he mentions Paz's interest in hearing his testimony of the events of that day. But he depicts Paz as locked into his own interpretation of the massacre: "nada de lo que dije ni de lo que pude tímidamente objetarle le hizo cambiar la interpretación que ya tenía bien formada de lo ocurrido el 2 de octubre, y que expondría poco después en *Posdata*: el surgimiento de la violencia indígena soterrada en la historia y en la vida de México" (Nothing I said, nothing I timidly objected, had any effect on the interpretation he had already settled on of what had happened on the second of October. This was the interpretation he would soon put forward in *Posdata*: the massacre as a bursting forth of the indigenous violence buried underneath the surface of Mexican life and history"). See Jorge Aguilar Mora, *La sombra del tiempo: Ensayos sobre Octavio Paz y Juan Rulfo* (Mexico City: Siglo XXI, 2010), 9. Paz, in turn, spoke dismissively of Aguilar Mora in a June 1, 1969, letter to Carlos Fuentes. Alluding to the objections to his interpretation of the Tlatelolco massacre, he singled out one person in particular. Even though he does not mention his name in this passage, there can be little doubt that the target of Paz's ire is indeed Aguilar Mora. "Otro de ellos" (Another one of my critics), Paz writes, "me dijo que mi alusión al pasado azteca no poseía la menor significación política. Es decir que, nada menos que

en nombre del materialismo histórico, para ese mequetrefe la historia no cuenta" (informed me that my references to the Aztec past had no political significance whatsoever. In other words, for this schmuck, speaking in the name of nothing less than historical materialism, history does not matter). See Adame, *Octavio Paz en 1968*, 143.
24. Aguilar Mora, *La divina pareja*, 60.
25. Bartra, *La jaula de la melancolía*, 159.
26. Rodríguez Ledesma, *El pensamiento político de Octavio Paz*, 313.
27. Héctor Aguilar Camín, "Octavio Paz: Recuento personal," in *Aire en libertad: Octavio Paz y la crítica*, ed. José Antonio Aguilar Rivera (Mexico City: Fondo de Cultura Económica, 2015), 73.
28. Domínguez Michael, *Octavio Paz en su siglo*, 336.
29. Quoted in Domínguez Michael, 337.
30. Adame, *Octavio Paz en el 68*, 107.
31. One commentator who focuses on the political rather than the mythological analysis Paz develops in *Posdata* is the Mexican political scientist Carlos Ramírez. See Carlos Ramírez, "Luz del pasado en el presente. Octavio Paz, politólogo," *Zona Octavio Paz*, https://zonaOctaviopaz.com/detalle_conversacion/122/luz-del-pasado-en-el-presente-Octavio-paz-politologo; and "Las estaciones políticas de Octavio Paz," *Zona Octavio Paz*, https://zonaOctaviopaz.com/detalle_conversacion/104/las-estaciones-politicas-de-Octavio-paz. The Chilean critic Miguel Enrique Morales also underlines the importance of the political thesis Paz puts forward in *Posdata*, which Morales summarizes as follows: "la necesidad de democratizar a México" (the need to democratize Mexico). In Paz's defense of democracy in *Posdata*, Morales sees a key turn in Paz's intellectual trajectory, a turn that will mark his thinking until the end of his career. See Miguel Enrique Morales, "Ideas para disentir de costumbres: *Posdata* (1970) y el giro en el pensamiento político sobre México de Octavio Paz," *Modern Language Notes* 135, no. 2 (March 2020): 441.
32. Paz, *Posdata*, 153.
33. García Cantú's response to *Posdata* appeared in "La cultura en México," the cultural supplement of *Siempre!* in March 1970. It was later included in a collection of the author's essays. García Cantú criticizes Paz for replacing a historical view of Mexico with a mythical one. What the Mexican poet is guilty of, he argues, is to "retroceder la concepción histórica y hacerla dócil ante el asombro que provocan los mitos" (back away from a historical point of view, weakening it in light of the astonishment caused by the realm of myth). See Gastón

García Cantú, "Posdata," in *Idea de México III, Ensayos 1* (Mexico City: Fondo de Cultura Económica, 1991), 319.
34. Paz and Orfila Reynal, *Cartas cruzadas*, 243.
35. Diana Sorensen is the rare critic who has probed this aspect of *Posdata*. She identifies the deterministic and totalizing elements of Paz's reading of the Tlatelolco massacre, but also emphasizes the importance of the concept of criticism in *Posdata*: "Critique (*la crítica*) as the 'acid' that dissolves images is identified as the vehicle for learning anew, for constructing different visions unbound by the weight of petrified images." See Diana Sorensen, *A Turbulent Decade Remembered: Scenes from the Latin American Sixties* (Stanford, CA: Stanford University Press, 2007), 67.
36. A number of recent critics continue the tradition established by García Cantú and Aguilar Mora of reading Paz as a mythifier. See Samuel Steinberg, *Photopoetics at Tlatelolco: Afterimages of Mexico, 1968* (Austin: University of Texas Press, 2016), 29, and Ignacio Sánchez Prado, *Naciones intelectuales: Las fundaciones de la modernidad literaria mexicana (1917–1959)* (West Lafayette, IN: Purdue University Press, 2009), 225–38. Steinberg focuses on Paz's response to the Tlatelolco massacre, whereas Sánchez Prado concerns himself with the mythifying aspects of *El laberinto*.
37. Steven Marcus, *Freud and the Culture of Psychoanalysis: Studies in the Transition from Victorian Humanism to Modernity* (Boston: George Allen & Unwin, 1984), 110.
38. Marcus, *Freud and the Culture of Psychoanalysis*, 38.
39. Paz and Orfila Reynal, *Cartas cruzadas*, 243.
40. See Grenier, *From Art to Politics*.
41. Adame, *Octavio Paz en 1968*, 83.
42. In a brief explanatory note prefacing *Conjunciones*, Paz informs the reader that Jiménez had asked him to write a prologue to his book.
43. Eli Zaretsky, *Secrets of the Soul: A Social and Cultural History of Psychoanalysis* (New York: Vintage Books, 2005), 317.
44. Zaretsky, 317–18.
45. Paz and Orfila Reynal, *Cartas cruzadas*, 48.
46. Norman O. Brown, *Life against Death: The Psychoanalytical Meaning of History* (Middletown, CT: Wesleyan University Press, 1959).
47. In order to make communal life possible, human beings, according to Freud, must place restrictions on sexual life, as well as restrain their natural aggressiveness. He notes that "it is impossible to overlook the extent to which civilization is built upon a renunciation of instinct,

how much it presupposes precisely the non-satisfaction (by suppression, repression or some other means?) of powerful instincts." Instinctual renunciation is a civilizational need; it also explains why what Freud calls "the programme of becoming happy" is, in his opinion, impossible to achieve. See Sigmund Freud, *Civilization and Its Discontents*, trans. James Strachey (New York: W.W. Norton, 1989), 51–52, 34.

48. Contemporary scholars suggest that "Tantrism" is more than anything a construction of the Western mind. Hugh B. Urban, for example, writes that the category "is largely a creation of modern Western thought, a joint construction of certain Indian texts, European Orientalist scholarship and the Western popular imagination." He also notes that the Orientalist construction of Tantrism oscillates between "denigration" and "sanitization." See Hugh B. Urban, "The Extreme Orient: The Construction of 'Tantrism' as a Category in the Orientalist Imagination," *Religion* 29, no. 2 (1999): 123–46. An assessment of the accuracy of Paz's depiction of Tantrism in *Conjunciones* goes beyond the scope of this work; nevertheless, it is clear that Paz neither denigrates nor sanitizes the practices he describes.

49. See "Por qué Fourier?" in Paz, *El ogro*, 208–11. In *Los hijos del limo*, Paz describes Fourier as an "anti-Freud" for his rejection of the idea that "la sociedad es represiva por naturaleza, como piensa Freud" (society is by its very nature repressive, as Freud believes). See Paz, *Los hijos del limo*, 106.

50. Octavio Paz, *La llama doble: Amor y erotismo* (Barcelona: Seix Barral, 1993), 5–7.

51. Sigmund Freud, *Sexuality and the Psychology of Love* (New York: Simon & Schuster, 1963), 58.

CHAPTER 6

1. For feminist critiques of Paz, see Norma Alarcón, "Traddutora, Traditora: A Paradigmatic Figure of Chicana Feminism," *Cultural Critique* 13 (Autumn 1989): 57–87; Sandra Messinger Cypess, *La Malinche in Mexican Literature* (Austin: University of Texas Press, 1991) 93–97, and *Uncivil Wars: Elena Garro, Octavio Paz, and the Battle for Cultural Memory* (Austin: University of Texas Press, 2012) passim; Alicia Gaspar de Alba, *[Un]framing the 'Bad Woman': Sor Juana, Malinche, Coyolxauhqui and Other Rebels with a Cause* (Austin: University of Texas Press, 2014), 44–50, 65–78, 261–271; Judy B. McInnis, "Octavio Paz: La Malinche as Symbol of Illegitimacy and Betrayal," *MACLAS* 8 (1995): 51–62; and

Marta E. Sánchez, *"Shakin' Up" Race and Gender: Intercultural Connections in Puerto Rican, African American, and Chicano Narratives and Culture (1965–1995)* (Austin: University of Texas Press, 2005), 29–32.

2. Silviano Santiago observes that Paz's *El laberinto* is the first work in the tradition of the Latin American essay on national identity that makes room for the figure of the woman. "Octavio Paz, es, si no me falla la memoria," (Octavio Paz is, if memory does not fail me), Santiago writes, "el primero de los intérpretes canónicos de América Latina que no esconde la *fémina* en los subterráneos de la hermenéutica patriarcal colonialista... no substrae la fuerte presencia de la mujer en nuestra América ni la camufla en la producción textual.... La dota de toda la riqueza de un *round character*, reverencia que hasta entonces el ensayismo latinoamericano solo delegara a personajes masculinos" (the first of the canonical interpreters of Latin America who does not hide women in the subterranean vaults of patriarchal and colonialist hermeneutics... he does not neglect the strong presence of women in our America, nor does he camouflage her presence in textual production.... He endows her with all the richness of a round character, a form of respect that in the Latin American essayistic tradition had until then been shown only to male characters). In short, Santiago regards the inclusion of women in Paz's discussion as significant in itself; moreover, he views the Mexican essayist's approach to the topic as rounded rather than demeaning. See Santiago, *Las raíces*, 148.

3. See Sánchez, *"Shakin' Up" Race and Gender*, 30.

4. The misreading of Paz's commentary on La Malinche and his depiction of gender relations in the Mexico of his day is widespread. However, there are some noteworthy exceptions to this tendency. Especially incisive is Anthony Stanton, who notes that "Some commentators, failing to grasp the rhetorical strategy at work (in *El laberinto*) have accused the author of actually believing in the inferiority of the female sex," adding that "To reproduce stereotyped attitudes and beliefs in this way is not to justify them." See Stanton, Introduction to *El laberinto de la soledad*, 25. On the question of Paz's feminism, it is also worth consulting Rubén Gallo, "Octavio Paz Reads *Moses and Monotheism*," in *Octavio Paz: Humanism and Critique*, ed. Oliver Kozlarek (New Brunswick, NJ: Transaction Publishers, 2009), 65–85.

5. See *La llama doble*, 58–60 for a discussion of Proust in which Paz corrects his earlier misreading.

6. An exception to this rule is an online text by Adriana González Mateos in which she claims, mistakenly in my view, that in the section of *El*

laberinto in which Paz alludes to the work of Simone de Beauvoir he reaches conclusions "a la[s] que ella no llega ni por asomo" (that she doesn't even come close to reaching). See Adriana González Mateos, "La imposibilidad de Simone de Beauvoir, o cómo Octavio Paz fue incapaz de leer uno de los libros cruciales del siglo XX," Academia, http://www.academia.edu/19543167/La_imposibilidad_de_Simone_de_Beauvoir_o_como_Octavio_Paz_fue_incapaz_de_leer_uno_de_los_libros_cruciales_del_siglo_XX. Accessed on 20 November 2020.

7. Paz, *Sor Juana*, 11.
8. See "Sor Juana Inés de la Cruz," in Octavio Paz, *Las peras del olmo* (Barcelona: Seix Barral, 1982), 34–48. In Spanish, the expression "pedirle peras al olmo" (asking for pears from the elm tree) means to expect the impossible. In English, one might speak of "reaching for the moon."
9. Paz, *Sor Juana*, 11.
10. See, for example, Gaspar de Alba, *(Un)framing the "Bad Woman,"* 322–23, and Pamela J. Rader, "Boys to Men: Redefining Masculinities in *Women Hollering Creek and Other Stories*," in *Sandra Cisneros's* Women Hollering Creek, edited by Cecilia Donohue (New York: Rodopi, 2010), 131–49.
11. See Gaspar de Alba, *(Un)framing the "Bad Woman,"* 258.
12. Gaspar de Alba describes Paz as "not the only one of Sor Juana's critics and biographers to declare that there was nothing 'abnormal' (to use their word) about Sor Juana." According to Gaspar de Alba, "not abnormal" for these critics equates with "not lesbian." This, of course, would mean that Paz was implying that homosexuality is "abnormal." See Gaspar de Alba, *(Un)framing the "Bad Woman,"* 44.
13. Paz, *La llama doble*, 213.
14. Paz, *Conjunciones*, 22.
15. For the claim that Paz feels threatened by homosexuality, see Gaspar de Alba, *(Un)framing the "Bad Woman,"* 48.
16. Paz, *La llama doble*, 121–22.
17. Octavio Paz, "La palabra edificante (Luis Cernuda)," in *Cuadrivio* (Mexico City: Joaquín Mortiz, 1965), 187.
18. Paz, "La palabra edificante," 187.
19. Paz, "La palabra edificante," 189.
20. Paz wrote in a similarly moving and clear-eyed way about the work of another important gay poet: Xavier Villaurrutia, a leading member of the *Contemporáneos* group, and one of Paz's mentors in the 1930s and 1940s. Many years later, Paz devoted a book to Villaurrutia. In it, he touches on Villaurrutia's homosexuality, celebrating the open way in which the older poet lived his sexual identity in a deeply homophobic society. He describes Villaurrutia as "un hombre que no tuvo miedo

de enfrentar sus inclinaciones eróticas a una sociedad dominada por un machismo feroz y obtuso" (a man who was not afraid to be open about his erotic inclinations in a society dominated by a ferocious and obtuse machismo). See Octavio Paz, *Xavier Villaurrutia en persona y en obra* (Mexico City: Fondo de Cultura Económica, 1978), 39–40.

21. Gaspar de Alba claims that Paz's argument is guided by a "homophobic logic." See Gaspar de Alba, *(Un)framing the "Bad Woman,"* 44.
22. Elena Poniatowska, widely regarded as one of Mexico's leading feminist authors, offers a striking (and heartening) departure from the anti-Pazian perspective described in this chapter. In *Octavio Paz: Las palabras del árbol* (1998), Poniatowska mixes reminiscences of her long friendship with Paz, generous commentary on his work, and excerpts from some of the many interviews she conducted with the Mexican poet over the years. Poniatowska also reproduces several letters Paz wrote to her in the 1950s and early 1960s. In one of them, written from Paris on May 25, 1960, Paz alludes to the vast changes that were taking place in the role of women in society. "Quizá el gran fenómeno del siglo XX" (Perhaps the most significant phenomenon of the twentieth century), he suggests, "no sea la física nuclear, ni el comunismo, ni Fidel Castro sino la liberación de la mujer" (will turn out to be not nuclear physics, Communism, or Fidel Castro, but women's liberation). Poniatowska also recalls that in 1971 Paz asked her to write an essay on the topic of abortion for the first issue of *Plural*. "Comprobé tu interés" (I could see how interested you were), she writes, addressing Paz in the second person, "por la suerte de las mujeres, tu feminismo que se ha acrecentado a través de los años, tu solidaridad" (in the situation of women, I recognized your feminism, which has become stronger over the years, and your solidarity). See Elena Poniatowska, *Octavio Paz: Las palabras del árbol* (Mexico City: Plaza & Janés, 1998), 80, 81.

CHAPTER 7

1. Fernando Vizcaíno, *Biografía política de Octavio Paz, o, La razón ardiente* (Málaga: Algazara, 1993), 18.
2. Vizcaíno, *Biografía política*, 73. Vizcaíno is referring to Paz's response to the David Rousset affair in Paris, which led him to publish a dossier dealing with the subject of the Soviet system of concentration camps in *Sur*. For a detailed account of Paz's response to Rousset's denunciation of the Soviet Union, see Klaus Meyer-Minneman, "Octavio Paz, David Rousset y el universo de los campos de concentración," *Literatura mexicana* 13, no. 1 (2002), 149–72.

3. Vizcaíno, *Biografía política*, 76.
4. For an account of Victor Serge's life, see Bill Marshall, *Victor Serge: The Uses of Dissent* (New York: Berg, 1992).
5. Vizcaíno, *Biografía política*, 55.
6. Vizcaíno, *Biografía política*, 76
7. Vizcaíno, *Biografía política*, 107. Roger Bartra and Carlos Monsiváis also make the point that Paz was always in dialogue with the Left. Bartra describes Paz as "un intelectual que escribe para la izquierda y cuyos mejores ideas y descubrimientos serán (y están siendo) apropiados por la izquierda" (an intellectual who writes for the Left and whose best ideas and discoveries will be (and are being) picked up by the Left). See Roger Bartra, *El reto de la izquierda* (Mexico City: Grijalbo, 1982), 114. Monsiváis, for his part, describes the Left as Paz's "interlocutores permanentes" (permanent interlocutors). He also criticizes Paz for turning the Left into a more homogeneous phenomenon than it actually was. See Carlos Monsiváis, *Adonde yo soy tú somos nosotros. Octavio Paz: crónica de vida y obra* (Mexico City: Ediciones Raya en el Agua, 2000), 85–97.
8. Guadalupe Nettel, *Octavio Paz: Las palabras en libertad*, trans. Eduardo Berti (Mexico City: Taurus / El Colegio de México, 2014), 139.
9. Nettel, *Octavio Paz*, 288.
10. Nettel, *Octavio Paz*, 296.
11. Nettel, *Octavio Paz*, 285.
12. Grenier, "Socialism in One Person," 49.
13. Grenier, *From Art to Politics*, 32.
14. Alberto Ruy Sánchez, *Una introducción a Octavio Paz* (Mexico City: Joaquín Mortiz, 1990), 107.
15. Jaime Sánchez Susarrey, *El debate político e intelectual en México* (Mexico City: Grijalbo, 1993), 13–76.
16. Aguilar Mora, *La divina pareja*, 46. Aguilar Mora, for his part, has remained consistent in his attacks on Paz. See, for example, Aguilar Mora, *La sombra del tiempo*, 13–82; "La fuga de la identidad: Crítica a la obra poética de Octavio Paz," in José Vicente Anaya, ed., *Versus: Otras miradas a la obra de Octavio Paz* (Zacatecas: Ediciones de Medianoche, 2010), 19–30; and "Paz y Quetzalcóatl," in *Se acabó el centenario*, ed. Gabriel Wolfson (Puebla: UDLAP, 2015), 213–21. Although there is much that one can learn from Aguilar Mora's critiques of Paz, his attacks sometimes take on a decidedly ugly tone. At a conference at the CIDE in Mexico City in November 2014, Aguilar Mora accused Paz, absurdly, of not knowing how to die. Some obvious questions come to mind. How does Aguilar Mora know how Paz died? Did he

have access to Paz's mind in the final period of the poet's life? And what constitutes, one might ask, a good death? Is Aguilar Mora confident that he will do better than Paz in confronting his demise? The best one can say about this mean-spirited, ad hominem attack is that Aguilar Mora decided to leave it out of the published version of his talk. See Jorge Aguilar Mora, "Es como si nos hubieran arrancado los párpados: Apostilla," in *Aire en libertad*, ed. José Antonio Aguilar Rivera (Mexico City: Fondo de Cultura Económica, 2015), 33–46.

17. Raymond Leslie Williams, "The Octavio Paz Industry," *American Book Review* 14, no. 3 (August-September 1992): 3, 10.
18. Enrique González Rojo, *Cuando el rey se hace cortesano: Octavio Paz y el salinismo* (Mexico City: Posada, 1990), 21.
19. Héctor Aguilar Camín, "Metáforas de la tercera vía: Sobre *El ogro filantrópico* de Octavio Paz," in *Saldos de la revolución: Cultura y política de México, 1910–1980* (Mexico City: Nueva Imagen, 1982), 223.
20. Rodríguez Ledesma, *El pensamiento político de Octavio Paz*, 137.
21. Enrique Krauze, "Octavio Paz: Facing the Century. A Reading of *Tiempo nublado*," trans. Sonja Karsen, in *Salmagundi* 70–71 (Spring-Summer 1986): 131–32.
22. Krauze, "Octavio Paz: El poeta y la Revolución," 247.
23. Krauze, "Octavio Paz: El poeta y la Revolución," 247. The Kronstadt rebellion was a left-wing uprising against the Soviet government that took place in March 1921 and was ruthlessly suppressed by government troops under the leadership of Leon Trotsky. It is often viewed as the first event to reveal the repressive nature of the Soviet regime.
24. See *Memorias de un homenaje: Octavio Paz, 1914–2014* (Mexico City: Conaculta, 2014), 46.
25. Armando González Torres, *Las guerras culturales de Octavio Paz* (Mexico City: Ediciones Colibrí, 2001), 80, 90.
26. González Torres, 110.
27. Domínguez Michael, *Octavio Paz en su siglo*.
28. Both essays were subsequently included in Paz's *El ogro filantrópico*.
29. Although Solzhenitsyn focuses more on describing than explaining the Soviet system of concentration camps, it is not surprising that Paz reached this conclusion about the function of the camps after reading *The Gulag Archipelago*. What is not clear, however, is why the two interpretations—the economic and the political—should be regarded as mutually exclusive. Why not assume that the camps served both political and economic goals? Indeed, recent research has drawn attention to the multifunctionality of the camps. For a discussion of "the interconnection of multiple functions in the Gulag," see Michael David-Fox, "Intro-

duction: From Bounded to Juxtapositional—New Histories of the Gulag," in Michael David-Fox, ed., *The Soviet Gulag: Evidence, Interpretation, and Comparison* (Pittsburgh, PA: University of Pittsburgh Press, 2016), 13–14.

30. In *The Gulag Archipelago*, responsibility for the horrors of the camps is attributed primarily to Lenin and Stalin. However, in attempting to explain why so many participated in the vast enterprise of persecution unleashed by the 1917 Revolution and why Communist repression produced such an elevated number of victims, Solzhenitsyn places the blame less on specific individuals than on the more abstract phenomenon of ideology. There can be little doubt that the Russian author's critique of ideology implies a critique of Marxism. See Aleksandr I. Solzhenitsyn, *The Gulag Archipelago, 1918–1956: An Experiment in Literary Investigation I-II*, trans. Thomas P. Whitney (New York: Harper & Row, 1974), 174.

31. For an account of Paz's role in the debate on Mexico's democratization, see Soledad Loaeza, "Octavio Paz en el debate de la democratización," in *Octavio Paz entre poética y política*, ed. Anthony Stanton (Mexico City: El Colegio de México, 2009), 155–97.

32. *Plural*, the monthly review of which Paz was the general editor from 1971 to 1976, gave considerable and consistently sympathetic coverage to Sakharov's activities as a dissident. See I. F. Stone, "La campaña de Sájarov," *Plural* 26 (November 1973): 16–18; Laurent Schwartz, "La lucha de Sájarov," *Plural* 45 (June 1975): 15–18; Anonymous, "Andrei Sájarov: Premio Nobel de Paz," *Plural* 50 (November 1975): 91–92. *Plural* also published two articles by Roy Medvedev on Solzhenitsyn's *The Gulag Archipelago*. In both pieces, Medvedev praises Solzhenitsyn while taking issue with some of his positions, such as Solzhenitsyn's refusal to differentiate between Lenin and Stalin. Medvedev uses his discussion of Solzhenitsyn's work to reaffirm his allegiance to Marxism. See Roy Medvedev, "Sobre 'Archipiélago Gulag,'" *Plural* 30 (March 1974): 8–11, and "El Gulag 2 de Solyenitsin," *Plural* 58 (July 1976): 76–80. However, *Plural* also published a sharp critique by I. F. Stone of Medvedev's study of Stalinism, published in an English translation in 1972 under the title *Let History Judge*. Stone's principal complaint is that Medvedev refuses to acknowledge that the seeds of Stalinism can be found in Leninism, perhaps even in Marxism. See I. F. Stone, "¿Puede cambiar Rusia?" *Plural* 7 (April 1972): 35.

33. Domínguez Michael notes that Paz took the idea of "una sola sociedad industrial dividida en dos bloques políticos" (a single industrial civilization divided into two political blocs) from Raymond Aron. See Domínguez Michael, *Octavio Paz en su siglo*, 358.

34. For an account of Paz's political thought that stresses his Cold War outlook, see Salvador Vázquez Vallejo, *El pensamiento internacional de Octavio Paz* (Mexico City: Miguel Ángel Porrúa, 2006).
35. Paz combines his defense of Third World national liberation struggles with strong criticism of the North Vietnamese regime, which, following the French journalist and historian Jean Lacouture, he describes as "el más stalinista del mundo comunista" (the most Stalinist of the Communist world). See Paz, *El ogro*, 268.
36. Labeling Paz a "reactionary" is common among leftist commentators. Here's one example from the period under discussion. In his book *Los intelectuales en México*, E. Suárez-Iñiguez reports that in an interview published in *Excélsior* in August 1972 Paz criticized Fidel Castro for being a traditional Spanish American *caudillo* (strongman). Suárez-Iñiguez also mentions that Paz maintained that, in spite of his negative evaluation of Fidel, it was imperative to defend the Cuban Revolution against its enemies. Even so, Suárez-Iñiguez concludes from Paz's statements about Cuba that Paz's anti-Stalinism was merely a disguise for his deep-seated anti-Marxism and anti-socialism, and that the Mexican poet had placed himself at the service of reactionary thought. The possibility that one can criticize dictatorial or totalitarian regimes from a leftist perspective simply does not occur to Suárez-Iñiguez. See E. Suárez-Iñiguez, *Los intelectuales en México* (Mexico City: Ediciones "El Caballito," 1980), 223.
37. The strongest critic of the Central American revolutions among the writers associated with *Vuelta* was Gabriel Zaid. See "Nicaragua: El enigma de las elecciones" and "Colegas enemigos: Una lectura de la tragedia salvadoreña," in Gabriel Zaid, *De los libros al poder* (Mexico City: Editorial Océano, 1998), 174–219, 220–69.
38. For an account of Paz's speech and the response to the speech both in the streets of Mexico City and among the intelligentsia, see Armando González Torres, "Octavio Paz en 1984: La querella del diálogo y el ruido," *Letras Libres* 154 (October 2011), http://www.letraslibres.com/mexico/Octavio-paz-en-1984-la-querella-del-dialogo-y-el-ruido.
39. Joel Whitney notes incisively that "Octavio Paz spoke out against American imperialism in Latin America throughout his career, but his outspoken opposition to Stalinism and revolutionary violence got him smeared as a Reaganite." See Joel Whitney, "Poetry and Action: Octavio Paz at 100," *Dissent*, March 25, 2014, https://www.dissentmagazine.org/online_articles/poetry-and-action-Octavio-paz-at-100.
40. Pablo Antonio Cuadra and Pedro J. Chamorro Barrios, "También en Nicaragua," *Vuelta* 60 (November 1981): 54–55.

41. Pablo Antonio Cuadra, "Documentos de Nicaragua: La lucha por la democracia," *Vuelta* 74 (January 1983): 55–56.
42. "El cierre de *La Prensa* en Nicaragua," *Vuelta* 117 (August 1986): 63.
43. Gilles Bataillon, "La Prensa intervenida," *Vuelta* 118 (September 1986): 64–65.
44. "América Latina y la democracia," in Paz, *Tiempo nublado*, 171.
45. "América Latina y la democracia," in Paz, *Tiempo nublado*, 184.
46. This essay was subsequently reprinted in *Pequeña crónica de grandes días* (1990). See "El diálogo y el ruido," in Paz, *Pequeña crónica*, 88.
47. Octavio Paz, "Contrarronda: México, Estados Unidos, América Central, etcétera," *Vuelta* 131 (October 1987), 17.
48. Astonishingly, and against all evidence, many on the Left continued to accuse Paz of calling for a US invasion of Nicaragua. In a debate with Alberto Ruy Sánchez, the novelist and Sandinista leader Sergio Ramírez claimed that Paz supported a US intervention in the Nicaraguan conflict. Ruy Sánchez invited Ramírez to point to a specific passage in Paz's writings where such support was expressed, something Ramírez was not able to do. See Jaime Perales Contreras, *Octavio Paz y su círculo intelectual* (Mexico City: Ediciones Coyoacán, 2013), 321.
49. The Spanish philosopher Fernando Savater recalls that Paz was overjoyed when the PSOE (*Partido Socialista Obrero Español*) came to power in Spain in 1982. "Tengo una imagen de él" (I have an image of him), he writes, "el día en que Felipe González ganó las elecciones. Él, que era un hombre bueno, ya un poco escéptico y crítico con todos los gobiernos, ese día estaba como un niño. . . . Vivía la emoción de ese progresismo no dogmático" (on the day Felipe González won the elections. Paz, who was a good man, already a bit skeptical and critical of all governments, was like a child on that day. . . . He was experiencing the excitement of that non-dogmatic progressivism). See Fernando Savater, "La ciudad como galaxia," in *Los rostros de Octavio Paz: Una antología crítica*, ed. Braulio Peralta (Mexico City: El Tapiz del Unicornio, 2017), 46.
50. For a summary of responses to the colloquium in the Mexican press, see Rodríguez Ledesma, *El pensamiento político de Octavio Paz*, 259–66. Rodríguez Ledesma gives a not very sympathetic account of Paz's political thought; nevertheless, he makes it clear that he finds many of the responses, which occasionally degenerated into personal insults and even threats directed at Paz, deeply offensive. Christopher Domínguez Michael registers his surprise at the "virulent" nature of the response from the Mexican Left, especially in light of what he calls "la impecable altura intelectual del encuentro" (the impeccable intellectual level of

the colloquium). See Domínguez Michael, *Octavio Paz en su siglo*, 447.
51. Octavio Paz and Enrique Krauze, eds., *Miradas al futuro*, La experiencia de la libertad 7 (Mexico City: Fundación Cultural Televisa, 1991), 88.
52. Paz and Krauze, *Miradas al futuro*, 96.
53. Octavio Paz and Enrique Krauze, eds., *Hacia la sociedad abierta*, La experiencia de la libertad 1 (Mexico City: Fundación Cultural Televisa, 1991), 36.
54. Paz and Krauze, *Hacia la sociedad abierta*, 112.
55. Octavio Paz and Enrique Krauze, eds., *El ejercicio de la libertad: Política y economía*, La experiencia de la libertad 5 (Mexico City: Fundación Cultural Televisa, 1991), 100.
56. Paz and Krauze, *El ejercicio de la libertad*, 100.
57. Paz and Krauze, *Miradas al futuro*, 27.
58. Paz and Krauze, *Hacia la sociedad abierta*, 32.
59. Paz and Krauze, *Hacia la sociedad abierta*, 112.
60. Paz and Krauze, *Hacia la sociedad abierta*, 62.
61. Octavio Paz and Enrique Krauze, eds., *El mapa del siglo XXI*, La experiencia de la libertad 2 (Mexico City: Fundación Cultural Televisa, 1991), 42.
62. An anti-capitalist discourse—focused above all on the spiritual poverty of Western civilization—was a constant feature of Paz's writing throughout these years. See, for example, Paz, *La otra voz*, 128.
63. Paz and Krauze, *Hacia la sociedad abierta*, 115.
64. Paz and Krauze, *Hacia la sociedad abierta*, 85.
65. Octavio Paz and Enrique Krauze, eds., *La palabra liberada*, La experiencia de la libertad 3 (Mexico City: Fundación Cultural Televisa, 1991), 17–18.
66. Paz and Krauze, *Miradas al futuro*, 117.
67. Paz and Krauze, *El mapa del siglo XXI*, 108.
68. Paz and Krauze, *Hacia la sociedad abierta*, 64–66.
69. Paz and Krauze, *El ejercicio de la libertad*, 107.
70. Paz and Krauze, *Hacia la sociedad abierta*, 159.
71. Gustavo Leyva Martínez is surely off the mark when he presents Paz as a follower of the economic liberalism of Friedrich von Hayek and furthermore states that Castoriadis was the only participant at the colloquium to criticize free-market economics. See Gustavo Leyva Martínez, "Octavio Paz: Poesía, historia y política en el horizonte de la modernidad en América Latina," in *Octavio Paz: México y la modernidad*, ed. Gustavo Leyva Martínez et al. (México: Contraste Editorial, 2014), 92, 95.

72. Paz and Krauze, *La experiencia*, vol. 5, 31.
73. Córdova's article appeared in *Uno más uno* on 31 August 1990. It was reprinted in Paz and Krauze, *Hacia la sociedad abierta*, 168–70.
74. In their account of the colloquium, Carlos Illades and Rodolfo Suárez follow in the footsteps of Cordera and Córdova. According to Illades and Suárez, "el énfasis estuvo en la victoria definitiva del capitalismo y de la democracia representativa, la imposibilidad de construir una modernidad distinta . . . y la muerte tanto del socialismo como del marxismo" (emphasis was placed on the final victory of capitalism and of representative democracy, on the impossibility of creating a different kind of modernity . . . and on the death of both socialism and Marxism). See Carlos Illades and Rodolfo Suárez, "La caída del socialismo y el campo intelectual mexicano," *Revista Horizontes Sociológicos* 2, no. 4 (July-Dec 2014): 60.
75. Octavio Paz, "Izquierda y derecha sesenta años después," *Vuelta* 168 (November 1990): 45.
76. José Antonio Aguilar Rivera describes the intellectual debate of the 1980s and 1990s in Mexico as "una Gran Distracción" (a Great Distraction). He charges socialist intellectuals with having an unrealistic conception of the kind of change that was possible in Mexico, but he also notes that liberal intellectuals were prone to exaggerating the threat posed by their leftist peers. "Como si la tarea de los intelectuales mexicanos de izquierda" (As if the actions of Mexico's leftist intellectuals), Aguilar Rivera writes, in what can be taken as a criticism aimed at Paz, "hubiera sido crucial para el mantenimiento del estado burocrático mexicano" (were crucial to sustaining the Mexican bureaucratic state). See José Antonio Aguilar Rivera, *La sombra de Ulises: Ensayos sobre intelectuales mexicanos y norteamericanos* (CIDE / Miguel Ángel Porrúa, 1997), 89.

CHAPTER 8

1. One of the few scholars to offer a detailed account of the conservative (or neoconservative) strain in Paz's thinking, and that of the *Vuelta* group as a whole, is Avital Bloch. However, her attempt to pin the "neoconservative" label on Paz and his colleagues is unsuccessful. Bloch makes distorted claims about Paz's positions on specific issues and about the political movements he supported. At one point in her essay, Bloch asserts that the attacks of the *Vuelta* writers on Communist regimes went hand in hand with support for right-wing

dictatorships. Anyone familiar with Paz's political views knows that this was simply not the case. In addition, Bloch depicts Paz's lifelong sympathy for *Zapatismo* as an example of his conservative outlook, ostensibly because *Zapatista* ideology was rooted in a reverence for Mexico's indigenous heritage. One can indeed connect Zapata's defense of tradition with conservatism, but surely Bloch knows that Zapata (and his contemporary heirs, including Subcomandante Marcos) are revered on the Left and reviled on the Right. See Avital Bloch, "The Journal *Vuelta* and the Emergence of Neoconservatism," in *Public Intellectuals in Contemporary Latin America*, ed. Avital Bloch, Rogelio de la Mora, and Hugo Cancino (University of Colima / Aalborg University, 2007), 148–68.

2. Paz himself commented repeatedly on the hostility expressed toward him by critics on the Left. In *Itinerario*, he notes that in spite of the frequency with which he criticized capitalist democracies, "mis adversarios no han dejado de llamarme 'derechista' y 'conservador'" (my adversaries have not stopped calling me a 'rightist' and a 'conservative'). See Paz, *Itinerario*, 110–11. Elsewhere, he complains that the label *reactionary*, which was often attached to his thinking, serves merely to deflect debate on the issues. "Reaccionario" (Reactionary), he points out in an interview with Braulio Peralta, "es un adjetivo, no una razón" (is an adjective, not an argument). See Braulio Peralta, *El poeta en su tierra: Diálogos con Octavio Paz* (Mexico City: Grijalbo, 1996), 44.

3. Gastón García Cantú offers a forceful expression of this point of view. In surveying Mexican history, he observes an alliance between the capitalists, the Church, and the United States, who together represent the right side of the political spectrum and undermine the nation's best interests. He interprets Mexican history as an ongoing struggle between "la Colonia y la Independencia" (the colonial period and Independence). "Vivimos la segunda" (We are living the latter), he says, "conquistándola todavía; la primera no ha concluido: retorna cada vez que la duda, la ignorancia o la política se desvían de los fines históricos de la nación" (and we are still trying to conquer it; the former has not yet concluded: it returns every time that the forces of doubt and ignorance, or political factors, deflect us from the historical goals of the nation). See Gastón García Cantú, *El desafío de la derecha* (Mexico City: Joaquín Mortiz / Planeta, 1987), 114.

4. Erika Pani notes that conservatism has not been much studied, in part because the contemporary scholarly community identifies overwhelmingly as liberal, progressive, or revolutionary. She also observes that

in Mexico conservatives have traditionally been seen as "los malos del cuento" (the bad guys in the story), resulting in a dismissive attitude toward conservative thought. See Erika Pani, ed., *Conservadurismo y derechas en la historia de México*, vol. 1 (Mexico City: Fondo de Cultura Económica, 2009), 12. Pani's own two-volume edited collection on conservatism and the Right in Mexico is an exception to this rule, marking an important shift toward serious scholarly research on Mexican conservatism.

5. "En cuanto a la derecha" (As for the Right), says Paz, "hace mucho que la burguesía mexicana no tiene ideas—sólo intereses" (for a long time, the Mexican bourgeoisie has had no ideas, only interests). See Paz, *El ogro*, 151. "Si vuelvo la cara a la derecha" (When I look to the Right), he states elsewhere in the same volume, "veo a gente atareada haciendo dinero" (I see people busy making money). See Paz, *El ogro*, 337. There are many more statements in this work and others revealing Paz's dismissive view of Mexican conservatism in the 1970s.

6. One critic who expresses disagreement with Paz's dismissiveness toward Mexican conservatives is Yvon Grenier. "Paz considered (incorrectly in my view)," Grenier writes, "that the Left had 'ideas' and the Right 'only interests.' What he says may be true for the authoritarian Right in Mexico and Latin America (which may well mean much of the Right), but not for the liberal Right or the democratic sectors of the conservative Right." See Yvon Grenier, "Octavio Paz and the Rise and Fall of the Literary Intellectual in Mexico," in *The Willow and the Spiral: Essays on Octavio Paz and the Literary Imagination*, ed. Roberto Cantú (Newcastle upon Tyne: Cambridge Scholars Publishing, 2014), 144.

7. Clearly, there are other approaches to the question of Paz's conservatism in addition to the two that will be developed here. One might ask, for example, to what extent Paz became culturally conservative, that is, more traditionalist in his aesthetic preferences, toward the end of his life. For an excellent discussion of Paz as a defender of traditionalism in the arts, see Flores, *Viaje de* Vuelta.

8. Enrique Florescano observes that in Mexico "la reconstrucción del pasado se ha vinculado de tal modo a las grandes convulsiones políticas e ideológicas que atraviesan su historia, que cada proyecto político que se ha presentado a la nación ha tenido como correlato una nueva interpretación y reconstrucción del pasado" (the reconstruction of the past has been so strongly linked to the great political and ideological upheavals running through the country's history that every political project that has emerged in Mexico has been tied to a new interpreta-

tion and reconstruction of the past). See Florescano, *El nuevo pasado mexicano*, 12. Florescano has written a number of important books on Mexican historiography. In addition to *El nuevo pasado mexicano*, see Enrique Florescano Mayet, *Ensayos sobre la historiografía colonial de México* (Mexico City: Departamento de Investigaciones Históricas, INAH, 1979), and Enrique Florescano, *Historia de las historias de la nación mexicana* (Mexico City: Taurus, 2002).

9. Florescano mentions the works of Fray Servando Teresa de Mier and Carlos María de Bustamente as examples of "el nacionalismo indigenista y antiespañol" (the indigenist and anti-Spanish nationalism) that went hand in hand with the struggle for independence in the early nineteenth century. See Florescano Mayet, *Ensayos sobre la historiografía*, 30.

10. According to Florescano, Alamán was convinced that Mexico's rejection of its Hispanic heritage in the decades after Independence was in large part responsible for the nation's difficulties, and in particular for the loss of a large part of its territory to the United States in the Mexican-American war. See Florescano, *Historia de las historias*, 376.

11. Florescano notes that "las interpretaciones más negras de la colonia, las diatribas más cargadas de pasión y de violencia se escriben y pronuncian entre 1910 y 1940" (it is during the years between 1910 and 1940 that the most negative interpretations of the colonial period, the most passionate and vehement diatribes against it, are written and pronounced), but he also draws attention to the fact that these negative interpretations provoked a reaction on the part of historians who wished to defend the Spanish role in Mexican history. See Florescano Mayet, *Ensayos sobre la historiografía*, 53. For the Hispanist reading of Mexican (and Spanish American) history in the decades after the Revolution, see the works of Carlos Pereyra, especially *Breve historia de América* (Madrid: M. Aguilar, 1930), and *México falsificado* (Mexico City: Editorial Polis, 1949).

12. Florescano explains that in the second half of the nineteenth century, in the works of authors such as José María Vigil, a new view of Mexico's past came to the fore, one that broke with the tendency to reject entire periods of the nation's history and sought instead to construct "una historia que uniera los contrarios pasados de la nación en un relato solidario" (a version of history that would unite the contrasting elements of the nation's past in a shared narrative). See Florescano, *Historia de las historias*, 349.

13. Paz, *Sor Juana*, 23–24.

14. Paz, "México y Estados Unidos," 145.

15. David Brading draws attention to the tension not between indigenism and conservatism that emerges from Paz's writings on the colonial period, but on that between his liberal nationalism—according to Brading, his dominant outlook—and traces of conservatism. Brading is struck by "la manera en que Paz mantuvo su interpretación liberal de la historia mexicana y a la vez dio cabida libremente a otro tipo de persistencia" (the way in which Paz stood by his liberal interpretation of Mexican history even while he made ample room for a different kind of persistence). The different kind of persistence is that of a Catholic Mexico that has endured from the days of the colony until the present. See Brading, *Octavio Paz y la poética de la historia mexicana*, 89.
16. Octavio Paz, "Americanidad de España," in *Primeras letras (1931–1943)*, ed. Enrico Mario Santí (Mexico City: Editorial Vuelta, 1988).
17. Javier Rico Moreno points out that in distancing himself from the anti-Spanish currents in Mexican intellectual life, Paz was also distancing himself from the "liberalismo antihispanista" (anti-Hispanic liberalism) professed by both his father and grandfather. See Javier Rico Moreno, *La historia y el laberinto: Hacia una estética del devenir en Octavio Paz* (México: Bonilla Artigas, 2013), 96.
18. Note the terms in which Lucas Alamán praised colonial society: "Este sistema de gobierno no había sido obra de una sola concepción, ni procedía de teorías de legisladores especulativos, que pretenden sujetar al género humano a los principios imaginarios, que quieren hacer pasar como oráculos de incontrastable verdad: era el resultado del saber y de la experiencia de tres siglos, y antes de llegar a los resultados que se habían obtenido, había sido menester pasar por largas y reiteradas pruebas" (this system of government was not the product of one single idea, nor did it emerge from the theories of speculating legislators, who presumed to chain the human race to imaginary principles, which they like to pass off as oracles of indisputable truth: on the contrary, it was the result of the knowledge and experience of three centuries, and before achieving the results that had been reached, it had been necessary to undergo long and repeated trials). This passage revolves around the contrast between a mode of government that grows slowly over time, and is rooted in wisdom and experience, on the one hand, and one that is made to fit a pre-established theoretical plan, on the other. Conservatives like Alamán obviously favored the former. See Lucas Alamán, *Historia de México*, 5 vols. (Mexico City: Editorial Jus, 1942), 1:61.

19. Although conservatives were often dismissive of the accomplishments of pre-Columbian civilizations, they liked to point out that the Spanish were much more humane in their treatment of the indigenous peoples of the New World than the British. Here is what Vasconcelos had to say about this subject: "Y sin duda, si en nuestro país no vencen los españoles, más tarde la tierra la hubieran ocupado los ingleses y la suerte de los naturales no hubiera sido mejor; todo lo contrario, allí está el ejemplo de los territorios en que ellos dominaron y en los cuales el indio quedó desposeído, excluído del trato humano, extinguido" (And without a doubt, if it had not been for the victory of the Spanish in our country, it would eventually have been occupied by the English and the fate of the natives would not have been any happier; on the contrary, we have the example before us of the lands they conquered and in which the Indians were dispossessed, excluded from humane treatment, extinguished). See José Vasconcelos, *Historia de Méjico*, 4th ed. (Mexico City: Ediciones Botas, 1938), 150.

20. In a 1967 essay on Latin American poetry, Paz restates his vision of the inclusive nature of colonial society: "en el orden colonial participaban, así fuese en la base de la estructura social, todos los habitantes" (all the inhabitants participated in colonial society, even if it was at the bottom of the social structure). See Paz, "¿Poesía latinoamericana?," 160. Late in his life, in his book on India, Paz is perhaps even more explicit in his defense of colonial society, or, better said, of certain aspects of that society. He writes the following: "La literatura sobre la dominación de españoles y portugueses abunda en rasgos sombríos y en juicios severos; sin negar la verdad de muchas de esas descripciones y condenas, hay que decir que se trata de una visión unilateral. No todo fue horror: sobre las ruinas del mundo precolombino los españoles y los portugueses levantaron una construcción histórica grandiosa que, en sus grandes trazos, todavía está en pie. Unieron a muchos pueblos que hablaban lenguas diferentes, adoraban dioses distintos, guerreaban entre ellos o se desconocían. Los unieron a través de leyes e instituciones jurídicas y políticas pero, sobre todo, por la lengua, la cultura y la religión. Si las pérdidas fueron enormes, las ganancias han sido inmensas" (The literature on Spanish and Portuguese rule is full of somber passages and severe judgments; without denying the truth of many of these descriptions and condemnations, it has to be said that they offer a one-sided vision. Not everything was filled with horror. On the ruins of the pre-Columbian world, the Spanish and Portuguese erected a grand historical edifice which, in large part, has remained standing.

They united many nations that spoke different languages, worshipped different gods, waged war on each other, or simply did not know each other. They were brought together by laws and political and juridical institutions, but, above all, by language, culture, and religion. The losses were huge, but the gains were immense). See Paz, *Vislumbres*, 116–17.

21. For Paz's thoughts in the 1970s on the colonial period in Mexican history, see "Nueva España: Orfandad y legitimidad" and "El espejo indiscreto." Observations on New Spain also appear in "Vuelta a *El laberinto de la soledad*," an interview with the French critic Claude Fell, and "Las ilusiones y las convicciones," an essay on the Mexican historian Daniel Cosío Villegas. All of these essays were collected in *El ogro filantrópico*.
22. Paz, *El ogro*, 61–62.
23. Paz, "Vuelta," interview by Claude Fell, 342.
24. Paz, "Vuelta," interview by Claude Fell, 345.
25. Paz, *El ogro*, 61.
26. Paz, *Sor Juana*, 37.
27. Paz, *Sor Juana*, 52.
28. Paz, *Sor Juana*, 67.
29. See Vasconcelos, *Historia de México*, 63.
30. Consider the following passage in which Vasconcelos explains what was at stake in the Conquest of Mexico: "El triunfo español crearía una era nueva y aumentaría una nación a la cultura del planeta. Si Moctezuma hubiese vencido, la crueldad, la brutalidad más espantosa hubiese seguido deshonrando esta tierra que hoy es, o podría ser, nuestra. En cambio, si los españoles vencían, quedaríamos incorporados a una fracción creadora de la humanidad, colaboradores de uno de los pueblos más ilustres de todos los tiempos" (The triumph of the Spanish would open the door to a new era and would add a new nation to planetary culture. If Moctezuma had triumphed, the most horrific cruelty and savagery would have continued dishonoring this land, which is now, or might be, our land. On the other hand, if the Spanish triumphed, we would be joined with a most creative portion of humanity, and we would become collaborators with one of the most illustrious people of all time). See Vasconcelos, *Historia de México*, 63.
31. Prior to 1997, the position of mayor of Mexico City was an appointive office. The winner of the 1997 election, and the first freely elected mayor of Mexico City, was Cuauhtémoc Cárdenas of the leftist *Partido de la Revolución Democrática* (PRD). Castillo Peraza ended in third place with 15.5 percent of the vote. For a report on the 1997 mayoral

election in Mexico City, see Julia Preston and Sam Dillon, *Opening Mexico: The Making of a Democracy* (New York: Farrar Straus and Giroux, 2005), 297–99. Domínguez Michael reports that Paz voted for Castillo Peraza. See Domínguez Michael, *Octavio Paz en su siglo*, 388.

32. See Peralta, *El poeta en su tierra*, 135.
33. Paz, "Izquierda y derecha."
34. Octavio Paz, "PRI: Hora cumplida," in *El laberinto de la soledad*, ed. Enrico Mario Santí (Madrid: Cátedra, 1993), 493.
35. Paz, "PRI: Hora cumplida," 494.
36. See Paz, "Ante un presente incierto: Historias de ayer," in *El laberinto de la soledad*, ed. Enrico Mario Santí (Madrid: Cátedra, 1993), 508.
37. Peralta, *El poeta*, 63.
38. Paz, "Las elecciones de 1994: Doble mandato," *Vuelta* 215 (October 1994): 9.
39. Soledad Loaeza, *Acción Nacional: El apetito y las responsabilidades del triunfo* (Mexico City: El Colegio de México, 2010), 17.
40. Loaeza, *Acción Nacional*, 44.
41. There is a tendency among some commentators to link the PAN exclusively to the rise of neoliberalism, ignoring its role in the advance of democracy in Mexico. See, for example, Renée de la Torre and Marta Eugenia García Ugarte, introducción to *Los rostros del conservadurismo mexicano*, edited by Renée de la Torre, Marta Eugenia García Ugarte, and Juan Manuel Ramírez Saíz (Mexico City: CIESAS, 2005), 11–31; and Dora Kanoussi, "Introducción al pensamiento conservador," in *El pensamiento conservador en México*, ed. Dora Kanoussi (Mexico City: BUAP / International Gramsci Society / Plaza & Valdés, 2002), 11–30.
42. For detailed, highly informative, and nuanced accounts of the PAN's role in twentieth- and early twenty-first-century Mexican political history, see two books by Soledad Loaeza: *Acción Nacional: El apetito y las responsabilidades del triunfo* and *El Partido Acción Nacional: La larga marcha, 1939–1994. Oposición leal y partido de protesta* (Mexico City: Fondo de Cultura Económica, 1999).
43. In his conversation with Revel, Paz explains that at one time he thought that the name "Acción Nacional" suggested the influence of Charles Maurras, the French monarchist and anti-parliamentarian (as well as anti-Semitic) author and politician. He now realizes that he was mistaken, and proceeds to offer the following profile of the PAN: "Eran católicos, conservadores, pero, sobre todo demócratas . . . se compone de personas que no son intelectuales: gente de la clase media, pragmática, hostil a la omnipresencia del Estado. Sus críticas

contra el partido único en el poder, el PRI, son las más escuchadas" (They were Catholic and they were conservatives, but above all they were democrats . . . the party is made up of people who are not intellectuals; they are members of the middle class, with a pragmatic outlook and a clear hostility toward the omnipresence of the state. Their attacks on the PRI and its monopoly on power are the most heeded). See Octavio Paz, "Miradas sobre el mundo actual," interview by Jean-François Revel, *Vuelta* 114 (May 1986): 31.
44. Paz, "Ante un presente incierto," 506.
45. Paz, "Ante un presente incierto," 506–7.
46. Christopher Domínguez Michael offers helpful commentary on this feature of Paz's thinking. "La biografía de Paz" (Paz's biography), he observes, "está marcada por un rechazo coherente y sistemático de toda ruptura violenta del sistema" (is characterized by a coherent and systematic rejection of any kind of violent break with the system). See Christopher Domínguez Michael, review of *El pensamiento político de Octavio Paz: Las trampas de la ideología* by Xavier Rodríguez Ledesma, *Vuelta* 235 (July 1996): 35–36. Domínguez Michael also reports that the dispute surrounding the results of the 1988 election caused divisions among Paz's closest collaboradores on the editorial board of *Vuelta*. See Domínguez Michael, *Octavio Paz en su siglo*, 459–60.
47. Paz, "Las elecciones de 1994," 13.
48. "México, después del 6 de julio," in Paz, *Obras completas*, 14:285.
49. In 1985, Paz complained that the PAN had failed to put forward "un proyecto nacional nuevo y viable que se ofrezca como una opción distinta a la del PRI. Las profesiones de fe democrática de sus voceros son valiosas y útiles; su programa en otros dominios es vago" (a new and viable national project that offers an alternative to the PRI. The professions of faith in democracy put forward by its spokespersons are useful and valuable; in other areas, the party's program is vague). See Paz, "PRI: Hora cumplida," 494.
50. In 1988, Paz argued that "el PAN tuvo y tiene graves limitaciones que hoy se han hecho cruelmente visibles. No ha penetrado en el México rural, especialmente en el centro y en el sur" (the PAN has suffered from and continues to suffer from grave limitations that have now been harshly spotlighted. The party has failed to connect with rural voters, especially in the center and south of the nation). See Paz, "Ante un presente incierto," 508–9.
51. Paz, "PRI: Hora cumplida," 494–95.
52. Peralta, *El poeta*, 63.

53. Paz, "Las elecciones de 1994," 231.
54. We have already noted that Paz voted for Carlos Castillo Peraza in the 1997 Mexico City mayoral election. Also worth mentioning is that Castillo Peraza participated in Paz's 1990 colloquium *La experiencia de la libertad*. That Castillo Peraza felt an affinity for Paz is clear from the title of one of his books: *El ogro antropófago y otros ensayos* (Mexico City: EPESSA, 1990).
55. "Alguien me deletrea," interview by Carlos Castillo Peraza, in Paz, *Pequeña crónica*.

CHAPTER 9

1. *El arco* was first published in 1956 and appeared in a revised and expanded version in 1967. I will be citing from the 1967 edition.
2. Paz, *Las peras del olmo*, 31.
3. Paz, *Las peras*, 54.
4. Paz, *Corriente alterna*, 5.
5. Paz, *El arco*, 108.
6. Paz, *El arco*, 187.
7. Paz, *Cuadrivio*, 88.
8. Paz, *El arco*, 110.
9. Paz, *El arco*, 110.
10. Paz, *Las peras*, 31.
11. Paz, *In/mediaciones*, 10.
12. Paz, *El arco*, 192.
13. Octavio Paz, *Puertas al campo* (Mexico City: UNAM, 1966), 96.
14. Paz, *Puertas al campo*, 103.
15. Paz, *In/mediaciones*, 108.
16. Paz, *In/mediaciones*, 164.
17. Paz, *Las peras*, 79.
18. Paz, *Las peras*, 73.
19. Paz, *El arco*, 40.
20. Paz, *Puertas al campo*, 43.
21. José Luis Fernández Castillo reads Paz's poetry as a response to what he calls "la crisis de la divinidad" (the crisis of divinity), by which he means the collapse of the belief in God as the stable foundation of all human knowledge. It offers a religious experience for a non-religious age. See José Luis Fernández Castillo, *El ídolo y el vacío: Octavio Paz y las transformaciones de lo divino* (Buenos Aires: Biblos, 2016).
22. For a roughly contemporaneous critique that zeroes in on the transformation of modern art into a battle of ideas about art, see Tom Wolfe, *The Painted Word* (New York: Farrar, Straus and Giroux, 1975).

23. See Octavio Paz, *Marcel Duchamp, o, El castillo de la pureza* (Mexico City: Ediciones Era, 1968), and *Apariencia desnuda: La obra de Marcel Duchamp* (Mexico City: Ediciones Era, 1973).
24. For a helpful account of romantic/symbolist aesthetics, primarily in the British and French contexts, one might consult Frank Kermode's *Romantic Image*, which came out the year after Paz published *El arco y la lira*. Consider, for example, the following summary by Kermode of the concept of art that prevailed in this tradition: "The work of art considered as having 'a life of its own,' supplying its own energy, and possessing no detachable meanings—yielding to no analysis, containing within itself all that is relevant to itself—the work of art so described invites an analogy with unconscious organic life, and resists, not only attempts to discuss it in terms of the intention of the artist or detachable 'morals' or 'prose contents,' but attempts to behave toward it as if were a kind of machine." The similarities with Paz's ideas about poetic autonomy are unmistakable. See Frank Kermode, *Romantic Image* (London: Routledge & Kegan Paul, 1957), 92.
25. In suggesting that Paz combines ideas from different sources, and that these ideas sometimes exist in a state of tension with each other, I am echoing several previous Paz critics. Enrico Mario Santí, for example, describes *El arco* as a work "[de] naturaleza ecléctica" (of an eclectic nature) and proposes that this eclecticism derives from the way Paz brings together "los atisbos filosóficos del surrealismo y la fenomenología existencialista" (the philosophical traces of surrealism and existentialist phenomenology). See Enrico Mario Santí, *El acto de las palabras: Estudios y diálogos con Octavio Paz* (Mexico City: Fondo de Cultura Económica, 1997), 241, 238. Evodio Escalante identifies three principal ingredients in Paz's poetics. "Cuando Octavio Paz redacta *El arco y la lira*" (When Octavio Paz composes *El arco y la lira*), he states, "se le entrecruzan tres franjas de pensamiento en apariencia inconciliables entre sí: la poética del surrealismo, la hermenéutica fenomenológica de inspiración germánica y la revolución política propugnada por Marx" (he combines three seemingly irreconcilable intellectual trends: surrealist poetics, German phenomenological hermeneutics, and the political revolution advocated by Marx). See Evodio Escalante, *Las sendas perdidas de Octavio Paz* (Mexico City: UAM-Iztapalapa / Ediciones Sin Nombre, 2013), 8. Anthony Stanton, for his part, speaks of "la totalización sincrética efectuada en *El arco y la lira*" (the syncretic totalization carried out in *El arco y la lira*) and of the book's "multiplicidad discursiva" (discursive multiplicity). Among the many threads Paz weaves together, Stanton singles out "la ontología temporal y la 'poética' de Martin Heidegger; [el] concepto

de lo sagrado, que proviene aquí de la fenomenología de la experiencia religiosa, elaborada por Rudolf Otto, y, por último... la noción de 'la heterogeneidad esencial del ser', tal como aparece en la prosa de Antonio Machado." (the ontology of time and the "poetics" of Martin Heidegger; the concept of the sacred, derived from Rudolf Otto's phenomenology of religious experience, and, finally, the notion of "the essential heterogeneity of being," as it appears in the prose writings of Antonio Machado). See Anthony Stanton, *El río reflexivo: Poesía y ensayo en Octavio Paz (1931–1958)* (Mexico City: Fondo de Cultura Económica, 2015), 402, 390. One of the guiding threads in Tom Boll's study of the influence of T. S. Eliot on Paz is the idea that the Anglo-American poet provided his Mexican counterpart with an example of how to work through the tension between a Symbolist aesthetics, on the one hand, and a poetics of engagement with history, on the other. See Tom Boll, *Octavio Paz and T. S. Eliot: Modern Poetry and the Translation of Influence* (London: Legenda, 2012), passim. My own view is that the main tension in Paz's theory of poetry is between the formalist/symbolist viewpoint, on the one hand, and the surrealist/revolutionary, on the other. Maya Schärer-Nussberger places her finger on the same tension I am pointing to when she speaks on the first page of her book on Paz of an alternation in his work between "poesía mágica" (magic poetry) on the one hand and "poesía formal" (formal poetry) on the other. However, she does not explore this conflict in depth, and ends up focusing her study on other aspects of Paz's work. See Maya Schärer-Nussberger, *Octavio Paz: Trayectorias y visiones* (Mexico City: Fondo de Cultura Económica, 1989), 11.

26. To get a sense of the unusual nature of the combination of perspectives in Paz, it is helpful to recall Peter Bürger's well-known thesis on the subject of avant-garde art. According to Bürger, the avant-garde aim of erasing the barrier separating art from life was conceived in *explicit opposition to* the ideal of aesthetic autonomy. In short, Paz links two approaches to art that, if we accept Bürger's thesis, were historically in conflict with each other. See Peter Bürger, *Theory of the Avant-Garde*, trans. Michael Shaw (Minneapolis: University of Minnesota Press, 1984), passim.

27. Gustavo Leyva Martínez criticizes Paz's position in this regard, speaking of the "excesiva demanda que Paz plantea a la propia poesía" (the exaggerated expectations Paz places on poetry itself). See Leyva Martínez, "Octavio Paz: Poesía, historia y política," 87.

28. The yoking together of poetry and revolution is nothing if not a totalizing idea. It is worth noting, nevertheless, that several critics have

linked Paz to anti-totalizing currents of thought such as postmodernism and deconstructivism. For a reading that puts Paz in conversation with postmodern theory and criticism, see Clara Román-Odio, *Octavio Paz en los debates críticos y estéticos del siglo XX* (A Coruña: tresCtres Editores, 2006). Roberto Hozven, for his part, tracks the deconstructivist elements in Paz's writing. See Hozven, *Octavio Paz: Viajero del presente*, 217–40.

29. One of the earliest critical examinations of Paz's poetry—and still one of the best—focuses on the Mexican poet's ties with surrealism. See Jason Wilson, *Octavio Paz: A Study of His Poetics* (Cambridge: Cambridge UP, 1979). For examinations of Paz's relationship to surrealism, see also Hugo Verani, *Octavio Paz: El poema como caminata* (Mexico City: Fondo de Cultura Económica, 2013), 68–84; and Manuel Ulacia, *El árbol milenario: Un recorrido por la obra de Octavio Paz* (Barcelona: Galaxia Gutenberg / Círculo de Lectores, 1999), 117–34.

30. Federico Fridman offers a rich exploration of Paz's idea of the poet as belonging to a clandestine and exclusive "brotherhood" that serves to buttress the poet's power in the public realm. Fridman's emphasis on the poet's separation from the wider community needs to be complemented by an awareness of the fact that Paz also promoted the idea—most notably in *El arco*—that everyone could be a poet. See Frederico Fridman, "The Remnants of the Poets' Brotherhood: Octavio Paz, Poetry, Theory, and the Question of Community," *Revista de estudios hispánicos* 52, no. 3 (October 2018): 837–66.

31. "Poesía, mito, revolución," in Paz, *La otra voz*.
32. "La otra voz," in Paz, *La otra voz*.
33. See, especially, Paz, *Los hijos del limo*, 89–114.
34. Paz, *La otra voz*, 138.

CHAPTER 10

1. For a helpful overview of this genre, see Paul Franssen and Ton Hoenselaars, ed., *The Author as Character: Representing Historical Writers in Western Literature* (Madison, NJ: Fairleigh Dickinson University Press, 1999).
2. For a history of literary and cinematic representations of Shakespeare, see Paul Franssen, *Shakespeare's Literary Lives: The Author as Character in Fiction and Film* (Cambridge: Cambridge University Press, 2016).
3. See the compilation of texts about Borges in Eduardo Berti and Edgardo Cozarinsky, ed., *Galaxia Borges* (Buenos Aires: Adriana Hidalgo, 2007).

4. See Alicia Gaspar de Alba, *Sor Juana's Second Dream: A Novel* (Albuquerque: University of New Mexico Press, 1999); Paul Anderson, *Hunger's Bride: A Novel of the Baroque* (London: Constable, 2005); and Mónica Zagal, *La venganza de Sor Juana* (Mexico City: Planeta, 2007).
5. Novels in which José Martí appears as a character include Daína Chaviano, *El hombre, la hembra y el hambre* (Barcelona: Planeta, 1998) and Francisco Goldman, *The Divine Husband: A Novel* (New York: Atlantic Monthly Press, 2004).
6. See César Aira, *El congreso de literatura* (Buenos Aires: Tusquets, 1997) and Alberto Fuguet, *Sudor* (Barcelona: Random House, 2016).
7. A number of critics have addressed the complicated story of the friendship between Paz and Fuentes, surely the two best-known Mexican authors of the twentieth century. See Alfonso González, "Octavio Paz y Carlos Fuentes: Encuentros y desencuentros," *Revista de la Universidad de México*, Nueva Época, no. 102 (August 2012): 14–18; Guillermo Sheridan, "Las cartas entre Octavio Paz y Carlos Fuentes: De Tlatelolco a Echeverría," in *Paseos por la calle de la amargura y otros rumbos mexicanos* (Mexico City: Penguin Random House / Debate, 2018), 73–144; and Domínguez Michael, *Octavio Paz en su siglo*, passim. The most thorough and illuminating treatment of the topic can be found in Malva Flores's *Estrella de dos puntas. Octavio Paz y Carlos Fuentes: Crónica de una amistad* (Mexico City: Ariel, 2020).
8. Carlos Fuentes, "How I Started to Write," in *Myself with Others: Selected Essays* (New York; Farrar, Straus and Giroux, 1988), 22.
9. Carlos Fuentes, "South of the Border," *Saturday Review*, 17 December 1960, 27.
10. See Luis Harss and Barbara Dohmann, *Los nuestros* (Buenos Aires: Sudamericana, 1969), 358.
11. See Richard Reeve, "Octavio Paz and Hiperión in *La región más transparente*: Plagiarism, Caricature, Or . . . ?" *Chasqui: Revista de literatura latinoamericana* 3, no. 3 (May 1974): 13–25. Reeve considers but in the end rejects the accusation that Fuentes was guilty of plagiarism. According to Reeve, Fuentes was not trying to copy Paz's ideas in his novel; rather, his aim was to recreate the ambience of the Mexican intellectual world in the early 1950s.
12. José Vázquez Amaral, "Mexico's Melting Pot," *Saturday Review*, 19 November 1960, 29.
13. Octavio Paz to José Bianco, 30 March 1959, José Bianco Papers, Correspondence, Folder 5, Manuscripts Division, Department of Rare Books and Special Collections, Princeton University Library.

14. For an anthology of texts by the members of the Hiperión group, and an introduction to their thought, see Guillermo Hurtado, ed., *El Hiperión: Una antología* (Mexico City: Universidad Nacional Autónoma de México, 2006).
15. Carlos Fuentes, *La región más transparente*, 2nd. ed. (Mexico City: Fondo de Cultura Económica, 1972), 68.
16. Fuentes, *La región*, 68–69.
17. Paz, *El laberinto*, 89.
18. Paz, *El laberinto*, 88.
19. Fuentes, *La región*, 281.
20. Fuentes, *La región*, 281.
21. Rafael Rojas describes Fuentes's ideas about the Mexican Revolution as "la variación conceptual de una conocida idea de Octavio Paz . . . que atribuía a la Revolución el efecto de una 'revelación del ser mexicano'" (the conceptual variation of a well-known idea put forward by Octavio Paz . . . who attributed to the Revolution the effect of a "revelation of the Mexican being"). See Rafael Rojas, "Fuentes entre dos revoluciones," in *Carlos Fuentes y el Reino Unido*, ed. Steven Boldy (Mexico City: Fondo de Cultura Económica, 2017), 140.
22. Luis Harss describes Zamacona as "un intelectual vacilante, ineficaz" (a vacillating, powerless intellectual). See Harss and Dohmann, *Los nuestros*, 353.
23. José Alvarado eventually became president of the Universidad Autónoma de Nuevo León. For a selection of his writings about Mexico City in the 1930s, and his memories of Octavio Paz, see José Alvarado, "En la mirada de José Alvarado," *Zona Octavio Paz*, https://zonaOctaviopaz.com/detalle_conversacion/206/en-la-mirada-de-jose-alvarado. Accessed on 20 November 2020.
24. Carlos Fuentes, "Mi amigo Octavio Paz," *El País*, 13 May 1998, elpais.com/diario/1998/05/13/cultura/895010411_850215.html.
25. Carlos Fuentes, "La desdichada," in *Constancia y otras novelas para vírgenes* (Mexico City: Fondo de Cultura Económica, 1990), 89.
26. Fuentes, "La desdichada," 82.
27. See Enrique Krauze, "La comedia mexicana de Carlos Fuentes," *Vuelta* 139 (June 1988): 15–27.
28. Carlos Fuentes, *Adán en Edén* (Mexico City: Alfaguara, 2009).
29. In a review of *Adán en Edén*, Fernando García Ramírez differs with critics who claim that Maximino Sol is Octavio Paz. But he expresses his disagreement in a way that amounts to a fierce criticism of Fuentes's view of Paz. "Me parecería una actitud cobarde" (I would judge

it to be a cowardly attitude), García Ramírez writes, "que Fuentes se refiriera, en una novela, a Octavio Paz, que fue su amigo y mentor por más de treinta años, como 'un hombre condenado a la traición de sus aduladores y ciego a la independencia de sus amigos'" (for Fuentes to refer in a novel to Octavio Paz, who was his friend and mentor for more than thirty years, as "a man fated to betray his flatterers and blind to the independence of his friends"). He goes on to offer several other examples of what he regards as inexplicably harsh observations about Paz. See Fernando García Ramírez, "*Adán en Edén* de Carlos Fuentes," *Letras Libres*, 30 April 2010, https://www.letraslibres.com/mexico/libros/adan-en-eden-carlos-fuentes.

30. For an account of the hostile reaction to Piazza's book in Mexican intellectual circles, see Volpi, *La imaginación y el poder*, 53–60. It is worth noting that Volpi himself exemplifies the type of reception he documents, given that he rebukes Piazza for exaggerating the cultural power of the group of intellectuals he portrays in his novel, a group that corresponds to the writers and artists gathered around "La Cultura en México," the cultural supplement of the weekly newsmagazine *Siempre!*

31. Luis Guillermo Piazza, *La mafia* (Mexico City: Joaquín Mortiz, 1967).

32. See Carlos Fuentes to Luis Guillermo Piazza, 18 February 1966, Box 120, Folder 14, Carlos Fuentes Papers, C0790, Manuscripts Division, Department of Rare Books and Special Collections, Princeton University Library. In an undated letter written in response to Fuentes's letter from Italy, Piazza responds enthusiastically to his friend's report. "Me regocija tu encuentro con Paz" (I rejoice in your meeting with Paz), he writes, "¡Qué bueno! Cuéntame más—Gozamos tus cartas con Monsi, hoy comeré con él, le pareció genial tu última" (How wonderful. Tell me more. We revel in your letters with Monsi, today I will have lunch with him, he thought your last letter was terrific). See Luis Guillermo Piazza to Carlos Fuentes, no date, Box 120, Folder 14, Carlos Fuentes Papers, C0790, Manuscripts Division, Department of Rare Books and Special Collections, Princeton University Library. It appears, however, that the friendship between Piazza and Fuentes did not survive the publication of *La mafia*. The last few letters from Piazza to Fuentes included in the folder in the Carlos Fuentes Papers containing correspondence between the two authors are full of desperate pleas for a response from Fuentes and insistent questions from Piazza as to whether he has done something to offend his friend. As far as one can tell, Fuentes did not respond to Piazza's letters. Many years later, he donated his correspondence with Piazza to the Princeton University Library.

33. Domínguez Michael points out that in the 1960s "Fuentes era más famoso que Paz" (Fuentes was more famous than Paz). See Domínguez Michael, *Octavio Paz en su siglo*, 282.
34. Enrique Serna, "La vanagloria," *Nexos*, 1 June 2007, https://www.nexos.com.mx/?p=12247.
35. Serna's short story "Borges y los ultraístas" focuses on the relationship between a glamorous and highly successful Latin American author and a struggling (and resentful) academic teaching at an American university. See Enrique Serna, "Borges y los ultraístas," in *Amores de segunda mano* (Xalapa, Veracruz: Universidad Veracruzana), 111–52.
36. Serna, "La vanagloria," 11.
37. Enrique Serna, *El miedo a los animales* (Mexico City: Joaquín Mortiz, 1995), 38.
38. Serna attacked Paz in his essays as well as his fiction. See Enrique Serna, *Genealogía de la soberbia intelectual* (Mexico City: Taurus, 2013), 157–61.
39. See Domínguez Michael, *Octavio Paz en su siglo*, 520.
40. King, *The Role of Mexico's Plural*, 28.
41. Juan García Ponce, *Pasado presente* (Mexico City: Fondo de Cultura Económica, 1993), 134.
42. The "real visceralistas" of Bolaño's novel are based on the "infrarrealistas," a group of young, avant-garde poets in the Mexico City of the 1970s with whom the author of *Los detectives salvajes* was affiliated. For an account of this period in Bolaños's life, see Montserrat Madariaga Caro, *Bolaño Infra 1975-1978: Los años que inspiraron* Los detectives salvajes (Santiago de Chile: RIL editores, 2010). One chapter of Madariaga's book is tellingly titled "¡Hay que acabar con Octavio Paz!" (We have to finish off Octavio Paz). See Madariaga, 47–63.
43. For critical approaches to *Los detectives salvajes* that focus on Bolaño's antagonism toward Paz, see José Agustín Pastén B., "De la institucionalización a la disolución de la literatura en *Los detectives salvajes*," *Revista canadiense de estudios hispánicos* 33, no. 2 (Winter 2009): 423–46, and Carmen de Mora, "El canon literario en *Los detectives salvajes*," *Romanische Studien* 1 (2015): 33–52.
44. Jordi Balada Campo speaks of Bolaño's "crítica virulenta de autores consagrados como Octavio Paz" (virulent criticism of consecrated authors such as Octavio Paz). See Jordi Balada Campo, "Roberto Bolaño frente al canon literario," *Romanische Studien* 1 (2015): 27–32. Heriberto Yépez claims that Bolaño "no soportaba a Paz" (could not stand Paz). See Heriberto Yépez, "De la índole crustácea de la poesía," in José Vicente Anaya, ed. *Versus: Otras miradas a la obra de Octavio*

Paz (Zacatecas: Ediciones de Medianoche, 2010), 220.
45. Roberto Bolaño, *Los detectives salvajes* (Barcelona: Anagrama, 1998).
46. Chris Andrews rightly observes that "Bolaño has a marked preference for drifting, discontinuous, and inconclusive narrative forms." Recognizing the presence of such traits in the Paz episode in *Los detectives salvajes* helps the reader grasp the nature of Bolaño's perspective on the Mexican poet. Nowhere in his novel does Bolaño present a forceful and assertive point of view. It is clearly a mistake, then, to read such a perspective into the episode about Paz, as some critics have chosen to do. See Chris Andrews, *Roberto Bolaño's Fiction: An Expanding Universe* (New York: Columbia University Press, 2014), 100. Christopher Domínguez Michael is one of the few critics to have grasped the ambiguous, open-ended quality of Bolaño's depiction of Paz in *Los detectives salvajes*, noting that "Bolaño establece una relación juguetona con la imagen de Paz" (Bolaño establishes a playful relationship with Paz's image). See Domínguez Michael, *Octavio Paz en su siglo*, 401. My approach to Bolaño is also indebted to Rubén Gallo, who presented an illuminating lecture at UCLA titled "Roberto Bolaño's Mexico City," 18 February 2014.
47. Federico Vite, *Fisuras en el continente literario*, 2nd ed. (Mexico City: Editorial Tierra Adentro, 2007).
48. Heriberto Yépez, *A.B.U.R.T.O.* (Mexico City: Random House Mondadori, 2005), 34.
49. Yépez, *A.B.U.R.T.O.*, 33.
50. One can observe traces of Paz's ideas in many sections of Yépez's book. Generally, Yépez does not acknowledge the links. However, in a section devoted to the Chicanos, Yépez recognizes Paz as an important precursor, commending him for the significant intuition he displayed in his depiction of the *pachuco*, while claiming at the same time that Paz failed to fully grasp his own insight. See Heriberto Yépez, *La increíble hazaña de ser mexicano* (Mexico City: Editorial Planeta / BOOKET, 2010), 242–44.
51. In an interview he gave shortly after the publication of *De puño y letra*, Ramos was not eager to confirm that Pascacio was Paz. "No necesariamente se trata de Paz" (It is not necessarily about Paz), he states, explaining that in writing the novel he was more interested in the general theme of the connections between the literary and political worlds in Mexico. There are many indications, however, beginning with the initials of Ramos's fictional poet, that the author of *De puño y letra* had Paz, more than anyone else, in mind. See Óscar Zapata, "Las buenas novelas son políticamente incorrectas," interview with

Luis Arturo Ramos, "Confabulario," cultural supplement of *El Universal*, 29 August 2015, https://confabulario.eluniversal.com.mx/las-buenas-novelas-son-politicamente-incorrectas.
52. Luis Arturo Ramos, *De puño y letra* (Mexico City: Ediciones Cal y Arena, 2015), 40.
53. Elena Garro, *Testimonios sobre Mariana* (Mexico City: Porrúa, 2006).
54. See Domínguez Michael, *Octavio Paz en su siglo*, 75.
55. Lucía Melgar's account of Garro's years in Paris helps the reader pinpoint the connections—as well as the differences—between the life and the work. See Lucía Melgar, "Elena Garro en París (1947–1952)," in *Elena Garro: Lectura múltiple de una personalidad compleja*, ed. Lucía Melgar and Gabriela Mora (Puebla: Benemérita Universidad Autónoma de Puebla, 2002), 149–72.
56. See Elena Garro, *Mi hermanita Magdalena* (Monterrey, Nuevo León: Ediciones Castillo, 1998)
57. The account of Magdalena's marriage echoes the account Garro gave of her own marriage to Paz, which she claims she was forced into against her will. See for example, Elena Garro, "Elena cuenta su historia: Fragmentos de cartas a Gabriela Mora," in *Elena Garro: Lectura múltiple de una personalidad compleja*, ed. Lucía Melgar and Gabriela Mora (Puebla: Benemérita Universidad Autónoma de Puebla, 2002), 283. Ángel Gilberto Adame provides evidence indicating Garro fabricated her version of the events that took place on the day of her marriage to Paz. See "La boda," in Ángel Gilberto Adame, *Octavio Paz: El misterio de la vocación* (Mexico City: Penguin Random House, 2015), 123–29.
58. The figure of the ill-tempered and abusive husband or lover appears frequently in Garro's fiction. One might think of Frank in *Reencuentro de personajes* or Pablo in "La culpa es de los tlaxcaltecas." These characters have clear resemblances with Augusto and Enrique. Nevertheless, there are insufficient links between Frank and Pablo and specific aspects of Garro's biography to justify identifying them as representations of Paz. See Elena Garro, *Reencuentro de personajes* (México: Grijalbo, 1982) and "La culpa es de los tlaxcaltecas," in *La semana de colores* (Xalapa: Universidad Veracruzana, 1964), 7–33.
59. Sandra Messinger Cypess argues that *Testimonio sobre Mariana* should be read not simply as a *roman à clef* "that describe[s] [Garro's] life with Paz and her bellicose attitude toward him," but rather as a critique of "Mexican *machista* society *in toto*." See Cypess, *Uncivil Wars*, 158.
60. Guillermo Sheridan provides the best account we have of the relationship between Paz and Garro in a long essay titled "Elena Garro: El

centro fugitivo." Sheridan's attempt to reconstruct the history of the couple's courtship and marriage is limited by his decision to use Paz's letters to Garro as his guide. This means that he has little to say about the periods for which there are no letters available; it also means that the focus is firmly on Paz. Nevertheless, the strength of Sheridan's account is that he writes with sympathy and understanding for both Paz and Garro. From the point of view of the present investigation, his narrative is especially helpful since it provides clues that help us understand why Garro portrayed her ex-husband in the way that she did. Put simply, a review of Paz's letters to Garro from the years 1935–1937 reveals an extraordinarily passionate but also intensely possessive lover and husband. Here is how Sheridan puts it: "el joven revolucionario, que admira el libre albedrío de las mujeres en las novelas de Lawrence, no estuvo por encima de su condición cultural de varón dominante, no supo sobreponerse al modelo de macho mandamás que tanto aborreció en su padre. Y el lector de Proust, que entiende bien el infierno de los celos de Swann, es incapaz de apreciar en sí mismo la dimensión de ese error esencialmente sádico: el del enamorado convencido de ser el único objeto de la libertad de su pareja. Y el lector de Nietzsche que celebra la 'danza en el aire' de la libertad ... le ordena que deje 'la danza y la locura'" (the young revolutionary, full of admiration for the freedom of the female characters in the novels of D. H. Lawrence, was not able to break out of the role of the dominant male instilled in him by his culture, nor was he able to overcome the model of the tyrannical macho figure he detested in his father. And the reader of Proust, who understands the hell of Swann's jealousy, is incapable of recognizing in himself the workings of that essentially sadistic error: that of the lover who is convinced that he is the only possible object of his partner's freedom. And the reader of Nietzsche who celebrates freedom's 'dancing star' ... commands her to abandon 'the dance and the madness.'" See "Elena Garro: El centro fugitivo," in Sheridan, *Los idilios salvajes*, 223. Sheridan also suggests that some of Paz's later essays on poetry and poets, and on the subject of love, show that he drew valuable lessons from his failed marriage to Garro.

61. In a March 30, 1959 letter to Bianco, Paz offers the following fulsome praise of a book by Garro, although with a touch of ambivalence at the end: "¿Recibiste el libro de Helena? ¿Qué te parece? A mí me sorprende y maravilla: ¡cuánta vida, cuánta poesía, cómo todo parece una piedra, un cohete, una flor mágica! Helena es una ilusionista. Vuelve ligera la

vida. Es hada. (Y también bruja: Artemisa, la cazadora, la siempre Virgen, dueña del cuchillo, enemiga del hombre)." Paz does not state the title of the book. It seems likely, however, that he is referring to *Un hogar sólido y seis piezas en un acto*, Garro's first book, first published in 1958. See Octavio Paz to José Bianco, 30 March 1959, José Bianco Papers, C0681, Manuscripts Division, Department of Special Collections, Princeton University Library. A few years later, Paz celebrated the publication of Garro's first novel, *Los recuerdos del porvenir* (1963), describing it as "una obra de verdad extraordinaria, una de las creaciones más perfectas de la literatura hispanoamericana contemporánea" (a truly extraordinary work, one of the most perfect creations of contemporary Spanish American literature). See Paz, *Puertas al campo*, 117. Still, Pedro Serrano rebukes Paz for having erased Garro from his autobiographical writings. See a section titled "Ocultamiento de Elena Garro," in Pedro Serrano, *La construcción del poeta moderno: T. S. Eliot y Octavio Paz* (Mexico City: UNAM / Conaculta / El Centauro, 2011), 175–84.
62. Paz, *Itinerario*, 47.
63. For an account of Paz and Garro's meeting with Bosch in Barcelona, see Elena Garro, *Memorias de España 1937* (Mexico City: Siglo XXI, 1992), 34–35. Both Paz and Garro assume that Bosch dies shortly after their meeting with him, as does Rivero Taravillo. Recent research indicates, however, that Bosch survived the Civil War and lived until at least 1991. See "José Juan Bosch Fontserè, la resurrección de la presencia," in Adame, *Octavio Paz: El misterio de la vocación*, 83–96.
64. Antonio Rivero Taravillo, *Los huesos olvidados* (Sevilla: Ediciones Espuela de Plata, 2014).
65. For an excellent account—far more nuanced than most—of the memory wars in Spain, see Jeremy Treglown, *Franco's Crypt: Spanish Culture and Memory Since 1936* (New York: Farrar, Straus and Giroux, 2013).
66. Fernando Vallejo, *Entre fantasmas* (Bogotá: Planeta, 1993).
67. Paz, *El arco y la lira*, 207.
68. Paz, *Corriente alterna*, 90.
69. Vallejo mentions Paz a number of times in *¡Llegaron!* (Mexico City: Alfaguara, 2015). However, the references are less frequent than in *Entre fantasmas*, and they do not add up to a distinctive perspective on the life and/or work of the Mexican poet, unlike what we see in the earlier novel.
70. Héctor Abad Faciolince, *El olvido que seremos* (Bogotá: Planeta, 2006), 193.

Bibliography

ARCHIVES

Manuscripts Division, Department of Special Collections, Princeton University Library: Elena Garro Papers; José Bianco Papers; Carlos Fuentes Papers; and the *Plural* Editorial Files

WORKS CITED

Abad Faciolince, Héctor. *El olvido que seremos*. Bogotá: Planeta, 2006.

Adame, Ángel Gilberto. *Octavio Paz: El misterio de la vocación*. Mexico City: Penguin Random House, 2015.

———, ed. *Octavio Paz en 1968: El año axial. Cartas y escritos sobre los movimientos estudiantiles*. Mexico City: Penguin Random House / Taurus, 2018.

Aguilar Camín, Héctor. "Metáforas de la tercera vía: Sobre *El ogro filantrópico* de Octavio Paz." In *Saldos de la revolución: Cultura y política de México, 1910–1980*, 207–34. Mexico City: Nueva Imagen, 1982.

———. "Octavio Paz: Recuento personal." In *Aire en libertad: Octavio Paz y la crítica*, edited by José Antonio Aguilar Rivera, 69–112. Mexico City: Fondo de Cultura Económica, 2015.

Aguilar Mora, Jorge. "Es como si nos hubieran arrancado los párpados: Apostilla." In *Aire en libertad: Octavio Paz y la crítica*, edited by José Antonio Aguilar Rivera, 33–46. Mexico City: Fondo de Cultura Económica, 2015.

———. *La divina pareja: Historia y mito en Octavio Paz*. Mexico City: Ediciones Era, 1978.

———. "La fuga de la identidad: Crítica a la obra poética de Octavio Paz." In *Versus: Otras miradas a la obra de Octavio Paz*, edited by José Vicente Anaya, 19–30. Zacatecas: Ediciones de Medianoche, 2010.

———. *La sombra del tiempo: Ensayos sobre Octavio Paz y Juan Rulfo*. Mexico City: Siglo XXI, 2010.

———. "Paz y Quetzalcóatl." In *Se acabó el centenario: Lecturas críticas en torno a Octavio Paz*, edited by Gabriel Wolfson, 213–21. Puebla: UDLAP, 2015.

Aguilar Rivera, José Antonio, ed. *Aire en libertad: Octavio Paz y la crítica*. Mexico City: Fondo de Cultura Económica, 2015.

———. *La geometría y el mito: Un ensayo sobre la libertad y el liberalismo en México, 1821–1970*. Mexico City: Fondo de Cultura Económica, 2010.

———. *La sombra de Ulises: Ensayos sobre intelectuales mexicanos y norteamericanos*. Mexico City: CIDE / Miguel Ángel Porrúa, 1997.

———. "Vuelta a Paz." *Nexos*, 1 January 2014. https://www.nexos.com.mx/?p=15722.

Aira, César. *El congreso de literatura*. Buenos Aires: Tusquets, 1997.

Alamán, Lucas. *Historia de México*. 5 vols. Mexico City: Editorial Jus, 1942.

Alarcón, Norma. "Traddutora, Traditora: A Paradigmatic Figure of Chicana Feminism." *Cultural Critique* 13 (Autumn 1989): 57–87.

Albala, Eliana. *El estilo ensayístico de Octavio Paz*. Mexico City: Centro de Investigación y Docencia en Humanidades del Estado de Morelos / Juan Pablos Editor, 2015.

Allen, Charles. "Who Owns India's History: A Critique of Shashi Tharoor's *Inglorious Empire*." *Asian Affairs* 49, no. 3 (2018): 355–69.

Allen, Douglas. *Mahatma Gandhi*. London: Reaktion Books, 2011.

Alonso, Carlos. *The Burden of Modernity: The Rhetoric of Cultural Discourse in Spanish America*. New York: Oxford University Press, 1998.

Alvarado, José. "En la mirada de José Alvarado." *Zona Octavio Paz*. https://zonaOctaviopaz.com/detalle_conversacion/206/en-la-mirada-de-jose-alvarado. Accessed on 20 November 2020.

Álvarez Garín, Raúl. *La estela de Tlatelolco: Una reconstrucción histórica del Movimiento estudiantil del 68*. Mexico City: Grijalbo, 1998.

Anaya, José Vicente. "Plagios de Paz en *El laberinto de la soledad*." In *Versus: Otras miradas a la obra de Octavio Paz*, ed. José Vicente Anaya, 51–61. Zacatecas: Ediciones de Medianoche, 2010.

———, ed. *Versus: Otras miradas a la obra de Octavio Paz*. Zacatecas: Ediciones de Medianoche, 2010.

"Andrei Sájarov: Premio Nobel de Paz." *Plural* 50 (November 1975): 91–92.

Asiain, Aurelio. "Octavio Paz en Japón, Japón en Octavio Paz." In *Japón en Octavio Paz*, edited by Aurelio Asiain, 9–56. Mexico City: Fondo de Cultura Económica, 2014.

Balada Campo, Jordi. "Roberto Bolaño frente al canon literario." *Romanische Studien* 1 (2015): 27–32.

Bartra, Roger. *El reto de la izquierda*. Mexico City: Grijalbo, 1982.

———. *La jaula de la melancolía: Identidad y metamorfosis del mexicano*. Mexico City: Grijalbo, 1987.

Bataillon, Gilles. "La Prensa intervenida." *Vuelta* 118 (September 1986): 64–65.

Baudrillard, Jean. *Amérique*. Paris: Le Livre de Poche, 1986.

Berlin, Isaiah. "The Decline of Utopian Ideas in the West." In *The Crooked Timber of Humanity: Chapters in the History of Ideas*, 20–48. London: John Murray, 1990.

Berti, Eduardo, and Edgardo Cozarinsky, ed. *Galaxia Borges*. Buenos Aires: Adriana Hidalgo, 2007.

Bianco, José. *La pérdida del reino*. Buenos Aires: Siglo XXI, 1972.

Blanco Aguinaga, Carlos. "El laberinto fabricado por Octavio Paz." In *De mitólogos y novelistas*, 5–25. Madrid: Turner, 1975.

Bloch, Avital. "The Journal *Vuelta* and the Emergence of Neoconservatism." In *Public Intellectuals in Contemporary Latin America*, edited by Avital Bloch, Rogelio de la Mora, and Hugo Cancino, 148–68. University of Colima / Aalborg University, 2007.

Bolaño, Roberto. *Los detectives salvajes*. Barcelona: Anagrama, 1998.

Boll, Tom. *Octavio Paz and T. S. Eliot: Modern Poetry and the Translation of Influence*. London: Legenda, 2012.

Bosteels, Bruno. *Marx and Freud in Latin America*. New York: Verso, 2012.

Brading, David A. *Octavio Paz y la poética de la historia mexicana*. Mexico City: Fondo de Cultura Económica, 2002.

Bradu, Fabienne. "Octavio Paz en perpetua ruptura." *Literatura Mexicana* 19, no. 2 (2008): 123–30.

———. *Permanencia de Octavio Paz*. Madrid: Vaso Roto Ediciones, 2015.

Brewster, Claire. *Responding to Crisis in Contemporary Mexico: The Political Writings of Paz, Fuentes, Monsiváis and Poniatowska*. Tucson: University of Arizona Press, 2005.

Brown, Judith M. *Nehru: A Political Life*. New Haven, CT: Yale University Press, 2003.

Brown, Norman O. *Life against Death: The Psychoanalytical Meaning of History*. Middletown, CT: Wesleyan University Press, 1959.

Brunk, Samuel. *The Posthumous Career of Emiliano Zapata: Myth, Memory, and Mexico's Twentieth Century*. Austin: University of Texas Press, 2008.

Brunner, José Joaquín Brunner. *América Latina: Cultura y modernidad*. Mexico City: Grijalbo, 1992.

Bürger, Peter. *Theory of the Avant-Garde*. Translated by Michael Shaw. Minneapolis: University of Minnesota Press, 1984.

Caistor, Nick. *Octavio Paz*. London: Reaktion Books, 2007.

Camayd-Freixas, Erik. "Introduction: The Orientalist Controversy and the Origins of Amerindian Culture." In *Orientalism and Identity in Latin America: Fashioning Self and Other from the (Post)Colonial Margin*, edited by Erik Camayd-Freixas, 1–18. Tucson: University of Arizona Press, 2013.

Camayd-Freixas, Erik, ed. *Orientalism and Identity in Latin America: Fashioning Self and Other from the (Post)Colonial Margin*. Tucson: University of Arizona Press, 2013.

Camus, Albert. *L'homme révolté*. Paris: Gallimard, 1951.

Cansino, César, Omar M. Gallardo, and Germán Molina Carrillo, ed. *Octavio Paz sin concesiones: 15 miradas críticas*. Puebla: Benemérita Universidad Autónoma de Puebla / Grupo Editorial Mariel, 2016.

Cantú, Roberto. "Points of Convergence: Ancient China, Modernity, and Translation in the Poetry and Essays of Octavio Paz, 1956–1996." In *Alternative Orientalisms in Latin America and Beyond*, edited by Ignacio López-Calvo, 2–28. Newcastle upon Tyne: Cambridge Scholars Publishing, 2007.

———. ed. *The Willow and the Spiral: Essays on Octavio Paz and the Poetic Imagination*. Newcastle upon Tyne: Cambridge Scholars Publishing, 2014.

Capetillo-Ponce, Jorge. "The Walls of the Labyrinth: Mapping Octavio Paz's Sociology through Georg Simmel's Method." In *Octavio Paz: Humanism and Critique*, edited by Oliver Kozlarek, 155–77. London: Transaction Publishers, 2009.

Castañón, Adolfo. *Tránsito de Octavio Paz (Poemas, apuntes, ensayos)*. Mexico City: El Colegio de México, 2014.

Castillo, Debra A. "Octavio Paz's Bread and Mole." *Hispanófila* 178 (December 2016). 153–66.

Castillo Peraza, Carlos. *El ogro antropófago y otros ensayos*. Mexico City: EPESSA, 1990.

Chaviano, Daína. *El hombre, la hembra y el hambre*. Barcelona: Planeta, 1998.

"El cierre de *La Prensa* en Nicaragua." *Vuelta* 117 (August 1986): 63.

Cooper, Daniel Solomon. *The Roots of Transformation: Octavio Paz and the Militant Americanist Awakening of Pablo Neruda*. PhD diss., University of California, Los Angeles, 2018.

Costa, Horácio. *Mar abierto: Ensayos sobre literatura brasileña, portuguesa e hispanoamericana*. Mexico City: Fondo de Cultura Económica / Facultad de Filosofía y Letras, UNAM, 1998.

———. "Poíesis y política: El modelo intelectual de Octavio Paz." In *Mar abierto: Ensayos sobre literatura brasileña, portuguesa e hispanoamericana*. 313–331.

Cuadra, Pablo Antonio. "Documentos de Nicaragua: La lucha por la democracia." *Vuelta* 74 (January 1983): 55–56.

Cuadra, Pablo Antonio, and Pedro J. Chamorro Barrios. "También en Nicaragua." *Vuelta* 60 (November 1981): 54–55.

Cypess, Sandra Messinger. *La Malinche in Mexican Literature*. Austin: University of Texas Press, 1991.

———. *Uncivil Wars: Elena Garro, Octavio Paz, and the Battle for Cultural Memory*. Austin: University of Texas Press, 2012.

David-Fox, Michael, ed. *The Soviet Gulag: Evidence, Interpretation, and Comparison*. Pittsburgh, PA: University of Pittsburgh Press, 2016.

de Mora, Carmen. "El canon literario en *Los detectives salvajes*." *Romanische Studien* 1 (2015): 33–52.

de la Torre, Renée, and Marta Eugenia García Ugarte. Introducción to *Los rostros del conservadurismo mexicano*, edited by Renée de la Torre, Marta Eugenia García Ugarte, and Juan Manuel Ramírez Saíz, 11–31. Mexico City: CIESAS, 2005.

de la Torre, Renée, Marta Eugenia García Ugarte, and Juan Manuel Ramírez Saíz, ed. *Los rostros del conservadurismo mexicano*. Mexico City: CIESAS, 2005.

Domínguez Michael, Christopher. *Octavio Paz en su siglo*. Mexico City: Aguilar, 2014.

———. Review of *El pensamiento político de Octavio Paz: Las trampas de la ideología* by Xavier Rodríguez Ledesma. *Vuelta* 235 (July 1996): 35–36.

Dorfsman, Marco Luis. *Heterogeneity of Being: On Octavio Paz's Poetics of Similitude*. Lanham, MD: University Press of America, 2015.

Durán, Javier. "Border Crossings: Images of the Pachuco in Mexican Literature." *Studies in Twentieth Century Literature* 25, no. 1 (Winter 2001): 140–172.

Enciso, Froylán. *Andar fronteras: El servicio diplomático de Octavio Paz en Francia (1946–1951)*. Mexico City: Siglo XXI, 2008.

Escalante, Evodio. *Las sendas perdidas de Octavio Paz*. Mexico City: UAM Iztapalapa / Ediciones sin Nombre, 2013.

Ferguson, Niall. *Empire: The Rise and Demise of the British World Order and the Lessons for Global Power*. New York: Basic Books, 2003.

Fernández Castillo, José Luis. *El ídolo y el vacío: Octavio Paz y las transformaciones de lo divino*. Buenos Aires: Biblos, 2016.

Flores, Malva. *Estrella de dos puntas. Octavio Paz / Carlos Fuentes: Crónica de una amistad*. Mexico City: Ariel, 2020.

———. *Viaje de* Vuelta: *Estampas de una revista*. Mexico City: Fondo de Cultura Económica, 2011.

Florescano, Enrique. *El nuevo pasado mexicano*. Mexico City: Ediciones Cal y Arena, 1991.

———. *Historia de las historias de la nación mexicana*. Mexico City: Taurus, 2002.

Florescano Mayet, Enrique. *Ensayos sobre la historiografía colonial de México*. Mexico City: Departamento de Investigaciones Históricas, INAH, 1979.

Franssen, Paul. *Shakespeare's Literary Lives: The Author as Character in Fiction and Film*. Cambridge: Cambridge University Press, 2016.

Franssen, Paul, and Ton Hoenselaars, ed. *The Author as Character: Representing Historical Writers in Western Literature*. Madison, NJ: Fairleigh Dickinson University Press, 1999.

Freud, Sigmund. *Civilization and Its Discontents*. Translated by James Strachey. New York: W.W. Norton, 1989.

———. *The Ego and the Id*. Translated by Joan Riviere. London: Hogarth Press, 1927.

———. *Sexuality and the Psychology of Love*. New York: Simon & Schuster, 1983.

Fridman, Federico. "The Remnants of the Poets' Brotherhood: Octavio Paz, Poetry, Theory, and the Question of Community." *Revista de estudios hispánicos* 52, no. 3 (October 2018): 837–66.

Fuentes, Carlos. *Adán en Edén*. Mexico City: Alfaguara, 2009.

———. "How I Started to Write." In *Myself with Others: Selected Essays*, 3–27. New York; Farrar, Straus and Giroux, 1988.

———. "La desdichada." In *Constancia y otras novelas para vírgenes*, 77–127. Mexico City: Fondo de Cultura Económica, 1990.

———. *La región más transparente*. 2nd. ed. Mexico City: Fondo de Cultura Económica, 1972.

———. "Mi amigo Octavio Paz." *El País*, 13 May 1998, elpais.com/diario/1998/05/13/cultura/895010411_850215.html.

———. "South of the Border." *Saturday Review*, 17 December 1960, 27.

Fuguet, Alberto. *Sudor*. Barcelona: Random House, 2016.

Gadre, Vasant G. "*Vislumbres de la India:* Viciadas por el prisma del pensamiento occidental de Octavio Paz." *Ciberletras* 5 (August 2001). www.lehman.cuny.edu/ciberletras/v05/gadre.html.

Gallardo, Omar M. "Octavio Paz: Poética y política de la revuelta mexicana." In *Octavio Paz sin concesiones: 15 miradas críticas*, edited by César Cansino, Omar M. Gallardo, and Germán Molina Carrillo, 215–35. Puebla: Benemérita Universidad Autónoma de Puebla / Grupo Editorial Mariel, 2016.

Gallo, Rubén. *Freud's Mexico: Into the Wilds of Psychoanalysis*. Cambridge, MA: MIT Press, 2010.

———. "Octavio Paz Reads *Moses and Monotheism*." In *Octavio Paz: Humanism and Critique*, edited by Oliver Kozlarek, 65–85. New Brunswick, NJ: Transaction Publishers, 2009.

———. "Roberto Bolaño's Mexico City." Lecture, Department of Spanish and Portuguese, UCLA, 18 February 2014.

García Cantú, Gastón. *El desafío de la derecha*. Mexico City: Joaquín Mortiz / Planeta, 1987.

———. "Posdata." In *Idea de México III, Ensayos I*, 318–22. Mexico City: Fondo de Cultura Económica, 1991.

García Monsiváis, Blanca. *El ensayo mexicano en el siglo XX: Reyes, Novo, Paz, desarrollo, direcciones y formas*. Mexico City: Universidad Autónoma Metropolitana, Unidad Iztapalapa, División de Ciencias Sociales y Humanidades, 1995.

García Ramírez, Fernando. "*Adán en Edén* de Carlos Fuentes." *Letras Libres*, 30 Abril 2010. https://www.letraslibres.com/mexico/libros/adan-en-eden-carlos-fuentes.

García Ponce, Juan. *Pasado presente*. Mexico City: Fondo de Cultura Económica, 1993.

Garro, Elena. "Elena cuenta su historia: Fragmentos de cartas a Gabriela Mora." In *Elena Garro: Lectura múltiple de una personalidad compleja*, edited by Lucía Melgar and Gabriela Mora, 281–99. Puebla: Benemérita Universidad Autónoma de Puebla, 2002.

———. "La culpa es de los tlaxcaltecas." In *Semana de colores*, 7–33. Xalapa: Universidad Veracruzana, 1964.

———. *Memorias de España 1937*. Mexico City: Siglo XXI, 1992.

———. *Mi hermanita Magdalena*. Monterrey, Nuevo León: Ediciones Castillo, 1998.

———. *Reencuentro de personajes*. Mexico City: Grijalbo, 1982.

———. *Testimonios sobre Mariana*. Mexico City: Porrúa, 2006.

Gaspar de Alba, Alicia. *Sor Juana's Second Dream: A Novel*. Albuquerque: University of New Mexico Press, 1999.

———. *(Un)framing the 'Bad Woman': Sor Juana, Malinche, Coyolxauhqui and Other Rebels with a Cause*. Austin: University of Texas Press, 2014.

Giraud, Paul-Henri. *Octavio Paz: Vers la transparence*. Paris: Presses Universitaires de France, 2002.

Goldman, Francisco. *The Divine Husband: A Novel*. New York: Atlantic Monthly Press, 2004.

González, Alfonso. "Octavio Paz y Carlos Fuentes: Encuentros y desencuentros." *Revista de la Universidad de México*, Nueva Época, no. 102 (August 2012): 14–18

González de Alba, Luis. *Los días y los años*. Mexico City: Ediciones Era, 1971.

———. *Tlatelolco, aquella tarde*. Mexico City: Ediciones Cal y Arena, 2016.

González Mateos, Adriana. "La imposibilidad de Simone de Beauvoir, o cómo Octavio Paz fue incapaz de leer uno de los libros cruciales del siglo XX." Academia, www.academia.edu/19543167/La_imposibilidad_de_Simone_de_Beauvoir_o_c%C3%B3mo_Octavio_Paz_fue_incapaz_de_leer_uno_de_los_libros_cruciales_del_siglo_XX. Accessed on 20 November 2020.

González-Ormerod, Alejandro. "Octavio Paz's India." *Third World Quarterly* 35, no. 3 (2014): 528–43.

González Rojo, Enrique. *Cuando el rey se hace cortesano: Octavio Paz y el salinismo*. Mexico City: Editorial Posada, 1990.

_____. *El rey va desnudo: Los ensayos políticos de Octavio Paz*. Mexico City: Editorial Posada, 1989.

González Torres, Armando. "Comerse al mundo: Octavio Paz y los peligros de la vocación." In *Aire en libertad: Octavio Paz y la crítica*, edited by José Antonio Aguilar Rivera, 131–49. Mexico City: Fondo de Cultura Económica, 2015.

_____. *Las guerras culturales de Octavio Paz*. Puebla: Secretaría de Cultura del Gobierno del Estado de Puebla, 2002.

_____. *Los signos vitales: Anacronismo y vigencia de Octavio Paz*. Mexico City: Libros Magenta, 2018.

_____. "Octavio Paz en 1984: La querella del diálogo y el ruido." *Letras Libres* 154 (October 2011). www.letraslibres.com/mexico/Octavio-paz-en-1984-la-querella-del-dialogo-y-el-ruido.

Grenier, Yvon. *From Art to Politics: Octavio Paz and the Pursuit of Freedom*. Lanham, MD: Rowman and Littlefield, 2001.

_____. "Octavio Paz and the Rise and Fall of the Literary Intellectual in Mexico." In *The Willow and the Spiral: Essays on Octavio Paz and the Poetic Imagination*, edited by Roberto Cantú, 137–55. Newcastle upon Tyne: Cambridge Scholars Publishing, 2014.

_____. "Socialism in One Person: Specter of Marx in Octavio Paz's Political Thought." In *Octavio Paz: Humanism and Critique*, edited by Oliver Kozlarek, 47–64. Bielefeld: Transcript Verlag, 2009.

Hale, Grace Elizabeth. *A Nation of Outsiders: How the White Middle Class Fell in Love with Rebellion in Postwar America*. New York: Oxford University Press, 2011.

Harss, Luis, and Barbara Dohmann. *Los nuestros*. Buenos Aires: Sudamericana, 1969.

Hillstrom, Kevin. *The Zoot Suit Riots*. Detroit: Omnigraphics, 2013.

Hozven, Roberto. *Octavio Paz: Viajero del presente. Otra vuelta*. Mexico City: Fondo de Cultura Económica, 2014.

Hurtado, Guillermo, ed. *El Hiperión: Una antología*. Mexico City: Universidad Nacional Autónoma de México, 2006.

Illades, Carlos, and Rodolfo Suárez. "La caída del socialismo y el campo intelectual mexicano." *Revista Horizontes Sociológicos* 2, no. 4 (July–Dec. 2014): 59–69.

Judt, Tony. *Past Imperfect: French Intellectuals, 1944–1956*. Berkeley: University of California Press, 1992.

Jullien, Dominique. *Récits du Nouveau Monde: Les voyageurs français en Amérique de Chateaubriand à nos jours*, Paris: Nathan, 1992.

Kanoussi, Dora. "Introducción al pensamiento conservador." In *El pensamiento conservador en México*, edited by Dora Kanoussi, 11–30. Mexico City: BUAP / International Gramsci Society / Plaza & Valdés, 2002.

Kermode, Frank. *Romantic Image*. London: Routledge & Kegan Paul, 1957.

Khan, Yasmin. "Gandhi's World." In *The Cambridge Companion to Gandhi*, edited by Judith M. Brown and Anthony Parel, 11–29. Cambridge: Cambridge University Press, 2011.

King, John. *The Role of Mexico's Plural in Latin American Literary and Political Culture: From Tlatelolco to the Philanthropic Ogre*. New York: Palgrave MacMillan, 2007.

Kolakowski, Leszek. "The Death of Utopia Reconsidered." In *Modernity on Endless Trial*, 131–45. Chicago: University of Chicago Press, 1990.

Kozlarek, Oliver, ed. *Octavio Paz: Humanism and Critique*. Bielefeld: transcript Verlag, 2009.

Krauze, Enrique. "La comedia mexicana de Carlos Fuentes." *Vuelta* 139 (June 1988): 15–27.

———. "Octavio Paz: El poeta y la revolución." In *Redentores: Ideas y poder en América Latina*, 135–295. Mexico City: Random House Mondadori, 2011.

———. "Octavio Paz: Facing the Century. A Reading of *Tiempo nublado*." Translated by Sonja Karsen. *Salmagundi* 70–71 (Spring-Summer 1986): 129–51.

Kushigian, Julia A. *Orientalism in the Hispanic Literary Tradition: In Dialogue with Borges, Paz, and Sarduy*. Albuquerque: University of New Mexico Press, 1991.

Lafaye, Jacques. *Octavio Paz en la deriva de la modernidad*. Mexico City: Fondo de Cultura Económica, 2013.

Lempérière, Annick. *Intellectuels, état et société au Méxique: Les clercs de la nation, 1910–1968*. Paris: L'Harmattan, 1992.

Lemus, Rafael. "Editando neoliberalismo: *Vuelta* en los años ochenta." In *Aire en libertad: Octavio Paz y la crítica*, edited by José Antonio Aguilar Rivera, 197–224. Mexico City: Fondo de Cultura Económica.

Leyva Martínez, Gustavo. "Octavio Paz: Poesía, historia y política en el horizonte de la modernidad en América Latina." In *Octavio Paz: México y la modernidad*, edited by Gustavo Leyva Martínez, Jesús Rodríguez Zepeda, Guillermo Flores Miller, Suzanne Islas Azaïs, and Jorge Rendón Alarcón, 13–131. Mexico City: Contraste Editorial, 2014.

Loaeza, Soledad. *Acción Nacional: El apetito y las responsabilidades del triunfo*. Mexico City: El Colegio de México, 2010.

———. *El Partido Acción Nacional: La larga marcha, 1939–1994. Oposición leal y partido de protesta*. Mexico City: Fondo de Cultura Económica, 1999.

———. "Octavio Paz en el debate de la democratización." In *Octavio Paz entre poética y política*, edited by Anthony Stanton, 155–97. Mexico City: El Colegio de México, 2009.

López-Calvo, Ignacio, ed. *Alternative Orientalisms in Latin America and Beyond*. Newcastle upon Tyne: Cambridge Scholars Publishing, 2007.

———. Introduction to *Alternative Orientalisms in Latin America and Beyond*, edited by Ignacio López-Calvo, viii–xiv. Newcastle upon Tyne: Cambridge Scholars Publishing, 2007.

———. Introduction to *One World Periphery Reads the Other: Knowing the 'Oriental' in the Americas and the Iberian Peninsula*, edited by Ignacio López-Calvo, 1–16. Newcastle upon Tyne: Cambridge Scholars Publishing, 2010.

———. *One World Periphery Reads the Other: Knowing the 'Oriental' in the Americas and the Iberian Peninsula*. Newcastle upon Tyne: Cambridge Scholars Publishing, 2010.

Madariaga Caro, Montserrat. *Bolaño Infra 1975–1978: Los años que inspiraron Los detectives salvajes*. Santiago de Chile: RIL editores, 2010.

Madrid-Barela, Arturo. "In Search of the Authentic Pachuco: An Interpretive Essay." *Aztlán* 4, no. 1 (Spring 1973): 31–60.

Mander, John. *Static Society: The Paradox of Latin America*. London: Victor Gollancz, 1969.

Marcus, Steven. *Freud and the Culture of Psychoanalysis: Studies in the Transition from Victorian Humanism to Modernity*. Boston: George Allen & Unwin, 1984.

Marshall, Bill. *Victor Serge: The Uses of Dissent*. New York: Berg, 1992.

McInnis, Judy B. "Octavio Paz: La Malinche as Symbol of Illegitimacy and Betrayal." *MACLAS* 8 (1995): 51–62.

Medina, Rubén. *Autor, autoridad y autorización: Escritura y poética de Octavio Paz*. Mexico City: El Colegio de México, 1999.

Medvedev, Roy. "El Gulag 2 de Solyenitsin." *Plural* 58 (July 1976): 76–80.

———. "Sobre 'Archipiélago Gulag.'" *Plural* 30 (March 1974): 8–11.

Melgar, Lucía. "Elena Garro en París (1947–1952)." In *Elena Garro: Lectura múltiple de una personalidad compleja*, edited by Lucía Melgar and Gabriela Mora, 149–72. Puebla: Benemérita Universidad Autónoma de Puebla, 2002.

Melgar, Lucía, and Gabriela Mora, ed. *Elena Garro: Lectura múltiple de una personalidad compleja*. Puebla: Benemérita Universidad Autónoma de Puebla, 2002.

Memorias de un homenaje: Octavio Paz, 1914–2014. Mexico City: Conaculta, 2014.

Mermall, Thomas. "Octavio Paz: *El laberinto de la soledad* y el psicoanálisis de la historia." *Cuadernos americanos* 156 (Jan.-Feb. 1968): 97–113.

Meyer-Minneman, Klaus. "Octavio Paz, David Rousset y el universo de los campos de concentración." *Literatura Mexicana* 13, no. 1 (2002): 149–72.

Milosz, Czeslaw, Octavio Paz, Claude Simon, and Derek Walcott. "Particularismos, universalismo, literatura." *Vuelta* 235 (June 1996): 7–16.

Monsiváis, Carlos. *Adonde yo soy tú somos nosotros. Octavio Paz: crónica de vida y obra*. Mexico City: Ediciones Raya en el Agua, 2000.

Morales, Miguel Enrique. "Ideas para disentir de costumbres: *Posdata* (1970) y el giro en el pensamiento político sobre México de Octavio Paz." *Modern Language Notes* 135, no. 2 (March 2020): 441–58.

Morse, Richard. *New World Soundings: Culture and Ideology in the Americas*. Baltimore, MD: Johns Hopkins University Press, 1989.

Nagy-Zekmi, Silvia. "Buscando el Este en el Oeste: Prácticas orientalistas en la literatura latinoamericana." In *Moros en la costa: Orientalismo en Latinoamérica*, edited by Silvia Nagy-Zekmi, 11–21. Madrid and Frankfurt: Iberoamericana / Vervuert, 2008.

Nettel, Guadalupe. *Octavio Paz: Las palabras en libertad*. Translated by Eduardo Berti. Mexico City: Taurus / El Colegio de México, 2014.

Ollé-Laprune, Philippe, and Fabienne Bradu, ed. *Una patria sin pasaporte: Octavio Paz y Francia*. Mexico City: Fondo de Cultura Económica, 2014.

Pani, Erika, ed. *Conservadurismo y derechas en la historia de México*. 2 vols. Mexico City: Fondo de Cultura Económica, 2009.

Parra, Max. *Writing Pancho Villa's Revolution: Rebels in the Literary Imagination of Mexico*. Austin: University of Texas Press, 2005.

Pastén B., Jose Agustín. "De la institucionalización a la disolución de la literatura en *Los detectives salvajes*." *Revista canadiense de estudios hispánicos* 33, no. 2 (Winter 2009): 423–46.

_____. *Octavio Paz: Crítico practicante en busca de una poética*. Madrid: Editorial Pliegos, 1999.

Paz, Octavio. "A fondo—Octavio Paz." Interview with Joaquín Soler Serrano. Televisión Española, 1977. http://www.rtve.es/alacarta/videos/a-fondo/Octavio-paz-fondo-1977/1349841/.

_____. *Al paso*. Barcelona: Seix Barral, 1992.

_____. "Americanidad de España." In *Primeras letras (1931–1943)*, edited by Enrico Mario Santí, 153–56. Mexico City: Editorial Vuelta, 1988.

_____. "Ante un presente incierto: Historias de ayer." In *El laberinto de la soledad*, edited by Enrico Mario Santí, 505–23. Madrid: Cátedra, 1993.

_____. *Apariencia desnuda: La obra de Marcel Duchamp*. Mexico City: Ediciones Era, 1973.

_____. *El arco y la lira: El poema, la revelación poética, poesía e historia*. 2nd ed. Mexico City: Fondo de Cultura Económica, 1967.

_____. "El arte de México: Materia y sentido." In *In/mediaciones*, 51–70. Mexico City: Seix Barral, 1979.

_____. "El caracol y la sirena (Rubén Darío)." In *Cuadrivio*, 9–65. Mexico City: Joaquín Mortiz, 1965.

_____. "Chiapas, ¿nudo ciego o tabla de salvación?" In *Obras completas*, vol. 14, 248–60. Mexico City: Fondo de Cultura Económica, 2000.

_____. *Claude Lévi-Strauss, o, El nuevo festín de Esopo*. Mexico City: Joaquín Mortiz, 1967.

_____. *Conjunciones y disyunciones*. Mexico City: Joaquín Mortiz, 1969.

_____. "Contrarronda: México, Estados Unidos, América Central, etcétera." *Vuelta* 131 (October 1987): 14–21.

_____. *Corriente alterna*. Mexico City: Siglo XXI, 1967.

_____. *Crónicas truncas de días excepcionales*. Edited by Antonio Saborit. Mexico City: UNAM, 2007.

_____. *Cuadrivio*. Mexico City: Joaquín Mortiz, 1965.

_____. "David Rousset y los campos de concentración soviéticos." *Sur* 197 (March 1951): 48–76.

_____. "La democracia imperial." In *Tiempo nublado*, 29–58. Barcelona: Seix Barral, 1986.

_____. "Dos apostillas: Asia y América." In *Puertas al campo*, 141–54. Mexico City: UNAM, 1966.

———. "Las elecciones de 1994: Doble mandato." *Vuelta* 215 (October 1994): 8–13.

———. "El espejo indiscreto." In *El ogro filantrópico: Historia y política, 1971–1978*, 53–69. Mexico City: Joaquín Mortiz, 1979.

———. *Los hijos del limo: Del romanticismo a la vanguardia*. Barcelona: Seix Barral, 1974.

———. *Hombres en su siglo*. Barcelona: Seix Barral, 1984.

———. *In/mediaciones*. Barcelona: Seix Barral, 1979.

———. *Itinerario*. Mexico City: Fondo de Cultura Económica, 1993.

———. "Izquierda y derecha sesenta años después." *Vuelta* 168 (November 1990): 45–46

———. *El laberinto de la soledad, Posdata y "Vuelta a* El laberinto de la soledad*."* Mexico City: Fondo de Cultura Económica / Colección Popular, 1993.

———. *The Labyrinth of Solitude*. Translated by Lysander Kemp. New York: Grove Press, 1985.

———. *La llama doble: Amor y erotismo*. Barcelona: Seix Barral, 1993.

———. *Marcel Duchamp, o, El castillo de la pureza*. Mexico City: Ediciones Era, 1968.

———. "México y Estados Unidos: Posiciones y contraposiciones." In *Tiempo nublado*, 139–59. Barcelona: Seix Barral, 198.)

———. "Miradas sobre el mundo actual." Interview with Jean-François Revel. *Vuelta* 114 (May 1986): 29–32.

———. *El mono gramático*. Barcelona: Seix Barral, 1974.

———. "El nudo de Chiapas," *Obras completas*, vol. 14, 245–48. Mexico City: Fondo de Cultura Económica, 2000.

———. *Obras completas*. 15 vols. Mexico City: Fondo de Cultura Económica, 1994–2003.

———. "Octavio Paz. De la revolución a la crítica." Interview with Enrique Krauze. In *Luz espejeante. Octavio Paz ante la crítica*, edited by Enrico Mario Santí, 673–90. Mexico City: Ediciones Era, 2009.

———. *El ogro filantrópico: Historia y política, 1971–1978*. Mexico City: Joaquín Mortiz, 1979.

———. *La otra voz: Poesía y fin de siglo*. Barcelona: Seix Barral, 1990.

———. "La palabra edificante (Luis Cernuda)." In *Cuadrivio*, 165–203. Mexico City: Joaquín Mortiz, 1965.

———. *Las peras del olmo*. Barcelona: Seix Barral, 1971.

———. *Pequeña crónica de grandes días*. Mexico City: Fondo de Cultura Económica, 1990.

———. "¿Poesía latinoamericana?" in *El signo y el garabato*, 153–65. Mexico City: Joaquín Mortiz, 1973.

———. *Posdata*. Mexico City: Siglo XXI, 1970.

———. "PRI: Hora cumplida." In *El laberinto de la soledad*, edited by Enrico Mario Santí, 485–503. Madrid: Cátedra, 1993.

———. *Primeras letras (1931–1943)*. Enrico Mario Santí, ed. Mexico City: Editorial Vuelta, 1988.

———. *Puertas al campo*. Mexico City: UNAM, 1966.

———. *El signo y el garabato*. Mexico City: Joaquín Mortiz, 1973.

———. *Sombras de obras*. Barcelona: Seix Barral, 1983.

———. *Sor Juana Inés de la Cruz, o, Las trampas de la fe*. Mexico City: Fondo de Cultura Económica, 1982.

———. *Tiempo nublado*. Barcelona: Seix Barral, 1986.

———. "El uso y la contemplación." In *In/mediaciones*, 7–23. Mexico City: Seix Barral, 1979.

———. *Vislumbres de la India*. Mexico City: Seix Barral, 1995.

———. "Vuelta a *El laberinto de la soledad*." Interview with Claude Fell. In *El laberinto de la soledad, Posdata y "Vuelta a* El laberinto de la soledad*,"* 319–350. Mexico City: Fondo de Cultura Económica / Colección Popular, 1993.

———. *Xavier Villaurrutia en persona y en obra*. Mexico City: Fondo de Cultura Económica, 1978.

Paz, Octavio, Ignacio Bernal, and Tzvetan Todorov. "La Conquista de México: Comunicación y encuentro de civilizaciones." *Vuelta* 191 (October 1992): 10–14.

Paz, Octavio, and Enrique Krauze. *El ejercicio de la libertad: Política y economía*. La experiencia de la libertad 5. Mexico City: Fundación Cultural Televisa, 1991.

———. *Hacia la sociedad abierta*. La experiencia de la libertad 1. Mexico City: Fundación Cultural Televisa, 1991.

———. *El mapa del siglo XXI*. La experiencia de la libertad 2. Mexico City: Fundación Cultural Televisa, 1991.

———. *Miradas al futuro*. La experiencia de la libertad 7. Mexico City: Fundación Cultural Televisa, 1991.

---. *La palabra liberada. La experiencia de la libertad 3*. Mexico City: Fundación Cultural Televisa, 1991.

---. *Las pasiones de los pueblos. La experiencia de la libertad 4*. Mexico City: Fundación Cultural Televisa, 1991.

---. *Las voces del cambio. La experiencia de la libertad 6*. Mexico City: Fundación Cultural Televisa, 1991.

Paz, Octavio, and Arnaldo Orfila Reynal. *Cartas cruzadas*. Mexico City: Siglo XXI, 2005.

Paz, Octavio, and Alfonso Reyes. *Correspondencia (1939–1959)*. Edited by Anthony Stanton. Mexico City: Fondo de Cultura Económica, 1998.

Perales Contreras, Jaime. *Octavio Paz y su círculo intelectual*. Mexico City: Ediciones Coyoacán, 2013.

Peralta, Braulio. *El poeta en su tierra: Diálogos con Octavio Paz*. Mexico City: Grijalbo, 1996.

---, ed. *Los rostros de Octavio Paz: Una antología crítica*. Mexico City: El Tapiz del Unicornio, 2017.

Pereyra, Carlos. *Breve historia de América*. Madrid: M. Aguilar, 1930.

---. *México falsificado*. Mexico City: Editorial Polis, 1949.

Piazza, Luis Guillermo Piazza. *La mafia*. Mexico City: Joaquín Mortiz, 1967.

Poniatowska, Elena. *La noche de Tlatelolco*. Mexico City: Ediciones Era, 1971.

---. *Octavio Paz: Las palabras del árbol*. Mexico City: Plaza & Janés, 1998.

Preston, Julia, and Sam Dillon. *Opening Mexico: The Making of a Democracy*. New York: Farrar, Straus and Giroux, 2005.

Quiroga, José. *Understanding Octavio Paz*. Columbia: University of South Carolina Press, 1999.

Rader, Pamela J. "Boys to Men: Redefining Masculinities in *Women Hollering Creek and Other Stories*." In *Sandra Cisneros's* Women Hollering Creek, edited by Cecilia Donohue, 131–49. Amsterdam: Rodopi, 2010.

Ramírez, Carlos. "Las estaciones políticas de Octavio Paz." *Zona Octavio Paz*. zonaOctaviopaz.com/detalle_conversacion/104/las-estaciones-politicas-de-Octavio-paz. Accessed on 20 November 2020.

---. "Luz del pasado en el presente. Octavio Paz, politólogo." *Zona Octavio Paz*. zonaOctaviopaz.com/detalle_conversacion/122/luz-del-pasado-en-el-presente-Octavio-paz-politologo. Accessed on 20 November 2020.

Ramos, Luis Arturo. *De puño y letra*. Mexico City: Ediciones Cal y Arena, 2015.

Reeve, Richard. "Octavio Paz and Hiperión in *La region más transparente*: Plagiarism, Caricature, Or . . .?" *Chasqui: Revista de literatura latinoamericana* 3, no. 3 (May 1974): 13–25.

Reyes, Alfonso. "Pasado inmediato." *Obras completas*, vol. 12. Mexico City: Fondo de Cultura Económica, 1983. 182–216.

Rico Moreno, Javier. *La historia y el laberinto: Hacia una estética del devenir en Octavio Paz*. Mexico City: Bonilla Artigas, 2013.

Rivero Taravillo, Antonio. *Los huesos olvidados*. Sevilla: Ediciones Espuela de Plata, 2014.

Rodríguez Ledesma, Xavier. *El pensamiento político de Octavio Paz: Las trampas de la ideología*. Mexico City: Plaza & Valdés, 1996.

Román-Odio, Clara. *Octavio Paz en los debates estéticos del siglo XX*. A Coruña: tresCtres Editores, 2006.

Rojas, Rafael. "Fuentes entre dos revoluciones." In *Carlos Fuentes y el Reino Unido*, edited by Steven Boldy, 139–58. Mexico City: Fondo de Cultura Económica, 2017.

———. *La polis literaria: El boom, la Revolución y otras polémicas de la Guerra Fría*. Mexico City: Penguin Random House / Taurus, 2018.

Roston, Murray. *The Search for Selfhood in Modern Literature*. New York: Palgrave, 2001.

Roy, Tirthankar. Review of *Inglorious Empire* by Shashi Tharoor. *Cambridge Review of International Affairs* 31, no. 1 (2018): 134–38

Rudnytsky, Peter L. *Freud and Oedipus*. New York: Columbia University Press, 1987.

Ruy Sánchez, Alberto. *Una introducción a Octavio Paz*. Mexico City: Joaquín Mortiz, 1990.

Said, Edward. *Orientalism*. New York: Pantheon Books, 1978.

Sánchez, Marta E. *"Shakin' Up" Race and Gender: Intercultural Connections in Puerto Rican, African American, and Chicano Narratives and Culture (1965–1995)*. Austin: University of Texas Press, 2005.

Sánchez Prado, Ignacio. *Naciones intelectuales: Las fundaciones de la modernidad literaria mexicana (1917–1959)*. West Lafayette, IN: Purdue University Press, 2009.

Sánchez Susarrey, Jaime. *El debate político e intelectual en México*. Mexico City: Grijalbo, 1993.

Santí, Enrico Mario. *El acto de las palabras: Estudios y diálogos con Octavio Paz*. Mexico City: Fondo de Cultura Económica, 1997.

———. "Introducción a *El laberinto de la soledad*." In *El acto de las palabras: Estudios y diálogos con Octavio Paz*. Mexico City: Fondo de Cultura Económica, 1997.

———. ed. *Luz espejeante: Octavio Paz ante la crítica*. Mexico City: Ediciones Era, 2009.

Santiago, Silviano. *Las raíces y el laberinto de América Latina*. Translated by Mónica González García. Buenos Aires: Ediciones Corregidor, 2013.

Savater, Fernando. "La ciudad como galaxia." In *Los rostros de Octavio Paz*, edited by Braulio Peralta, 27–50. Mexico City: El Tapiz del Unicornio, 2017.

Schärer-Nussberger, Maya. *Octavio Paz: Trayectorias y visiones*. Mexico City: Fondo de Cultura Económica, 1989.

Schwartz, Laurent. "La lucha de Sájarov." *Plural* 45 (June 1975): 15–18.

Schwarz, Roberto. *Misplaced Ideas: Essays on Brazilian Culture*. New York: Verso, 1992.

Séjourné, Laurette. *Pensamiento y religión en el México antiguo*. Mexico City: Siglo XXI, 1957.

Serna, Enrique. "Borges y los ultraístas." In *Amores de segunda mano*, 111–52. Xalapa, Veracruz: Universidad Veracruzana.

———. *Genealogía de la soberbia intelectual*. Mexico City: Taurus, 2013.

———. *El miedo a los animales*. Mexico City: Joaquín Mortiz, 1995.

———. "La vanagloria." *Nexos*, 1 June 2007. https://www.nexos.com.mx/?p=12247.

Serrano, Pedro. *La construcción del poeta moderno: T. S. Eliot y Octavio Paz*. Mexico City: Conaculta, 2011.

Sheridan, Guillermo. "Cartas de un Hijo Pródigo (a Octavio G. Barreda)." In *Habitación con retratos: Ensayos sobre la vida de Octavio Paz 2*, 92–99. Mexico City: Ediciones Era, 2015.

———. "Cartas supersónicas entre Paz y Fuentes." *Letras libres* (14 December 2015). https://www.letraslibres.com/mexico-espana/cartas-supersonicas-entre-paz-y-fuentes.

———. *Habitación con retratos: Ensayos sobre la vida de Octavio Paz 2*. Mexico City: Ediciones Era, 2015.

———. *Los idilios salvajes: Ensayos sobre la vida de Octavio Paz 3*. Mexico City: Ediciones Era, 2016.

———. "Las cartas entre Octavio Paz y Carlos Fuentes: De Tlatelolco a Echeverría." In *Paseos por la calle de la amargura y otros rumbos mexicanos*, 73–144. Mexico City: Penguin Random House / Debate, 2018.

———. *Poeta con paisaje: Ensayos sobre la vida de Octavio Paz 1*. Mexico City: Ediciones Era, 2004.

Silva-Herzog Márquez, Jesús. "Sílabas enamoradas." In *La idiotez de lo perfecto: Miradas a la política*, 155–87. Mexico City: Fondo de Cultura Económica, 2006.

Solzhenitsyn, Aleksandr I. *The Gulag Archipelago, 1918–1956: An Experiment in Literary Investigation I-II*. Translated by Thomas P. Whitney. New York: Harper & Row, 1974.

Sorensen, Diana. *A Turbulent Decade Remembered: Scenes from the Latin American Sixties*. Stanford, CA: Stanford University Press, 2007.

Stanton, Anthony. *El río reflexivo: Poesía y ensayo en Octavio Paz (1931–1958)*. Mexico City: Fondo de Cultura Económica, 2015.

———. Introduction to *El laberinto de la soledad* by Octavio Paz. Edited by Anthony Stanton. Manchester: Manchester University Press, 2008.

———, ed. *Octavio Paz entre poética y política*. Mexico City: El Colegio de México, 2009.

Steinberg, Samuel. *Photopoetics at Tlatelolco: Afterimages of Mexico, 1968*. Austin: University of Texas Press, 2016.

Stone, I. F. "La campaña de Sájarov." *Plural* 26 (November 1973): 16–18.

———. "¿Puede cambiar Rusia?" *Plural* 7 (April 1972): 35.

Suárez-Iñiguez, E. *Los intelectuales en México*. Mexico City: Ediciones "El Caballito," 1980.

Tannenbaum, Frank. *Peace by Revolution: An Interpretation of Mexico*. New York: Columbia University Press, 1933.

Taylor, Charles. *Sources of the Self: The Making of the Modern Identity*. New York: Cambridge University Press, 1989.

Tharoor, Shashi. *Inglorious Empire: What the British Did to India*. London: Hurst & Company, 2016.

Tocqueville, Alexis de. *Democracy in America*. Two vols. Translated by Henry Reeve. Edited by Francis Bowen. Mineola, NY: Dover Publications, 2017.

Todorov, Tzvetan. *The Conquest of America: The Question of the Other*. Translated by Richard Howard. New York: Harper & Row, 1984.

Treglown, Jeremy. *Franco's Crypt: Spanish Culture and Memory Since 1936*. New York: Farrar, Straus and Giroux, 2013.

Trevelyan, Raleigh. "One Nation under Many Gods." Review of *In Light of India* by Octavio Paz, translated from the Spanish by Eliot Weinberger. *New York Times Book Review*, 30 March 1997. 25.

Ulacia, Manuel. *El árbol milenario: Un recorrido por la obra de Octavio Paz*. Barcelona: Galaxia Gutenberg / Círculo de Lectores, 1999.

Urban, Hugh B. "The Extreme Orient: The Construction of 'Tantrism' as a Category in the Orientalist Imagination," *Religion* 29, no. 2 (1999): 123–46.

Vallejo, Fernando Vallejo. *Entre fantasmas*. Bogotá: Planeta, 1993.

———. *¡Llegaron!* Mexico City: Alfaguara, 2015.

Van Delden, Maarten. "The Real Nation and the Legal Nation." In *Carlos Fuentes, Mexico, and Modernity*. Nashville, TN: Vanderbilt University Press, 1998.

Van Delden, Maarten, and Yvon Grenier. *Gunshots at the Fiesta: Literature and Politics in Latin America*. Nashville, TN: Vanderbilt University Press, 2009.

Vasconcelos, José. *Breve Historia de Méjico*. 4th edition. Mexico City: Ediciones Botas, 1938.

Vázquez Amaral, José. "Mexico's Melting Pot." *Saturday Review*, 19 November 1960, 29.

Vázquez Vallejo, Salvador. *El pensamiento internacional de Octavio Paz*. Mexico City: Miguel Ángel Porrúa, 2006.

Veliz, Claudio. *The New World of the Gothic Fox: Culture and Economy in English and Spanish America*. Berkeley: University of California Press, 1994.

Verani, Hugo. *Octavio Paz: El poema como caminata*. Mexico City: Fondo de Cultura Económica, 2013.

Vizcaíno, Fernando. *Biografía política de Octavio Paz, o, La razón ardiente*. Málaga: Editorial Algazara, 1993.

Viswanathan, Gauri. *Masks of Conquest: Literary Study and British Rule in India*. New York: Columbia University Press, 1989.

Vite, Federico. *Fisuras en el continente literario*, 2nd ed. Mexico City: Editorial Tierra Adentro, 2007.

Volpi, Jorge. *La imaginación y el poder: Una historia intelectual de 1968*. Mexico City: Ediciones Era, 1998.

Weber, Max. *The Protestant Ethic and the Spirit of Capitalism*. Translated by Talcott Parsons. New York: Charles Scribner's Sons, 1958.

Whitney, Joel. "Poetry and Action: Octavio Paz at 100." *Dissent*, March 25, 2014. www.dissentmagazine.org/online_articles/poetry-and-action-Octavio-paz-at-100.

Williams, Raymond Leslie. "The Octavio Paz Industry." *American Book Review* 14, no. 3 (August-September 1992): 3, 10.

Wilson, Colin. *The Outsider*. New York: Jeremy P. Tarcher / Putnam, 1982.

Wilson, Jason. *Octavio Paz: A Study of His Poetics*. Cambridge: Cambridge University Press, 1979.

Wolfe, Tom. *The Painted Word*. New York: Farrar, Straus and Giroux, 1975.

Wolfson, Gabriel, ed. *Se acabó el centenario: Lecturas críticas en torno a Octavio Paz*. Puebla: UDLAP, 2015.

Womack, John, Jr., *Zapata and the Mexican Revolution*. New York: Vintage Books, 1968.

Yépez, Heriberto. *A.B.U.R.T.O.* Mexico City: Random House Mondadori, 2005.

———. "De la índole crustácea de la poesía." In *Versus: Otras miradas a la obra de Octavio Paz*, edited by José Vicente Anaya, 217–49. Zacatecas: Ediciones de Medianoche, 2010.

———. *La increíble hazaña de ser mexicano*. Mexico City: Editorial Planeta / BOOKET, 2010.

Zagal, Mónica. *La venganza de Sor Juana*. Mexico City: Planeta, 2007.

Zaid, Gabriel. "Colegas enemigos: una lectura de la tragedia salvadoreña." In *De los libros al poder*, 220–69. Mexico City: Editorial Océano, 1998.

———. *De los libros al poder*. Mexico City: Editorial Océano, 1998.

———. "Nicaragua: el enigma de las elecciones." In *De los libros al poder*, 174–219. Mexico City: Editorial Océano, 1998.

———. "Un espíritu excepcional." In *Octavio Paz sin concesiones: 15 miradas críticas*, edited by César Cansino, Omar M. Gallardo, and Germán Molina Carrillo, 19–23. Puebla: Benemérita Universidad Autónoma de Puebla / Grupo Editorial Mariel, 2016.

Zapata, Óscar. "Las buenas novelas son políticamente incorrectas." Interview with Luis Arturo Ramos. "Confabulario," cultural supplement of *El Universal* (29 August 2015) confabulario.eluniversal.com.mx/las-buenas-novelas-son-politicamente-incorrectas.

Zaretsky, Eli. *Secrets of the Soul: A Social and Cultural History of Psychoanalysis*. New York: Vintage, 2005.

Index

À la recherche du temps perdu (Proust), 136–37
Abad Faciolince, Héctor, 260–61
abortion, 196–97
A.B.U.R.T.O. (Yépez), 245–46
Adán en Edén (Fuentes), 230–31
águila y la serpiente, El (Guzmán), 39
Aguilar Camín, Héctor, 109–10, 156, 172, 174
Aguilar Mora, Jorge, 108–9, 155–56
Aguilar Rivera, José Antonio, 274–75n68, 301n76
Alamán, Lucas, 180, 181, 189, 190, 305n18
Alexis de Tocqueville Prize, 33
alienation, 65
Allen, Charles, 282n9
Allen, Douglas, 281n7
Alonso, Carlos, 272–73n39
Alvarado, José, 315n23
Álvarez Garín, Raúl, 53
"América Latina y la democracia" (Paz), 170–71
"Americanidad de España" (Paz), 183–84
Andrews, Chris, 318n46
anthropology, 4
arco y la lira, El (Paz), 3, 199, 200–207, 209, 215–18, 279–80n57
arielismo, 279n49
Aron, Raymond, 297n33

atheism, 196–97
authoritarianism, 28, 33
authors as literary characters
  overview of, 222–23
  Fuentes as, 222, 231–32, 233–34, 239
  Garro as, 254–55, 256–57
  See also Paz, Octavio, as literary character
automatic writing, 3
avant-garde art, 4, 24, 27, 232–33, 241, 312n26
Aztecs, 46, 105, 106–8, 110–13

Balada Campo, Jordi, 317–18n44
Bartra, Roger, 109, 295n7
Bataillon, Gilles, 170
Baudrillard, Jean, 278n40
Beauvoir, Simone de, 137–38
Bell, Daniel, 5, 172, 176
Berlin, Isaiah, 38
Bernal, Ignacio, 283–84n14
Bianco, José, 5, 224, 251–52, 254–55, 320–21n61
Bioy Casares, Adolfo, 251–52
birth control, 196–97
Bishop, Elizabeth, 205
Blake, William, 28, 98, 216
Blanco Aguinaga, Carlos, 267n8
Bloch, Avital, 301–2n1
Bolaño, Roberto, 240–45, 255

Boll, Tom, 311–12n25
Borges, Jorge Luis, 5, 99, 222
"Borges y los ultraístas" (Serna), 317n35
Bosch, José Juan, 255–59
Brading, David, 268n13, 287n19, 305n15
Bradu, Fabienne, 5, 266n4
Breton, André, 3, 4, 216–18
Brodsky, Joseph, 157–58
Brown, Judith M., 281–82n8
Brown, Norman O., 117–23
Brunk, Samuel, 271n16
Buddhism, 121–23
Bürger, Peter, 312n26
Burns, Archibaldo, 251–52
Burroughs, William, 232

Cabrera Infante, Guillermo, 5
campesinos (peasantry), 42–43
Camus, Albert, 4, 26
Cantú, Roberto, 79
Capetillo-Ponce, Jorge, 268n11
capitalism, 64–65, 75–76, 174–77
Carballo, Emmanuel, 238, 239
Cárdenas, Cuauhtémoc, 192, 307n31
Cárdenas, Lázaro, 193, 272n35
Carranza, Venustiano, 43
Castañón, Adolfo, 5, 266n4, 285–86n10
caste system, 84–85
Castillo, Debra, 275–76n11
Castillo, Donald, 170
Castillo Peraza, Carlos, 63, 172, 178, 190–91, 197
Castoriadis, Cornelius, 172, 173, 174–75, 176, 177
Castro, Fidel, 298n36
Catholicism, 185–90, 196–98
Centro Mexicano de Escritores, 239
Cernuda, Luis, 143–44
Chamorro Barrios, Pedro J., 169
Chicanos, 30
Christianity, 83–84, 121–23, 126. See also Catholicism

Cold War, 168–72
Colletti, Lucio, 172, 175
Colosio, Luis Donaldo, 194, 237–38, 245–46
Communist revolutions, 31–38, 57, 157–58
Comte, Auguste, 74
concentration camps, 2
Conjunciones y disyunciones (Paz), 29, 94–95, 116–18, 119–23, 142–43, 147
conservatism and Paz
  colonial period in Mexican history and, 181–90
  criticisms of, 179–80
  Partido Acción Nacional and, 180–81, 190–98
  views of rebellion and revolution and, 11
  See also the Left and Paz
Constancia y otras novelas para vírgenes (Fuentes), 229–30
Contemporáneos group, 4, 293–94n20
"Contrarronda: México, Estados Unidos, América Central, et cetera" (Paz), 171
Cordera, Rolando, 172, 177
Córdova, Arnaldo, 172, 173, 177
Corriente alterna (Paz)
  overview of contents of, 95
  comparison between East and West in, 94–97
  on fragment, 265n15
  on India, 80
  on Marxist theory, 60
  on poetry, 208–9
  on rebellion and revolution, 11, 27, 34–36, 38, 45, 49
  on utopianism, 56
  on women's liberation movement, 127
Cortés, Hernán, 104
counterculture of the 1960s
  critique of the Western tradition and, 98

counterculture of the 1960s (*continued*)
  Paz and, 2, 12, 26–30, 62, 117, 127, 179
craftsmanship, 210–13
Cuadra, Pablo Antonio, 169–70
Cuadrivio (Paz), 199
"Cuantía y valía" (Paz), 208–9
Cuauhtémoc, 105
Cuban Revolution, 49, 298n36
Cuesta, Jorge, 4
Cuevas, José Luis, 232
"culpa es de los tlaxcaltecas, La" (Garro), 319n58
Cypess, Sandra Messinger, 319n59

Daoism, 117
Darío, Rubén, 59
De puño y letra (Ramos), 247–48
"Death of Utopia Reconsidered, The" (Kolakowski), 38
"Decline of Utopian Ideas in the West, The" (Berlin), 38
"democracia imperial, La" (Paz), 67–68, 278n32
democracy, 163–67, 178, 190–96
Democracy in America (Tocqueville), 278n32
"desdichada, La" (Fuentes), 229–30
detectives salvajes, Los (Bolaño), 240–45
días y los años, Los (González de Alba), 53–54
Díaz, Porfirio, 40. *See also* Porfiriato
Díaz Ordaz, Gustavo, 2
Dirección de Difusión Cultural, 239
Domínguez Michael, Christopher
  on Aron, 297n33
  on Bolaño's depiction of Paz, 318n46
  on Fuentes and Paz, 317n33
  Paz and, 5
  on Paz's relationship with the Left, 158–59, 309n46
  on Paz's view of Tlatelolco massacre, 110

Donoso, José, 232
Dorfsman, Marco Luis, 267n9
Duchamp, Marcel, 211

educational systems, 82–83
Edwards, Jorge, 172
Eliot, T. S., 203, 311–12n25
Elizondo, Salvador, 239
English (language), 83
Enlightenment, 26, 39–40, 56, 57, 114–15
Entre fantasmas (Vallejo), 259–60
eroticism and erotic love, 124–25, 128, 135–38, 142, 147–50
Escalante, Evodio, 311–12n25
"espejo indiscreto, El" (Paz), 62, 64
"Everything and Nothing" (Borges), 222
Excélsior (newspaper), 298n36
existentialist philosophy, 3
experiencia de la libertad, La (The experience of liberty, 1990), 172–78, 310n54

Fehér, Ferenc, 172
Fell, Claude, 101–2, 188
feminism
  criticism of Paz and, 128–37, 150–51
  Garro's *romans à clef* and, 253–54
feminism in Paz's writings
  love and, 128, 135–38, 147–50
  social position of women and, 128–35
  Sor Juana Inés de la Cruz and, 138–42, 144–47
  support for, 127–28
Ferguson, Niall, 282n9
Fernández Castillo, José Luis, 310n21
fiesta, 22–26, 39, 65–66, 69, 103–4, 133–36
filosofía de lo mexicano (philosophy of Mexicanness), 225
Fisuras en el continente literario (Vite), 244–45
Florescano, Enrique, 271–72n16, 303–4n8&12

Fourier, Charles, 123–24
Fox, Vicente, 193–94
France, 2, 3, 33, 51–54, 61, 279–80n57
Franqui, Carlos, 172
French Revolution, 220–21
Freud, Sigmund, 4, 101–2, 103–16, 118–19, 123, 124–26
Fridman, Federico, 313n30
Fuentes, Carlos
    as literary character, 222, 231–32, 233–34, 239
    Paz and, 4, 5, 223–31, 267n8, 288–89n23
    Revista mexicana de literatura and, 238

Gadre, Vasant G., 281n6
Galbraith, John Kenneth, 5
Gallo, Rubén, 286n15, 318n46
Gandhi, Mahatma, 80, 81, 82
García Cantú, Gastón, 113–14, 302n3
García Márquez, Gabriel, 232, 245
García Monsiváis, Blanca, 287n16
García Ponce, Juan, 238–40
García Ramírez, Fernando, 315–16n29
García Terrés, Jaime, 239
Garro, Elena
    Bosch and, 256
    illness of, 79
    as literary character, 254–55, 256–57
    Paz and, 263n3, 269n15
    romans à clef by, 248–54
Gaspar de Alba, Alicia, 293n12, 294n21
genealogy, 101
Geremek, Bronislaw, 172
Gide, André, 2
González de Alba, Luis, 53–54, 287n17
González Mateos, Adriana, 292–93n6
González Rojo, Enrique, 156
González Torres, Armando, 158, 264–65n10
Gorbachev, Mikhail, 153
Goya, Francisco, 56

Great Britain, 80–84
Grenier, Yvon, 57, 115–16, 154–55, 303n6
Gulag Archipelago, The (Solzhenitsyn), 157–67
"Gulag: Entre Isaías y Job" (Paz), 160
Guzmán, Martín Luis, 39

Harss, Luis, 224, 315n22
Harvard University, 5
Hayek, Friedrich von, 300n71
Heidegger, Martin, 3
Heller, Agnes, 172
hermeneutics of suspicion, 101–2, 208–9
Hernández, Luisa Josefina, 239
hijos del limo, Los (Paz), 1, 199, 213–14, 291n49
Hillstrom, Kevin, 266n5
Hinduism, 84
Hiperión circle, 225
Hispanic orientalism, 98–99
history, 62–63
Un hogar sólido y seis piezas en un acto (Garro), 320–21n61
homme révolté, L' (Camus), 26
homosexuality, 141–47
Howe, Irving, 5, 172, 177
huesos olvidados, Los (Rivero Taravillo), 255–59
human sacrifice, 107

Ignatieff, Michael, 172
Illades, Carlos, 301n74
India, Paz as diplomat in, 2–3, 46, 79–80, 98
India in Paz's writings
    comparison between East and West and, 80, 83–90, 93–97, 98, 117, 121–23
    criticism of, 99–100
    identity and otherness and, 80, 90–94
    impact of the West on, 80–84
    orientalism and, 98
individualism, 85–86

infrarrealismo, 317n42
International Congress of Writers for the Defense of Culture (Paris, 1935), 153
Itinerario (Paz)
  on conservative ideology, 302n2
  on Neruda, 263n1
  on *pachuco*, 268–69n14
  on rebellion and revolution, 32, 36–38, 47, 48

Japan, 79
jaula de la melancolía, La (Bartra), 109
Jiménez, Armando, 117, 142–43
jornada, La (newspaper), 191–92
Juana Inés de la Cruz, Sor, 138–42, 144–47, 222
Juárez, Benito, 132
Jullien, Dominique, 278n40

Kemp, Lysander, 274n65
Kermode, Frank, 311n24
Kerouac, Jack, 232
King, John, 239
Kolakowski, Leszek, 38, 172
Komárek, Valtr, 172
Kornai, János, 172–73
Korotich, Vitaly, 172
Krauze, Enrique
  experiencia de la libertad, La, colloquium and, 172
  Fuentes and, 230
  Paz and, 5, 32, 49–50
  on Paz's relationship with the Left, 157–58, 159
Kropotkin, Peter, 81
Kushigian, Julia A., 98–99

laberinto de la soledad, El (Paz)
  overview of, 1
  on colonial period in Mexican history, 103–6, 108, 133–36, 183, 184–88, 189–90

laberinto de la soledad, El (Paz) (*continued*)
  conservative ideology in, 156
  context of, 26–27
  on *fiesta*, 22–26, 65, 69, 103–4, 133–36
  Freudian ideas in, 103–6, 108, 115–16
  on love, 128, 135–38
  on masks and masking, 132–33
  on Mexican revolution and post-revolutionary regimes, 38–42, 43, 44–46, 47, 49–50
  on modernity, 76, 77
  on *pachuco*, 11–19, 22, 25–27, 30
  Paz on, 58–59
  on *Porfiriato*, 73–74, 184–85, 227
  región más transparente, La (Fuentes) and, 225–29
  on religion, 197–98
  on social position of women, 128–35, 148, 150–51
  on Sor Juana Inés de la Cruz, 138–39
  on "El sueño de la razón produce monstruos" (Goya), 56
  on United States, 19–22, 66–67, 76, 77
  writing of, 61
  on *Zapatistas* (Mexican Revolution), 115
Lacouture, Jean, 298n35
Lafaye, Jacques, 278n32
Lambert, Jean-Clarence, 52–53, 111–12
Left, the, and Paz
  as conflictive relationship, 2, 11, 152–57, 171–72, 179–80
  experiencia de la libertad, La, colloquium and, 172–78
  notion of post-ideological period and, 191
  Sandinista Revolution and, 168–72
  Solzhenitsyn and, 157–67
  See also conservatism and Paz
Lempérière, Annick, 268n12
Leninism, 161–62

Lévi-Strauss, Claude, 285n6
Leyva Martínez, Gustavo, 300n71, 312n27
liberalism, 115–16
Libro de buen amor (Ruiz), 121
Life against Death: The Psychoanalytical Meaning of History (Brown), 117–23
llama doble: Amor y erotismo, La (Paz), 103, 123–26, 143–44, 147–50
¡Llegaron! (Vallejo), 321n69
Loaeza, Soledad, 192–93
López Portillo, José, 193
López Velarde, Ramón, 203, 205
López-Calvo, Ignacio, 99
love, 123–26, 128, 135–38, 142, 147–50

Macaulay, Thomas Babington, 1st Baron Macaulay, 83
Machado, Antonio, 202
MacLeish, Archibald, 204
mafia, La (Piazza), 231–35
Malinche, La, 104, 105, 128, 133–36, 150–51
Mallarmé, Stéphane, 232
Mander, John, 279n47
Manea, Norman, 172
Manrique de Lara y Gonzaga, María Luisa, 146
Marcus, Steven, 114
Marcuse, Herbert, 117
Mariátegui, José Carlos, 58
Martí, José, 58, 222
Martínez, José Luis, 4
Marx, Karl, 4, 33
Marxism
   on alienation, 65
   experiencia de la libertad, La, colloquium and, 172–78
   historiography and, 63
   Paz and, 4, 32, 36, 59–60, 101–3, 113–14, 157, 167, 179
masculinity, 129

masks and masking
   Paz on, 23, 39, 40, 103–4, 132–33
   región más transparente, La, (Fuentes) on, 227–28
Maurras, Charles, 308–9n43
Medvedev, Roy, 163, 297n32
Melgar, Lucía, 319n55
mercantilism, 188–89
Merquior, José Guilherme, 172, 177
"mesa y el lecho, La" (Paz), 62, 68
mescaline, 95–96
Mesoamerican civilizations, 46, 89–93, 105, 106–8, 110–13, 181–83
Mexican identity
   Bartra on, 109
   Hiperión circle and, 225
   región más transparente, La (Fuentes) and, 225–29
   United States as Other and, 58
Mexican identity in Paz's writings
   behavioral poles of, 38–39
   compared to United States, 19–22, 60–62, 68–69, 70–77
   comparison between East and West and, 80, 86–91
   fiesta and, 22–26, 39, 65–66, 69, 103–4, 133–36
   Freudian ideas and, 103–16
   pachuco and, 13–19, 27
   question of national identity and, 58–61
   religion and, 21–22, 197–98
   as rooted in history, 69–73
   social position of women and, 128–35
   United States as Other and, 58
   See also *El laberinto de la soledad* (Paz)
Mexican Revolution (1910–1920)
   historiography on, 43–44

Mexican Revolution (1910–1920)
   (*continued*)
   Paz on, 31–33, 38–51, 55–56, 57, 69,
      179, 182–83
   región más transparente, La (Fuentes)
      on, 227–29
"México: modernidad y
   patrimonialismo" (Paz), 50–51
"México y Estados Unidos: Posiciones y
   contraposiciones" (Paz), 60–61, 62,
   63–66, 68–69, 278n32
Mi hermanita Magdalena (Garro), 252–54
Michaux, Henri, 95–96, 260
Michnik, Adam, 172
miedo a los animales, El (Serna), 237–38
Milosz, Czeslaw, 172
Mitterand, François, 33
modernity in Paz's writings
   comparison between Mexico and
      United States and, 75–77
   India and, 82–83, 89–90
   individualism and, 86
   Mexico and, 89–90
   Protestantism and, 75
   rebellion and, 26–29, 34, 36–38
   Solzhenitsyn and, 162–63
Molotov-Ribbentrop Pact (1939), 153
Monsiváis, Carlos, 172, 231–32, 295n7
Montes de Oca, Marco Antonio, 205
Morales, Miguel Enrique, 289n31
Morse, Richard, 76
multiculturalism, 62

Nagy-Zekmi, Silvia, 99
national identity
   Paz on, 58–61, 167
   Solzhenitsyn on, 167
   See also Mexican identity in Paz's
      writings
National Museum of Anthropology
   (Mexico City), 112

Nazism, 162
Nehru, Jawaharlal, 80, 81–82
neoliberalism, 193
Neruda, Pablo, 1–2, 230
Nettel, Guadalupe, 154
Nicaragua, 168–72
Nietzsche, Friedrich, 4, 101–2
Nobel Prize, 6
noche de Tlatelolco, La (Poniatowska),
   54–55, 287n17
normality, 141–42
Nueva picardía mexicana (Jiménez), 117,
   142–43
Nuño, Juan, 172

Ocampo, Silvina, 251–52
Octavio Paz (Poniatowska), 294n22
Oedipus complex, 104–5
ogro filantrópico, El (Paz)
   on colonial period in Mexican
      history, 180, 183
   conservative ideology in, 156–57
   on feminism, 127
   on love, 147
   on Puritanism, 64
   on rebellion and revolution, 47
   on Solzhenitsyn, 160–61
olvido que seremos, El (Abad Faciolince),
   260–61
Orfila Reynal, Arnaldo, 51–52, 113–14,
   117–18, 287–88n22
orientalism, 98
otra voz, La (Paz), 77, 199, 208–9, 219, 220
Outsider, The (Wilson), 26

pachuco, 11–19, 22, 25–27, 30, 318n50
pacifism, 81
Pani, Erika, 302–3n4
Parra, Max, 43
Partido Acción Nacional (PAN), 180–81,
   190–98

Partido de la Revolución Democrática (PRD), 307n31
Partido Revolucionario Institucional (PRI), 44–47, 46, 48–49, 190–93, 194–95
Pasado presente (García Ponce), 238–40
Paso, Fernando del, 236
passive resistance, 81
Pasternak, Boris, 206
Paterson (Williams), 203
patrimonialism, 188
Paz, Octavio
   career as a diplomat, 2–3, 46, 61, 79, 98
   criticisms of, 6–8
   major influences on, 101
   significance of, 1–5
   See also specific works and themes
Paz, Octavio—as literary character
   overview of, 222–23, 261
   in *Adán en Edén* (Fuentes), 230–31
   in *A.B.U.R.T.O.* (Yépez), 245–46
   in *De puño y letra* (Ramos), 247–48
   in "La desdichada" (Fuentes), 229–30
   in *Los detectives salvajes* (Bolaño), 240–45
   in *Entre fantasmas* (Vallejo), 259–60
   in *Fisuras en el continente literario* (Vite), 244–45
   in *Los huesos olvidados* (Rivero Taravillo), 255–59
   in *La mafia* (Piazza), 231–35
   in *Mi hermanita Magdalena* (Garro), 252–54
   in *El miedo a los animales* (Serna), 237–38
   in *El olvido que seremos* (Abad Faciolince), 260–61
   in *Pasado presente* (García Ponce), 238–40
   in *La pérdida del reino* (Bianco), 254–55

Paz, Octavio—as literary character (*continued*)
   in *La región más transparente* (Fuentes), 223–29
   in *Testimonios sobre Mariana* (Garro), 248–52
   in "La vanagloria" (Serna), 235–37
Paz Solórzano, Octavio, 266n4
Peace by Revolution (Tannenbaum), 43–44
Pellicer, Carlos, 205
Pensamiento y religión en el México antiguo (Séjourné), 287–88n22
Pequeña crónica de grandes días (Paz), 76–77
Peralta, Braulio, 191, 192, 196, 302n2
peras del olmo, Las (Paz), 139
pérdida del reino, La (Bianco), 254–55
Pereyra, Carlos, 190
perfil del hombre y la cultura en México, El (Ramos), 287n16
Pfandl, Ludwig, 140
Piazza, Luis Guillermo, 231–35, 255
Plural (journal, 1971–1976), 4–5, 160, 235, 238, 297n32
"Poesía, mito, revolución" (Paz), 33, 218–19, 219–20
Poesía en voz alta (Poetry Out Loud; theater group), 238, 239
"¿Poesía latinoamericana?" (Paz), 306n20
"poeta y la Revolución, El" (Krauze), 157–58
poetry and poetic autonomy in Paz's writings
   criticism of, 209–14
   defense of, 199–209
   political interests and, 205–7
   romantic/symbolist aesthetics and, 214
   transformative power of, 215–21

Pollock, Jackson, 204
"Polvos de aquellos lodos" (Paz), 160–67
Poniatowska, Elena, 287n17, 294n22
"¿Por qué? Fourier?" (Paz), 147
Porfiriato
    Paz on, 40, 48–49, 73–74, 101–2, 184–85, 226–27
    La región más transparente (Fuentes) on, 226–27
Posdata (Paz)
    criticism of, 108–15
    on democracy, 194
    Freudian ideas in, 103, 106–15
    on modernity, 77
    on rebellion and revolution, 28–29, 42–43, 45–46, 47–49, 53
    on Tlatelolco massacre, 107–15
    on United States, 276n13
Positivism, 74
Pound, Ezra, 203
Prensa, La (newspaper), 169–70
progress, 28
Protestant Ethic and the Spirit of Capitalism, The (Weber), 277n24
Protestantism, 75, 117, 122–23
Proust, Marcel, 136–37
psychoanalysis in Paz's writings
    Brown and, 117–23
    Freudian ideas and, 4, 101–2, 103–16, 124–26
Puertas al campo (Paz), 91–92
Purdy, James, 232
Puritanism, 64–66

racial discrimination, 17
Ramírez, Sergio, 299n48
Ramos, Luis Arturo, 247–48
Ramos, Samuel, 287n16
Reagan administration, 170–71, 193
"Rebelión, revuelta, revolución" (*Corriente alterna*, Paz), 11

rebellion and revolution in Paz's writings
    changing views of, 11
    Communist revolutions and, 31–38, 57
    counterculture of the 1960s and, 12, 26–30
    fiesta and, 22–26, 39
    May 1968 uprising in Paris and, 51–53
    Mexican Revolution and, 31–33, 38–52, 55–56, 57, 69
    Mexican student movement and, 52–53, 54–55
    modernity and, 26–29, 34, 36–38
    pachuco and, 11–19, 22, 25–27, 30
    poetry and, 215–21
    post-revolutionary regimes and, 32–33, 34–35, 44–47
    Zapatista rebellion (1994) and, 31–32, 56–57
recuerdos del porvenir, Los (Garro), 320–21n61
redemption, 16–18
Reencuentro de personajes (Garro), 319n58
Reeve, Richard, 314n11
región más transparente, La (Fuentes), 223–29
Reich, Wilhelm, 117
religion in Paz's writings
    colonial period in Mexican history and, 185–90
    comparison between East and West and, 83–84, 95–97, 117, 121–23
    early interest in, 4
    Mexican identity and, 21–22, 197–98
    Partido Acción Nacional and, 196–98
    utopianism and, 36–38
    See also Catholicism; Protestantism
repression, 103–4, 118–23, 124–25
Revel, Jean-François, 172, 175, 194
Reverdy, Pierre, 213–14

Revista mexicana de literatura (literary journal), 238, 239
revolution. *See* rebellion and revolution in Paz's work; *specific revolutions*
Reyes, Alfonso, 4, 43–44, 58–59
Rico Moreno, Javier, 305n17
Rimbaud, Arthur, 98
Rivero Taravillo, Antonio, 255–59
Rodó, José Enrique, 58, 279n49
Rodríguez Ledesma, Xavier, 109, 156–57, 299–300n50
Rodríguez Monegal, Emir, 52
Rojas, Rafael, 270–71n7, 315n21
romans à clef, 222, 248–55
Romantic Image (Kermode), 311n24
romanticism
  counterculture of the 1960s and, 98
  on love, 136–37
  Paz and, 26, 28–29, 57, 98, 115–16, 136–37
  poetic autonomy and, 214
  rebellion and, 28–29
Rousset, David, 2, 154, 160–61, 294n2
Roy, Rāmmohun, 83
Rudnytsky, Peter, 105
Ruiz, Juan, 121
Russian Revolution (1917–1923), 32, 57. *See also* Communist revolutions
Ruy Sánchez, Alberto, 155, 299n48

Said, Edward, 98
Sakharov, Andrei, 163
Salinas de Gortari, Carlos, 6–7, 50, 77, 246
Salmagundi (journal), 157–58
Salvadoran Civil War, 168–72
Sánchez Prado, Ignacio, 290n36
Sánchez Susarrey, Jaime, 155
Sánchez Vázquez, Adolfo, 172, 173
Sandinista Revolution, 168–72

Santí, Enrico Mario, 267–68n10, 286n15, 311–12n25
Santiago, Silviano, 268–69n14, 269n20, 292n2
Sarduy, Severo, 5, 99
Sarmiento, Domingo, 58
Sartre, Jean-Paul, 2, 260
Saturday Review (literary magazine), 224
Savater, Fernando, 299n49
Schärer-Nussberger, Maya, 311–12n25
Scherer García, Julio, 110
Schlegel, Friedrich, 216
Schwarz, Roberto, 272–73n39
Second Sex, The (Beauvoir), 137–38
Segovia, Tomás, 4
Séjourné, Laurette, 287–88n22
Semprún, Jorge, 172, 173–74
Serge, Victor, 153
Serna, Enrique, 235–38
Serrano, Pedro, 320–21n61
Serrano Plaja, Arturo, 263n1
sexual revolution, 29–30, 117
sexuality, 124–25, 141–47
Shakespeare, William, 209, 222
"Shakespeare's Memory" (Borges), 222
Sheridan, Guillermo, 5, 266n4, 319–20n60
Shmelev, Nikolai, 172
Silva-Herzog Márquez, Jesús, 275–76n11
sin, 16–18
Sloterdijk, Peter, 172
social reform, 81
solitude, 21, 59, 135–36
Solzhenitsyn, Alexander, 157–67
Sontag, Susan, 5, 232
Sor Juana Inés de la Cruz, o, Las trampas de la fe (Paz), 139–42, 144–47, 182, 183, 188–89
Sorensen, Diana, 290n35
Soriano, Juan, 239

Soviet Union, 2, 153–54, 168, 180. *See also* the Left and Paz
Spanish Civil War, 2, 255–59
Spencer, Herbert, 74
Stalinism, 157, 162
Stanton, Anthony, 41, 292n4, 311–12n25
Steinberg, Samuel, 290n36
Stone, I. F., 297n32
structuralism, 4
student movement, 51–55, 274n63. *See also* Tlatelolco massacre (Mexico City, 1968)
Suárez, Rodolfo, 301n74
Suárez-Iñiguez, E., 298n36
Subcomandante Marcos (Rafael Sebastián Guillén Vicente), 246
sublimation, 118–23
"sueño de la razón produce monstruos, El" (Goya), 56
Sur (Argentine journal), 2, 5, 161, 251–52
surrealist movement, 3, 28, 216–18, 219
Switzerland, 79
symbolism, 214

Tablada, Juan José, 201
Tannenbaum, Frank, 43–44
Tantrism, 117, 122–23
Tarde, Gabriel, 226
Taylor, Charles, 275n69
technology, 81
Tempest, The (Shakespeare), 209
Testimonios sobre Mariana (Garro), 248–52, 253–54
Tharoor, Shashi, 282n9
Thatcher, Margaret, 176, 193
Thomas, Hugh, 172
Thoreau, Henry David, 81
Tiempo nublado (Paz), 36, 38, 127–28, 170–71
Times Literary Supplement (literary review), 64

Tlatelolco, aquella tarde (González de Alba), 287n17
Tlatelolco massacre (Mexico City, 1968), 2, 28, 46, 54–55, 106, 107–15
Tocqueville, Alexis de, 85–86, 278n32, 278n40
Todorov, Tzvetan, 283–84n14
Tolstaya, Tatyana, 172
Tolstoy, Leo, 81
Tomlinson, Charles, 116–17
Trevor-Roper, Hugh, 172, 173
Trotsky, Leon, 153

UNAM (Universidad Nacional Autónoma de México), 239
unconscious, 101, 107–9, 113–15, 116
United Kingdom, 193
United Nations (UN), 61, 79
United States
  neoliberalism in, 193
  as Other, 58
  Paz in, 61–62
  Sandinista Revolution and, 170–71
United States in Paz's writings
  compared to Mexico, 19–22, 60–62, 68–69, 70–77
  comparison between East and West and, 80, 87–88
  history as natural evolution and, 63–65, 70–71
  as inorganic society, 65–67, 70–71, 74
  modernity and, 75–77
  as outside of history, 67–68
  role in Latin America of, 170–71
Universidad Nacional Autónoma de México (UNAM), 239
Uno más uno (newspaper), 177
Urban, Hugh B., 291n48
"uso y la contemplación, El" (Paz), 209–13
utopianism, 34–38, 56, 117, 119–20, 123–24

Vallejo, Fernando, 259–60
"vanagloria, La" (Serna), 235–37
Vargas Llosa, Mario, 5, 172, 174, 175–76, 177, 232
Vasconcelos, José, 58, 180, 190, 306n19
Vázquez Amaral, José, 224
Velázquez, Diego, 121
Veliz, Claudio, 279n49
Venus del Espejo (Velázquez), 121
Vietnam War, 167, 168
Vigil, José María, 304n12
Villaurrutia, Xavier, 4, 293–94n20
Villoro, Luis, 172
violence, 34–35
Virgin of Guadalupe, 105
Vislumbres de la India (Paz)
  overview of contents of, 79–80
  comparison between East and West in, 80, 83–90, 98
  on identity and otherness, 80, 90–94
  on impact of the West on India, 80–84
Viswanathan, Gauri, 282n10
Vite, Federico, 244–45
Vivekananda, Swam, 84
Vizcaíno, Fernando, 152–54
Volpi, Jorge, 54, 316n30
Vuelta (journal, 1976–1998)
  García Ponce and, 238
  Krauze on Fuentes in, 230
  Paz and, 4–5, 31, 168–72, 177–78, 235, 283–84n14
  Sandinista Revolution and, 168–72
  Todorov and, 283–84n14

Weber, Max, 188, 277n24
Westphalen, Emilio Adolfo, 205
Whitney, Joel, 298n39
Wieseltier, Leon, 172
Wilde, Oscar, 214
Williams, Raymond Leslie, 156
Williams, William Carlos, 203
Wilson, Colin, 26
Wolfe, Tom, 232
Womack, John, Jr., 271–72n16

Yépez, Heriberto, 245–46

Zaid, Gabriel, 6, 298n37
Zapata, Emiliano, 41–43, 45, 69, 182–83, 266n4
Zapatista rebellion (1994), 31–32, 56–57, 194–95, 237–38
Zaretsky, Eli, 117
Zedillo, Ernesto, 194–95, 236

www.ingramcontent.com/pod-product-compliance
Lightning Source LLC
Chambersburg PA
CBHW051205300426
44116CB00006B/449